# RELIGION, STATE, AND SOCIETY IN MEDIEVAL INDIA

# RELIGION, STATE, AND SOCIETY IN MEDIEVAL INDIA

Collected Works of S. Nurul Hasan

Edited and with an Introduction by
*Satish Chandra*

**OXFORD**
UNIVERSITY PRESS

# OXFORD
### UNIVERSITY PRESS

YMCA Library Building, Jai Singh Road, New Delhi 110 001

Oxford University Press is a department of the University of Oxford.
It furthers the University's objective of excellence in research,
scholarship, and education by publishing worldwide in

Oxford  New York

Auckland Cape Town Dar es Salaam Hong Kong Karachi
Kuala Lumpur Madrid Melbourne Mexico City Nairobi
New Delhi Shanghai Taipei Toronto

With offices in

Argentina Austria Brazil Chile Czech Republic France Greece
Guatemala Hungary Italy Japan Poland Portugal Singapore
South Korea Switzerland Thailand Turkey Ukraine Vietnam

Oxford is a registered trademark of Oxford University Press
in the UK and in certain other countries

Published in India
By Oxford University Press, New Delhi

ISBN-13: 978-0-19-566765-3
ISBN-10: 0-19-566765-4

Typeset in Pratap 10.5/12
by Excellent Laser Typesetters, Pitampura, Delhi 110 034
Printed in India by Pauls Press, New Delhi 110 020
Published by Manzar Khan, Oxford University Press
YMCA Library Building, Jai Singh Road, New Delhi 110 001

# Contents

# Preface

Saiyid Nurul Hasan was a rare combination of academic abilities and intellectual dedication. He was an excellent teacher who spoke in a clear and convincing style. Under his guidance for the first time University Grants Commission set up an Advanced Centre of History (Medieval) in this country at Aligarh Muslim University. Nurul Hasan contributed not only to teaching and research but also to building up a good history library at Aligarh.

When Nurul Hasan became Education Minister, he recognized education on rational and professional lines. He established the Indian Council of Historical Research and several other institutions. Though he wrote many pieces, particularly on agrarian history, only a few could be published in his lifetime because of his preoccupation with institutional work. In keeping with the dignity of college and university teachers, he made their salary structure respectable.

Professors Hasan Mahmud and A. R. Khan collected Nurul Hasan's articles and the Indian Council of Historical Research was asked to publish them, but this could not be done. Later the Nurul Hasan Foundation approached the Editorial Committee of the Comprehensive History of India Society for the publication of this valuable collection. The Committee accepted it and the Oxford University Press agreed to bring it out. The press copy has been prepared by the OUP and finally edited by Professor Satish Chandra. On behalf of the Editorial Committee of the Comprehensive History of India I thank Professor Satish

Chandra, Secretary, Editorial Committee, Comprehensive History of India Society, for the Introduction, and also Professors Hasan Mahmud and A. R. Khan for their efforts.

R. S. SHARMA
Emeritus Professor
Dept. of History, Patna University
and Founder Chairman
Indian Council for Historical Research
New Delhi

# Introduction

Saiyid Nurul Hasan (1921–93), played an important, even a leading role in giving a new direction to history writing in India, immediately before, and after Independence. His vision of history was shaped by the 'nationalist' Allahabad school of history writing, Marxism to which he was attracted during his student days, and his family traditions. His family belonged to Ghazipur (Eastern UP), and had the hereditary title of *pesh-imams*. During the time of Shuja-ud-Daula, the successor of Nawab Burhan-ul-Mulk, the family moved to Fyzabad, and at the instance of his famous queen, Bahu Begum, were appointed pesh-imams there. His maternal grand uncle, Sir Wazir Hasan, was a leading lawyer, and was appointed Judge of the Lucknow bench of the Allahabad High Court. His father, Syed Abul Hasan, was a civil servant, and served as a District Settlement Officer, and was later appointed Chairman, Court of Wards, which dealt with the taluqdars of Awadh, their problems of succession, internal administration, etc. Thus, the family had one foot in Islamic tradition, and the other in modern times. While his father was a Settlement Officer, Nurul Hasan moved with him from village to village, and came to know at first hand the pattern of village life, and the working of the revenue system. This stood him in good stead in his later study of the Mughal revenue system.

After obtaining a brilliant first division in history at the Allahabad University in 1942, Nurul Hasan chose not to follow the family tradition of government service, but joined the History Department of the Lucknow University. The salaries of university teachers, in fact teachers in general, had reached a nadir at that time, both on account of the effects of the economic crisis of 1929, and the British government's disdain of university teachers following a rapid process of Indianization of education. Perhaps, it was this experience which made Nurul Hasan pushing for a rapid upward revision of university and college teachers' salaries shortly after he became the Minister of Education at Delhi.

After the end of World War II, Nurul Hasan joined the Oxford University, and obtained the degree of D.Phil under the supervision of the noted scholar, H. A. R. Gibb. The subject of his thesis was, 'Chishti and Suhrawardi *silsilahs* in North India During the thirteenth–fourteenth Centuries'. Although the thesis has not been published, the present writer was one of the few persons privileged to read it. While tracing the growth of these silsilahs to the specific socio-political conditions obtaining in the region, Nurul Hasan argued that their growth was also closely linked with the interests of the state and the ruling classes, which tried to utilize the prestige of the Sufi saints to establish their own political credibility and support base, especially among various sections of the Muslims. The so-called refusal of the Chishti saints to have anything to do with the state cannot be accepted at its face value, for they received indirect support from the state by way of gifts (*futuh*) from the leading nobles. Again, the primary purpose of these Sufi saints was to provide spiritual solace to the Muslims, not to convert the 'infidels'. By painstakingly collecting evidence, Nurul Hasan tried to rebut the belief that many eminent Sufi saints had settled down in 'enemy country' (*dar-ul-harb*) for purposes of conversion. In many cases, fame acquired by these saints was a later phenomenon in which political calculations also played a part. Thus, Nurul Hasan tried to place the Sufi movements in India in their socio-economic, and historical context.

After returning from Oxford, in 1949 Nurul Hasan moved to the History Department of the Aligarh Muslim University. Although the Aligarh Muslim University was in a shambles following the partition of the country in 1947, and the widely held feeling that the students and staff of the University had actively campaigned for the Partition, and should be taught a lesson, the University had a strong core of nationalists, many of them

Marxists, who had taken a stand in opposition to the demand for Pakistan, sometimes in disregard of their personal safety. Among these was the noted historian, Professor Muhammad Habib, Head of the Departments of History and Political Science. The Government of India, led by Jawaharlal Nehru, too, was keen to rehabilitate the University, and appointed as Vice-Chancellor of the University the noted nationalist and Gandhian, Dr Zakir Husain, who was later to become the Vice-President, and then President of India.

It was in these circumstances that Nurul Hasan tried to give a new shape to history, especially Medieval Indian history. The approach which he fashioned was later dubbed the 'Aligarh School of History', although there was a wide difference of opinion and approaches to history in the faculty. It was, however, a period of intense debate and research. I was fortunate to join it as a Reader in 1953, and spent eight fruitful years there.

In the latter part of his life, Nurul Hasan shifted from writing history to helping in shaping history. After being a nominated, and then an elected member of the Rajya Sabha, he became the Minister of State for Education in 1971. Thereafter, except for a brief stint of being Professor of History at the Delhi University in 1977–78, he held various posts of distinction—Vice Chairman, Council of Scientific and Industrial Research; Ambassador to the Soviet Union; and Governor of West Bengal, Orissa, and again West Bengal. He died while in harness in 1993 at Calcutta (now Kolkata). However, during this period, his interest in history remained abiding, as is borne out by the papers and address which he delivered. Many of these have been included in the present collection.

## Approach to History

Trained under Sir Shafaat Ahmad Khan who was one of the founders of the Indian History Congress, Dr R. P. Tripathi and Dr Tara Chand who had set the tone of the Medieval Indian History at Allahabad, Nurul Hasan considered history to be a powerful means of national integration, and of building a society free of religious or sectarian violence and bitterness. He always fought for a holistic view of history, where all aspects of life— political, economic, social, religious and cultural would be seen in an integrated manner, and in perspective. This led him to take a strong stand against the communal approach to history. He also fought against the distortion of Indian history by the colonial rulers, who had put forward a narrow view of history, partly out of their own narrow Eurocentric view of history, and partly out of a desire to serve imperial ends.

Thus, in his Presidential address to the Medieval section at the Indian History Congress at Delhi in 1961 (No. 2 in the present collection), Nurul Hasan attacked the traditional British point of view put forward by Peter Hardy from the School of Oriental and African Studies that 'apartheid was the dominant ideal in Medieval India, in default of cultural victory'. Nurul Hasan argued that 'The tendency to assume that the main basis of social division, or the *leit-motif* of social action, whether in the field of politics or of culture was religion, can hardly be justified', and that 'such a view could not be upheld either on the basis of available data, or on the fact that while Hindus and Muslims did have differences, the differences of thought and outlook between Hindus and Muslims belonging to a particular class or region, were not so marked as members of the same community belonging to different regions or social back ground'.

In essence, he rejected not only the Two-Nation theory, and Hindu 'fundamentalism' favouring a unicultural approach to Indian history, but also the notion that the amorphous body of the Hindus, or of the Muslim *umma* formed some kind of a corporate body. He brought out their division into various social and economic groups or regions, each of which had specific religio-cultural forms and outlook despite an over-all unity. This dual aspect led to a new study of categories such as 'Islamic conquest', 'Muslim era' or even the term 'Muslim'. In a scholarly Introduction to the book *India's Islamic Traditions, 711–1750* (OUP 2003) Richard M. Eaton underlines this point, criticizing the 'tendency, found in much scholarly writing in Europe and North America during the nineteenth and twentieth centuries, to collapse religion with culture, and to conflate both of these with civilization and even territory'. He goes on to say, these in turn, 'were construed into mutually exclusive civilizational/territorial units.'

Nurul Hasan always acknowledged his debt to the Marxist school of historiography, but he did not consider it to be a rigid dogma. His emphasis was on 'objective and genuine search for truth'. He warned against basing one's research on a priori hypotheses. He refused to consider relationships of production as the 'determining factor' in Indian history. In his own words:

On the basis of our existing knowledge of medieval Indian history it would be premature to try and decide whether religion, or ideas, or relationships of production or any other factor played the determining role in the history of the period.

Specifically, Nurul Hasan rejected Henry Maine's idea, later accepted by Marx, of the Indian villages being some kind of isolated, self-sufficient republics, and of the 'objectively progressive role' of the British in breaking down their isolation. In his study of rural life, he saw the village as continually developing, and involved in a wider network of economic relations. Hence, he rejected the concepts of 'Oriental Despotism' or 'Asiatic Mode of Production' which were based on a static social mould.

For Nurul Hasan, the essence of history was change, and the task of the historian was to analyse the process of change, establishing relationship between social, economic, political, religious, cultural and intellectual factors. This also implied a multi-disciplinary approach.

Nurul Hasan laid considerable emphasis on regional studies in Indian history. Early in his career he had toyed with the idea of different linguistic entities in India constituting sub-nationalities, working towards nationhood (No. 9). This was in 1944 when the question of Indian independence, and the form and structure of a future India Union—multinational, federal, loose association, confederal, etc. were very much under discussion. With the adoption of a semi-federal constitution, and the subsequent formation of states on a linguistic basis, this question has receded into the background (although the question of cultural pluralism or position and role of Muslims in India has, if anything, come to the forefront). Interestingly, some western scholars have tried to revive the idea of multinationalism in medieval India, and to present the growth of Maratha and Sikh movements as examples of the growth of nationalism which became an important factor in the disintegration of the Mughal empire.

That regionalism was always an important factor in Indian history was well recognized by Indian historians. Many of them linked it to what were called 'centripetal and centrifugal tendencies'. However, this term or concept was later given up because of its absence of linkages with any specific social groups. It is hardly relevant to point out that nationalism in Europe grew in a particular socio-economic context, viz. the growth of capitalism. Its revival by some western scholars is again an attempt to apply western terms in a vastly different context. In part, this problem has arisen because of uncritical translation of terms like *qaum,* or regional entities such as 'Marathas' into 'nations'. It is also linked to the 'firm' theory, or rise of the banking firms, and moneyed elements in Medieval India. How far these elements were conscious of, or promoted 'regional nationalism' needs specific study. In this context, the role of caste as legitimizing social aspirations, and of social formations such as zamindars has received some attention in Indian writing.

Nurul Hasan considered that regional history did not mean political history, or the doings of local rulers or chiefs at a lower, regional level. While emphasizing the remarkable unity in the broad pattern of socio-economic development, culture and administrative institutions in India, he was of the opinion that 'the trends of historical change in the country would remain sadly incomplete unless the details are studied at the regional level' (No. 3). This implied in depth study of the working of the administrative machinery, land relations, pattern of agricultural production, organization of trade and handicrafts, position of social classes, groups etc. at the regional level.

Nurul Hasan also laid emphasis on growth of towns, city morphology, and the role of business communities (Nos 4 and 5). For him, there was no sharp dividing line between towns and the rural areas—they supplemented and supported each other. He would not, thus, agree with the notion that the towns in Medieval India were an index of the exploitation of the country-side by a small, urban elite. That towns exploited the countryside was accepted by the French historian, Fernand Braudel who also said that 'Towns generate expansion and are themselves generated by it'. The question is; was this applicable to the Western World only? Anticipating Braudel, in the sixteenth century Abul Fazl had said, 'People that are attached to the world collect in towns without which there would be no progress.'

## The Ruling Class and Rural Economy

A major subject of interest for Nurul Hasan was the nature of the ruling class, and its role in state and economy. He divided the ruling class the Medieval India into two segments—the amirs, and the zamindars. He did undertake some study of the former (Nos 10, 11) but was of the opinion that in order to understand the nature and dynamic of the Indian society, it was necessary to understand first the nature of the rural society. This had to begin with understanding the structure and role of the dominant or ruling class, the zamindars. His analysis of zamindars, his division of the zamindars into three categories—autonomous chieftains, intermediary zamindars and primary zamindars, bringing out the hierarchical nature of the zamindars and of their being widespread both in the jagir and the khalisa lands, (No. 12) was a pioneering work, which has helped to understand the basic structure of Indian society, and opened the way for a deeper study of rural society. Caste is linked to it, but the basic structure was based not on caste, but on relations of production.

The role of the zamindars in the assessment and collection of revenue is borne out in a number of papers included in this collection—Revenue Administration of the Jagir of Sahsram by Farid (Sher Shah) (No. 16), Three Studies of the Zamindari System (No. 13), and Thoughts on Agrarian Relations in Medieval India (No. 21). Nurul Hasan's approach has led to a more intensive study of the role of zamindars in different region, by scholars such as A. R. Kulkarni, N. A. Siddiqi, B. R. Grover and many others. However, it is necessary to keep in mind the dialectical nature of the role of the zamindars—their role as backbone in revenue administration, and an essential role in the expansion and improvement of cultivation, as also of being exploiters and being the main source of administrative difficulties and local opposition which the central government had to face. Insufficient realization of this dual nature has, perhaps, led a modern writer, Andre Wink, to consider local opposition, which he calls *fitna*, to be the major factor in rural life in Medieval India. In his opinion, the main task of the central government was to 'manage' this fitna. For him, the question of centralization carried out by the Mughals had little relevance.

Nurul Hasan and Begum Nurul Hasan's article, in association with S. P. Gupta, on 'Pattern of Agricultural Production in the Territories of Amber', and 'Prices of Food Grains in the Territory of Amber' (Nos 17, 18) based on the *arhsattas*, broke new ground, and also corrected some widely held but wrong notions. Making use of the method suggested by the noted mathematician-cum-historian, D. D. Kosambi, these articles plotted out the area under the production of different crops, based on records mentioning the state share in *jinsi* (kind or sharing) and *zabti* (cash-rates). They showed that 'the rate of land revenue demanded from the cultivators in princely states was hardly different from that demanded by the Mughals'. This was a clear refutation of the views of the French traveller, François Bernier, who had deeply influenced Marx's thinking, and also many modern writers on agrarian history, such as W. H. Moreland. In their opinion, the Mughal agrarian system was so oppressive as to ruin cultivation, and cause the flight of peasants to the territories of the Hindu rajas. This is also the view of the noted scholar, Irfan Habib, and is widely considered to be the view of the 'Aligarh School' of historians.

These quantitative studies also showed that the village was not an isolated unit, because the prices of a particular crop in one pargana, influenced the prices and the area sown under a particular crop in the neighbouring areas. In recent years, the publication of S. P. Gupta's *The Agrarian System of Eastern Rajasthan*, Dilbagh Singh's *States, Landlords, Peasants: Rajasthan in the eighteenth Century,* and a number of other monographs have provided further evidence to support Nural Hasan's point of view regarding the agrarian situation under the Mughals.

Nurul Hasan's lectures on the agrarian system, delivered at the Patna University in 1971 (No. 21), raises a few questions which have not yet been answered, or dealt with adequately. One: with zamindars present everywhere, and collecting and paying land-revenue either to the agents of the state in *khalisa*, or to the agent of the *jagirdar* in his *jagir*, was there double-exploitation? Nurul Hasan argued that theoretically it was not so because the state realized the full share of the land revenue due, which was supposed to be half of the production, and the share of the zamindar, and the local village officials, assesses, etc. were paid out of this. He agreed that this could be violated. The question is: what was the range and magnitude of these violations? How effective was the state machinery in checking these violations?

If not, what options did the peasants have except flight, appeal to higher authorities, or, as the last resort, rebellion? Two: what was the role and extent of influence of the more affluent sections in rural society, the section he calls *halmirs*, that is, those who had a surplus of oxen and ploughs? These were a section of what have been called *khud-kasht* and which Nurul Hasan called free peasants or primary zamindars. Were these the sections which invested in land to improve cultivation, while the zamindars in general were more intent on expanding cultivation? Can it be said that these two sections—the intermediary zamindars, and the halmirs or the richer sections of the khud-kasht, appropriated the major benefits of the Mughal policy of expansion and improvement of cultivation? I have attempted to answer some of these questions elsewhere. But a great deal remains to be done.

In recent writings, the role of the moneyed sections, both urban and rural—the bankers, the *ijaradars*, the new breed of zamindars who were out to gather money by all means possible, have led some to talk of 'portfolio capitalism', while some others see in it a growing convergence between these sections whose basic motives were merchantilist, and the East India Company which was 'the most consistent advocate of merchantilism'. P. J. Marshall, in his Introduction to *India in the Eighteenth Century*, even talks of an 'intermediate state', as if these 'intermediate' elements had acquired state power, or were on the verge of doing so.

It is hardly possible to examine these theories within the conspectus of this brief Introduction. It does, however, show that the old colonial theory of India being a stagnant society before the arrival of the British is dead and buried. The efforts of Nurul Hasan and some of his writings brought together here, can be said to have played a part in this much delayed demise of an antediluvian theory.

Finally, did the peasant society have the capacity to transform itself to a higher, that is, capitalist stage? Nurul Hasan considered this to be one of the 'ifs' of history which professional historians avoided. However, he did not believe that the limits of rural development had been reached in India by the seventeenth century. He maintained that money economy and handicraft productions were growing in the country. Simultaneously, he believed that 'the decay of the system had already started and the process of this decline would have necessarily led to the overthrow of the system and to the emergence of something different.' He went on to say, 'if this process (of growth) had not been disrupted by foreign rule, maybe it would have grown into a full fledged industrial society' (No. 4).

## Religion and Political Processes

Despite his preoccupation with rural society, Nurul Hasan was from the beginning, deeply involved in the study of religious movements and religions personages. We have already referred to his D.Phil, thesis on the Chishti and Suhrawardi saints in north India During the Thirteenth-fourteenth Centuries. It is hoped that the Nurul Hasan Foundation would take early steps to have this thesis which, despite lapse of time still has relevance, to be published.

The first research article which Nurul had published in 1943 interestingly enough, was the *Mahzar* of Akbar (No. 7). The article was not so much to rebutt Vincent Smith's contention that Akbar was influenced by the Western concept of Papacy, and that the decree had invested him with the 'attribute of infallibility', since this had been done effectively by many others such as Buckler, Roy Choudhary and S. R. Sharma. He studied the issues which the orthodox Muslim opinion, represented by Badauni, and which continue to influence orthodox Muslim thinking in India and Pakistan. Among these sections, it has been held that it was 'a dishonest document' since it declared Akbar to be a *mujtahid,* thereby permitting him to interpret Holy laws whereas he was hardly literate. Nurul Hasan has cited evidence to show that according to orthodox opinion, the position of Imam was higher than a mujtahid, and that the decree gave freedom to the Emperor, in case there was difference of opinion among the mujtahids, to choose any one of them 'for the welfare of mankind and proper functioning of the administrative affairs of the world'. Interestingly, the Pakistan historians, S. M. Ikram, and S. A. Rashid who was formerly Professor of History at the Aligarh Muslim University, hold that 'studied carefully and dispassionately, it appears to be a major constructive effort, fully in conformity with the Islamic Law and providing a basis for adjustment of temporal government and the Shariat'. But the authors go on to say that in practice it 'became an excuse of unrestrained autocracy'. Thus, the entire ground of debate has been shifted. However, their attempt to shift the ground of debate has hardly convinced the orthodox elements.

Nurul Hasan also took issue with Muslim orthodoxy for their eulogizing Shaikh Ahmad Sirhindi (No. 8) who was a narrow dogmatist, and was bitterly opposed to Akbar's policy of sulh-i-kul, and of associating Hindus in the task of government. That he was unable to influence any sizeable section in the nobility and that there was hardly any opposition when Jahangir imprisoned him showed that Akbar had built more strongly than he is often given credit for. But the orthodox ulama remained unreconciled to Akbar's liberal policies, and their demand for the strict observance of the sharia was an example of the perennial struggle in India between the forces of liberalism and orthodoxy. The actual support from different social groups these elements enjoyed is a subject of more sustained research.

There has always been a strong anti-femininist strain in the Indian historical writings. Thus, Minhaj Siraj praises Razia for administrative skill, etc. but considers them useless because of her sex. Likewise, all the faults and failures of Jahangir are often attributed to the evil influence and intrigues of Nurjahan. In a well-argued article (No. 11), Nurul Hasan refutes the argument that Nurjahan formed a 'junta' in association with Asaf Khan and Shahjahan which divided the court into two and goaded Shahjahan into rebellion. He showed this opinion was based either on the writings of Sir Thomas Roe who had no access to court circles, or to works written during the reign of Shahjahan. The article is a classic example of how sources needed to be examined critically in order to sift controversial issues, or to controvert widely held, but erroneous notions.

It is hardly necessary to dwell on Nurul Hasan's insistence on using original source material including documents for writing history. The search for sources took him to many universities and Bibliotheques—Oxford, the British Museum, Bibliotheque Nationale, Paris, Tubingen, to mention only a few. He took great efforts to bring as many photocopies of sources as possible to Aligarh in order to make it a real centre for research. He was conscious of the value of European and early British records— the Amini Report, the Fifth Report, papers such as those starting with the question: *'Chist Zamindar'* (What is a zamindar?) brought

together in the huge collection of Persian volumes, the correspondence between various British administrative protagonists
such as Philip Francis, which, till now, have hardly been used for
a better understanding of the structure of Indian society, and its
working. To this may be added the writings and papers of many
of the British and European settlers/adventurers, such as du
Jardin (No. 25) which he introduced for the first time. Despite
the rigid division of history into Ancient, Medieval and Modern
periods of history in Indian universities, such approaches are a
pointer to the direction in which research in Indian history is
moving, or needs to be moved.

Through his papers and addresses scattered over a period of
fifty years, Nurul Hasan shows a mind which was both critical and
wide-ranging in readings and interests. Above all, he was strongly
opposed to a narrow, communal interpretation of history. His
emphasis on the integrative multi-cultural, composite nature of
India's ethos and historical traditions is best summed up in the
words of one of his favourite Urdu poet, Khwaja Mir Dard:

> Shaikh ka'ba ho ke pahuncha
> Ham kunisht-i-dil men ho,
> Kalp, manzil eh thi,
> Tuk rahi ka khel tha.

The Shaikh went via the Ka'ba,
While I took the route of the Temple of the Heart,
Dard, the destination was the same,
Only the path was different.

Nurul Hasan may be considered the best example of what
may be called 'Awadhi culture' in which tradition and modernity
are combined, and friends and associates, irrespective of their
personal or religious background, are treated on par with the
family—both loved and respected.

As his old friend and associate, S. Gopal, wrote in Nurul
Hasan's Obituary, 'he remained to the end a historian of the
finest tradition of Oxbridge-rational as well as romantic, scep-
tical but always sympathetic'.

SATISH CHANDRA
Secretary
Editorial Board
Comprehensive History of India

# PART I

# THE HISTORIAN'S TASK

# 1

## *Indian History*
### A Synoptic View*

One of the most significant developments in historical studies since Independence has been the growing interest in social and economic development. While detailed studies will necessarily be confined to some small aspects of social or economic history, I am happy to note that the concept of social change in its broader aspect has not been ignored by our scholars. Social or economic history is, therefore, no longer looked upon as parallel in nature but as integral part of the study of society as a whole—its material activity, mode of production, social organization, political life, ideological trends, and religious institutions. All these aspects are essentially interrelated and form the basis of social organization. Similarly, our scholars have been devoting a good deal of attention to the study of the dynamics of society and the process of social change. Today we know much more about the factors that accelerated or retarded the process of social transformation, the stages through which society passed, and the direction that it took. Our country has, because of its large size and variety of environment, seen the emergence of local cultural traditions. It has also been subjected to influences from abroad. The interaction of these varied cultures and social institutions has led to the emergence of a synthesis, to its richness, and to its characteristic unity in

* General President's Address, *Proceedings of Indian History Congress*, XXXIV Session, Chandigarh, 1973, pp. 1–9.

diversity. But this cultural interaction has, on the one hand, been influenced by social processes and conflicts, and, on the other, it has given to social conflicts, the appearance of cultural conflicts. This particular feature which is attracting the attention of our historians has, at the same time, created difficulties and pitfalls. Many of the social and political tensions of today are sought to be reflected backwards in the interpretation of history. But this difficulty is not confined to the historians of India living in our own country. Many writers on Indian history abroad are equally carried away by their political prejudices. I have every confidence that the muse of history will guide our scholars to retain their objectivity and scientific outlook so that the value of their work is not vitiated by extraneous considerations or passions and prejudices.

To study the foundations of Indian society and culture we have to begin from the beginning. The transformation of Indian society from savagery to civilization has been studied by many distinguished archaeologists. A great deal of work has been done in the field of prehistory. I only hope that the line of investigation undertaken by Kosambi of combining the anthropological method with that of archaeology is pursued with greater vigour by the Indian scholars.

Out achievements in the field of proto-history are, however, more substantial. The numerous excavations that have been carried out in recent years, particularly by university departments, have enabled us to understand more clearly the sequence of social development during the proto-historic period. If we take the Harappan culture as the base, we are today in a better position to know more about the cultures that preceded it and those that followed it. The culture of ochre colour pottery appears to have links with pre-Harappan culture even though it seems to have evolved in the upper Ganga-Yamuna doab almost independently and contemporaneously with the Harappan culture. The black and red ware culture of central India seems to be independently developed by the tribals who still survive in these regions. If anthropological evidence is taken into account and studied alongside the archaeological finds and geological data, it would appear possible that these tribal people of central India extended their 'booleys' over vast areas of the Gangetic plain going as far east as Bihar, possibly even Bengal. Its spread in Rajasthan, Gujarat, and the south Narmada areas is, of course, well established. Thanks to the keen interest taken by our archaeologists, our knowledge of the chalcolithic culture of this period is today much better. The emergence of the painted grey ware culture towards the end of the second millennium BC and its spread in the upper Ganga-Yamuna valley extending further eastwards up to Varanasi has been carefully studied. There seems a great deal of agreement among archaeologists that this culture can be associated with the Aryans. Of special significance is the fact that the people of painted grey ware culture not merely brought with them tamed horses but also introduced iron and iron technology, which brought about major social changes. As iron and iron technology began to spread eastwards, and as richer deposits of iron were discovered, we find the emergence of settled agriculture, of towns and settled villages and, consequently, of new social institutions as well as ideological and religious trends. The work done on the social origins of Buddhism and on the growth of society from about the sixth to the seventh centuries BC has been of great significance. One may not entirely agree with the view that it marks the beginning of slavery, but, I think, it has been established that by this time class divisions appear unmistakably. The significance of early empires and of money economy has also been noticed by our historians.

Recent years have seen significant discoveries belonging to the first three centuries of the Christian era. A large number of urban sites have been unearthed not only in Central Asia but also in India. It is surprising that the Kushana levels are in a flourishing condition both in and outside India. This will have to be accounted for. Since the Kushana empire extended over India, Pakistan, Afghanistan, Iran, and Soviet Central Asia, coordinated and sustained efforts will have to be made by the archaeologists and historians of all these countries to study the cultural heritage of the period.

Excavations during the last twenty-five years have certainly established the cultural sequence in chronological order, and made possible the period-wise identification of the main traits of material culture. But since almost all of them have been vertical, they do not give us much idea about the communal life, or the organization of society and economy. It is now time that we undertook horizontal excavations at least at a few selected places with a view to determining the nature of rural or urban settlement as the case may be. We need to know quite a lot about the planning of houses, about the position of kitchen, storeroom, etc.

Apart from this, I would venture to suggest that these studies are inadequate in two important prospects. Firstly, the process of social change which seems to be clearer for north India, is not so clear for south India. I hope that the archaeologists will devote special attention to the archaeological studies of south India for the proto-historic period. The second deficiency is that our archaeologists have not been given adequate facilities to study the interrelationship between the growth of cultures in northern India with those of the neighbouring countries. I am glad that the Government of India has initiated a programme of bilateral archaeological agreements with neighbouring countries. I fervently hope that universities will develop expertise in the study of the archaeology of neighbouring countries. I would also urge the archaeologists and historians of ancient India to devote greater attention to researches in the historical geography of the period.

A strong case has been made for indicating the beginnings of feudalism in India from about the sixth century AD, but we do not know whether there was any difference between feudal and pre-feudal society in regard to technological equipment. The growing number of tools and implements discovered as a result of excavations and their representation in sculpture and painting should enable us to study this subject more carefully. Any number of dates have been suggested for the beginning of the medieval age in India, and the most fashionable is the one which links it up with the coming of the followers of Islam in this country. True, the coming of Islam introduced some changes into the country, but in many ways even under the Turkish rulers, the old feudal society continued, land grants grew in numbers, castes continued to proliferate, and regional trends in art, literature, and language continued to be strengthened.

I do not want to enter here into controversy regarding the applicability of the word feudal to Indian society. It is very clear from all accounts that a large share of the surplus produced by the peasant in medieval India went to the sultan and his amirs, although the process of cultivation and the rural life was controlled by the zamindar. The amirs could not exist independently of the zamindar. This is a system which could be described as feudal if we totally modify the definition of feudalism. Considerable work has been done by scholars in clarifying the nature of property relations in medieval India, the working of the *jagirdari* system and of the village community, and the social relations prevailing at that time.

It has been suggested that the Turks gave a fillip to the process of urbanization in the country. It seems that the processes of urbanization, which included the establishment and growth of large towns as well as *qasbas* was largely the result of the new forms of agrarian relationships which were developed. Large centralized empires which were sustained by the system of revenue assignments, known as the *iqtadari* system and large standing armies created a considerable demand for handicraft products and facilitated internal as well as external commerce. These factors stimulated the process of urbanization. In a sense, urbanization also reflects the expansion of money economy and of commodity production. The major changes influenced cultural trends as well as political institutions and policies. During recent years, extremely valuable studies have been undertaken into the nature and organization of medieval nobility, of the *zamindari* system and of agrarian relations in general.

The discovery of a whole mass of documentary sources has brought a new dimension to medieval studies which are no longer confined to the chronicles. These documents are rich in statistical data. New methods are being evolved to analyse and interpret these data in spite of the fact that the series of figures is neither continuous nor full. Based on these data, quantitative assessments are being made, though I must confess, quantification can hardly replace the need for historical judgement and insight. I earnestly hope that systematic effort will be made by historians to utilize the documentary material and the statistical data included therein, for, it must be admitted, only a very small fragment of them has yet been studied.

Today we are in a position to know much more about village life and about the elements that constituted rural society. This has been a development of great significance which will enable us to understand the nature of agrarian society more fully. With the outlines of social organization becoming clear through the study of the documentary material, both Indian and foreign, our scholars are now beginning to utilize religious as well as secular literature, paintings and architecture, and sources of other types to fill in the details. I feel gratified that archaeological studies are now being utilized to study more adequately medieval society. I hope that greater attention will be paid to the utilization of such sources.

I may venture to offer a few suggestions here. The volume of documentary evidence that has been discovered is so large that it is totally beyond the reach of individual scholars. Unless the work of referencing and calendaring of documents is undertaken on a large scale, the utilization of this material would remain inadequate. Would it be too much to expect that our distinguished university professors would award PhD and MPhil degrees to those young scholars who take up the calendaring of documents?

While discussing the importance of original documents for the study of medieval history, I may be forgiven for reiterating my earlier plea that the European documentary sources should also receive greater attention than they have done in the past. I am not only referring to British, French, Portuguese, and Dutch sources but also to the documents in Persian and Indian languages prepared for the foreign merchants and administrators. I am glad that the Indian Council of Historical Research is aware of the problem. I trust that our young scholars will come forward to avail of the opportunities offered by the Council for studying these fields.

There is a good deal of discussion regarding the crisis of the Mughal empire and its underlying social and economic causes. In this context the question has been raised whether the medieval Indian society could have been transformed into an industrial or a capitalist or even a modern society if the British and the other Europeans had not intervened. The belief that basically the social relationships in India remained constant and that there was no change in the Indian society till the arrival of the British is no longer accepted by historians. However, we are still not clear about the nature of the change, the direction of the change, and the factors which caused the change. These problems have so far been analysed largely from the viewpoint of the working of the rural economy or the growth of money economy in the country. The larger question whether the technique of agricultural production was undergoing any change has not so far been adequately investigated.

It appears that, medieval society in our country was able to make positive achievements up to a point, but it was not able to maintain the tempo of scientific and technological advance. It stagnated and suffered because science and technology could not keep pace with the advance taking place in the West. It is possible that the rapid growth of science and technology in the West was accelerated because land and agriculture could not keep on yielding greater wealth at a fast enough rate, and hence trade, particularly overseas trade, triggered off the movement for scientific and technological advance. In India, on the other hand, the belief that by bringing more and more land under cultivation, enough wealth could be obtained, kept the ruling class in a state of euphoria and hence it did not feel compelled to discover new technology. The ideological climate and the prevailing system of beliefs also seem to have discouraged scientific thought and investigation.

There has been a great deal of interest in recent times in the study of science and technology from the ancient down to the medieval period. These studies have to be intensified and related to the social processes. It would also be necessary to study the history of handicrafts, commodity production, internal trade, and the extent of the use of money in the late Mughal times. It is obvious that such studies will have to be mostly regional, and only when considerable spadework has been done in this direction can we take a synoptic view of the developments in the country as a whole.

Although modern Indian history is not the field of my study, I would like to put forward some suggestions for your consideration. The early history of modern India is still a study of conflicts between Indian princes and the British rulers and their European rivals. In order to shift the focus to the development of Indian society during the period, careful studies will have to be made regarding the social basis of the various principalities which arose in the country at the time, and the impact of British policies on different sections of society. Attention needs to be paid to the position of the tribals and the poorer section of the peasantry which apparently were hit hard by the British administrative and economic policies, and as a result they repeatedly rose in rebellion.

During the 1960s, a number of studies have been made on the impact of utilitarian ideas on the development of administration in India. However, they do not take into account the social and economic milieu in which these administrators were trained in England or the Indian conditions in which they operated. In some works British administration is regarded the fountainhead of all changes in India, and even important changes in social structures are attributed to the activities of the bureaucrats. It is for scholars to find out whether indigenous elements played no part in the process of social change in our country. There have also been some studies of the attitudes of various groups to different kinds of problems, particularly of castes and communities. While such studies do contribute to an understanding of Indian society as a whole, the tendency to explain major social, economic, and political changes primarily in terms of castes, communities, or amorphous 'elite' groups, is fraught with dangers.

The rise of the middle class and other allied groups has aroused considerable interest amongst scholars. In analysing these and other social changes, many Indian historians have adopted approaches which have emanated from abroad. There can certainly be no objection to adopting methodologies developed outside the country if they help us to comprehend the historical reality better. But we should be careful in importing concepts which do not really fit into the framework of Indian society.

Enough attention has not yet been paid to the study of such different segments of society as merchants, artisans, peasants, agricultural labourers, and industrial workers. Although useful work has been done on the development of British agrarian policies, hardly any work has been done on the life and condition of the peasants, or of the peasant movements of the time. These, as well as the study of the development of individual villages, would enable us to understand the problem of the breakdown of the traditional village society in some depth.

The statistical data regarding population, trade, agricultural production, monetary trends, etc., which are available in continuous series from about the middle of the nineteenth century have yet to be studied by Indian historians. The method of quantitative analysis would undoubtedly provide fresh insight into the trend of the development of Indian society and economy in the nineteenth century.

One of the most popular subjects which has drawn the attention of foreign and Indian scholars working on modern India is the history of the freedom movement. For understandable reasons, this subject did not attract too many people when the struggle for freedom was going on. Even historians who at one time were critical of the freedom movement have now become its admirers. But we notice some unfortunate trends in the study of the history of the national movement.

The basic tendencies based on religion, language, caste, community, region, etc., which at one time were highlighted in order to deny India's claim to independence are now being projected in a manner as to prove that the national movement was bereft of all signs of idealism. That it possessed a strong element of unity and solidarity, is sought to be denied. It is thereby attempted to establish that the attainment of freedom was not the result of the struggle of the Indian people and their leaders, but was in the nature of a gift. Attempts have been made to utilize historical documents to prove this point. It is obvious that it would be a great disservice to the cause of objective history if such distortions are not exposed and corrected.

The primary responsibility for researches in the history of India must rest on Indian scholars and the Indian History Congress has to play a pre-eminent role in ensuring that this responsibility is adequately discharged. It is the only national forum which has been providing organized guidance and leadership in this field for a long time and I have no doubt that it would assume greater responsibilities in the future. I am happy that the Indian Council of Historical Research is supplementing its work. The decision of the Council to make students and teachers aware of recent trends and new methods in the writing of history and to translate standard monographs into the various regional languages is welcome. It is obvious that more and more material will have to be made available to teachers and students working in universities and colleges in various Indian languages. In several universities doctoral theses are being submitted in languages of the state. These in turn would have to be made available to the people using the other regional languages.

It is also one of our main responsibilities to popularize the latest research methods in history. Unless our historians are well grounded in both theory and statistics, they cannot make much contribution to social and economic history. Proficiency in the language of the source-material is extremely important for a student of history. It becomes very difficult to use sources in a period of transition, such as the eighteenth century, when these are so diverse and are found in so many languages. For such types of study, we badly need teamwork. Teamwork can be intra-subject, inter-subject, interdepartmental, and inter-university depending on the theme and the nature of the subject. I think that the Indian History Congress and the Indian Council of Historical Research can play an important part in organizing such collective and cooperative work.

Lastly I would like to draw your attention to the need of developing in India the study of history of other countries. There is no doubt that during the 1950s, a large number of books of Indian history are being produced in India, but the study of non-Indian history is very weak in our country. To stimulate interest in this field the Indian History Congress decided to introduce a section on non-Indian history. At present because of paucity of original sources available in India, we can carry on research on such bits of non-Indian history as are marginally related to the main currents of Indian history and as can be studied on the basis of sources available in our archives. For example, we can work on the British use of Indian men and material in extending their power and prestige in different parts of Asia and Africa. But in future we have to think of a few places where we could collect sources regarding certain areas of Asian history, European history, African and Latin American history.

# 2

## Medieval Indian History
Danger of Communal Interpretation
and the Need for Reconsidering Priorities *

It is almost a truism to say that objectivity and a genuine search for truth are necessary for the proper pursuit of knowledge. Most historians will agree that it would be dangerous to base one's research on a priori hypotheses, or to look for only such facts as seem to fit into one's preconceived notions, or to 'explain away' inconvenient data. Even with the best of will, the ideal of absolute objectivity is difficult to attain. But the capacity for dispassionate study, impartiality in the selection of data, and the attempt to see things in their proper historical perspective are nevertheless qualities to be cultivated as a discipline if a true understanding of the past is to be made possible.

Unfortunately, these accepted canons of historiography are not always applied to the study of medieval Indian history. Only too often there is a tendency to look at the history of this period through the coloured glasses of communalism. The picture of conflict between followers of different religions gets out of focus, and the vision of historical processes becomes distorted. That there were conflicts on religious issues or that there were powerful separatist cultural movements among the different communities which at times engendered mutual antagonism is undeniable. But at the same time, the existence of opposite

* Presidential address, Medieval India, *Proceedings of Indian History Congress*, XXIV Session, Delhi, 1961, pp. 107–13.

trends, the trends in favour of unity and cultural synthesis, should not be underestimated either. In any case, it would be perilous to assume that conflict between religious communities was the central theme around which the drama of medieval Indian history revolved.

It is regrettable that forces of communalism, revivalism, and chauvinism have deeply corroded the political life of this sub-continent in modern times; it is even more disconcerting that those who pursue communal politics look for a justification of their present policies from history. They project their own conceptions in the understanding of the past, and seek to identify themselves with such medieval trends as appear to them to be akin to their emotions. Since the historian cannot remain aloof from the various political trends, it is understandable that some of them are unable to escape the influence of such an outlook in their historical writing.

I would not presume to criticize the writings of well-known scholars in this respect. But I venture to mention a few examples of how even some famous historians have permitted their assumptions to appear as axiomatic, not requiring academic scrutiny. In his Introduction to the *History of Freedom Movement* published by a Board of Editors appointed by the Government of Pakistan, I. H. Qureshi has criticized the Mughal government in the following words:

It was a crime to lull the Muslims into believing that the maintenance of the Empire was not their primary responsibility. Even more disastrous was the encouragement of the feeling that tolerance implied the belief that all religions were merely different paths; all equally good, for reaching the same God. This was an even more potent cause of the demoralization and degeneration of the Muslims, especially their acceptance of subtle non-Islamic ideas. Indeed this was the darkest period in the history of Indian Islam.[1]

Not entirely dissimilar is the approach of the distinguished Indian historian, R. C. Majumdar. In a study on historical writing organized by the School of Oriental and African Studies, London, the learned scholar states:

The newly acquired ideal of a 'secular State' is opposed to all known facts of Indian history. But it is sought to be buttressed by a new conception of Indian history and culture, which recognizes no distinct

Hindu or Muslim culture in modern India, and looks upon these, along with European or Western culture, as so many streams meeting together only to mingle and lose their separate entities in the sea of Indian culture. The Muslims, however, repudiate any such idea, and Islamic culture is not only recognized as a distinct entity, but has been formally adopted as the basis of the new State of Pakistan. In India, however, a small but gradually increasing class of influential persons now fight shy of the term 'Hindu' as a designation of a cultural unit, and only think in terms of an Indian culture. Whatever may be the value of such an idea in shaping India's culture, it becomes positively dangerous when it encroaches upon the domain of Indian history and seeks to ignore the existence of Hindu culture as one of the most potent and patent facts of Indian history even today.[2]

The tendency on the part of certain Indian or Pakistani historians to be influenced by religious prejudices, though hardly justifiable, is at least understandable. However, many Western historians and institutions are also emphasizing the irreconcilability of Hindu and Muslim cultures. It was hoped that with the end of the British rule in India, the imperialist attempt to present medieval Indian history as the story of an unending struggle between different communities would also end. But it appears that according to some Western historians, the policy which culminated in the establishment of Pakistan requires a continuing justification. Introducing the section on 'Islam in Medieval India' in the Columbia University publication, *Sources of Indian Tradition*. Peter Hardy of London explains his standpoint thus:

...neither educated Muslims nor educated Hindus accepted cultural co-existence as a natural prelude to cultural assimilation. Thus long before British rule and long before modern political notions of Muslim nationhood, the consensus of the Muslim community in India had rejected the eclecticism of Akbar and Dara Shikoh for the purified Islamic teachings of Shaikh Ahmad of Sirhind and Shah Wali-Ullah. Cultural apartheid was the dominant ideal in medieval Muslim India, in default of cultural victory.

While emphasizing the danger of the influence of a communal outlook, I have no desire to minimize the importance of avoiding other prejudices. If any scholar were to deny the significance of the role of religious conflict altogether, he would be equally guilty of distorting history. Similarly, scholars have to be on their guard against the uncritical acceptance of other 'ready-made' theories, such as the mechanical application of the materialist interpretation of history, or tendency to apply current norms to judge the trends of an earlier period. Hasty generalizations on the basis of inadequate data, such as Wittfogel's theory of Oriental despotism, have to be subjected to the scrutiny of historical criticism.

On the basis of our existing knowledge of medieval Indian history, it would be premature to try and decide whether religion, or ideas, or relationships of production or any other factor played the *determining* role in the history of the period. The tendency to assume that the main basis of social division, or the leitmotif of social action, whether in the field of politics or of culture was religion, can hardly be justified on the basis of the available data. During the medieval period, there were many things which the Hindus, and similarly the Muslims, had in common with their co-religionists in the country. At the same time, common bonds between the members of the two communities belonging to the same region, or to the same class seem to be equally, if not more powerful. The differences in thought and outlook between Hindus and Muslims belonging to a particular class and region do not seem to be so marked as between the members of the same community belonging to different regions or social background. Religious affinity or antagonism influenced the actions of individuals or groups on some occasions, but in many more cases, decisions were influenced by political, economic or other motives and interests.

Thus while recognizing the importance of the study of religious factors and regional groupings, a balanced understanding demands the study of Indian society as a whole, giving due weight to the interplay of all the various factors: political, economic, social, technological, geographical, ethnic, cultural as well as religious.

Since medieval Indian society was mainly agricultural, the foremost need is to study the agrarian relations subsisting therein. Some valuable work has been and is being done in this field at Aligarh and elsewhere but much more detailed research, especially on a regional basis, has yet to be done. The commonly held opinion that there was no substantial change in the nature and extent of agricultural production requires a fuller examination. It is true that there does not seem to be much change in production technique, nor was there an appreciable extension of irrigation works, but the growth in the cultivation of 'cash crops' especially indigo, cotton, sugarcane, and later tobacco, must have affected village economy. Another significant development was the extension of cultivation to many areas which had been covered by forests. This could not have taken place by the individual effort of the peasant: there is some evidence to suggest that it was generally organized by the zamindars. Both these factors could have led to changes in the system of agricultural production, but the extent and nature of this change is not yet clear.

Another major development during the medieval period was the growth of the practice of the peasants paying revenue in cash, but neither the extent of the cash nexus nor its economic consequences have been adequately studied. Similar is the case with the question of land tenure. It seems that by and large peasants had acquired alienable rights in landholding within certain limits, but the question of the relationship of the individual peasant with the village community requires elucidation, as also the question of the rights of the ruling class over the peasant (apart from the right to realize the revenue). The distinction between *raiyati* and zamindari villages, the de facto control of state officers over peasants in zamindari villages, and the right of the peasant to appeal to government authorities against the decisions of the zamindars, are questions requiring careful scrutiny. The role of caste (among Hindus as well as Muslims) in village economy, the position of landless agricultural labourers (including those whose holdings were very small), and the related question of the factors which contributed to migrations from villages to towns when pressure on land was not considerable, have still to be adequately studied. Though problems of the modes of assessment of land revenue, its magnitude and incidence, and the machinery of collection have been analysed to some extent, another aspect requiring attention is the tendency of the tax on agricultural produce to develop into land rent. How far did this change actually take place is not yet clear, but perhaps the concept of *nasaq* and the growth of the *ijara* were bound to lead to this process. These are only some of the problems of village economy that require the attention of research workers. An understanding of these problems is essential if the history of the overwhelming majority of the common people is to be reconstructed.

No proper study of the agrarian system or of the nature of the state and its polity is possible without an adequate understanding of the position of the ruling classes. In medieval India, the ruling classes comprised two main groups: the nobles (amirs) and the zamindars. The nobles were high officers of state to whom the state's share of land revenue was assigned in lieu of services performed by them. During the Sultanate period they were usually called *muqtis* or *iqtadars*, while under the Mughals, they were the *jagirdars* and *mansabdars*. Though the broad nature of the nobility is known, detailed studies have yet to be made. Some valuable work is being done at Aligarh on the composition, character, and political role of the nobility, but a careful study of the working of the *jagirdari* system has still to be undertaken. In many of the monographs and articles, formulations regarding the jagirdari system have been made which appear to be wide off the mark, even on the basis of the data hitherto available. For example, the administrative duties and functions of the jagirdars and the relationship between them and other officers such as *faujdars*, *amins*, and *amils*, are frequently misunderstood and their importance underestimated.

The failure of Akbar to pay his officers cash salaries, perhaps inevitable at the time, the payment of the overwhelming majority of mansabdars by *jagirs*, the inflation of the nobility and the demand for higher *mansabs* resulting in a shortage of jagirs produced a crisis in the ruling class as well as in the economy of the country. This crisis not only led to a decline of Mughal polity but also intensified bitterness between various social, ethnic, religious, and regional groups. The consequences of this crisis were far-reaching for the Mughal empire as well as for Indian society generally. It is therefore hoped that the scholars would devote their special attention to the study of the institutions of the nobility and jagirdari.

The other important element of the ruling class was that of the zamindars. Unfortunately little attention has been paid by historians to a systematic study of the nature and character of the institution of zamindari or of the role of the zamindars in the history of the period. However, even on the basis of the meagre studies on the subject, it would not be unjustifiable to put forward the tentative suggestion that no understanding of medieval politics, or of medieval economy or culture can be considered adequate till questions connected with the zamindari system have been properly examined.

I have used the term zamindar in the same broad sense in which it was used in Mughal chronicles and documents, viz., all hereditary landed interests, excluding the peasants. The term was intended to cover a very wide range of landed interests, from ruling princes enjoying independence or autonomy to petty intermediaries. The classification of these rights, acquired in the course of centuries from ancient times and undergoing constant change, has not advanced far beyond the stage when it was first investigated by Grant and others in the last quarter of the eighteenth century, while the process of this change has hardly received much attention.

It seems that on the eve of the Turkish conquest, the socio-political structure was essentially pyramidical: the Rajput empires and kingdoms exercizing varying degrees of overlordship and control over local chiefs, many of whom, perhaps a majority being non-Rajput belonging to indigenous tribes or lower castes. The Turkish rulers overthrew as many of the bigger chiefs as they could, and tried to obtain the recognition of their suzerainty from the rest on varying terms and conditions, the smaller chiefs remaining generally undisturbed. Between the thirteenth and the fifteenth centuries, however, there appears to be a wholesale displacement of the local chiefs of the lower castes by the Rajputs. It is unlikely that this process would have taken place without the support or connivance of the authorities of the Sultanate. If this assumption is correct, it would seem that close political and economic links were established between the Sultanate and the Rajput aristocracy. With the break-up of the Tughluq empire, the local Rajput chiefs began to play an increasingly important part in politics. At the same time, attempts were made by the sultans to curtail the administrative and economic powers of the petty zamindars. Nevertheless local administration remained largely vested in zamindars of different types.

Akbar gave a new turn to imperial policy towards the zamindars. While ensuring that the ruling chiefs accepted his paramountcy, he initiated the policy of recruiting them to the ranks of the nobility. The large-scale influx of hereditary chiefs into the administrative machinery brought about important changes in the nature and character of the state. This policy was continued by his successors, and while it strengthened the state, it also created tensions between nobles who had no hereditary rights and the ruling chiefs who had been included in the nobility.

Though the Mughals continued to base their administration on the zamindari system, they sought to increase the hold of the central government over the zamindars, achieving a large measure of success. But the opposite tendency was also at work. Many of the chieftains extended their states, hereditary collectors of land revenue tended to become large zamindars, the *ijaradars*, the holders of *madad-i-maash* grants and even many of the officials had come to acquire zamindari rights. Many documents of sale or purchase of these rights during the seventeenth and eighteenth centuries have come to light suggesting transfers of these rights on a large scale. There are also indications that some of those who purchased these rights were traders or businessmen. These changes must have affected village society considerably.

The decline of local autonomy and the establishment of a centralized empire might have stimulated the growth of a money economy and contributed to the rise of a unified market, apart from bringing political and other benefits. On the other hand, the loss of local autonomy had its obvious disadvantages. In any case, since the centralized state based itself on the zamindari system, the decline of centralization was perhaps inevitable. Moreover, the effects which the pyramidical structure had on the life of the common people in the villages are by no means clear. Perhaps the central authority, by placing curbs on the power of the zamindars, was able to restrict the exploitation of the peasantry. At the same time, it is also possible that the peasant had to bear the dual burden of the zamindar and the jagirdar, and thus suffered more. May be that some of the powerful political movements which were led by zamindars of various types were able to attract a considerable peasant following for this very reason.

The cultural role of the zamindars also requires careful investigation. In view of their close association with the state, they appear to have acted as a link between the cultural traditions of the courts and the common people. Since many of the zamindars served as officials in different parts of the empire, their outlook could not have remained narrowly local or parochial. The development of a composite cultural tradition owed not a little to the zamindars. On the other hand, their patronage of local cultural activity seems to have strengthened the traditions of conservatism.

I have taken the liberty of sharing my thoughts with you at some length on the question of agrarian relations to illustrate the point that in spite of the very valuable work that has already been done in medieval Indian history, a great deal remains to be examined before we are able to perceive, even dimly, the outlines of the historical processes of the period. While interpretative works are necessary, and while general histories have to be written re-evaluating our existing knowledge of the subject, with minor changes here and there, the major task before research workers is to concentrate on the investigation of the different aspects of Indian society. Such 'burrowing' expeditions into details are not likely to produce spectacular results, but in this way we will be able to lay the foundations on which the edifice of a scientific history can be raised.

I will not presume to enumerate all the various fields which require urgent study, but I venture to suggest some of the other topics which may be fruitfully examined on a priority basis.

Though some useful work has been done on the pattern of trade and industry during the seventeenth–eighteenth centuries, adequate study of this aspect for the earlier period has not been made. Unless attention is paid to this problem, it will not be possible to understand why Indian trade and industry could not keep pace with western European progress, why the growth of a middle class was retarded, why Indian towns could not develop into cities of the Western type, and why in spite of a favourable balance of trade, Indian industry and commerce fell under the domination of the Europeans.

One of the major factors which facilitated European domination was scientific and technological superiority, achieved even before the Industrial Revolution. Though the spirit of scientific enquiry was not wanting in the Mughal empire, and though some advance in technology is noticeable, it is perhaps symbolic of the medieval Indian outlook that neither Akbar nor his successors showed any interest in the two most significant inventions of the Western world: the mechanical clock and the printing press. We must examine the corpus of scientific knowledge and the state of technology during the period in order to study the problem mentioned above. Fortunately, work has already been started in the field under the auspices of the National Institute of Sciences.

Although a good deal of valuable research has been done on political history and the administrative institutions of the period, only the outlines have emerged so far. Detailed studies of the internal working of the administrative machinery, together with its tensions and stresses and their impact on policies and problems, have yet to be carried out. These studies will enable us to understand with greater clarity the nature and character of the state and the fundamental problems of its polity.

I have ventured to stress mainly the importance of the study of socio-economic factors and the problems of state and polity. This does not mean that I am underestimating the importance of cultural movements. Some very useful studies on various aspects of cultural life have been published, but a great deal remains to be done. In this respect, a fruitful line of investigation would be to undertake comparative studies of different cultural trends and to examine their interaction. However, unless cultural phenomena are seen against the social background, the sense of perspective may be lost.

One of the factors which has circumscribed research work so far is the limitation imposed by the nature of the source material. Our studies have been mainly based on the Persian chronicles and the accounts left by foreign travellers. Their value and importance are undeniable, and these will continue to be the principal sources of our information. Nevertheless, their inadequacy is only too evident: the scope of historiography has changed so much since medieval times that it would be unrealistic to expect medieval writers to supply us information on the life of the common people, or to explain in detail the working of administrative institutions, or to provide economic data. Moreover, it is not always easy to judge how far their statements have been coloured by their political, religious or social prejudices, or their sources of reliable information.

Furthermore, statements of facts are so deeply intermixed with expressions of personal opinion that it is difficult to distinguish one from the other. Every effort has therefore to be made to supplement the data contained in such works from all other possible sources. Fortunately, a great mass of documentary material is still extant. The two largest collections of documents of the Mughal period are in the Rajasthan State Archives and the Central Records Office of Hyderabad. A rich collection of administrative documents has recently been acquired by the National Archives of India. The vast volume of the records of the European commercial firms as well as missionary societies, lodged in different places in India and abroad, also contain a wealth of information on the seventeenth century. These large collections, along with numerous smaller collections, lie scattered in various offices, religious institutions, commercial houses, and with private individuals. Only an infinitesimal fraction of these documents has so far been utilized by historians. Even though it is not possible to assess the value of these unexplored sources fully, it is a safe assumption that their proper utilization will materially alter our understanding of medieval history. May I venture to suggest that a scheme for the handlisting and calendaring of the collections of documents should be sponsored by the Indian History Congress in collaboration with the Union and state governments, the universities and learned societies.

Even the utilization of the documentary material is not likely to provide the historian with adequate data to reconstruct the history of the common people. A new methodology of research has to be evolved to tackle this problem. Bits and pieces of information scattered in innumerable pages of books and documents have to be fitted together to provide an outline of medieval society; evidence of a later date has to be used judiciously in the process of 'working backwards'; techniques of sociological and anthropological investigation have to be employed, and methods of statistical analysis have to be used where figures are available.

Work on these lines will perhaps be beyond the capacity of most individual workers. Cooperative effort will therefore become more and more necessary. One of the most important

methods of achieving this cooperation without in any way cir-
cumscribing the historical judgement and imagination of scholars, is to undertake the preparation of works of reference.
Biographical and geographical dictionaries, glossaries of terms,
bibliographical studies, historical maps, editions, annotations,
and translations of texts, selections of documents, etc. will
considerably facilitate the study of the more complex historical
processes.

Lastly, it is worthwhile repeating the obvious requirement of
research workers in the field of medieval Indian history, namely,
the need for a proper linguistic equipment. It would be unwise
for a scholar to depend only on translations. He must have at
least a working knowledge of the languages in which the bulk
of the source material is to be found. But in our endeavour to
break fresh ground and taking the study of the subject on a still
higher plane, we cannot afford to ignore the extremely valuable
contribution of distinguished historians, and of the lines of work
indicated by them.

## Notes and References

1. *A History of the Freedom Movement: Being the Story of Muslim Struggle for
the Freedom of Hind-Pakistan*, 1707–1947, Karachi, 1957, Vol. I, p. 34.

2. C. H. Philips, ed., *Historians of India, Pakistan, and Ceylon*, London,
1961, pp. 426–7.

3. Wm. Theodore de Bary, ed., *Sources of Indian Tradition*, Columbia
University Press, New York, 1958, p. 370.

# 3

# *Perspective on Regional History*
## Medieval Punjab*

While fully sharing the approach that regional history should not
be permitted to be influenced by chauvinistic and separatist
considerations, I would like to emphasize the importance of the
study of regional history for the study of the history of India as
a whole. Ours is a large country with considerable variations in
its different regions. At the same time, the existence of major
differences notwithstanding there is a remarkable unity in the
broad pattern of socio-economic development, culture, and administrative institutions. The understanding of the significant
trends of historical change in the country would remain sadly
incomplete unless the details are studied at the regional level.
In fact, most detailed studies are possible only at that level, such
as the working of the administrative machinery, land relations,
pattern of agricultural production, organization of trade and
handicraft, and position of social classes and groups. These
regional studies will be meaningful only if they are undertaken
in the context of the history of the whole country, for only then
can the significance of the different features be understood and
the distinctiveness appreciated. Even the problems of regional
history would arise in the mind of the scholar only as a part of
the study of the history of the country as a whole, for the process

---

* Presidential Address, Medieval Punjab, *Punjab History Conference*, Ist
Session, Patiala, 1966, *Proceedings*, pp. 73–81.

of social change and the factors motivating it can hardly be observed within the narrow field of a region.

I may be forgiven if by the Punjab I refer neither to the territory of the present Indian state of that name, nor even of the Punjabi *suba* which many friends think should be established. The Punjab, the land of the five rivers, is a geographical as well as a historical entity. More or less, the Punjab comprised the territory included in the British province of that name and included the Punjab hill states and Jammu. Geographically, this comprised the five doabs, the basin of the upper Ghaggar, and the northern hill areas economically connected with the plains. It is true that during the medieval period, the territory to which I have referred did not form part of a single political unit. Even since Mahmud of Ghazni made Lahore a province of his empire, his governors and descendants made several attempts to bring the entire territory up to Delhi under their control. But their authority over the hill areas, the territory between the Sultlej and the Yamuna, and over Multan was by no means continuous or stable. During the Sultan-ate period, Multan, Dipalpur, and Lahore were generally under separate governors while the Cis-Sutlej region remained administratively cut off from rest of the Punjab. For a time, Multan was governed by an independent dynasty. Under Akbar and his successors, the region was divided between the subas of Lahore and Multan, while the *sarkar*s of Sirhind and Hissar Firoza formed part of the suba of Delhi with the Sutlej forming the boundary. But inspite of the administrative fragmentation, the Punjab had developed during the medieval period a personality of its own. It was culturally and socially distinct from the Ganga-Yamuna doab in the east, Kashmir in the north, the territory of Roh[1] in the west and Rajputana in the south. It is true that within this region there were variations from place to place and from one social group to the other, but these variations do not militate against the broader historical unity of the Punjab. In fact, no one had ever seriously questioned this unity until the British imperi-alists decided to partition it on the basis of religion.[2] Notwith-standing the madness which gripped the people of the region in the wake of Partition, the affectionate memories of the glory of united Punjab still move the heart of the common people.

To the superficial observer, the history of the Punjab during the medieval period is marked by several distinctive features, each of which needs to be studied with great care. I shall refer to only a few of these features. First and foremost, society in the Punjab during the Middle Ages is characterized by the powerful survivals of tribal organization. The tribe (*qaum* or *zat*), the clan (*qabila*) and smaller groups of cognatic relatives dominated social relations, and materially influenced relationships of production. Administration and policies also revolved round tribal organizations. Tribal society retained many of its basic pastoral characteristics even where agriculture and trade were highly developed. The region of Dipalpur remained comparatively backward agriculturally during most of the medieval period, and, therefore, it was only natural that the pastoral features should be more pronounced there. Wealth was counted in terms of head of cattle, and the tax was widely collected on the basis of cattle rather than land or agricultural production. But even in areas where agriculture was developed, revenue was often taken in terms of individuals or cattle. For example, Babur writes about the territory roughly corresponding to the modern district of Jhelum, that:

One tribe is called Jud and the other Jaujuha. From old times they have been the rulers and inhabitants of this hill, and of the *ils* and *uluses* which are between Nilab and Bhera; but their power is exerted in a friendly and brotherly way. They cannot take from them whatever they please. They take as their share a portion that has been fixed from very remote times.... They give a *Shahrukhi* for each head of cattle and seven *Shahrukhes* are paid by each master of a family.... The chief man amongst them gets the name of Rai; his younger brothers and sons are called maliks.

During the Mughal period agriculture was further extended and the state provided considerable encouragement, including the extension of irrigation works. According to Abul Fazl, irrigation in the suba of Lahore was chiefly from wells. Later canals were also constructed. With the extension of cultivation the system of assessing revenue per bigha of land under cultivation (*zabti* system) was also extended while the *ghalla-bakhshi* system was further developed in the province of Multan. Notwithstanding these changes, the tribal pattern continued and produced a new form of feudalism. There were areas where a dominant tribe would be of zamindars while the peasants or occupancy tenants would be of another tribe; in both cases vestiges of communal, tribal or clan rights would continue. Simultaneously in many cases individuals of a tribe tended to acquire rights of overlordship over the other members of the same tribe. Then there were peculiar institutions like that of the *dhok*. The number of small zamindars who let out land to tenants and simultaneously carried on cultivation themselves, appears to be much larger in the Punjab than in the Ganga valley or Rajputana. These developments also appear to be connected with the continuance of the tribal system.

The complexity of the socio-economic relationship in the Punjab appears to have been accentuated because many new tribes seem to have come to the region during the medieval period and established themselves in a position of superiority over the tribes which had held control earlier. These tribes were some time pushed out, but were generally depressed and made to accept inferior positions. This tribal tussle and the changes in the state of tribes very probably continued throughout the medieval period. Even the position as recorded in the *Ain-i-Akbari* had undergone appreciable changes by the eighteenth century. A careful study of the tribal organization of the Punjab will open new vistas of research in different aspects of Indian history—political, economic, social as well as cultural.

Not only was the agricultural fertility of the Punjab 'rarely equalled' in the words of Abul Fazl, but also its trade was highly developed. Lahore, which became during the Mughal period one of the biggest cities of the country, could boast of 'the choicest production of Turkistan, Persia, and Hindustan' and was considered as the 'resort of the people of all countries whose manufactures present an astonishing display' (*Ain-i-Akbari*). Multan had also become a great centre of international trade, passing not only through the overland route to Qandhar, but also through the Indus to Arab countries beyond the seas. Although it had somewhat declined by the second half of the seventeenth century, its commercial importance is mentioned even by Thevenot. No worthwhile study has yet been made of the volume, nature, pattern, organizations or the economic significance of this trade.

Abundant agricultural surplus and extensive trade led to the twofold development of growth of science and technology on the one hand and the expansion of manufactures on the other. Even a preliminary study made so far has revealed that Lahore had become a great centre of mathematical sciences and scientific instrument-making during the seventeenth century. The family of Ustad Isa of Lahore, the architect of the Taj Mahal, was well-known for mathematics and science, and is credited with the compilation of a number of scientific works. Astrolabes manufactured in Lahore were considered to be among the best in the East. Similarly, there are tantalizing references to the extensive existence of handicrafts and manufactures, and to the skill of the Punjabi craftsmen. Researches in these fields are bound to be rewarding.

From the point of view of political history, the study of relationship of the chieftains with the representatives of the central government deserves particular attention. The important part played by the Rajput rajas of the hill states is undeniable but it has been only inadequately studied. Also, not enough is known about the political role of important tribal chiefs such as the Gakkars. The Baluchi incursions into the Punjab and the acquisition of territory by them seem to be very important, but not much is known about them. Incidentally the main Baluchi centre, Derajat, does not figure in the revenue list given by Abul Fazl, even though they had definitely accepted Mughal suzerainty. Is it a fact, as tradition puts it, that they paid no land revenue? If so, why not?

While the Baluchi immigration into the Punjab left permanent marks, it is difficult to detect the lasting signs of many other incursions. It is known that many 'ghazis'[3] from Central Asia came to the Punjab with the Ghaznavid armies and settled here. What happened to them and who are their descendants? Throughout the thirteenth and the fourteenth centuries, the Mongols kept on raiding India. Most of the raids were checked in the Punjab. In fact the military commanders of the Punjab who were entrusted with the responsibility of defending the Sultanate from the Mongol raiders played a very important part in the politics of Hindustan. But it is not known whether the Mongol attacks or their defeat left any durable marks on the history of the Punjab. We also know that partly as a result of the Mongol attacks, and partly due to the expansion of the Chughtai power in Afghanistan, there were large scale immigrations of Afghan tribes from Roh to India. It is, however, surprising that comparatively few of these Afghan clans settled down in the

Punjab permanently. The considerable Afghan settlement during the fifteenth and sixteenth centuries in the Punjab, dwindles appreciably in the seventeenth century whereas further east and in the south this tendency cannot be observed.

The Punjab has been the great home of religious movements in the Middle Ages. Shaikh Ali Hujviri, the author of *Kashful Mahjub*, a major theoretical work on Sufism, lived in Lahore in the Ghaznavid period and died there. Bahauddin Zakariya established the Suhrawardi order at Multan which became particularly important when his grandson, Ruknuddin, received favours from the Tughlaq sultans. Shaikh Farid-ud-din Ganj-i-Shakar, the famous Chishti, established himself at Ajodhan, later called Pakpattan, and his family became very influential. Another Suhrawardi saint, Saiyid Jalal-ud-din Bukhari, called Makhdum Jahanian Jahangasht, was held in great esteem by Firoz Tughlaq and consequently, his headquarters in Uchh acquired considerable importance. A very large number of the Muslim tribes of the Punjab claim that their ancestors were converted to Islam by one or the other of these saints. In spite of careful study of the records of these Sufi saints, I have failed to get any evidence of their missionary activities. It is quite possible that later Muslims considered it more 'respectable' to attribute the conversion of their ancestors to the miraculous powers of a famous saint rather than to some mundane motive, and hence such stories are to be regarded as apocryphal. But the question remains, when were these tribes converted and why did they change their faith? It is obvious that the common people could not have changed their faith for any ideological reason, nor were they converted by the 'argument of the sword'. There is no such evidence on record. Moreover, why was the 'argument of the sword' not applied near Delhi? Considering that many of the tribes which were converted belonged to the economically deprived sections of society, the temptation of material gain could have been a likely factor. Perhaps, this phenomenon can be explained in socio-economic terms, but that requires further investigations.

During the Mughal period, the Punjab was simultaneously the home of a militant revivalist Muslim movement and of a tolerant liberal movement. Shaikh Ahmad Sirhindi, the regenerator of the second millennium to his followers, spearheaded an intolerant and chauvinistic movement. Because of his influence over the Afghan tribes settled in the Punjab, and of his attempt to utilize, in the fashion of the Jesuits, the grandees of the empire, he was thrown into prison by Jahangir, and when released he preferred to stay at the court to avoid further trouble. His disciple Shaikh Adam of Banur had to leave the country because his activities among the Afghan tribesmen were considered to be prejudicial to the state.[4] Very different in character was the Qadiri centre of Lahore. The outlook of Mian Mir and Mulla Shah has been popularized by Dara Shikoh, who incidentally held for long the governorship of Lahore. What were the social roots of their contradictory movements and from where did they receive sustenance are interesting problems for investigations.

The most significant religious movement to have emerged from the Punjab is undoubtedly the Sikh movement. Guru Nanak made an explicit attempt to unify the Hindus and Muslims, and certainly succeeded in synthesizing within his own teachings, the essential concepts of Hinduism and Islam. His message was essentially for the common man, and his identification with the message was so complete that in his teachings, and in the idiom that he used, the life and struggle of the peasant find a reflection.[5] Naturally, a great deal has been written about Guru Nanak and on the Sikhs by many scholars, yet, even this subject deserves further and careful study. What were the socio-economic origins of the early followers of Guru Nanak and his spiritual successors? What aspects of the Guru's teaching attracted them most, if it can be assured that masses during the medieval period changed their faith because of individual ideological predilections. Alternatively, what were the other reasons and the mechanics of the spread of Sikhism? Even the frequently answered question regarding the transformation of a tolerant religious community into a militant sect, deserves further investigation. Neither Jahangir's treatment of Guru Arjan, nor the attitude adopted by Aurangzeb provide an adequate explanation for the emergence of this powerful movement. A more careful examination of the social, economic, and political factors might alter our understanding of the transformation.

I have ventured to refer to only some of the major problems of the history of the Punjab during the medieval period which I feel deserve fuller study. Such investigation will simultaneously

be of value in understanding the wider historical processes in
the country. There is however one major difficulty in conducting
such studies. The destiny of the Punjab being so closely linked
up with the rest of the country, there is no worthwhile medieval
history or chronicle dealing exclusively with the region. The
historical data regarding the Punjab have therefore to be culled
from the general medieval chronicles. Apart from the difficulty
of collecting evidence which is widely scattered, there is the
more serious problem of the scope of the medieval chronicles
being materially different from the things we wish to study.
Consequently bits and pieces of information have to be collected and inference drawn. The detail even though meagre and
incomplete, has to be carefully analysed with the help of the
modern apparatus of historical investigation. This data has to
be supplemented with sources of other types such as administration manuals, *insha* collections, accounts left by foreign
travellers, religious literature, and the few original documents
extant. In fact, the Punjab is not as fortunate as Rajasthan or
Hyderabad in this respect. However, in the records preserved
at Bikaner and Hyderabad, valuable references are available to
the developments in the Punjab. I do hope that a sufficient
number of scholars will acquire adequate linguistic proficiency
to be able to use these documents and sources.

The inadequacy of sources makes it necessary for scholars
to employ the difficult as well as dangerous technique of working
backwards that is, studying the earliest definite data available
and then proceeding to examine to what extent was the earlier
situation similar. For example, the evidence collected by the
early British administrators regarding the tribes or the land
system can be a useful point of 'working backwards' in time.
Along with this is the task of conducting sociological and anthropological field investigations and the collection of oral traditions
and folklore, before society changes further and even the blurred
memories are completely obliterated. The recently developed
technique of utilizing sociological and anthropological evidences
as sources of history, though by no means free from objection,
can be usefully employed for whatever it is worth. Unfortunately
it will not be possible for our scholars to conduct any field
investigations outside of the border, or even to utilize the records
available there, until the present political situation lasts. Let us

hope that the communal frenzy which has been fanned by external forces will subside and all facts of the true personality of the Punjab can be freely studied.

## Notes and References

1. Abbas Khan defines the territory of Roh as the Afghan region between Attock and Siwi, with the Indus as its eastern boundary. See, *Tarikh-i-Shershahi*, B. P. Ambashtya, English transl. Patna, 1972, p. 9.

2. It is significant that in the course of the earliest studies conducted by the British administrators, the observation has generally been made that cultural differences on grounds of religion are of a comparatively minor nature. Cf. *Punjab District Gazetteers*.

3. For the term 'ghazi' see, C. E. Bosworth, *The Ghaznavids*, Edinburg, 1963, p. 114.

4. For an interesting study of Shaikh Ahmad and his disciple, see A. A. Rizvi's book, *Muslim Revivalist Movement in Northern India in the Sixteenth and Seventeenth Centuries*, Agra, 1965, pp. 202–60, 384–8.

5. Irfan Habib's paper, 'Evidence for Sixteenth Century Agrarian Conditions in the Guru Granth Sahib', in *Indian Economic and Social History Review*, Vol. I, 1964, pp. 64–72.

# 4

~~~

# *Value and Importance of*
# *Urban History**

The value and importance of urban history has always been recognized by all students of history. But the nature of work done in the field till Independence was hardly substantial. Since Independence, interest has certainly been increasing and some extremely important studies have been undertaken. Among the earliest scholars to take up the study of growth and classification of towns during the Mughal period was I. P. Gupta, who started his work under the guidance of Satish Chandra. Soon after that came the work of H. K. Naqvi. Following her, S. C. Misra literally and metaphorically exposed new avenues of research when he took up with his colleagues the excavation and the interpretation of the ruins of Champaner. A few other scholars have published interesting studies which throw light on the urban history of medieval India. J. S. Grewal and Indu Banga, by undertaking the study of Batala, have thrown new light on the problems of urban history. While fully appreciating the excellence of the work already done, I may be permitted to point out that this is a field which requires a far more intensive study than has been undertaken so far.

Our archaeologists have uncovered the remains of Harappan cities. They have shown that these towns had stores of food

* Inaugural Address, Seminar on Urban History, in J. S. Grewal and Indu Banga, eds, *Studies in Urban History*, Guru Nanak Dev University, Amritsar, 1981, pp. 1–7, 206–9.

grains, that they were centres of trade with far-off lands of Mesopotamia, etc. that they had a hierarchical social system, monarchical polity, and perhaps an established religion. But the nature and extent of the dependence of Mohenjodaro and Harappa on trade, particularly on Mesopotamia, and their importance as collecting centres for goods and articles from as far north as Badakhshan and as far south as perhaps the Deccan as well as the Yamuna-Sutlej divide has not been fully understood. There are several questions which remain unanswered. How was agriculture able to generate sufficient surplus to maintain an urban population? How was the surplus extracted from the producers? What did the town-dwellers do for a living? What did they manufacture and trade in, etc.?

For almost a thousand years or perhaps more we do not find any evidence of urban settlements. The ochre-coloured pottery people of the Ganga valley were almost certainly nomadic. The habitational remains of the black and red ware people indicate that these were villages or hamlets or just camping sites of the groups of people undertaking, what Kosambi has called, 'boolies'. At none of the painted grey ware sites remains of permanent dwellings have been discovered. They seem to be essentially a pastoral people who took to shifting cultivation. It is not until the sixth century BC, with the emergence, on a large scale, of settled agriculture, the use on an extensive scale of iron, of northern black polished wares and the punch-marked coins, that definite evidence of the existence of urban centres is to be found.

Several questions arise from these observations. Why did urban centres decline? Why did they not develop again for such a long time? Was there a decline in agricultural production, at any rate in the accumulation of agricultural surplus? If so, why? The painted grey ware people had technological advantage over their predecessors in two respects. They knew the use of iron and also used horses. Why did they take so long to develop settled agriculture and build towns? By the time Christ was born, both north and south India had well-developed towns, well-organized handicraft production, and extensive trade including foreign trade. Money economy had taken firm root and gold was being extensively used. Urban development of ancient India seems to have reached its high watermark in the Gupta Age. However, what factors contributed to the rise of towns? How was agricultural surplus extracted so that it reached the towns? What was the extent of manufacture and trade? What was the occupation of the town-dwellers? These and many other related questions have been raised but inadequately answered so far. With the emergence of feudal relationships, the position of towns seems to be undergoing a change. It appears that in northern India, urban decline had set in and continued at least till the thirteenth century. However, there is no indication that the trade of coastal regions and the accumulation of gold in south India, which was a result of the extensive overseas trade, suffered any decline. How can these developments be explained? What was the direction in which the economy was moving? If Al-Biruni is to be believed, urban morphology was undergoing a change. But I am not certain whether it is possible to accept fully the interpretation which the late Muhammad Habib has given.[1] Similarly, in the light of the analysis made by R. S. Sharma and B. N. S. Yadav, it seems difficult to accept some of the observations of Lallanji Gopal in this regard.[2] A more intensive and detailed research would fill in many gaps in our knowledge and help resolve some of the controversies.

It seems that from the fourteenth century onwards, there is a rapid process of urbanization, a process that became accelerated in the sixteenth and seventeenth centuries. Although a few towns and even cities declined, such as Champaner, Hampi, and Fatehpur Sikri, many cities expanded enormously, so that they became comparable with the biggest in the world. A very large number of medium size cities grew up, while growth in the number of small towns is phenomenal. Bernier had stated that cities suddenly expanded when the imperial camp was established there and became deserted when the emperor left, but many modern scholars have satisfactorily proved that the Indian cities and towns during the period were fairly stable.

In spite of the illuminating studies so far undertaken, many problems still need to be clarified. We know that during the medieval period land was plentiful and the state provided every encouragement to the agriculturists to expand cultivation. Further, a great deal of manufacturing activity and handicraft production was being carried on in villages. Therefore, why did people move to towns and which sections of the agricultural community migrated? What proportion of the total population lived in cities and towns? Were migrations to towns seasonal? Did the urban people retain close ties with their original homes in villages? There are many other problems which are of equal significance, which perhaps need a second look or deeper analysis.

We find two rather interesting and apparently contradictory developments during this period. On the one hand, we observe that the trade and manufacture were basically stimulated and encouraged by the feudal set-up of the medieval empire— whether it was internal trade or external trade. We know for certain, as has been shown by scholars like N. K. Sinha, and as is obvious from the writings of many authors of Persian, in reply to questions put to them by the East India Company and its officers late in the eighteenth century, that the decline of the Mughal empire contributed appreciably to the decline of, if I may inaccurately translate into English, 'the people of substance', the nearest equivalent of the Persian expression which has been used. We know that within twenty-five years of the transfer of *diwāni* to the East India Company, the trade of Bengal and the manufacture of Bengal had declined considerably. We know that within fifteen years of the annexation of Oudh, the population of Lucknow declined from around a million to about two hundred thousand and that people migrated to the villages or went back to their own villages. Therefore, we observe that the existence of a centralized feudal monarchy with all its trappings and the impact that it had on the various categories of zamindars and the *ashrāf*, the gentry had something to do with the growth and expansion of handicrafts, trade, and consequently of towns.

We also know that in spite of the widespread production of handicraft goods in the villages, the towns did remain, throughout this period, major centres of production as well as of collection of manufactured articles and trade. But the decline of feudalism leads to a sudden decline of many of the towns specially in upcountry and a definite decline in handicraft production, particularly in textiles. It is only party due to competition with the industry of Lancashire. The industry of Lancashire had not become a force in the eighteenth century. It became a force in the nineteenth century. But at the same time, we find observations already towards the close of the eighteenth century, that handicraft production as well as trade had begun to decline appreciably.

On the other hand, there is the phenomenon that with the feudal accumulation and centralization, people of substance begin to grow richer and begin to organize production on a massive scale. I have ventured to suggest somewhere that society during this period contained within itself the germs of a possible transformation to a capitalistic mode of production and that if this process had not been disrupted by foreign rule, may be it would have grown into a large-scale industrialized society. I am aware of the fact that many of my very distinguished friends, specially Irfan Habib, strongly disagree with my formulation. However, whether the transformation could have taken place or not, the fact still remains that we do find the growth of merchant houses, the growth of organized production on a comparatively large scale in different parts of the country, particularly on the western coast. So these are two rather contradictory observations which need to be resolved as a result of intensive studies.

I am afraid, I know very little about the second half of the nineteenth and the early twentieth century but it seems to me quite clearly that the nature and the process of urbanization during this period was qualitatively different from the nature and type of urbanization during the medieval period. The impact of industrialization, of world market, of colonialism, and of imperialist drain is very clearly noticeable. There are some changes for the better and many changes are for the worse. All these have to be examined, and examined with great care.

The role of religion has also been examined in the growth of cities. Religion has no doubt played a very important part in our history. Therefore, it would be wrong on our part to ignore it. However, studies have shown that the part played by religion was within limited parameters, and that there were other factors which played no less a significant part in the growth as well as in the fall of cities.

And this brings me to a very important point: our cities grew up with a cosmopolitan population, with different religions, with people coming from different parts of the country, and keeping themselves aloof from each other and yet not, in any way, escaping the influence of the different sections on one another.

Even in a place like Delhi, the period of transition, the period of decline is extremely significant and important. The conflict between Punjabi Muslims and the people of Delhi, I think, is a very significant aspect of the study of the towns. It has been brought out in the context of Delhi as it has been brought out in the Punjab and Maharashtra, that when clashes take place, they are not necessarily clashes between one community and another, but other factors begin to play an important part.

We have also seen the growth and rise of a colonial town into one of the biggest metropolises of the world with all its present problems, its filth, its squalor, its cultural beauty, and its intellectual prowess. I am talking of Calcutta. And Calcutta is not merely the capital of Bengal. As its former Chief Minister pointed out in one of the meetings of the National Development Council, Calcutta was the biggest Assamese town, it was the biggest Oriya town, it was the biggest Bihari town, it was one of the biggest of UP towns. Calcutta grew as a major cosmopolitan city because it served a very wide hinterland. But the poverty and the squalor of Calcutta arose, to a very great extent, from the fact that its second grade sector of industry did not grow rapidly enough, and even where it does grow it is not basically the industrial occupation and employment which grew. The tertiary sector is a substandard, economically depressed sector, which had grown, and, therefore, we could not have taken for granted the fact that if the percentage of population in the secondary sector grew it would automatically solve the problems of poverty.

I would like to draw attention to one other major factor. During the medieval period urban culture had already developed its own peculiarity and speciality. My mother tongue which is very much the product of an urbanized culture and society, namely Urdu, is itself an evidence of a gap and a wide gap, between the culture of the villages and the sophistication of the towns. I have another personal advantage: my roots lie in the villages. I can speak the Purbi dialect, rather enjoy hearing it even if I do not speak it as well. My grandmother preferred to speak in the village dialect even in the Legislative Council of the United Provinces. What is the significance of this cultural dichotomy? What did it mean? This is another aspect of urban history that I hope the scholars would attend to.

I would like to close my observations with an appeal for greater interdisciplinary studies. For far too long the scholars of various disciplines have worked on their own. The historians, at least the more experienced, always talk of using the methods of the economists, the sociologists, the anthropologists, and so on. But speaking at least for myself I know how shallow is my own knowledge of economics, of sociology, and of anthropology. It would be presumptuous on my part to criticize the scholars of economics, sociology, and anthropology. Although many of them started from the discipline of history, they seem to be getting away from this discipline, and many schools of thought have begun to thrive which have totally rejected the historical method, and those who do not consciously reject the historical method make reference to historical phenomena without the discipline of history. Quite obviously, single individuals can not obtain mastery over all these disciplines. Therefore, what is needed is teamwork, for specialists in different fields taking up projects jointly, so that some of these problems could be solved and newer problems raised. It is only in this way that we will make progress.

## Notes and References

1. Mohd. Habib, Introduction to Elliot and Dowson's *History of India* Vol. II (revd) ed., K. A. Nizam, Aligarh, 1952, pp. 36–68.

2. Lallanji Gopal, *The Economic Life of Northern India*, AD 700–1200, Delhi, pp. 133–6.

# 5

## Historian and the Business Communities*

Over three hundred years ago, Bernier wrote that in India there was no middle state.[1] What did he mean by this statement? Surely he could never have meant that there were no merchants or businessmen in India. Obviously, he was arguing the case for France when he made this statement that Indian cities were like large military camps; they shrank when the king left with his army; they expanded when the king was there. In other words, the suggestion of Bernier was that the importance of cities was principally and primarily due to the presence of imperial armies and their hangers-on.

But the fact was the other way round. Large cities in India attracted the attention of the administrators because they were important centres of trade and manufacture; it was not necessarily due to their political or administrative set-up or military importance that they existed or expanded. Any number of cities can be mentioned from the Mughal period which politically were not major centres. I will deliberately not quote the example of Ahmedabad, because Ahmedabad was established as a political capital. But surely during the eighteenth century its importance was far greater as a commercial city than as an administrative centre. Its political importance continued because it was a major centre of business. Likewise, Amritsar

* Printed in Dwijendra Tripathi, ed., *Business Communities of India: A Historical Perspective*, Manohar, Delhi, 1984, pp. 1–8.

was never a major political centre. It had its religious importance but apart from it, it continued to be a very important centre of trade and commerce even though it was away from Lahore which was more important politically.

Modern scholars have collected a great deal of evidence to show that the business communities were numerous and trade was flourishing in pre-British India. Debate among historians today seems to be whether this class of merchants and businessmen could have brought about a transformation in medieval Indian society, particularly in its mode of production. In other words, could this class have industrialized India if the British rule had not been superimposed? Even though the contemporary implications of this question cannot be ignored, I hope that the Indian historians have the intellectual discipline to look at it from the point of view of the evidence and theories rather than its implications for the India of today.

Unfortunately for us, a very large number of our historians have found it convenient to study only the published records of the European trading companies, particularly those that were either written into English or translated into English, and form their opinions on that basis. No one can deny the value of these records and the immense amount of information that they contain. But because of the partial character of these records, an unfortunate impression has gained ground that non-agrarian activity was largely conditioned by the European trade and European trading communities. As more and more records are becoming available to us, most Indian historians are coming round to the view that external trade formed but a very small part of the mercantile activity of the Indians. Today it is no longer a controversial issue among Indian historians that European trade formed only a small part of the total volume of trade or the total manufacture in pre-British India. If we are observant a good bit of evidence is available on our traditional economics. Only we have not always looked at our source materials as carefully as we ought to have done.

A recent collection of edicts of the Mughal era[2] contains an extremely fascinating *farman* or *nishan* of Nurjahan Begum about a *katra*. What is a katra? It is a word used in relation to innumerable cities, large and small and dates back to the medieval period. The word katra has a definite meaning today.

But we can assume that it had the same meaning three hundred or four hundred years ago. The farman I have referred to makes it absolutely clear what a katra was and what its role was in trade and commerce. If we do not use the English translation of *Ain-i-Akbari* and *Ain-i-Kotwali* but read the original, we can understand much more about the city and how it was governed and what was the morphology of a Mughal city and what was the role that was played by the mercantile community in administering the city. *Ain-i-Kotwali* refers to two very interesting institutions: one is the head of the *Muhalla*, viz. *Mir-i-Muhalla*, and the other is the head of what had been translated as a craft guild. Craft guilds are known to have played important roles in the governance of the city in the ancient and the early medieval period, but we do not have enough information about them in the medieval period. When we come across works like *Ain-i-Akbari*, we know much more about the organization of the city and the part played by the mercantile community and business classes in civic life.

There are other works which are known and read but unfortunately not adequately utilized for understanding the nature and the role of the business communities. I am referring in particular to a well-known autobiographical account written in Hindi by Banarasi Das during the reign of Shahjahan under the title of *Ardh Kathanak*,[3] though there is a some controversy about its exact title. The writer had no pretensions to scholarship although he was a well known and very devout Jain merchant. It is a delightful account. He wrote it when he was fifty-five, signifying the mid-point in his lifespan, and the book is supposed to contain an account of the first half of his life. Written in poetic form, it contains great deal of valuable information.

Several other chronicles and memoirs provide valuable information on the position and role of the business communities. Very helpful in understanding this phenomenon is a group of works that were written at the instance of the British for the benefit of the British officials in India. As we are aware, when the English East India Company acquired the rights of *diwani* in 1765, it was very keen to find out what were the rights of different sections of people and what were local customs and institutions. Written in Indian languages, some of these were translated into English which were used by Ranajit Guha to write his delightful book, the *Rule of Property for Bengal.*[4] But I would urge you to have a look at the originals, as the translation does not have the same flavour as the originals; sometimes the sense has undergone a change when rendered into English. Mercifully the originals are intact. According to these accounts also, the merchant community was extremely numerous and economically important. After the British rule was established, it, or a section of it, started losing its importance.

Still more important than these accounts is a class of documents which are coming to light every day and are enabling us to understand the functioning of socio-economic institutions. The *Khatapatras* located in an Ahmedabad library belong to this class. Recently an interesting study on the Nagarsheth of Ahmedabad based on these documents has been published.[5] Likewise, S. A. I. Tirmizi has published some documents relating to the Jagatseths.[6] They indicate that when Jagatseth the second died and his successor was recognized as Jagatseth the third by the British, he wanted the title of raja and the governor general was inclined to oblige him. But the question arose whether the governor general had the right to confer the title. The right was vested in Shah Alam. Now, Shah Alam by 1793 was not the most powerful sovereign that the world knew. Even though his sway did not extend beyond Palam, a suburb of Delhi where we have the aerodrome today, it was he, and not the powerful governor general, who, according to the time honoured custom, could confer the title.

I have myself had the occasion to see the du Jardin Papers in the Bibliotheque Nationale in Paris which I have briefly introduced in the form of a paper (Chapter 25 in this volume).[7] Originally I thought that the du Jardin Papers comprised eleven volumes. Now I have gone through twenty-three volumes and still do not know whether I have seen the last of the volumes. One of the volumes contains *taqavi* documents. Taqavi, as you know, is a form of agricultural credit which in the eighteenth century was given in accordance with the principle of *Sood Sawai.* That is to say that for a hundred rupee loan, one had to return, possibly in kind but not always in kind, a quarter per cent more at the next harvest. So if the taqavi was taken at the beginning of a *rabi* season, that is to say that if it was taken in November, it was to be repaid some time in April or May. The rate of interest, thus, worked out to be more than 50 per cent which by any standard was exorbitant. It is commonly believed that the taqavi was given by the state. But in these papers it becomes quite clear that neither the *Hakim*, who represented the state, nor the Raja of Etah gave the taqavi. It was given by one Daniel du Jardin, a French merchant settled in what are now the districts of Aligarh and Etah.

These papers cover the period from 1778 to 1788, that is just before the British rule was established. These regions had certain dealings with Farrukhabad which started coming under the British domination around 1785. The British did not take kindly to du Jardin and he had to pull out. Finally what happened to him is not known to me because all documents ceased after 1788 though Aligarh itself did not come under the British control until 1803. One of the volumes deals with *hundi*s and we have several volumes of *bahi*s and *khata*s which in modern terminology would be equivalent to journals and ledger books. These records also tell us about a number of other features—what was the type of insurance, what was the type of business and so on. I have tried to categorize the type of functions that the businessmen performed not only on the basis of the du Jardin Papers but on the basis of other evidence that I have found elsewhere.

The first was *malzamini*—standing surety for the payment of revenue. This was a very important function of the business community. Precisely how much commission or *batta* they got for malzamini is not known to me. My suspicion is that it would have differed from time to time, from area to area, and according to the personality and the credit-worthiness of the person for whom surety was undertaken.

The second was agricultural credit; taqavi in some cases, in other cases direct credit by the comparatively well-to-do village headman—*Mukhia, Mandal, Patel, Patil* or *Desai*. If the *khudkashta* was large, the credit would be given to the person who actually cultivated the land or who got the land cultivated or arranged it to be cultivated. The merchant community granted credit when large amount of liquid cash was needed which neither the Hakim, the representative of the state, nor the zamindar was in a position to advance.

The third major function was *ijara* or revenue farming which was a common feature of the medieval economy. Beginning with the twilight years of the Mughals, however, we find a new feature emerging in this age-old system. The merchants themselves started sowing cash crops on land taken on ijara. To put it differently, the merchants used the ijara land for growing cash crops and thereby making profit. In fact, increase in cash crops was by and large accompanied by the increase in the ijara land and most of the persons taking ijara were people belonging to the business community. Some of these, in course of time, became zamindars and gave up their mercantile pursuits. I know some families who from the time of Farrukhsiyar became pure zamindars and gave up all business activities which their ancestors had pursued. It seems to me that the mercantile class started taking ijara around the middle of the eighteenth century.

Then the next important function of the business communities was grain trade. Approximately 50 per cent of the grain produced in a village was given away to others in one form or the other. A sharecropper had to part with 50 per cent of the produce to the owner of the land; a portion of it would go to various hereditary village officials like the *chaudharis*, *qanungos*, and to the *jagirdar* or the state. The process entailed conversion of produce into cash as has been pointed out by several scholars. Although Akbar gave full freedom to the tax-payer to pay the revenue in cash or in kind, more often than not the payment was made in cash. Now, if the revenue was to be paid in cash then the produce had to be sold fairly near the place of production; and if it was to be paid in kind then also it would be sold. Whatever the circumstances, it is the merchants who brought the grain and carried on trade in it. So the trade in food grains was an important source of their wealth. The du Jardin Papers indicate that their margin of profit was considerable. I do not want to cite figures because I am not quite certain about the accuracy of these figures but the margin of profit was undoubtedly considerable. It would amount to hundreds and thousands of rupees per year in a single pargana.

Another source of merchants' profit was exchange. The revenue could be paid in any currency but it was to be deposited in the imperial treasury in the standard currency. For changing the money into standard currency the merchants were allowed batta or commission. Then there was the question of transmitting money from one place to the other not only for imperial expenses but also for trade. In some of these documents I have seen the actual hundis through which the money was transmitted. Yet another function that the merchants performed was to provide for the supplies to the armies in the event of expedition. In fact, the entire Mughal system or medieval system depended on the capacity of these people to meet the needs of the military.

The merchants also gave advances to handicraftsmen. There is plenty of evidence in original records of the advances that were given by the businessmen to the artisans. And it was the responsibility of the merchants to market the goods produced by the artisans. In fact, the artisans accepting the advances were required to sell their goods to their creditors. If an artisan tried to do otherwise, disputes inevitably arose, as several documents bear out. So in the process of production and distribution, the merchants played a very important role. Finally, they acted as comprador of foreign companies. They acted as their gumashtas, and served as their interpreters or *dubhashis*.

While dealing with the past of the Indian business communities, one should be very careful in interpreting certain words in the documents, for the words may have different meanings in different regions. For instance, the word *mahajan* denoted an association of merchants in Ahmedabad, playing a crucial role in the life of the city, while in north India it referred to an individual merchant. It seems to me that in the latter sense also, the mahajans were so called because they performed important economic functions. They enjoyed some concessions also. They were taxed lightly in order that they did not run away. Those who were called *sarraf* or *shroff* or *sheth*, likewise, performed some specific role. Today, any businessman of substance is called sheth or seth, but I have a suspicion that the *sheth* in the past discharged some administrative or economic function. The basis of my suspicion is that the word sheth is used whenever administrative duties are mentioned, whether it is nagarsheth or jagatseth. It is probable that other common nouns such as gumashta and *purchunee* and *pansari* had different connotations. It seems to me that a distinction was always maintained between the wholesaler and the retailer and the retailers carrying on the trade in different objects were known by different names.

All this suggests that historical enquiries into the antecedents and growth of business communities would unfold several aspects of our socio-economic life about which we still know very little. There is a great deal of materials which remain unused or which have been used only partially. To use them with profit and to use them with care is both a challenge and an opportunity to the historian.

## Notes and References

1. F. Bernier, *Travels in the Moghul Empire*, AD 1656–1668, 2nd rev. ed., V. A. Smith, London, 1934, p. 252.

2. S. A. I. Tirmizi, *Edicts from the Mughal Harem*, New Delhi, 1979, pp. 29–30.

3. Banarasi Das, *Ardha Kathanak*, Bombay, 1970.

4. Ranajit Guha, *Rule of Property for Bengal*, New Delhi, 1981.

5. D. Tripathi and M. J. Mehta, eds, 'The Nagarsheth of Ahmedabad: History of an Urban Institution in a Gujarat City', in *Indian History Congress Proceedings*, 39th Session, Hyderabad, 1978, pp. 481–96.

6. S. A. I. Tirmizi, *Indian Historical Vistas*, New Delhi, 1979, pp. 29–30.

7. S. Nurul Hasan, 'Du Jardin Papers: A Valuable Source for the Economic History of Northern India, 1778–88', *Indian Historical Review*, Vol. V, Nos 1–2 (July 1978–January 1979), pp. 187–99 (Chapter 25 in this volume).

# PART II

STATE, RELIGION, AND
THE RULING CLASS

# 6

## Aspects of State and Religion in Medieval India*

I am grateful to the authorities of St Stephen's College for having asked me to deliver this year's I. H. Qureshi Memorial Lecture. I had the privilege of knowing Professor Qureshi and had had the opportunity of many fruitful discussions on historical subjects while he was still in India and later when we met on a few occasions in England. In spite of sharp differences of opinion on many issues, I was deeply impressed by his profound scholarship and his immense personal charm. I have chosen to speak on some aspects of state and religion in medieval India, a subject on which Professor Qureshi has written so much. I cannot, however, presume to cover this vast subject in the short time at my disposal. I shall, therefore, confine myself to highlighting a few points which appear to me to be significant in understanding this interesting subject.

Medieval societies, in many parts of the then civilized world, were organized on the basis of almost autonomous principalities. The people living in these principalities owed personal loyalties to the prince. The state comprised principalities which the prince or the king would bring under his own authority whether by conquest or on the basis of inheritance. In some parts

* I. H. Qureshi Memorial Lectures delivered on 20 and 21 March 1991 at St Stephen's College, Delhi. Published in *Man and Development*, September 1992, pp. 83–93.

of the medieval world, principalities were joined together by dynastic marriages. Political legitimacy depended upon either the right of conquest or of the personal claim of the prince.

Consequently, in many parts of the world the religion of the prince was considered to be the religion of the state. Let us take a few examples from Europe. The Wars of Religion in Central Europe which had erupted with the emergence of Protestantism in the sixteenth century were finally ended by accepting the principle that the religion of the king would be deemed to be the religion of the people of the kingdom. During the same century, in England, the religion of the king or queen was accepted as the religion of the state. Roman Catholics were persecuted when Henry VIII broke with the Pope. During the reign of his daughter, Queen Mary, Roman Catholicism was re-established as the state religion and Protestants were subjected to persecution. After her death, during the time of Queen Elizabeth I, Protestantism again became the established religion of the English state.

In Asia too, this concept was in existence in one form or another even though it was not always explicitly acknowledged. As late as the twentieth century, a princely state in India was considered to be a Muslim state if the ruler was a Muslim or a Hindu state if the ruler was a Hindu. For example, Hyderabad was considered to be a Muslim state because its ruler, the Nizam, was a Muslim, even though the overwhelming majority of the population was Hindu. Consequently, the ruler was supposed to be bound by the laws and principles of his own religion and was expected to enforce these throughout his dominion.

When the Sultanate of Delhi was established in the thirteenth century, the sultans who were Muslims were expected by the jurists (*ulama*), and many others among their co-religionists who were their followers, to rule according to the laws, dictates, and the precepts of Islam. Those laws and precepts had been developed and evolved for communities where the bulk of the people were Muslims. No theoretical framework existed for a state where the bulk of the subjects were non-Muslim even though the ruler was a Muslim.

Before discussing the situation in a country like India let us briefly recall that even in territories where the king as well as most of his subjects were Muslims, the canonical law (*shariat*) was not and could not be fully enforced. It may be recalled that immediately after the end of the rule of the first four or pious caliphs, the Muslim rulers were accused of having deviated from the path of the true faith. In fact, the Omayyad Caliphate was overthrown on the excuse that it had deviated from the true path. The Il-Khanid empire of Persia was not administered according to the principles of Islam even after the rulers had been converted to that faith early during the fourteenth century. The old traditions of Chingiz Khan and many of the traditions of pre-Islamic monarchy were mingled with Islamic precepts and the state was run more on the basis of political or military consideration than in accordance with the teaching of Islam.

## Islamic Law Not Applicable

Such being the case in countries where both the ruler and the ruled were Muslims, it stands to reason that a country where most of the people were non-Muslims while the ruler was Muslim, the state could not be administered in accordance with the Islamic religious law.

At a time when Islam provided a powerful binding force for the ruling classes, the sultan naturally claimed that he was following the dictates of religion. In many cases he would take some demonstrative steps to show to his co-religionists that he was ruling in accordance with the laws of Islam. Apart from the empathy which it evoked among the Muslims for the sultan, the religious law or the *shariat* was the only check on unbridled autocracy. An appeal to religion was also sometimes made to overcome the contradiction between the interest of the nobility and the king.

To understand the nature of the medieval state in India we have to keep in view the fact that the power of the sultan depended upon the support that he could get from the nobility (*amirs*) and on the latter's military strength. The armed contingents of the nobles generally comprised troops who were his co-religionists and quite frequently were his kinsmen. The nobles did not enjoy any hereditary or territorial rights. They depended for their position on the pleasure of the sultan. They could be transferred, promoted, demoted or even dismissed by the sultan. At the same time, the nobles resisted the attempts of the king to become all powerful. While the nobles were dependent on the king, there was also a contradiction between their ambition and the authority of the king. The king naturally wanted to keep the nobles under his control and took all possible steps to see that they did not transgress his authority. But at the same time the king's power and authority depended on the strength of his nobles and the loyal support that they would extend to him. There was thus interdependence between the nobility and the king as well as conflict of interest between the two. With the change of each ruling dynasty, the bulk of the nobility lost power and a new nobility came in its place. In this situation of interdependence as well as contradiction, religion provided an important ideological link which held the Sultanate together.

But sultans were reluctant to be bound by the *shariat* law not only because it circumscribed their political and military authority but also because it would not have been practicable for the sultan to administer his kingdom in accordance with the *shariat* law, since the bulk of the people living in India were non-Muslims.

## Practical Political Reality Recognized

One may bear in mind the fact that in most parts of the country where the power of the sultan was strong the bulk of the people remained non-Muslims. The Quranic injunction that there can be no compulsion in the matter of faith (*La-Ikrah Fiddin*) and the principle taught by the Prophet of Islam when he concluded a truce with the Quraish of Mecca, known as the Peace of *Hudaibiya* that Muslims should live in peace with the non-Muslims, could not be ignored by the sultan. Along with these principles of the Quran and Sunna there was the practical political reality that administration in India could not be based on the shariat.

This was realized very early in the history of the Sultanate. It is recorded in *Sahifa-i-Naat-i-Muhammadi* that one day the ulama of the Court of Iltutmish (1211–36) went to the sultan and said that since the Brahmins were the worst enemies of the Prophet of Islam, devotion to the Prophet enjoined upon the King of Islam to force the Brahmins either to change their faith or to suffer execution. Iltutmish was rattled to receive this demand from the court ulama. He replied that he would give an answer the following day. The next day the king's minister told the ulama that since the Muslims in the kingdom were so few as to be like 'salt in food', their demand could not possibly be met in such a situation. However, he said, when the situation changed and the population of the Muslims increased, it might be possible to act according to the demand of the ulama.

Iltutmish, it seems, had to face the demands of compliance with the shariat on other occasions also. His contemporary in Delhi was the famous Sufi saint, Shaikh Qutb-ud-Din Bakhtiyar, commonly called Kaki. Shaikh Qutb-ud-Din was very fond of listening to religious music (Sama') which the orthodox ulama decreed was impermissible in Islamic society. A demand was made that action be taken against the saint. The latter escaped punishment because under the rule, officers of the sultan could not enter a house without a householder's permission.

According to a conversation attributed to Sultan Balban (1266–86), Iltutmish used to say that it was not practicable for a king to observe the commands of the faith (dindari). It was enough if he could be defender of the faith (dinpanahi). Balban then went on to say that as far as he himself was concerned, he not only could not observe the religious commandments (dindari) he could not even act as defender of the faith (dinpanahi). He felt that it would be enough for him if he could dispense justice (adl).

Dispensing even-handed justice had been considered to be the most important virtue of a good king. The pre-Islamic Persian ruler Anushirwan was held in high esteem by the Muslims because he was believed to be a just ruler. They called him Nawshirvan-i-Adil. The earlier Indian tradition also had laid a great deal of emphasis on justice and considered it as being the most important of kingly virtues. In fact, in the sixteenth century, although Sher Shah had claimed credit for his various achievements, and merit for having acted according to the faith (though only on a few occasions), his epitaph bears the verse that during the reign of Sher Shah such justice was dispensed that the tiger and the goat drank water from the same stream.

Early during the fourteenth century, Sultan Alauddin Khalji is reported to have made the explicit statement that 'I do not know whether or not my action is in accordance with the law. Whatever I considered to be proper for my kingdom that I decreed'. *Jahandari* or statesmanship was thus considered to be independent of *dindari* or observance of the faith. Alauddin Khalji's successor Qutbuddin Mubarak Shah claimed to be a caliph in his own right. His contemporary, the famous Shaikh Nizamuddin Auliya, however, avoided his company as he had avoided that of Sultan Alauddin.

After the Khaljis were overthrown, Sultan Muhammad, son of Sultan Ghiyasuddin Tughlaq, ascended the throne. He avoided giving too much authority to the Muslim jurists. Instead, among the scholars who had his ear were philosophers and logicians. Neither of these branches of knowledge was liked by the theologians. In fact, even with a Sufi saint like Shaikh Nasiruddin Mahmud, commonly called *Chiragh-i-Delhi*, his relations were not cordial.

Muhammad-bin-Tughlaq's successor, Firuz Shah, tried to repair his relations with the ulama. In his *Futuhat-i-Firuz Shahi* he claimed to have enforced religious commandments. He also took other demonstrative steps to prove his orthodox bona fides. But notwithstanding these few cases, a close examination of his long reign shows that his administration was no more in accordance with the *shariat* law than those of his predecessors. Incidentally, it may be mentioned that the first important book on Indian classical music in Persian, which has survived, was written during his reign and is entitled *Ghuniyat-ul-Muniya*. Although the famous Amir Khusrau was deeply versed in Indian music and contributed to it, no book written by him on Indian music has survived.

The Lodi sultans were proud of their being Afghans and gave a position of pre-eminence to their kinsmen. Although they occasionally claimed to act in accordance with the shariat, in actual fact they gave precedence to Afghan traditions, apart from their political interests.

## Interdependence and Conflict of Interests

The principal source of wealth, and hence of power, of the medieval Indian state was agriculture. The bulk of the village elders, the landholders, the revenue officials, as well as the cultivators (*khots*, *muqaddams*, *chaudhuris*, *balahars*) were non-Muslims. Upon their well-being (*khushhali*) and the prosperity of the village (*abadani*) depended the wealth and power of the state. Since the state was keen to appropriate the agricultural surplus, it was anxious to see that the agriculturist was well-off and satisfied. But at the same time the state did not want these classes to become so strong as to be able to resist the collection of the surplus. The agriculturists benefited from the peace that was ensured by the centralized state. At the same time they frequently resisted the appropriation of the surplus by the state and became contumacious (*zortalab*). There was thus an interdependence as well as conflict of interest between the agriculturists and the state.

This situation of interdependence as well as of conflict was even more pronounced in the case of the chieftains and princes (*rajas*, *rais*, *rawats*, etc.). They were also by and large non-Muslims. The state depended on them for military support, for the maintenance of law and order in the countryside, and for help in the collection of revenue. Except in case of rebellion or other hostile action by the chieftains, political and military interest demanded that the state should maintain friendly relations with them. In the same way, in their own interest, the sultan and his nobles could not, and did not, resort to bigotry and intolerance, nor did they risk antagonizing the chieftains by subjecting them to shariat law.

Trade, commerce, and industrial production, so important for the well-being of the state, were mostly in the hands of non-Muslims. Over the centuries, partly because of the policies followed by the state, these activities received a great fillip. As money economy started reaching the villages, *banias*, *mahajans*, *sarrafs*, etc. acquired even greater importance in the political, economic, and social life of the state. Members of this class stood surety for the revenue and administrative officers (*malzamini*), gave agricultural credit (*taqavi*), provided loans to the nobles, and sometimes even to the sultan himself. Many nobles, and later the sultan as well, employed non-Muslims to manage their finances and accounts, and to man the revenue administration. These functions were performed by them over and above the functions of traders, merchants, bankers, and industrialists. The logic of the situation demanded that the state should look after them in its own interest. Imposition of the *shariat* law would have created difficulties.

## Muslims Not a Monolithic Community

Muslims in India did not form a homogeneous monolithic community during the Sultanate and the Mughal periods. Ethnic, linguistic, regional, and class differences played a very important part in their lives and prevented the emergence of a unified Muslim *umma* as visualized by the *shariat.* Occasional appeals to common religious bonds served only a limited purpose. During the thirteenth century, for example, the sultan and the umara belonged to a narrow circle of Turks (*Turkan-i-Chihlgani*). In fact Balban once removed from an important office a person who was a weaver by caste (*julaha*). This is one of the earliest examples of the caste system entering Muslim society. The Turks who had made India their home began to take pride in being 'Indian Turks' who spoke in *Hindui.* One famous example of this is the verse of poet Amir Khusrau, who wrote:

*Turki-i Hindustani-yam, man Hindawi guyam sukhan*
*Shakkar-i Misri na daram kaz Araf guyam jawab.*

Amir Khusrau mentions that different languages had been developed in different parts of the country. There is evidence that these regional or provincial languages had become the mother tongue of even those Muslims whose ancestors had immigrated from abroad. For example, Shaikh Fariduddin Ganji-i-Shakar composed poetry in Punjabi, while Shaikh Wajihuddin Gujrati wrote in Gujrati. Muslim rulers and many of the literati, who had come from outside India, wrote in Deccani, which was the prototype of modern Urdu. Qa'im, an eighteenth-century poet wrote:

*Qa'im main ghazal taur kiya rekhta wama*
*Ek bat lachar si yeh zabani Dakkani thhi*

Mulla Da'ud composed in Hindi in the fourteenth century his famous poem *Chandayan* describing the story of Laurik and Chanda. Malik Muhammad Jaisi wrote his famous *Padmavat* in Awadhi during the reign of the Surs, while Abdur Rahim Khan-i-Khanan, who was of Turkoman origin, will always be remembered for his poem written in Braj Bhasha.

With the establishment of the provincial sultanates, links between the Hindus and Muslims became closer in the different localities. A regional polity emerged in various parts of India with a shared language and culture as well as political interests. Throughout the Middle Ages, streams of immigrants came to India and settled down here. Many of them came as they had to leave their homes because of political turmoil in Central Asia or Persia; others came to build for themselves a brighter future. The immigrants had ethnic and linguistic differences, for example, Turks or Tajiks, Iranis or Turanis, Afghans or Khurasanis. These differences occasionally turned into feuds which were carried on by their families for generations.

## Converts Retain Cultural Traits

And then there was the large body of Indian Muslims, usually converts to Islam. Many of these belonged to a single caste or professional group who retained their cultural traits even after conversion to Islam. However, some of these tried to improve their social status by claiming descent from a well-known Islamic religious or cultural personality. For instance,

*Awwalan naddaf budem ba'adahu gashtem Shaikh*
*Ghalla chun arzam shawad imsal Saiyid mi shawem.*

(I was born a cotton-dresser,
Later, I became a Shaikh,
This year, if corn becomes dearer,
I shall become a Saiyid.)

On the whole, the bulk of the Indian Muslims retained the culture of their castes or professions. They remained distinct from the descendants of the immigrants who began to be classified as Saiyid, Shaikh, Mughal, and Pathan. These later social groups retained their distinct identity and considered themselves superior to the Indian Muslims, who were considered inferior because they were thought to be lower in the Hindu caste hierarchy. They, however, quite often claimed equality with the Hindu upper castes.

In this background the appeal of the Islamic shariat was limited so far as the ruling class in the sultanate was concerned. This may explain why there was a de facto dichotomy between dindari and jahandari. Notwithstanding occasional appeals to the shariat, the political, economic, and military policies were not determined according to religious law.

While the traditions established earlier in the Sultanate of political, economic, and military policies being determined irrespective of the dictates of the *shariat* were continued during the Mughal period, a new theoretical framework of administration and politics gradually emerged. This was mainly during the reign of the Emperor Akbar (1556–1605). As is well-known, Akbar was unlettered but from his boyhood he had been placed under a tutor who left a deep imprint on his thinking. The name of the tutor was Mir Abdul Latif Qazwini. He was a man of liberal views who was influenced by Sufi ideas. He was the son of Mir Yahiya Qazwini who had been the Qazi of Qazwin of the capital of Shah Tahmasp Safavi's empire. Someone complained to Shah Tahmasp, who was a bigoted Shia, that Mir Yahiya was a Sunni. He was, therefore, dismissed and thrown into prison. His son, Mir Abdul Latif, accompanied by his brother, came to the Mughal court where he was appointed as Akbar's tutor. Many orthodox Sunnis accused Mir Abdul Latif of being a Shiite heretic. I have mentioned these details to show that Akbar's tutor was acceptable neither to the bigoted Shias nor to the bigoted Sunnis. Under his tutor Akbar studied the *Masnawi* of the famous Persian poet Maulana Rumi. A particular section of the Masnawi, it is believed, had especially appealed to Akbar. According to it, God told the Prophet Moses that he had been sent to unite mankind and not to divide it. God told him that he had given to each people their own faith in their own language particularly those of Sind and of Hind. These should not be interfered with.

## Poetry of Hafiz

Akbar was also deeply impressed by the poetry of the famous Persian poet Hafiz, especially by those verses which reflected broad human sympathy and liberal outlook. Consequently, soon after assuming the reins of power, Akbar took many important decisions which reflected his tolerant attitude, even though he still claimed to be acting faithfully according to the *shariat*. Mention may be made here of his abolition of *Jizya*, the pilgrim tax on the Hindus, appointment of Hindus to high places, showing tremendous confidence in those Rajput princes with whom he had contracted matrimonial alliances, and gradually absorbing in the category of his nobles more and more Hindus. Akbar had started organizing regular religious discourses at his court from 1572. Initially, in these discourses only the Muslim ulama were invited. Gradually Akbar felt dissatisfied with the narrowness of their vision and their bigoted outlook. He, therefore, started calling to these discourses Hindus, Jains, Parsis, Christian, etc. The leaders of these religions were treated with tremendous consideration by Akbar whose own outlook became more liberal, tolerant and catholic. However, at this time the orthodox ulama were still able to indulge in acts of bigotry.

In 1579, Akbar, it seems, took the final step to change the religious outlook of the state. He first asked the leading ulama of the court to submit a petition (*Mahzar*) which interalia stated that in his capacity as *Imam-i-Adil* (the just ruler), he (Akbar) was not bound by the interpretation of the shariat as given by the jurists of a particular school of *Fiqh* (religious law). This doctrine was, however, qualified by the proviso that the king's decisions were in conformity with the explicit injunctions of the Quran and Sunnat of the Prophet. Having thus freed himself from the obligations to be bound by the rulings of the ulama, Akbar started implementing the Sufi doctrine of *Sulhikul*. This doctrine implied that all religions were equal. Akbar subscribed to the view reflected in the famous verse of *Fughani-Shirazi*:

*Dar Haqiqat nasab-i Ashiq O Mashuq Yakist*
*But Fuzulan Sanam O Barhmani Sakhta and;*
*Yak Chiragh Ast Darin Khana ki Az Partwai An*
*Har Kuja Mi Nigaram Anjumani Sakhta and.*

In reality, the lover and the beloved are but one.

It is only the misguided who considered the idol to be separated from the Brahmin.

In reality there is only one light in this House whose reflection has illumined many a gathering.

As a symbol of his respect for all religions, Akbar ordered that the festivals of the different religious communities be observed at the court. The policy of the absorption of non-Muslims in the administrative and military hierarchy began to be pursued with greater vigour and even the highest ranks were thrown open to the Hindus. The policy of matrimonial alliances too received greater impetus.

## People of All Religions Equal

The great classics of Indian philosophy and religion were translated into Persian, particularly the Mahabharata and the Ramayana. Selections of the Upanishads were also translated into Persian; so were other literary and scientific works of Sanskrit. Thus the Mughal state moved considerably to a theoretical position where people of all religions were considered to be equal in the eyes of the state.

The importance of this is to be seen in the context of the then contemporary world in which religious bigotry and intolerance were considered to be virtues. Notwithstanding the end of the bitter War of Religion between the Catholics and the Protestants in Europe, religious intolerance characterized the policy of many of the European states in the sixteenth century. This was the time of the Inquisition, of the burning at the stake of the heretics. Intolerance led to the massacre of the Huguenots in Paris on St Bartholomew's Day (1572). Nearer home, Abdullah Khan Uzbeg and his descendants in Central Asia considered it their duty to suppress Shiite heresy. In Persia, the Shiite Safawid emperor, Tahmasp, was equally intolerant of the Sunnis. The Ottoman emperor Sulaiman, who ruled in the second half of the sixteenth century, claimed that enforcement of the shariat was an important aspect of his state policy.

Akbar's policy of not discriminating against the non-Muslims and of deliberately laying down detailed rules of governance and administration without any reference to the shariat, was resented by a section of the orthodox Muslims. We know how critical the famous historian Abdul Qadir Badauni was of the emperor's policy. Well-known and influential orthodox Muslim saint, Shaikh Ahmad Sirhindi, condemned this policy of Akbar in strong words and showed great relief when Akbar died. He then expressed the view that Akbar's successor Jahangir would restore the shariat to its position of supremacy. Akbar's foster-brother and one of the premier nobles, Mirza Aziz Koka, went away without permission to Mecca because he was dissatisfied with Akbar's religious policy. He, however, came back a few years later and gave full support to Akbar.

The policy of Akbar created misgivings among a section of non-Muslims too. Akbar's favourite noble, Raja Man Singh, was baffled by the religious practices and innovations which began to be followed at the court. The Jesuit fathers thought that Akbar was on the point of accepting Christianity but was prevented from doing so because of the fear of revolt by the Muslim nobles. The fathers were particularly impressed by the veneration Akbar showed to Virgin Mary, by the permission he gave for the construction of churches, and even the permission to convert people to Christianity. It may be observed that not only Hindus but Muslims were also converted to Christianity.

Generally, however, the reaction of the non-Muslims to the important changes in the religious policy of the state had a positive effect. Not only was Akbar successful in winning the loyalty of a large section of the Hindus but also of getting them to accept the legitimacy of the Mughal emperor. A small incident perhaps reveals the thinking of a contemporary Hindu who was not attached to the court. A merchant by the name of Banarasi Das in his autobiography writes that he was in Jaunpur when the news of Akbar's death reached him. The people cried with pain and were overwhelmed with grief.

## Religious Differences Tolerated

During the reign of Jahangir (1605–28), Akbar's religious policy was generally continued. Religious tolerance was on the whole maintained. In fact Jahangir, in his *Memoirs*, claimed credit that while the Turanis persecuted the Shiites, the Safawids persecuted the Sunnis, during the reign of his father and in his own reign religious differences were tolerated. We have the instance of a Muslim servant of a Mughal Christian officer being converted to Christianity. Jahangir ordered that the servant be given a stipend of two rupees per day when he became convinced that this person had changed his faith of his own free will and individual conviction. Jahangir took a great deal of trouble to go twice to meet a learned but recluse sanyasi, Jadrup Gosain, and enjoyed talking to him about Vedantic philosophy of monism, which he found to have a great deal of similarity with the Islamic concept of *Wahdaniyat*. Hindus continued to be absorbed in the imperial service and reach the highest position. The young ruler of Amber, Maharaja Jai Singh, was even given the title of Mirza (Imperial Prince). When the ruler of Mewar accepted the overlordship of the Mughal emperor, his son Kunwar Karan was treated with great respect and honour at the Mughal court.

Jahangir, however, had certain idiosyncrasies in religious matters which constituted a deviation from the accepted policies of his father. In an angry letter which Mirza Aziz Koka wrote of Jahangir, he accused the emperor of not trusting the Rajputs and the Turanis in the same manner as his father used to, but instead showing greater confidence in the Shaikhzadas and Persians. Jahangir permitted unwarranted action against Guru Arjun Dev even though he sought to justify it on political grounds. He ordered the learned and frail Shiite *Qazi* Nurullah Shustari to be beaten with lashes when he thought that the Qazi was being hypocritical in declaring his religious faith. The Qazi succumbed to his injuries. His death was applauded by a section of bigoted Sunni ulama. But this section could not have been pleased when Shaikh Ahmad Sirhindi was thrown into prison, allegedly for showing disrespect to the pious Caliph.

Many saints thanked their lucky stars when on being summoned at the court they could get back unharmed. Although the slaughter of a cow during the conquest of Kangra seems to be the result of political motivation, it is unlikely that such an action would have been permissible during the reign of Akbar.

## Political Motivation

During the reign of Shahjahan (1628–58), while the policies laid down by Akbar and Jahangir were generally followed, far greater concessions were made to Islamic orthodoxy. For example, Mirza Raja Jai Singh continued to be treated by the emperor with affection and friendship. Nevertheless, he began to be addressed as *Muti-ul-Islam* 'subservient to Islam'. The system of prostration at the court was abolished on the ground that the practice was un-Islamic; and in its place the *Chahar Taslim* was introduced. It may be noted that even this was a deviation from the orthodox Islamic practice of salutation, which was *As-salam-O-alaikum* without bowing the head. At the same time Shahjahan virtually treated Dara Shikoh as the heir-apparent, and during his prolonged illness, he put Dara in charge of the affairs of the state. Dara Shikoh was a man of pantheistic views. He wrote the famous book, *Majmaul Bahrain* or the Mingling of Two Oceans, a book which showed the similarity between Sufi thought and Vedantic precepts. Orthodox Muslims disapproved of the views and action of Dara Shikoh but Dara had the support and backing of his father as well as of the bulk of the nobility. It may also be mentioned here that Shahjahan had sought to impose restrictions on the construction of new temples as well as of their renovation. But there is also evidence that new temples were constructed during his reign, and that Shahjahan gave grants for the maintenance of some temples.

The reign of Aurangzeb (1658–1707) appears to have seen a reversal of Akbar's religious policies. In some respects it was so. His imposition of the Jizya could not have been liked by his non-Muslim subjects, even though no record of any serious resistance to the imposition of Jizya exists. Military action against a non-Muslim was considered to be a jihad, but most of the military campaigns had been undertaken against Muslim sultans. While there are cases on record of some temples having been demolished for one reason or another, many grants were given for the upkeep and maintenance of temples. Hindus continued to occupy positions of importance in imperial service and enjoyed the trust and confidence of the emperor. But a few demonstrative acts of submission to religious orthodoxy, such as banning of music at the court, were undertaken. It may, however, be mentioned that under Aurangzeb's direct patronage a large number of books were written in Persian on classical Indian music, and a textbook was prepared on Indian Hindu science (*Tuhfat-ul-Hind*) for the education of an imperial prince.

## Mughal Overlordship Accepted

Jizya was abolished soon after Aurangzeb's death. The later Mughal emperors, though weak generally, sought to maintain the traditions continued from Akbar's time. The policies initiated by Akbar and continued in a greater or lesser measure by his successors did lead to acceptance of the overlordship of Mughal emperors by the non-Muslim princes and chieftains as well as by the common people. In fact, Robert Orme, who was sent by the East India Company to Bengal, wrote in 1753 that he was surprised that the Hindus had accepted the rule of the

Muslims. For example, when after 1772, the Maratha chieftain, Mahadaji Scindia gained supremacy at the court of Shah Alam II, he made the Mughal emperor issue a *farman* appointing the Peshwa as his *Wakil-i-Multaq* and himself as the Wakil's deputy. Scindia was certainly in a position to overthrow the Mughal emperor but he chose not to do so and became a servant of the empire. Towards the end of the eighteenth century, when the famous banker of Bengal, Jagat Seth died, his successor (Harak Chand Jagat Seth) claimed the title of Maharaja and of Jagat Seth from the Mughal emperor, who at that time wielded no political or military authority. Even in the nineteenth century, as late as in 1837, in far off Kutch, coins issued by the Rana bore the name of the Mughal emperor. In 1857, those who rose in rebellion against the British decided to accept the nominal leadership of the Mughal emperor, Bahadur Shah Zafar. Bahadur Shah's political authority had not extended even to the city of Delhi.

It would thus be seen that Mughal empire had gained fairly wide acceptability among the non-Muslims. It had not merely practised religious toleration, showed respect for all religions and practised very little discrimination against non-Muslims in public offices, but also generally sought to separate the affairs of the state from the affairs of the faith.

# 7

## *The* Mahzar *of Akbar's Reign**

Vincent Smith has given us a novel interpretation of the *Mahzar* signed by the important *ulama,* of Akbar's reign and issued in September 1579. He seems to be labouring under the impression that Akbar wanted to usurp the spiritual leadership of the Indian Muslims and as such the document was illegal. In this connection, he makes two more assertions: that Akbar was influenced by the western European conception of Papacy; and, that the decree invested him with the 'attribute of infallibility'.[1]

Buckler,[2] Roy Choudhury,[3] and S. R. Sharma[4] have examined Smith's views and have criticized him effectively (the last-mentioned scholar has probably gone a little to the other extreme).[5] But still a further examination of the views of Smith will be of some interest.

### The Legal Validity of the Document

The Mahzar contains the following assertions:

   (a) that Akbar was the *Khalifa* of the age;
   (b) that the rank of the Khalifa[6] is higher than that of a *mujtahid*;
   (c) that in case of a difference of opinion among the mujtahids, Akbar can select any one opinion; and
   (d) Akbar himself may issue decrees which do not go against the *nass*.[7]

* *Journal of UP History Society*, Vol. XVI, July, 1943, pp. 125–37.

Let us now examine all these points and find out whether they are legal or illegal according to the Hanafi or Shafaii systems of law.

The first assertion is that Akbar was the Khalifa. The orthodox Sunni law envisages the election of the caliph. The legists have described the qualifications of the electors, of the candidate and the method of election. Mawardi, Qazi Baizawi, and Ghazali[8] state that a candidate should possess the following qualifications: (i) spotless integrity, (ii) requisite juridico-political knowledge to pronounce judgement in difficult cases, (iii) freedom from physical defects and infirmities, (iv) necessary insight for governing the people and conducting affairs of state, (v) courage and boldness in defending Muslim territory and in fighting infidels, (vi) maturity (bulugh), (vii) male sex, and (viii) descent from the family of Quraish. The qualifications of electors are: spotless integrity and the capacity for judging the qualifications for the leadership of the State. On the question of the method of election, although theoretically all Muslims could participate, yet in practice, an election by prominent men of the capital was recognized as legal and valid. Some legists think that an election effected by five men of position might be looked upon as legal, while even the conception of 'election by force' had entered the law.

The Mahzar may be considered to have confirmed the election of Akbar to Khilafat and the election was quite in accordance with the conditions mentioned above. The ulama who signed the document were theoretically eligible for being the electors. So far as the qualifications of Akbar go, he had all the qualifications except one, viz., descent from Quraish. In the manner of election, there was only one difficulty, viz., according to theory there cannot be two caliphs in the same community at one time.

The history of Islam furnishes sufficient precedents which provide a solution of the two difficulties mentioned above in accepting the validity of Akbar's election. The Ottoman caliphs were not of Quraish descent and yet the Hanafi legists had accepted the position. W. S. Blunt[9] has summarized the chief arguments of the Hanafi ulama in support of the Ottoman dynasty. Two points are of considerable interest. The first is the right of sword, 'the Khilafat being a necessity, it was also necessary that the de facto holder of the title be recognized as such *until a claimant with a better title should appear*.[10] This argument has also a bearing on the second difficulty of there being two caliphs at a time. Secondly, election, that is, the sanction of a legal body of elders. It was argued that as the *ahl-i-aqd* had been removed from Madina to Damascus, thence to Baghdad and Cairo, and finally to Constantinople, the election of the Ottomans became valid. It may be noted that the signatories of the Mahzar probably considered themselves the ahl-i-aqd, as may be seen from the following words in the preamble to the Mahzar:

Whereas Hindustan has now become the centre of security and peace and the land of *adl* and beneficence, a large number of people, especially learned ulama and great lawyers who are the guides of salvation and the leaders in the path of knowledge, having left the countries of *Arab* and *Ajam* have turned towards this land and accepted it as their home....[11]

On the question of there being two Caliphs at a time, the legal position that if a caliph has been recognized by 'acknowledgment by force', the acceptance is only provisional, has already been mentioned. But here again practice had rejected the theory. There was a Khilafat at Cardova and Granada right from AD 755 to 1492, that is, during the time that Abbassids and Fatamids were the caliphs. Hence from AD 910 to 1171 there were three caliphs. According to some legists, this position is not irregular. They hold that if oceans or insurmountable mountains separate two communities, both can have their own caliphs.

After all, we have to recognize that in the fifteenth and sixteenth centuries, the only claim to Khilafat was one of sword. The Ottomans had defeated some obscure descendant of the Abbassids, and thus claimed their title. Timur had defeated the Abbassid caliph of Baghdad, had assumed the title of caliph and had transferred the capital to Samarqand. Therefore, theoretically, the position of the Ottomans was in no way better than that of Akbar.[12]

Thus according to the accepted legal practice of Sunni Muslims, Akbar's title to caliphate may be considered as valid.

The next question is whether the rank of a caliph is higher than that of a mujtahid.[13] The Sunni theology is quite clear on the question of the *complete* and the unconditional supremacy of the caliph over all Muslims. The following traditions (*ahadis*), taken from authoritative Hanafiite and Shafaiite collections, will justify the above-mentioned assertion:

Whoever obeys the Amir obeys me; and whoever rebels against him, rebels against me.[14]

After me will come rulers; render them your obedience, for the ruler is like a shield wherewith a man protects himself; if they are righteous and rule you well, they shall have their reward; but if they do evil and rule you ill, then punishment will fall on them and you will be quit of it, for they are responsible for you, but you have no responsibility.[15]

It is indispensable for every Muslim to listen to, and approve the orders of the Imam, whether he likes or dislikes, so long as he is not ordered to sin and act contrary to *nass*; then when he is ordered to sin, he must neither attend to it nor obey it.[16]

He who forsakes obedience to the Imam will come before God on the Day of Judgment without a proof of his faith; and he who dies without having professed to Imam, dies as the people of ignorance.[17]

These four sayings of the Prophet establish the complete superiority of the caliph and as such subordinate the *Mujtahidin*[18] to the caliph, as well as give him the right to issue decrees, not in contravention of the nass, which would be binding on all Muslims.

Although in his capacity as caliph, Akbar was certainly entitled to choose between any of the opinions of the ulama, as an ordinary Muslim too he enjoyed that right. The companions of the Prophet did not blame the people for following opinions other than their own.[19]

The author of *Taqrir*[20] sees no objection in a man picking out from each school what is agreeable to him.[21] Abu Yusuf himself thinks that a sovereign could exercise the power of selection and discretion.[22]

Thus in view of the well-known opinions on the theory and practice of Sunni law, it is clear that the Mahzar was valid. It is really surprising how Smith got the impression that it was a decree of 'infallibility' because even if Akbar were the Mujtahid, the legal effect of *Ijtihad* is that the opinion tendered is *probably* right though there is the possibility of error.[23] The suggestion that Akbar was following the pattern of Papacy is too baseless to be commented upon since the conception of Khilafat is essentially Islamic. In view of this we may presume that Smith's condemnation of the Mahzar is really based on a lack of information.[24]

## The Historical Significance of the Document

On the question of the historical significance of the Mahzar, a peculiar theory has been put forward by Buckler. He says that the Mahzar 'was intended to fix the position of Akbar in the Muslim world by eliminating the religious or political control of Persia but without committing him to the allegiance of the Ottoman Khalifa.'[25] This theory was examined by R. P. Tripathi[26] and its weaknesses were effectively pointed out. A more recent writer, M. Roy Choudhury, has stated[27] that Tripathi's criticism of Buckler is not convincing, but he has given no arguments. It will, therefore, be the attempt of the writer of this paper to examine some of the opinions of Roy Choudhury and Buckler.

The argument of Roy Choudhury may be summed up as follows:

He (Akbar) intended to devise some means of freeing himself from the politico-religious pretensions of Iran and religious hegemony of Rum.... Thus very slyly the Imami-i-Adil of Hindustan was placed above the *mujtahids* of Persia.

Further he says that the Mahzar made the orders of the sultan binding on the *whole* nation, thus bringing the Shias under his authority. He goes on to say, 'The word "nation" was a new introduction in political terminology'. And finally, comes the statement that 'the Mahzar began by giving the Emperor Akbar the dignity of the Imam-i-Adil, a title which no one, be he a Shia or a Sunni, could object to'.[28]

With one part of the statement that it was a challenge to Ottoman pretensions, it is difficult to disagree. Akbar was certainly not prepared to admit the legal supremacy of the Ottoman sultans, nor was he willing to permit his own Muslim subjects to owe an allegiance to any one but himself and especially not to a rival sultan. Badaoni has reported an incident which lends support to this view, that was about an objection raised by Qutbuddin as to 'what would the King of the West, as the Sultan of Rum, say if he heard all this?' And the retort of Akbar was that the objector was probably an agent of the Sultan of Rum.[29] Tripathi too has accepted the view that the Mahzar was a challenge to the pretensions of the Sultan of Rum.[30]

In spite of all the numerous pages written by Buckler and Roy Choudhury, giving details of the relations of the Safavids and the Timurides of India, there is nothing to show that Akbar or even Humayun ever regarded themselves or were ever regarded by the Iranis as in any way inferior to the Shah of Iran. It is difficult to imagine how and from which source the two scholars got the idea that there was 'a religious or political control of Persia'. There is no evidence of any 'politico-religious pretensions of Iran' *at the time of Akbar,* including the days of Bairam Khan.

Tripathi has shown that 'there is no evidence to show that Persia exercized any religious or political control over the Mughal emperors of India'.[31] Only two or three points are reproduced here. The *Afzalut Tawarikh* reproduces a letter written by Shah Tahmasp in reply to that of Humayun. In a short note added by the Shah in his own pen, he calls him, 'My brother, the tribunal of majesty Humayun Badshah'. Arif Muhammad Qandahari says that *Khutba* was read in the name of Akbar as *Amirul Muminin* in AH 986, that is a year before the Mahzar. Moreover, the inscription of the names of the four caliphs on the coins of Humayun and Akbar definitely prove the absence of any control by the Shah of Iran, because such an inscription *would be most unpalatable to a Shia.*

This confusion has probably arisen due to the use of the expression mujtahid. Buckler propounded his whole theory because of this misunderstanding and Roy Choudhury took the cue. Buckler writes that 'the Mughal ulama simply placed Akbar above the Mujtahidin—the Shiah ulama of Persia—and there-fore, beyond Persian religious jurisdiction'.[32] Due to the popular Sunni theory of *insdad-i-bab-i-ijtihad* (to which reference has already been made), the term mujtahid is not generally used by the Sunnis and is common only to the Shia ulama. But Sunnis recognize ijtihad and the Hanafites have even classified them into numerous groups.[33] Many writers,[34] of whom some are modern, are of opinion that even *Ijtihad-i-kamil* is still possible. Ghazali too has defined ijtihad and its categories at length.[35]

Therefore, it is not correct to think that the use of the expression mujtahid in the Mahzar refers to the Shias only, and much less to the 'Shia ulama of Persia'. Hence the statement of Roy Choudhury that 'Imam-i-Adil of Hindustan was placed above the mujtahid of Persia' is based on some misconception.

Roy Choudhury also states that the Shias could not object to Akbar being given the title of '*Imam-i-Adil*'. This statement too is unwarranted. The Shia theory of *imamate* is clear. The Shias recognize either twelve Imams or seven Imams. The *isna-asharis*, or the believers in twelve Imams, who form a majority of Shias in India and Iran, believe that the twelfth Imam is still living though he is in hiding and that he would appear some day. No Shia can, therefore, recognize any one else as the Imam. And since the Shias could not recognize Akbar as the Imam, therefore, according to the Shia law, they *could not be* brought under the authority of Akbar.

Another minor mistake has crept in Roy Choudhury's book and that is the use of the word 'nation' in the Mahzar, to which the author has attached some importance. The original text of the document does not contain an equivalent of 'nation'. Lowe has translated it inaccurately. Buckler has pointed out this mistake,[36] but it has probably escaped the attention of Roy Choudhury.

Before concluding, let us see what the actual significance of the document is.[37] It is not possible to discuss the historical significance of the *Mahzar* at any length in the course of this short article. Only certain suggestions are given which may be considered by the readers.

One point, first stated by Buckler, has already been discussed, viz., that Akbar wanted to challenge the legal supremacy of the Ottoman sultan and to countenance all claims of the latter to the obedience of the Muslims in the Mughal empire. Sixteenth century a time when trade and commerce was flourishing, bringing economic prosperity to individual states and greater contact between the western Asian powers. This was also the time when, like Europe, four great powers had emerged, each battling for supremacy in western Asia.[38] The Ottoman empire had become strong and aggressive. The Khutba was being read in the name of the Ottoman sultan in Mecca and Medina. He was claiming the allegiance of all Muslims throughout the world. The Safavid dynasty had strengthened itself, and under Shah Tahmasp it was no less aggressive. It was trying to win over the sympathies of Indian Shias. The Uzbegs had become formidable under Abdullah Khan and enjoyed the support of the ulama of that seat of Muslim culture, Samarqand, which Timur had made the *Darul Khilafa*. Students of the political history of this period know how keenly Akbar was interested in Asiatic politics and how much he wanted to establish the supremacy of the Mughals not only in India but also much beyond her frontiers. Tripathi has aptly said that Akbar's idea was of universal kingship. This keen rivalry between the four powers is well reflected in the literary and cultural duels of the period.

And this leads us to the second point. The Muslim states had been defining their religious policy throughout Asia. Abdullah Khan Uzbeg had banned all schools of law except the Hanafi school. The Shahs of Iran were the ardent upholders of Shiaism and recognized no other branch of law. The Ottomans were no less bigoted in their outlook. It was, therefore, left to the son of the founder of *Din Panah*, to one fed on the liberal traditions of Maulana Rum and Hafiz, to one living in the midst of a great cultural upsurge thrown up as a result of the growing unity of Hindus and Muslims, of Shias and Sunnis, to declare that the Mughal empire would be the monopoly of no one sect, no one school, no *one* group of mullahs. This document is an enunciation of the religious policy of the Mughals vis-à-vis those of the Safavids, Uzbegs or the Ottomans. It released the Mughal empire from the shackles of sectarianism. The Mughal empire, being more liberal and cultured in its outlook, began to have an attractiveness for the intellectuals and freedom-loving people throughout the world of Islam.

Turning to India itself, we find that the mullahs had formed a class of their own and had become very powerful. The history of their securing power goes back to the days of the Umayyads, who being ignorant of the tenets of Islam, utilized the aid of the scholars of religion in interpreting the law. The Abbassids, since they had appealed to the slogan 'back to orthodoxy', naturally gave much power to the ulama, who began to transform themselves into a class, influencing and even controlling the day-to-day administration. The Safavids too had needed the aid of the ulama, and gave them much power. But soon the latter became too powerful even for their sovereigns. In India also, the ulama were fairly powerful. Alauddin had to make a conscious attempt to ignore them while other monarchs[39] too resented the political influence of the ulama class. The worst about the mullahs was that they could easily be influenced by rich and powerful nobles (by fair means or foul) and conspire against the sovereign. Since they were the custodians of religion, they exercised much influence over the masses and could excite them. It was, therefore, necessary that the religious *supremacy* of the ulama be abolished. This document placed the sovereign above the machinations of the ulama class and hence indirectly deprived the nobles of their last possible chance of fighting the growing concentration of power in the hands of the sovereign. It would not be correct to presume that Akbar himself was in any danger of an effective opposition by the ulama. But Akbar was creating a *machinery* of state, a *mechanism* of administration that would move on by its inherent tempo even after his death.

Finally, we come to the imperial aspect of the question. The Mughal empire was rapidly expanding, bringing into its fold men of various religious views and cultures. It was bordering on Shia states, on Sunni states, on Mahdavi states. The activities of the state were fast developing and incorporating the functions of a 'culture' state. Under these circumstances since the administration of state had to be uniformly carried out, it was open to Akbar to depend solely on any one school of law (even one interpreter of that law). However, his experiences with Shaikh Abdun Nabi and Abdullah Sultanpuri were none too happy. Hence he had to follow some other course. What could that be? Badaoni himself tells us that on every question there was so much difference of opinion that it was impossible to find one's way out. Akbar, therefore, had to exercise his own judgement. His criterion in making decisions was to be the 'good of the inhabitants of the world'. The policy of Akbar was to make all his subjects feel that it was their empire. This could be made possible only when the emperor had the ears of all (Muslims in first instance) and the basis of his administration was the welfare of the empire.

## Notes and References

1. *Akbar, the Great Mogul,* London, 1917. 'Before he made up his mind to renounce Islam, he wanted to follow a middle path and to seek peace by constituting himself the supreme judge of all differences between rival Muslim doctors'. He then mentions Sheikh Mubarak's hint that Akbar might become the temporal as well as the spiritual head of the people and writes, 'Six years later time was considered ripe for extending the autocracy of Akbar from the temporal to the spiritual side by making him

Pope as well as King' (p. 178). Then again: 'Probably it was suggested by the information then becoming available concerning the position of the Pope in western Europe... (Akbar) practically was invested with attribute of infallibility' (p. 179).

2. F. W. Buckler, *JRAS*, 1924, p. 591.

3. *Din-i-Ilahi*, Calcutta (1941).

4. *Religious Policy of the Mughal Emperors*, Oxford University Press, 1940.

5. Ibid.: 'The decree was only a manifestation of Akbar's anxiety to be considered a good Muslim', p. 40.

6. The words used in the document itself are *Sultan-i-Adil* and *Amirul-Muminin*. But the intention of the signatories was clearly to call Akbar a *Khalifa*. Badaoni says, 'The subject matter of the document was the settling of the absolute superiority of the just Imam over the *Mujtahids*.' In *Muntakhab-ul-Tawarikh*, Vol. II, p. 270. Arnold writes, 'The names and title Caliph, *Imam* and *Amirul Muminin* are very commonly used to denote the same person. The title *Sultan* was used by the Ottomans' *Caliphate*', p. 203. Buckler and R. P. Tripathi, *Some Aspects of Muslim Administration*, p. 156, support this view.

7. *Nass* means the explicit statements of the Quran and the *Hadith*.

8. Mawardi, *Caliphate*; Kazi Baizawi, *Tawilul Anwar*; Ghazali, *Ihya*; Ibn Jama, *Tahrir-ul-Akham*; Khuda Baksh, *Orient Under the Caliphs*; T. W. Arnold, *The Caliphate*; *Encyclopedia of Islam*.

9. W. S. Blunt, *Future of Islam*, p. 66; Hughes, *Dictionary of Islam*.

10. See *Sharh-ul-Mawaqif*.

11. Badaoni, *Bibliotheca* text, Vol. II, p. 271. The translation of Lowe is inaccurate.

12. Tripathi writes: 'From the historical point of view the claims of Akbar were probably higher and certainly not inferior to those of the Ottoman Sultan', op. cit., p. 143.

13. A *Mujtahid* is also called *Naib-i-Imam*.

14. *Kanz-ul-Ummal* by Ali bin-Hisamuddin Al-Mutaqqi, Hyderabad text, 1894, Vol. III, No. 2999. The work is one of the authoritative Hanafiite Collections of Traditions, and is regarded as one of the *Mutun-i-Mu'tabara*. It contains 46,681 sayings of the Prophet.

15. Ibid., No. 2580.

16. *Mishkat-ul-Masabih* by Abdullah Muhammad bin Al-Khateeb Tabrizi, Book XVI, ch. I. The work is regarded in India as one of the standard Shafaiite works.

17. Ibid.

18. According to *Sahih-al-Bokhari*, the gate of complete *ijtihad* has been closed (*Insdad-i-bab-al-ijtihad*). Therefore, Akbar was not placed over the *full Mujtahids* but *mujtahids* of the third category, that is, those on particular questions.

19. Shawkani, p. 253.

20. *Al-Taqrir* by Akmaluddin Muhammad, al-Babarti, the great Hanafite scholar who wrote a commentary on *Usul-al-Pazdawi.*

21. Badaoni himself thought that a Hanafi could accept the decisions of a Maliki Qazi. On the question of *muta*, he says: 'Should at any time a Qazi of the Maliki sect decide that Muta is legal, it is legal *according to common belief* even for the *Hanafis* and *Shafaiis.*' Op. cit., Vol. II, p. 207.

22. Abu Yusuf, *Kitabul Kharaj*, quoted by Tripathi, op. cit., p. 132, note 7.

23. Ghazali, *op. cit.*, Vol. II, p. 354.

24. It is curious that Smith is shocked in this case although Henry VIII did something much worse. Cf. *Act for the Submission of the Clergy*, 1534. The clergy promised that 'they will never from henceforth presume to attempt, allege, or put in use, or enact or promulgate...any new canons, constitutions...unless his majesty do give his most royal assent and authority in that behalf'. *Tudor Constitutional Documents*, ed. by Tanner, pp. 22–3.

25. Buckler, *JRAS*, 1924.

26. Tripathi, op. cit., Appendix, pp. 156–8.

27. M. L. Roy Choudhury, op. cit., p. 119.

28. Ibid., pp. 111–14,

29. Badaoni, op. cit., p. 274.

30. Tripathi, op. cit., p. 143.

31. Ibid., p. 156.

32. Buckler, *JRAS*, 1924, p. 593.

33. E.g., Ibu Abidin.

34. E.g., Al-Zarkashi, Hyder Effendi, Ibn-Hazm, etc.

35. Ghazali, op. cit., Vol. II, p. 351.

36. Ibid., p. 592.

37. The writer of this paper gratefully acknowledges the suggestions given by R. P. Tripathi, Professor of History, Allahabad University for this paper.

38. The history of Europe in the sixteenth century has a striking resemblance with the history of contemporary Asia. There, four powers had emerged as strong monarchies in the beginning of the century—Spain, France, England, and the Holy Roman Empire. They all fought each other for supremacy in Europe. Since the Church was a very powerful force in politics, they all tried to control the Papacy. Hence the Italian wars.

39. E.g., Sher Shah who is reported to have said once, 'Hasan Baba, what shall I do, for my heart has been rent into pieces by the actions of these Mullahs: I wish to send them all to the gallows'. (*Daulat-i-Sher Shahi*, 17th *farman.*)

# 8

～◦◦～

# Shaikh Ahmad Sirhindi and Mughal Politics*

Shaikh Ahmad Sirhindi[1] was one of the greatest religious leaders of his times. His followers included some of the principal
nobles[2] as well as a large number of common Muslims. He may
be regarded as the symbol of a powerful tendency that had
appeared in the reign of Akbar, the tendency of Muslim reaction
which was strengthened in the seventeenth century. He provided
the ideological basis of this tendency and took an active part in
furthering it. Thus even though the historical records may be
lacking in any visible proof of his direct political influence, it
would be interesting to study the political attitude of the Shaikh
as revealed in his letters to the important political personalities
of the period.[3]

A few words may be said about the then prevailing tendencies
before we actually examine Shaikh Ahmad's ideas and teaching. Akbar's reign marks the culmination of an epoch in which
a common Hindu-Muslim culture was growing in different parts
of the country. The dominant religious tendencies, both among
the Muslims as well as Hindus, had many common points.
These were, as is well-known, the Sufi movement and the Bhakti
cult. Politically, the endeavour of Akbar was to make the Mughal
state the common concern of Hindus and Muslims.

---

* *Proceedings of Indian History Congress*, VIII Session, Annamalainagar, 1945,
pp. 248–57.

But the very success of this tendency accentuated opposite tendencies. The Bhakti movement in Maharashtra assumes, at this period, an anti-Muslim character. The followers of Guru Nanak gradually shed away their catholicity and assumed the nature of a militant sect. Similarly, among the Muslims, there was a feeling of revolt against the existing trends of Sufism with its tolerance and freedom of individual worship. There was a cry 'Islam has become impure', 'Muslims are being influenced by kafirs'. Thus the slogan, 'Back to original Islam', was raised. The beginning of the second millennium had revived the idea of a regenerator. The Mahdavi movement,[4] although professing a different set of beliefs, was the product of a similar trend. The leadership of this tendency was, however, assumed by the Naqshbandi movement.[5] A large number of Muslim nobles who were either dissatisfied with the growing influence of Hindu nobles or subsequently of the Persian nobles, found themselves in complete agreement with this movement and extended to it their full support. It was precisely this group of nobles which turned the scales in favour of Jahangir during the controversy between Salim and Khusro for succession.

## Dissatisfaction with Akbar's Reign

Shaikh Ahmad was extremely dissatisfied with the policy of Akbar. In a letter to Shaikh Farid (Murtaza Khan) during Jahangir's reign he writes,

You know what sufferings the Musalmans have undergone in the past. The conditions of the Muslims in the past ages had never been worse than this; that the Muslims should follow their creed, and the kafirs should follow their path. In the previous reign the kafirs became so preponderant that in the land of Islam they promulgated orders of *kufr*, while the Muslims were unable to give Islamic orders; and if they did so, they were executed.[6]

Shaikh Ahmad was definitely in favour of the accession of Jahangir. He rejoiced in the news of Jahangir's accession, and wrote:

Today when the news of the rise of the Islamic state and the accession of the king of Islam has reached all, the followers of Islam considered it their duty to offer their support and aid to the king and to guide him in the propagation of the faith and the strengthening of the religion—whether this assistance is given with the hands or with the tongue.[7]

Shaikh Ahmad's devoted disciple Murtaza Khan played a leading role in favour of Jahangir in the Council of nobles convened by Khan-i-Azam at the time of Akbar's death.[8] And again it was Shaikh Farid who extracted from Jahangir the promise to defend Islam as a price of the support given by the nobles.[9]

The reactions of Shaikh Ahmad on the accession of Jahangir and during the early part of his reign are worth noting. High hopes were raised in his heart that the new regime would propagate the shariat. In his letters he unfolded his political ideas. The main points are summarized below.

## Importance of Shariat

Unlike the Sufic preachers, Shaikh Ahmad laid great stress on the importance of the propagation of the shariat by the state. In a letter to Khan-i-Azam he says: 'Sages have said that the *Shara*' is always under the sword, and the triumph of the *Shara*' depends on the Kings'.[10] He again emphasized this point in a letter to Jahangir himself when he wrote that the propagation of the *Shara*' depended on him.[11] He makes his argument very clear in the following words: 'The king stands in the same relation to the world as the heart stands to the body. If the heart is sound, the body is also well. If, however, the heart is in a bad way, the body also suffers. *Thus the welfare of the world* depends on the goodness of the King.'[12]

These ideas were somewhat different from the prevalent Sufic notions. The Sufis believed primarily in their individual salvation, and in the moral persuasion of the masses. Shaikh Ahmad, however, holds a contrary view. He considers the scholars of *Shara*' who propagate the Shariat as definitely superior to the Sufis.[13] And he holds that propagation of the *Shara*' is possible mainly with the backing of the state. To Khan-i-Azam he writes: 'Khwaja Ahrar used to say that his task was to propagate the Shariat. That was why he frequented the company of kings and *through them propagated the Shariat*.'[14] For this reason Shaikh Ahmad too maintained cordial relations with the nobles of the realm and concentrated on cultivating their friendship.[15]

He kept on pressing the nobles to exercise their influence on the king for the propagation of the Shariat. He says: 'In the new regime it is the duty of the nobles and the ulama to restore the glory of Islam. If the king is indifferent, and even his companions keep aloof from the problem, the fate of the Muslims would become pitiable.'[16] He is more explicit in his letter to Khan-i-Azam: 'Your word is effective and your adherence to Islam is respected among your equals. You should therefore make an attempt. At least the laws of *kufr* which are prevalent among the Muslims should be abrogated.... In the previous regime the religion of Muhammad was looked upon with hostility. In the present regime there is no open enmity. If there is any, it is due to ignorance.'[17]

This ignorance, therefore, he sought to combat. The elements mainly responsible for this ignorance on the part of the kings were the 'vicious ulama', 'The company of the worldly ulama is like a deadly poison. Their mischief is contagious... In the past the calamity that befell Islam was due to the machinations of these very people. It is they who have been misleading the kings.'[18] When therefore he heard that the king had decided to appoint four prominent ulama at the court to advise on religious questions, he was very pleased. But he cautioned his friends among the nobles that they should allow only such ulama to be appointed as were deeply religious and strict followers of the *Shara'*.[19]

The main mission of the life of Shaikh Ahmad was to establish the supremacy of the *Shara'* in the Muslim state. In almost all his letters addressed to the political personalities, there is the utmost emphasis on following the *Shara'*. In a letter to Murtaza Khan on the occasion of the appointment of the ulama at the court (referred to above), he says that they should 'enunciate the law of Islam so that no order is passed in contravention of the *Shara'*.[20] Again to Khan-i-Khanan he writes that 'in all matters the decisions of the truly religious ulama should be followed.'[21]

The Shariat has to be interpreted by the Sunni ulama on the basis of the Book (*kitab*), the tradition (*sunnat*) and the consensus of the community (*ijma-i-ummat*). There should be no attempt to seek rational justification of the religious laws, because one who tries to do so 'denies the greatness of the

Prophet'. In this connection it was imperative, according to Shaikh Ahmad, that first of all the beliefs be corrected according to the Sunni faith, and heretical tendencies be combated. In a long letter to Khan-i-Jahan, he urges him to conform strictly to the Sunni faith, enunciates its main tenets and beliefs, asks him to keep aloof from the other sects and requests him to speak from time to time to the king about it.[23] Almost the same advice is repeated to Murtaza Khan, Mirza Badiuz Zaman, Darab Khan, Hakim Fathullah, Khizr Khan Lodi, Fath Khan Afghan, and Khan-i-Khanan.[24]

Whenever action was taken to enforce the Shariat, he expresses satisfaction and appreciation. For example, he thanks and praises Qulich Khan for having promulgated a number of orders in accordance with the *Shara'* and congratulates him that during his tenure of office at Lahore, 'religion has been strengthened'.[25] He pleads for the appointment of *Qazis* so that the Shariat may be properly enforced.[26] On the other hand he unequivocally condemns all state institutions in contravention of the *Shara'*. His abhorrence of such activities was so great that he even refused to visit Delhi during the season of *Navroz*.[27]

## Opposition to Heretical Tendencies

The establishment of the supremacy of the *Shara'* involved, according to Shaikh Ahmad, a crusade against the heretics and the infidels. Let us first examine his ideas towards the heretics. In a long letter to Hakim Fathullah he violently attacks the non-Sunni sects, especially the Shias.[28] To Murtaza Khan his advice is to avoid the company of heretics altogether, as that was 'even worse than the company of infidels'.[29] The Shaikh also wrote a pamphlet refuting the beliefs of Shiism, entitled '*Radd-i-Rawafiz*'. Presumably this sustained campaign against Shiism was mainly directed towards the Shiite Persian nobles. The Shaikh was keen that heresy be put down, and for this reason wanted to enlist the sympathies of the nobles. In a letter to Khan-i-Khanan he writes: 'The followers of this (Naqshbandi) Order have become helpless in this land, and many people have fallen a victim to Shiite heresy. Your aid is solicited in this connection.'[30] The execution of Qazi Nurullah Shustari, the Shia Qazi of Akbar's reign, was presumably at the instance of the Shaikh.[31]

# Tirade Against Kafirs

Much more violent however was his tirade against the non-Muslims (kafirs). According to the Shaikh, Muslims should have no truck with the non-Muslims, not even social contacts. He emphasizes this point in a number of letters. For example, to Khan-i-Khanan he writes: 'Muslims have been instructed to regard kafirs as enemies.'[32] He expands his ideas in a letter to Murtaza Khan as follows:

One who respects the kafirs, dishonours the Muslims. Respecting them does not merely mean honouring them, but giving them a place in one's company and talking to them. Like dogs they should be kept away and if there is any worldly business which cannot be attained without them, then without taking them into confidence, only minimum contact should be established. The height of Islamic sentiment is to forego worldly profits and have no relationship at all with them.[33]

Shaikh Ahmad wanted to translate his religious hatred of the non-Muslims into the realm of politics. He considers the state ruled ·over by a Muslim as an Islamic state. Such a conception was fundamentally different from the theory of the Mughal state. The Mughal theory, at its best under Akbar, strove that the state should not remain the monopoly of any one religion, or race or group. Different religions and racial groups had been associated with administration, and the affairs of the state were being run more and more in harmony with the sentiments of the different elements of society. An administration which was tending to assume the character of a non-sectarian common concern was strongly disapproved by the Shaikh. He could not tolerate 'infidels' issuing orders of '*kufr*' in the 'land of Islam', and considered such a state to be one of helplessness and degradation for the Muslims.

He, therefore, urged an uncompromising policy. The non-Muslim should have no place in the administration; they should be reduced to a state of degradation and humiliation. Utmost harshness should be shown to them—this was, in short, his recommendation for the treatment of non-Muslims.[34] A few extracts from his letters will clearly reveal his main ideas on the subjects. In a letter to Murtaza Khan he writes, 'Obedience to the Prophet lies in the fact that the Islamic law be followed and the traditions of infidelity be obliterated. Islam and kufr are the negation of each other.... God has ordered, "O Prophet launch a crusade against the kafirs and disbelievers and suppress them".[35] Again, he repeats, his ideas as follows, 'Launching a crusade against the kafirs and treating them with harshness is one of the essential needs of religion'.[36] His bitterness reaches a climax when he writes, 'Every man has got some desire in his heart. The uppermost desire in the heart of this *faqir* is that the enemies of God and the Prophet be dealt with severely.... (This writer) has repeatedly invited you to perform this function and considers it to be one of the most important duties.... Every open and hidden effort should be made for their destruction.'[37]

## Views on *Jizya*

As has already been noticed, he was very keen that the infidels be kept in a state of degradation and humiliation. He looks upon *jizya* not as a monetary contribution for defence in lieu of personal service, as some jurists and writers have argued. He wanted the imposition of the jizya as an emblem of the subjugation of the non-Muslims. He elaborates this point in a letter to Murtaza Khan: 'The main reason for taking *jizya* is to degrade and humiliate them, so much so that because of its fear they may not be able to dress well and live in grandeur.... It does not behove the kings to stop *jizya*. God has instituted it to dishonour them. It is intended to bring them into contempt and to establish the honour and might of Islam.'[38]

## Appreciation of Measures Against Non-Muslims

Any blow at the non-Muslims was deeply appreciated by the Shaikh. His letter to Khan-i-Azam is characteristic of this sentiment. He writes, 'May God help you in upholding the law of Islam and give you victory over its enemies.... At such a critical juncture, we find in you a welcome personality...the verbal crusade that you are waging is the greatest of crusades (*Jihad-i-Akbar*), and consider it to be higher than the crusade of bloodshed'.[39] Similarly to Sadr-i-Jahan he writes, 'The promulgation of Islamic orders and the news of the dishonouring of the enemies of Faith has gladdened hearts of Muslims'.[40] He congratulated Murtaza Khan for having dishonoured the Hindus and destroyed their idols during the Kangra campaign. Perhaps his ideas emerge most sharply when he expresses his pleasure at the execution of Guru Arjan. He says that whatever may have been the motives of execution, it was a matter for satisfaction, since it involved the degradation of the infidels and the glory of Islam.[41]

## Growth of Shaikh Ahmad's Influence and His Imprisonment

Such in brief were the ideas of Shaikh Ahmad on politics. As observed before, he sought to extend his influence among the nobles and in the army. The Sunni nobles found these ideas in consonance with their political ambition. The supremacy of the Shariat and the subordination of the temporal authorities to the dictates of the ulama could act as a check on the autocracy of the king, something which must have been very welcome to most of the nobles. The tirade which Shaikh Ahmad launched against those ulama who justified Akbar's absolutism on the basis of the legal theory which had grown during the Abbasid period, could have undermined the religious sanction of royal autocracy. And as has already been mentioned, the attacks on Hindus and Shias could have helped in ousting the Persian and Hindu nobles from the much coveted higher posts. Whatever might have been the reasons, Shaikh Ahmad did begin to exercise an influence over an important section of the nobles.

In the army and in the administrative staff too, he carried on his propaganda. He appointed Shaikh Badruddin as his chief *khalifa* in the army. In almost all his letters to the important nobles we find that he is making a recommendation for the appointment to some post for one of his followers. Such concentrated efforts at a time when the minds of the people were only too well prepared to receive such ideas, produced effective results. His influence grew so much that even the king was alarmed, and decided to bring the situation under control.[42] In 1619, he was summoned to the court on the charge of claiming superiority over the first caliph, Abu Bakr. It is obvious that this was a trumped up charge. In a long letter to Hakim Fathullah, the Shaikh denied the charge and as a proof, referred to the

letter which he had written to the Hakim a few years before,
stating that Abu Bakr was superior to everyone else including
Ali.[43] There is a another proof which points that the authorities
knew it fully well that the Shaikh did not really consider himself
superior to Abu Bakr. Shaikh Mirak, who was Prince Khurram's
tutor, once went to Sirhind and questioned Shaikh Ahmad. Shaikh
Ahmad denied the charge and produced the letter in question.
Shaikh Mirak returned quite satisfied on the score.[44] Moreover,
considering the religious policy of Jahangir, it may be presumed
that the Shaikh would not have been persecuted only because of
his religious pretensions, even if the charges against him were
true. The Naqshbandi records also state that Jahangir jailed him
for refusing to perform *sijdah*. Probably it was to this incident
that Beni Prasad refers in his book.[45] Jahangir however makes
no reference to this incident in his *Memoirs*.[46] It is quite possible
that it may not have occurred because he had already abolished
sijdah for the Qazis and the ulama.

The Shaikh was however sent to Gwalior prison. But even
during his confinement he urged his followers not to do anything
against the state, probably because the Shaikh believed that the
success of his programme depended on the cooperation of the
King who was after all much more amenable to the influence of
the ulama than his father. The statement of some of the followers
of Shaikh Ahmad that he actually dissuaded Mahabat Khan from
revolting on this issue is not supported by facts.[47] However, the
way Jahangir mentions the occasion of the release of the Shaikh
two years later ('It was reported that the Shaikh had repented')
also shows that he was not dissatisfied with his conduct.

The Naqshbandi writers go on to say that the king apologized
to the Shaikh and promised to carry out the following programme
outlined by the Shaikh: abolition of the sijdah, reconstruction of
the mosques that were destroyed, permission for cow slaughter,
appointment of Qazis and censors to enforce the *Shara'*, introduction of jizya, and suppression of heresy and innovation.[48]
There is no contemporary evidence to show that either the king
expressed regret for his conduct or that he gave the pledge
demanded by the Shaikh. On the other hand, Jahangir writes
that the Shaikh expressed regret. It is also known that no action
was taken in accordance with the demands of the Shaikh as
enunciated above.

## Significance of His Imprisonment and Release

It would not be incorrect to say that both the imprisonment as well as the release of the Shaikh were due to political causes. The dissatisfaction against the Nurjahan junta had been increasing and this dissatisfaction had assumed a religious anti-Shiite colour. The dissatisfied nobles included Prince Khurram and Mahabat Khan. The latter was closely associated with the Naqshbandi order. (It may be recalled that there was trouble over the marriage of Mahabat Khan's daughter with the son of Khwaja Umar Naqshbandi.) Close affinity between these dissatisfied nobles and Shaikh Ahmad is not inconceivable. The imprisonment of the Shaikh was undoubtedly done under the influence of the Nurjahan junta, and his release was one of the measures taken to assuage the agitated Sunni opinion during these troubled times. This incident is sufficient in itself to prove the influential position which Shaikh Ahmad had come to acquire as the spiritual leader of the pan-Islamic tendency.

## Notes and References

1. Born in 1563 and died in 1624, he has been called 'Mujaddid Alf-i-Sani' or the Regenerator of the Second Millennium. He was the virtual founder of the Naqshbandi order in India.
2. E.g., Murtaza Khan, Islam Khan, Mahabat Khan, Mirza Badi-uz-Zaman, Darab Khan, etc.
3. *Maktoobat-i-Imam-i-Rabbani*, Nawal Kishore Press, Cawnpore, 1906, 3 Vols.
4. Maulana Abdul Kalam Azad's evaluation of the Mahdavi movement would be found of interest, see *Tazkira*.
5. Mirza Hakim, Akbar's younger brother, had organized his rebellion in 1581 on the slogan of 'the defence of religion'. Incidentally he was also a follower of the Naqshbandi order.
6. *Maktoobat*, Vol. I, letter no. 47. Also see letter no. 81 addressed to Lala Beg.
7. Ibid.
8. Asad Beg, *Waqaya*. B.M. III, 979b.
9. Accordingly, the leading nobles (Murtaza Khan), having been sent by the others as their representative, came to the Prince and promised, in all their names to place the kingdom in his hands provided that he would swear to defend the law of Mahomet. Ibid. In this context, see S. A. A. Rizvi, ed., *Muslim Revivalist Movements in North India*, Agra, 1965, pp. 216–21.

10. *Maktoobat,* Vol. I, letter no. 65.

11. Ibid., Vol. I, letter no. 47.

12. Ibid., Vol. I, letter no. 47.

13. Ibid., letter to Murtaza Khan, Vol. I, no. 48.

14. Ibid., Vol. I, letter no. 65.

15. E.g., he regards Murtaza Khan as a patron; he is anxious to regain the favour of Hakim Fathullah when the latter is annoyed; he humours and flatters, and at times admonishes Khan-i-Khanan and Khan-i-Azam to maintain his influence over them.

16. Ibid., letter to Sadr-i-Jahan, Vol. I, no. 195.

17. Ibid., Vol. I, letter no. 65. Similarly to Murtaza Khan he writes: 'It is expected from your gentle self that since God has given you complete nearness to the king, you will make every overt and covert effort to propagate the shariat of Muhammad.' Letter no. 47.

18. Ibid., Vol. I, letter no. 47.

19. Ibid., letter to Murtaza Khan (No. 53) to Sadr-i-Jahan (No. 194).

20. Ibid., letter no. 53.

21. Ibid., letter no. 70.

22. Ibid., letter to Khan-i-Khanan, no. 214.

23. Ibid., Vol. II, letter no. 67.

24. Ibid., Vol. I, letters nos. 69, 71, 75, 80, 94, 193, 213; Vol. II, letter no. 87.

25. Ibid., Vol. I, letter no. 76. See also letter to Sadr-i-Jahan, no. 194.

26. Ibid., letters no. 103 and 195.

27. Ibid., letter no. 44. In a subsequent letter he repeats his arguments: 'Today when the king of Islam is no longer as kind to the infidels, the custom of *kufr* cannot be looked upon with equanimity by the Muslims', letter no. 194.

28. Ibid., letter no. 80.

29. Ibid., letter no. 54.

30. Ibid., Vol. II, letter no. 62. This letter confirms the view taken by the author of *Maasir-i-Umara* that Khan-i-Khanan had genuinely discarded Shiism. The Khan-i-Khanan however remained unorthodox all his life, and Shaikh Ahmad admonished him frequently. Cf. Vol. I, letters nos 23, 68, 214, Vol. II, Nos 8, 62 and 66.

31. *Jahangir-i-Mujaddidia,* p. 43.

32. *Maktoobat,* letter no. 23.

33. Ibid., letter no. 163.

34. The scope of the present paper prevents an examination of the factors which led to rise of this tendency, or its evaluation, or a comparison with the corresponding non-Muslim movements. The writer hopes to undertake an exhaustive examination of these points in the book he is contemplating to write on 'Some Popular Muslim Religious Movements in Medieval India'.

35. Ibid., letter no. 163.
36. Ibid., letter no. 193.
37. Ibid., letter no. 269, cf. letter no. 165.
38. Ibid., letter no. 163, cf no. 193.
39. Ibid., letter no. 65.
40. Ibid., letter no. 194.
41. Ibid., letters nos. 193 and 269.
42. Khwaja Kamaluddin's work *Ruzat-ul-Qaiyyaumia* gives a detailed account of the life of Shaikh Ahmad. This account, though full of inaccuracies, is substantially the same as appears in other contemporary or later works.
43. *Maktoubat*, Vol. I, letter no. 202. The letter referred to is no. 80.
44. Dara Shikoh, *Safinatul Auliya* (Nawal Kishore Press), pp. 197–8.
45. Beni Prasad, *History of Jahangir*, OUP, 1922, Appendix B, p. 450.
46. *Tuzuk-i-Jahangiri*, edited by Md. Hadi.
47. B. A. Faruqi also makes the same statement (p. 25). The students of history need no proof of the fact that Shaikh Ahmad was released much before Mahabat Khan's *coup de main*.
48. Rauzat ul-Qaiyumiya, ff. 77a–78b.

# 9

〰️

# The Problem of Nationalities
# in Medieval India*

The history of India indicates that in the political sphere, two opposite tendencies have been in operation and their conflict has defied solution. One of them is the attempt to establish a centralized government over the whole country; and the other is the equally strong counter-tendency—the tendency towards decentralization. The Mughal empire which had almost succeeded in establishing a stable empire, floundered on this very rock. Various explanations have been given by scholars of history of this conflict between centrifugal and centripetal tendencies. One point, however, has not received the attention that it deserves. The object of this paper is to focus the attention of scholars on this point.

Perhaps the main reason why a centralized government could not succeed in India was that in this land of ours, as a result of the peculiar historical forces in operation, a number of nationalities have been in the process of formation, and their full development was incompatible with the existence of a strong central government. Here an attempt has been made to trace the forces which helped in the formation of northern Indian nationalities. It is not possible, of course, to deal with a profound subject like this in the course of such a short paper. This paper leaves aside the detailed historical facts of the

* *Proceedings of Indian History Congress*, VII Session, Madras, 1944, pp. 370–6.

period and contains only a few formulations on the basis of the broad outlines of the subject. Its purpose would be served if these formulations are carefully examined by scholars of history and either improved upon, amended or rejected. The writer of the paper himself considers them as mere tentative suggestions indicating lines of study.

It is difficult to find a commonly accepted definition of nationality. But a few observations may safely be made. First, the conception of nationhood is essentially modern, although the factors which shape a nation have been historically evolved. Secondly, as far as most of the modern nations are concerned, their emergence as nations follows the rise of commercial capitalism. In view of these observations, Stalin's definition of a nation may be regarded as a fairly workable proposition. He says that 'A nation is a historically evolved stable community of language, territory, economic life and psychological make-up manifested in a community of culture.' Obviously, the mere accumulation of a common language or culture does not convert a people into a nation, just as it is not correct to say that the Germans, who spoke the same language and enjoyed a similar culture as early as say the fifteenth century, constituted a nation. Nations are definitely the results of historical processes. If we look at the fully developed nations of the world, we shall notice that people living in contiguous territories draw near each other as a result of certain historical forces, and then at a particular stage of economic development, they are welded into the bonds of nationhood. The British, French, German, Italian, and American nations arose in the wake of capitalism. But in these countries we notice the rise of a single nation. There were certain other countries where as a result of the dissolution of feudalism and the rise of capitalism, a number of nationalities arose in a single state, for example, the Balkans, the pre-revolutionary Czarist empire or the Austro-Hungarian empire, which may be considered as multinational states. What is the reason that a similar stage of economic development leads to the evolution of some uni-national and some multinational states? An explanation of this phenomenon may be sought in the fact that in these multi-national states, as a result of certain historical forces, people living in different areas had been developing along divergent lines of cultural process. The coming of industrial economy gave shape to this submerged, and till then indistinct tendency of separate development.

It will not be correct to compare India with uni-national states like Britain or France. On the question of national development, India would bear better comparison with the Russian empire. India has not yet sufficiently progressed economically as to provide opportunities for her various nationalities to develop fully. Indian nationalities are still in the process of evolution, although some elementary economic progress and the struggle for freedom have helped in the process.

On the eve of the establishment of Turkish rule, the economic foundations of Indian society were laid on the system of village economy. Every village could on the whole be considered a self-contained unit. There was no direct relation between one village and another to infuse among them any sense of unity. Their only affiliation to each other was that sometimes they happened to be ruled by the same raja. Even politically large tracts did not possess common governments as the country was divided into a number of small states, ruled over by the head of one clan or another.

The establishment of Turkish rule created a new situation. The whole of northern India was brought under the political sway of one central government. The political fragmentation of the country disappeared, and, at least politically, large areas came into closer contact with each other. The Muslims, at this stage, however, were still a distinct unit. Their political and economic organization and their cultural traditions were different from the rest of Hindustan. In order to maintain their rule in an alien land, they maintained their separate existence.

At a time when the means of communication were not developed, it was difficult for a central government to keep its grip over a country of such vast distances, split up by so many natural barriers. The empire was therefore parcelled out to a number of *subadar*s or *jagirdar*s, who soon began to enjoy virtual autonomy. So long as these provincial governors felt that they would not be able to maintain their political domination without the support of the central government, they owed it allegiance. But the moment they felt secure in their own provinces and felt that the central government was not strong enough to coerce them, they proclaimed their independence. One of the first governors to proclaim independence was Tughril Beg, the governor of Bengal, who rebelled against Balban.

These governors realized that in order to strengthen their own position against the central government it was necessary for them to develop close political and cultural affinities with the local elements. This became all the more necessary because these *provincial* rulers had to face a dual conflict—with the central authority and with those local elements who wanted to win back political power. If we study the history of the provincial dynasties, we shall find that they did not have much difficulty in counteracting local opposition. The local Hindu rajas felt that being unable to overthrow the provincial chief, the best alternative for them was to make an alliance with him, since he was in need of their help and was prepared to share power with them. Moreover, it was in any case better for them that the political centre of gravity should remain near them, rather than they be treated as mere 'provincial'. Thus we notice that fairly close relations were developing between Hindu upper classes and the provincial rulers. Probably, the best illustration of the dual conflict and its solution is furnished by the history of Bengal.

Under these political circumstances, two other tendencies were in operation which facilitated the process of formation of nationalities. One of these tendencies was economic and the other was cultural.

The *jagirdari*[1] system dealt a blow to the system of village economy. Some of its effects are clearly visible, for example the gradual reduction of the isolation of villages. Secondly, the separate political rule of the rajas and along with them the domination of the higher castes tends to disappear. From the point of view of the masses, the tyranny of the local chief also comes to an end. There is no symbol of tyranny before their very eyes, whom they could perceive. To the common people the new government was on the whole largely impersonal.

An important consequence of these factors was that the political and economic interests of the people living in the provinces tended to become common. These common political and economic interests bound the Hindus and Muslims living in the provinces in common ties.

The above should not be taken to mean that the formation of different nationalities is visible at this stage. What is noticeable is that common interests are helping to prepare a psychological make-up among people with sufficient potential homogeneity who could ultimately under favourable circumstances, rise as a nationality. The preconditions of national evolution are being created at this stage. Of course, in some areas this tendency is more marked than in the others.

In the cultural sphere, the lessening of village isolationism and the disappearance of small independent states, and along with them the domination of the higher castes, led to the weakening of the belief in several tribal gods and deities. Polytheism began to yield place to some form of the ultimate unity of godhead, one God, who is the god of all, as one king who was supreme in that entire area. Before this Supreme God, all men are equal, just as before the sultan, *Thakur, Ahir,* Brahmin and Sudra all were equal, even though all were in subjection. It is true that many centuries earlier Sankara had preached monism, his theory of *advaitvada* being logically the most perfect form of idealism the East has yet produced. But the teachings of Sankara were too non-material, abstract, and they did not reach the masses. The social conditions of this later age, however, led to a mass drift towards some form of monotheism. In certain areas, as in Bengal, large number of people, particularly from among the followers of later Buddhism, were converted to Islam. In other areas, masses become the devotees of the preachers of the bhakti *marga.* From the thirteenth to the fifteenth century, preachers of the cult of bhakti spread over a very large area, in Bengal, Gujarat, the Punjab, Sind, UP, and central India—almost everywhere. There is no doubt that the ascendant Hindu religious movement of this period was the bhakti movement, preaching the brotherhood of man and the unity of godhead. Similarly, if we look at the popular Muslim religious movements of this period, we find that they are dominantly Sufic movements. It is significant that the popular Hindu and Muslim preachers are stressing those things which promote ideological affinities between their respective followers.

It should again be remembered that national development was not taking place in various regions with the same speed. Certain areas such as Bengal or Gujarat developed earlier in this respect than the others. Similarly, the pattern of development too was not the same everywhere. In Maharashtra, for example, the Muslim domination was weak, and therefore in that area the national development was not based on the fusion of Hindu and Muslim culture. Still the other considerations hold good on a broad plane in that area also.

To resume the theme, let us see how the formation of nationalities finds expression in the cultural sphere. The evolution of a distinctive national culture is clearly visible in the provinces of Bengal and Gujarat. Let us take for example the question of national language and architecture. Bengali language is a living symbol of the unity of Hindus and Muslims in Bengal. The rise of Bengali as a full-fledged literature may be said with some truth to have dated from the establishment of an independent Muslim Bengal. The same can be said about Gujarati literature. Similarly, in the realm of architecture, a similar tendency can be noticed. The Muslims had brought with them certain distinct Arab, Iranian, and Turkish traditions of architecture; the more important of these distinctive features were: the dome, the arch, and the minaret. If we look at the buildings built by the Slave and Khilji rulers, we shall find in them an incontinuity, a distinct heterogeneity. But both Gujarat and Bengal in their own way solved the problem of mixing the two styles of architecture. The Muslim and non-Muslim features of architecture have been blended so effectively that each building appears to be a homogeneous whole. The Jama mosque at Ahmedabad and the Adina mosque at Gaur are fine specimens of the Gujarat and Bengal styles.

This evolving national consciousness manifested itself politically as well. Just a few examples may here be considered. During the first kingship of Humayun when Askari was made the subedar of Gujarat, he is reported to have been thinking in terms of independence and Hindu Beg agreed with him. An explanation of this may be found in the fact that Askari and Hindu Beg may have realized that the Mughal government would have better chances of success in Gujarat if there were an independent Gujarat ruler rather than if he were subject to Delhi. Similarly, during the second kingship of Humayun, he is reported to be thinking in terms of creating twelve semi-autonomous provincial states, while the king himself was to have toured from one centre to the other. We might also consider the abnormal difficulties which Akbar had to face in conquering

Gujarat and Bengal as expressions of growing national consciousness.

During the sixteenth century, the coming of a new form of economy accelerated the process of the formation of nationalities. The hitherto submerged growth of national characteristics began to take definite shape.

This new form of economy was the rise of merchant capital in India. In the sixteenth century trade and commerce developed tremendously. The growth of merchant capital lends almost universally to the rise of commodities of money values. These effects were noticeable in India as well. The rise of money values can be judged from the fact that in most cases during the days of Sher Shah and Akbar, revenue began to be collected in cash. The developing economic bonds and the improvement of the means of communication consequent upon this, made national demarcations very distinct. It is significant that both Bengal and Gujarat were pioneers in the field of trade and commerce.

Akbar's attempt was to synthesize the growing unity between the Hindus and the Muslims in different national regions into an all-embracing unity on an all-India scale. He tried to prevent the Mughal empire from becoming the monopoly of any single race or nationality. Therefore, on the one hand he associated Rajputs, Iranians, etc. in addition to the Turks and Mughals in the administration, on the other hand he established a provincial administration under which the provincial nationalities found some scope for development.

But from this very period two opposite tendencies are visible. On the one hand, as a result of the rise of merchant capital, of the benevolent provincial administration of the Mughals, and the peace offered by the empire, various nationalities began to take shape; on the other, certain Indian and foreign Muslim nobles, fearing that political power may go out of their hands, begin to encourage these tendencies among the Muslims which might keep them apart from the Hindus. Politically, this effort manifested itself in the struggle between Salim and Khusrau or between Aurangzeb and Dara. This section of the Muslim nobility was partly successful in its efforts. Culturally, this tendency manifested itself in the rise of the Naqshbandi movement, the movement of Mujaddid Alf-i-Sani, who tried to prevent the fusion between the Hindus and the Muslims and who sought to draw Sufism nearer the fold of orthodox Islam. It is worth noting that this Muslim revivalism was strongest in the Punjab.

This section of the Muslim nobles sought to maintain the domination of the central government over the various provincial regions under the slogan of enhancing the glory of Islam. On the other hand, by promoting conditions for the rise of nationalities, the Mughal empire helped to generate forces whose rise could only be at the expense of the empire itself. Thus after a time, the existence of the empire demanded the prevention of the growth of nationalities. Therefore, the conflict between the Mughal empire and the various national units was the logical outcome of historical forces.

In view of the fact that the Muslim revivalist section was most concerned with the maintenance of the imperial unity at the expense of the nationalities, it could easily dominate the empire and being revivalist in its own ideology, it carried on its work in the name of Islam. Therefore, in the case of dominantly Hindu nationalities, their struggle against the empire adopted the form of Hindu religious struggle, for example, the struggle of the Maharattas.

It is significant that in the days of Aurangzeb, the Mughal empire did not have to face individuals or mere dynasties, but national groups, most of whom had developed potential national characteristics, for example, the Maharattas, the Sikhs, the Rajputs, the Bundelas, the Bengalis, and the Jats. To hold Aurangzeb personally responsible for the dissolution of the Mughal empire is to ignore the basic historic forces. It disintegrated because a number of national groups were striving for independence, and their rise had been facilitated by the conditions created during the empire. This is the historical significance of the fall of the Mughal empire.

Thus we find that towards the last days of the Mughal empire a distinct tendency is noticeable; among people living in geographically contiguous areas and speaking the same language, common bonds are growing and conditions have definitely been created in which as a result of later historical forces (e.g. economic progress and freedom movement) the emergence of distinct nationalities becomes possible.

Of course, the development of nationalities has been unequal. It is true that some of these national groups contained germs of future progress, and therefore, economic development and the struggle for freedom helped in their evolution considerably. Certain other peoples, due to economic or political reasons, fell into an eclipse, and would arise again under favourable economic and political conditions.

## Note and Reference

1. The term jagirdari system has been used to denote the Indian form of feudalism.

# 10

# New Light on the Relations of the Early Mughal Rulers with their Nobility*

In considering the relationship between the early Mughal rulers and their nobility, it is essential to grasp fully the nature of medieval Indian nobility. This is necessary because sometimes even in the context of Indian history, the word 'nobility' is used in its European connotation. The medieval Indian nobility was fundamentally different from the European feudal aristocracy. In Europe, the feudal lord was the hereditary owner of land. He kept his own private army and was expected to give military aid to the king. The source of his political power, that is, land and private army could be inherited by him. His position, therefore, did not depend solely on the goodwill of the king.

The Indian noblemen, however, did not own land, a factor which made all the difference. Since they were not the hereditary owners of land, they depended for their political position on the influence they could wield on the king. That influence itself depended primarily on the military importance of individual nobles, that is, on their military utility to the king. Each empire was founded as the result of a sort of a military alliance between a group of military leaders (sometimes leaders of tribes, and sometimes of heterogeneous groups) and a chief,

* *Proceedings of Indian History Congress*, VII Session, Madras, 1944, pp. 389–97.

who was probably the ablest amongst them, to put him on the throne. When that chief became the monarch, and the rule of his dynasty was established, the revenues of different parts of the country were assigned to different nobles. It was essential for maintenance of the political power of that particular group of nobles that the rule of the dynasty which it had placed on the throne, should continue because, whenever the empire of one dynasty was overthrown by another group of nobles supporting a different dynasty, the entire aristocracy which was associated with the overthrown dynasty was likewise swept off the political arena. For example, the Afghan military leaders had combined to support the Lodis to establish an empire in India. But when Ibrahim Lodi was defeated and the Mughals established their own empire, the bulk of the Afghan nobility did not find a place in it. Similarly, after the defeat of Humayun, almost all the Mughal nobles lost their positions. Such a phenomenon is almost unimaginable in the history of Europe.

The absence of the system of landed estates was the result chiefly of three factors—the particular system of economy prevailing in India, the tribal nature of the social organization of the rulers, and the laws of Islam. The traditional system of economy in India hampered the growth of the idea of private ownership of land by the landlords. The village communities generally, although not explicitly, regarded land as communal property. It was assigned by custom to different families for cultivation. The noble was, therefore, not the proprietor of land, but the revenue collector, who also supervised local administration and gave military aid to the king. The peasants, when they paid revenue, did not do so in recognition of the proprietary rights of the nobles.[1]

The social system of the invaders strengthened this idea. The Turks, the Afghans, and the Mughals all inherited a tribal culture, as a result of which they did not build up the institution of landed private property in India. The law of Islam with its strong disapproval of the private ownership in land and its conception that all land belongs to God and to the community also contributed to discourage the growth of individual ownership of productive land by one who did not cultivate it himself. It was because of these factors that the tribal social system of the Turko-Mongols did not break down when it came into contact with the agrarian economic system. The peculiar economy of India allowed the tribal system to grow. In the absence of landed property, the nobles did not become attached to any particular tract of land. Their position did not depend on their being in control of a particular territory, but on their military capacity.

The nobles of the early Mughal rulers were military leaders of such a type. They had been assigned *jagirs* and *iqtas* by Babur and Humayun. There were frequent transfers of the jagirs of even the most influential nobles by the monarch,[2] and in the event of the death of a nobleman, his jagirs were assigned to other military leaders.[3] Thus, the position of the Mughal nobles depended on their capacity as military leaders (whether or not of tribes) wherever they went and whatever territory they ruled.[4]

In consequence of the considerations described above, there arose an interdependence of the monarch and nobles on each other. No monarch could remain on the throne without the support and cooperation of his nobles. Similarly, the position of the nobles depended on the influence they could wield over the king. This interdependence contributed in some measure to another social phenomenon—that of conflict between the king and his nobles. Since the power of the nobles was ultimately a share of the royal power, it could be increased only at the expense of the latter. Hence we find that there is a continuous attempt on the part of the nobles, once they establish themselves in the country, to minimize the control that could be exercised over them by the king. The nobles therefore had an almost universal tendency of resisting the attempts of the king to become all powerful. The kings on the other hand tried their very best to increase their domination over the nobles.

Babur was able to keep under control his nobles although he was socially quite free with them. But in spite of the various attempts of Humayun to increase his prestige and power, he was never really able to become politically supreme. Humayun inculcated certain peculiar notions of kingly glory and divinity so that he might be in a position to raise himself above his nobles. The following examples will illustrate this tendency in Humayun's activities. While in Bengal he is said to have put a veil on his face so as to create a halo of divinity around himself.[5] Jauhar[6] tells us another interesting story which reveals this mentality further. While Humayun was retreating from Chausa, a nobleman, Mir Fakhr Ali, happened to march ahead of him. Humayun was so enraged that he threatened to punish the noble severely. As a counterpart of this desire of Humayun to raise his social position, we find some examples showing a desire on his part to increase his political strength vis-à-vis the nobles. There is, for example, an attempt to reorganize the central government and to classify the nobles according to grades. Khwandmir tells us how he established four central depart-ments,[7] which was probably with a view to exercise some sort of control over the administration of various parts of the country by the nobles. All these departments were subsequently placed under a sort of prime minister (Amir Owais Muhammad being the first incumbent). We are also told that some sort of grades were introduced among the nobility, which, according to S. K. Banerji, was the first attempt at the organization of the *mansabdari* system.[8] These measures were really intended to increase the dependence of the nobles on the king.

But in spite of these efforts, and in spite of the various attempts at conciliation made by Humayun,[9] we find that the nobles were trying to become as independent as possible. Kamran, Askari, Hindu Beg, almost every governor had grown practically inde-pendent, and Humayun was not in a position to exercise any effective control over them. Towards the close of the first period of Humayun's kingship when it appeared that his fortunes were on the wane, many of his nobles resorted to acts of disloyalty which sometimes even amounted to rebellion.[10] The numerous instances of disloyalty, notwithstanding a few examples of devo-tion shown by some nobles to Humayun, amply demonstrate the fact that Humayun was not able to exercise as much control over his nobles as had been exercised by Babur.

There were mainly three causes why Humayun was not able to control his nobles effectively and receive their full coopera-tion. Firstly, there was the difference between the personality of Babur and Humayun. The latter was not able to inspire faith and awe in his nobles. His defeats increased the lack of confidence in his leadership among his nobles. Secondly, the task of Babur was to found an empire. Upon his ability to do so depended the wealth and power of the nobles. Therefore, the nobles helped him in their own interest. When Humayun came to the throne, the initial task of founding the empire was over. The nobles felt that if they allowed Humayun to become too strong, their own political power would by jeopardized. Therefore, their own political power would depend, they thought, on preventing Humayun from becoming strong.[11] Thirdly, the traditions of the Mughals divided the loyalties of the nobles. Although they owed a general loyalty to the ruling house, they were not always loyal to any particular individual. In the absence of the law of primogeniture and due to the prevalence of the Mongol tradition of dividing the 'kingdom' among different sons of the ruler,[12] the members of the Timurid family, or the Mirzas, felt themselves justified in claiming a sort of equality with Humayun. These people refused to realize the gravity of the situation, did not unite, and 'opposed the central government not as puppets in the hands of nobles but as prime movers in the contest'.

The disunity among the Mirzas kept the nobility divided. In order to increase their own political power, groups of nobles would sometime back up one member of the ruling house, sometime the other. The opportunism of the nobles, which was inherent in their class due to the characteristic nature of its institution, made them side either with Humayun, or with Askari or with Kamran. But they tried their best to support the winning party. Even such devotees of Humayun as Yadgar Nasir Mirza, Hindal, Kasim Husain Sultan Uzbek, Tardi Beg deserted him at one time or the other, while among the officers of Kamran, even a trusted follower like Qaracha Khan tried to seek favour with Humayun when the latter conquered Kabul.[13]

This excessive opportunism and adventurism among the nobles of Humayun's reign is totally understandable. The nobles did not have much landed property and could not bequeath their social and political position. There was no guarantee that their sons would enjoy the social position won by themselves. Their position as well as that of their family could be seriously jeopardized if the monarchs were unfavourable to them. Therefore, they considered it prudent not to back up the losing member of the ruling family. Defeat tended to disorganize them completely.

A by-product of the opportunism of the nobles was defeatism, that is, an indecent eagerness to accept defeat in the face of even slight difficulty. This was partly accentuated by the absence of territorial loyalty among the nobles. The loss of any particular tract of land was not vital to their power. They could always hope to win it back, or to conquer some other territory instead. And partly this tendency of the nobles was encouraged by their peculiar class position. In order to build up their class power, they did not give Humayun their full cooperation. When, largely due to the lack of this cooperation, Humayun suffered defeats, they started deserting him. It was only when Humayun's fortunes definitely improved, due to other circumstances, that nobles started flocking back to 'the victorious standards of the world conquering monarch'.

Finally, another social phenomenon might have influenced the action of Humayun's nobles in refusing him full cooperation. That was the beginning of the decay of the village system. The self-sufficient village communities had resisted in the previous centuries the attempts of the state to collect revenue, and the collection of revenue quite frequently required military expeditions. Hence there was a constant use of force, and resultantly there was greater necessity of state support to the nobles. The village resistance was now weakening because the decay of the village system had begun. This may be judged from two new features. Firstly, efforts were being made to collect revenue from the peasants *individually* and not from the headman of the village for the village as a *whole*. This shows that individual cultivation was becoming more frequent and communal ties in the village were breaking down. Secondly, realization of revenue in *money* instead of in kind was becoming more frequent. This shows that there was a general increase in the use of gold, probably due to the increase in trade and commerce and the growth of towns. Gold converted the articles produced directly for consumption into commodities and it thus established individual cultivation and weakened the village system. Since the village system was becoming weak, the nobles might have started coveting the hereditary ownership of land.

Thus, to sum up, the following characteristic features are noticeable among the nobles of Humayun. They did not possess any hereditary vested interests. They were a heterogeneous crowd[14] and could not combine even to protect their class interests, and they were imbued with a spirit of opportunism and adventurism. Therefore, they were greatly dependent on the king for their political position.

These characteristics led to certain contradictions in the class position of the nobles. These contradictions were as follows. Since the position of the nobles depended on the king, it was necessary that they should support a king who was favourable to them. But if the king, as a result of their support, became too strong, then their own power would decline (for reasons explained above). Hence when they supported the king, they strengthened the rival of their own power and dealt a blow to their own potential power. If, on the other hand, they did not give the monarch their full cooperation so as to secure power for their own class, they undermined the very basis of their strength, that is, if as a result of the lack of their cooperation, the ruling dynasty with which they were associated was overthrown, then they would also lose whatever power they had enjoyed.

In the days of Humayun these contradictions became very acute. The nobles of Humayun did not give the sovereign their full cooperation so that the monarch might not become too strong for them. When largely as a result of this lack of cooperation, and sometimes even of hostility, Humayun started suffering defeats, they quickly deserted him. The result was that the Afghan nobility, which had been displaced by the Mughals, took advantage of this lack of cooperation among the Mughals, united under Sher Khan and made a bid for the capture of power. They succeeded in defeating Humayun, and with the latter's defeat, the entire Mughal nobility had to leave India and to seek refuge in Afghanistan.

This misfortune made them realize that it was essential to re-establish the Mughal empire in India before they could wield any political power. Therefore, they decided to rally round Humayun. But they made a final attempt to safeguard their political interest by means of a compromise. The occasion for this arose in 1550. In that year Humayun proposed that all the nobles should take an oath of loyalty to him. They were prepared to do so, but Haji Muhammad Khan (who very likely represented the general sentiment, as he was the leader of a group and subsequently became Humayun's *Vakil-i-dar*) demanded that 'His Majesty should likewise take an oath that whatever we, his well wishers recommend for his interest, he will consent to perform'.[14] Hindal objected to this 'insolence' on the part of a 'servant' but Humayun took the oath.

This compact, if it may by so called, marks an interesting development in Indian constitutional history. It was an attempt on the part of the monarch as well as the nobles to resolve the crisis. The nobles, by taking the oath, recognized that unless the Mughal monarchy were established, Mughal nobility could not have any power; while the king, if he had to reign, must give full consideration to the wishes of his nobles. There is every reason to believe that Humayun tried to act up to his promise. Whenever his nobles insisted on anything, he generally accepted their advice against his own wishes, for example, his giving up of the project of invading Kashmir, or the punishment meted out to Kamran. Humayun even reprimanded Akbar when his nobles complained about the prince.[16]

On return to India, Humayun tried to give a constitutional form to his promise. He planned to divide his empire into a number of autonomous provinces, each under a governor. The king himself would not have a force of more than twelve thousand. The king was to stay at various centres by turns to keep up the unity of the empire without reducing the autonomy of the *subadar*s.[17] This plan was intended to provide a solution of two important problems: (a) the conflict between the central government and the nobles; and (b) the continuous attempt on the part of the provinces, backed up by their provincial vested interests, to be free from an overpowering and dominating all-India centre.

But this entire scheme, including the promise given by Humayun to respect the wishes of a united nobility failed. The reasons of its failure were firstly, the death of Humayun; and secondly, the presence of serious external dangers to the infant Mughal state, which demanded greater centralization and the presence of a strong monarch. Thirdly, the serious conflict among the nobles themselves. Fourthly, the growth of trade and commerce which tended to unify different parts of north India. And, lastly, the dominating personality of Akbar which could never tolerate such a compromise. He established a strong monarchy which made the nobility completely subservient to it.

Thus, the relationship between Babur and Humayun with their nobles reveals the inherent contradictions of the early Mughal nobility, and the fact that if it wanted to maintain its social position, it had to surrender its political power.

## Notes and References

1. P. Saran has discussed this question at length in his book, *Provincial Government of the Mughals*, Delhi, 1952, pp. 328–33.

2. E.g., a single *jagir*, that of zamindar, was successively held by such influential noblemen as Tardi Beg, Bahadur Khan Shaibani, and Ismail Beg Doldai. *Maasirul Umara*, Vol. I, pp. 64, 384, 466.

3. E.g., on the death of Haji Md. Khan, his *jagirs* were distributed, Ghaznin having been assigned to Bahadur Khan. Shortly afterwards, Ghaznin was assigned to Hindal, while on the latter's death, it was given to Akbar. *Akbarnama*, p. 311 et seq.

4. This was amply demonstrated during the flight of Humayun from India, vide *Akbarnama*, and Jauhar, *Tazkiratul Waqiat*.

5. Badaoni, *Muntakhabut Tawarikh*, Vol. I, p. 446.

6. *Tazkiratul Waqiat*, f. 32a.

7. *Qanuni Humayuni*, pp. 48–50.

8. S. K. Banerji, *Humayun Badshah*, Vol. II, p. 366.

9. By means of numerous gifts, distribution of treasures, permission accorded to senior nobles to sit in court, increase in the salary of nobles after the first victory over Afghans, attempt to placate Kamran by giving him Hisar Firoza, or the increase in the pay ot Askari's officers during retreat from Bengal, see *Akbarnama* and *Tazkiratul Waqiat*.

10. Details may be seen in Banerji's admirable monograph on Humayun. Here are just a few examples: refusal of Zahid Beg to take up command in Bengal; the designs of Khusrau Kokaltash, Haji Md. Khan, and Zahid Beg who joined Nuruddin Md. Mirza and offered the throne to Hindal; the refusal of nobles to rally round Humayun when the latter gave the call for battle at Chausa (*Tazkiratul Waqiat*, f. 24a); persuasion of Kamran by Amir Khwaja Kalan to return to Lahore on the eve of the battle of Kanauj; the unpardonable cowardice shown by nobles during the battle of Kanauj (Mirza Haidar, *Tarikhi-Rashidi*); see also *Akbarnama* and *Tazkiratul Waqiat*.

11. Khusrau Kokaltash, Zahid Beg, and Haji Md. actually advised Kamran not to go to the aid of Humayun after having crushed the rebellion of Hindal, so as to prevent the emperor from becoming too strong (*Akbarnama*).

12. *Cf.* Division of the Kingdom of Sultan Abu Saeed Mirza, Babur's grandfather, among his sons.

13. *Akbarnama*, Vol. I, p. 244.

14. Among the nobles of Humayun were Turanis, Iranis, Afghans, Uzbeks, Mughals, and others.

15. *Akbarnama*, Vol. I, p. 302.

16. *Akbarnama*, Vol. I, p. 316.

17. Ibid., p. 356.

# 11

∽∾

## The Theory of the Nurjahan 'Junta'
### A Critical Examination*

Beni Prasad, in his learned work *A History of Jahangir*, has put
forward the theory that a 'junta' consisting of Nurjahan Begum,
I'timad-ud-Daula, Asaf Khan, and Prince Khurram became
dominant at the Mughal court shortly after the marriage of
Nurjahan with Jahangir and remained so till 1620.[1] It broke up
when Nurjahan realized that Shahjahan, with his domineering
nature, would relegate her to the background if he were to
succeed to the throne. She therefore decided to supersede him
by a more pliable instrument, Shahriyar, whose marriage was
arranged with her daughter, Ladli Begum. The 'junta' consoli-
dated its power by filling most of the vacancies in the imperial
service with its own creatures to an extent that its 'favour was
the sole passport to honour and rank'. This naturally aroused
the jealousy and hostility of the other nobles.[2] Consequently, the
court was split into two factions during this period: the adher-
ents of the Nurjahan 'junta', and the rival party whose candidate
for the throne was Khusrau.[3] Beni Prasad attributes to the
working of the 'junta' the following reasons: rapid rise in the
*mansab*s of I'timad-ud-Daula, and his family;[4] interruption in the
promotion of Mahabat Khan between 1612 and 1622 (and
presumably in the career of others like him);[5] imprisonment of

* *Proceedings of Indian History Congress*, XXI Session, Trivanduram, 1958,
pp. 324–35.

Khan-i-A'zam;[6] extraordinary rise of Khurram;[7] eclipse of Parvez;[8] and the varying fortunes of Khusrau.[9]

The above theory requires a careful examination, because, if accepted, it would imply that from quite early in the reign of Jahangir, the 'junta' started intriguing in its selfish interests (thus ignoring the interests of Jahangir) and that the party groupings at the court centred round the 'junta' and its opponents. A close examination of the sources and the sequence of events, however, suggests that this theory cannot be substantiated.[10] Consequently, the nature of the groupings at the court, the internal stresses within the nobility, and the role of the emperor have to be analysed further for a proper understanding of the principal political events during the period.

This theory is based principally on the European sources, notably on the statements of Sir Thomas Roe. He definitely refers to the existence of a 'junta' consisting of Nurjahan, I'timad-ud-Daula, Asaf Khan, and Shahjahan, in the context of Shahjahan's attempt to secure the custody of Khusrau in 1616,[11] and where he asserts that the main strength of Khurram lay in the support which he received from Nurjahan.[12] It is quite obvious that the information of Roe and the other foreigners is based upon rumours that were circulating about Khusrau, Khurram, and Nurjahan and hence his observations cannot be relied upon entirely. However, it is significant that from the end of 1616, rumours became current of an estrangement between Nurjahan and Shahjahan, and of an alliance between the former and Khusrau. Such rumours became quite common in 1617 and again in 1619, as will appear from the following statements:

1616—Rumour of an alliance between Asaf Khan and Khusrau.[13]

12–12–1616—Sultan Khusrau shall marry 'Nur Mahal's daughter and have liberty and that all factions will adhere to him.'[14]

21–8–1617—Nur Mahal and Asaf Khan, by their father's advice came out to make peace with Khusrau and alliance and with infinite joy his liberty is expected.[15]

25–8–1617—Report of a feast of Khusrau with Nurjahan and the likelihood of an alliance which would bring about Khusrau's liberty and Khurram's downfall.[16]

17–9–1619—Rumour that the emperor had displaced prince Khurram.[17]

30–9–1619—Rumours of Khurram's disgrace and Khusrau's liberty. Raising of him (Khusrau) will be the fall of the other whose high expectations would by no means be induced to conformity.[18]

Taken as a whole, the above statements suggest that from the end of 1616, the relations between Nurjahan and Shahjahan were not particularly cordial. The other European sources refer to Nurjahan's immense influence, or to the popularity of Khusrau and Shahjahan's hostility towards him, but provide no evidence of factional alliance between Nurjahan and Shahjahan.[19]

Among the Persian sources, Mu'tamad Khan strongly complains of the excessive influence of Nurjahan and of the fact that all her relations and friends got posts and appointments in the state, and the choicest *jagirs* of Hindustan were in the hands of those who were related to or associated with her.[20] There is, of course, no question of Mu'tamad Khan suggesting any factional alliance between Nurjahan and Shahjahan. On the other hand, he is keen to prove that Nurjahan was hostile and unjust to Shahjahan for selfish reasons. Since it appears that both his works (viz., the third volume of the *Iqbal Nama-i-Jahangiri* and the *Ahwal-i-Shahzadagi-i-Shahjahan Padshah*) were written during the reign of Shahjahan, his prejudice against Nurjahan is quite understandable.[21] Kamgar Husain, who wrote his *Ma'asir-i-Jahangiri* in 1630, also adopts the same line of argument.

The little known *Tawarikh-i-Jahangir Shahi* of Wali Sirhindi, written in the fourteenth year of Jahangir's reign, was composed for the purpose of winning imperial favour.[22] It contains eulogies to Jahangir, I'timad-ud-Daula, Asaf Khan, the prince, and some of the nobles. But significantly enough, it makes no mention of Nurjahan, thus casting a doubt on the view that she exercised undue influence even before 1620. Kami Shirazi's *Fath Nama-i-Nurjahan Begum*[23] written at Kabul in 1625–6, deals with the rebellion of Mahabat Khan, and as such contains no reference to or suggestion of any factional alliance between Nurjahan and Shahjahan during the earlier period. *Intikhab-i-Jahangir Shahi,* identified by Elliot as the fragment of a contemporary work, appears on a close internal examination to be a source of doubtful authenticity, compiled at a much later date.[24] But the anecdote mentioned even in this source cannot be considered as supporting the 'junta' theory. The anecdote is summarized as follows.[25]

In the presence of Khan-i-Alam and Khan-i-Jahan, Mahabat Khan complained to Jahangir against the excessive influence exercised by Nurjahan. He also pleaded for the release of Khusrau from perpetual confinement[26] and for entrusting him to one of the confidants of the emperor. The safety of the emperor and the peace of the empire depended on the life of Khusrau. Khan-i-Alam and Khan-i-Jahan corroborated the statement and the next day Jahangir entrusted Khusrau to Khan-i-Jahan with permission to pay his respects at the court. Khusrau was also given a horse to ride.[27] For a few days after Mahabat Khan left Jahangir at Pakli, the latter was careful, but on reaching Kashmir he again fell under the control of Nurjahan.[28]

Apart from the fact of the doubtful authenticity of the work, and the extreme unlikelihood of a noble complaining to Jahangir about Nurjahan in 1620, the incident presents certain other difficulties in regard to the 'junta' theory. Firstly, Mahabat Khan was with Jahangir for about three weeks in February, 1620,[29] but before this time, restrictions on Khusrau had already been relaxed. Secondly, this piece of evidence can be used in support of the 'junta' theory only if it is proved that in 1620, Nurjahan was using her influence to keep Khusrau in confinement, presumably in the interest of Shahjahan. However, as has been shown later, Shahjahan's demand for taking Khusrau with himself to the Deccan, and the betrothal of Shahriyar to Ladli Begum at about the same time, indicate mutual suspicion between Shahjahan and the court circles. It seems that Shahjahan's taking custody of Khusrau was sought to be counteracted by the betrothal of Shahriyar to Ladli Begum. It will thus be seen that the direct evidence of a factional alliance between Shahjahan and Nurjahan is of an extremely dubious nature.

We may now examine the facts and events which Beni Prasad has sought to explain in terms of the 'junta' theory. The rapid rise in the mansabs of I'timad-ud-Daula and his family cannot be denied. But the rise in their mansabs becomes particularly marked from 1616. Till early in 1616, the mansabs held by the family were—I'timad-ud-Daula, 6000/3000; Asaf Khan, 4000/2000; Itiqad Khan, 1500/500; and Ibrahim Khan, 2500/2000. However, the rise of this family should be seen in the light of the historical circumstances of the times. It was customary from the time of Akbar that high mansabs were given to many members of the families of the leading nobles.[30] Jahangir continued the tradition, and I'timad-ud-Daula's was not the only family many of whose members received high mansabs.

Soon after his release, Khan-i-Azam was given the mansab of 5000 in 1615, which was raised to 7000 in 1616, in the same year as the mansab of I'timad-ud-Daula was raised to 7000/5000. Khan-i-Azam's son, Jahangir Quli Khan, was raised to the mansab of 2500/2000 in 1615 and appointed Governor of Allahabad in that year. In 1617, he was appointed Governor of Bihar, a post he held till 1619. Khan-i-A'zam's younger son, Khurram (Kamal Khan), held the mansab of 2500, while his brother, Abdullah was raised to 1000/300 in 1618. Similarly, Khan-i-Khanan reached the mansab of 7000/7000 in 1618, one year before I'timad-ud-Daula reached that mansab. He continued as the *de facto* commander of the Deccan throughout this period.[31] His son, Shah Nawaz Khan, was raised to 5000/2000 2–3h in 1618, the year in which Asaf Khan was raised to 5000/4000 2–3h. Khan-i-Khanan's other sons were also given high mansabs. The combined mansab of 'Abdullah Khan Firuz Jung and his family had reached 12,000 *sawars du aspa sih aspa* in 1613, which compared not unfavourably with the combined mansab of I'timad-ud-Daula and his family in 1616.[32]

Though Mahabat Khan's personal mansab was not raised beyond 4000/3500 after 1612, in 1614 he was given additional jagir worth 3 *kror* dams.[33] He was given *du aspa sih aspa* rank in 1615 which had to be curtailed later when he did not bring to muster the required contingent.[34] It should also be remembered that though he had been entrusted with the command of Mewar, he had not achieved much. However, during this period, Mahabat Khan was by no means relegated to the background. He was sent to bring back Khan-i-Azam from the Mewar campaign.[35] He was also entrusted with important missions to the Deccan. In 1617, he was appointed to the very important command of Kabul, to bring under control the continuing tribal unrest.[36] His son, Amanullah, was raised to the mansab of 1000/600 in 1615, to 1500/400 in 1619 and 2000/1500 in 1620. Again it was on his recommendation that the mansab of Mubariz Khan was raised to 2000/1500 and Sardar Afghan was appointed to 1000/400.[37] After the custody of Khusrau was taken from Ani Rai Singh Dalan, the latter was raised in 1618 to the mansab of 2000/1600. Early in 1620, at the request of Mahabat Khan, he was posted to serve in the Bangash campaign.[38] If the *Intikhab-i-Jahangir Shahi* is to be believed, Mahabat Khan was by no means out of favour with Jahangir. During the period under review, a very large number of nobles received promotion. A few of the nobles, apart from those mentioned earlier, who were promoted were: Khwaja Jahan 3000/1000 (1614), 3500/2200 (1615), 5000/2500 (1619), 5000/3000 (1620), held the governorship of Agra. Khan-i-'Alam, on return from embassy to Persia, mansab raised to 5000/3000 (1620). Khwaja Ab'ul Hasan 4000/2000 (1618), 5000/2000 (1620), held the post of Mir Bakhshi. Qilij Khan 6000/5000 (1611) appointed Governor of Kabul; his son Chin Qilij, appointed Governor of Gujarat. Murtaza Khan 6000/5000 (1613), governorship of Punjab, continued to remain in favour and held a position of influence. Khan-i-Jahan Lodi was obviously very much in favour and held the governorships of Agra and Multan, during the period. Mirza Rustam Safavi's mansab was raised to 5000/1500 in 1618. Bahadur Khan raised to 5000/4000 in 1620. Similarly great favour was shown to Dilawar Khan, Bir Singh Deo Bundela, Suraj Singh, Khan-i-Dauran, Muqarrab Khan, Sadiq Khan, Saif Khan, Amanat Khan, Rizavi Khan, Keshav Das Maru, Ram Dad Kachhwaha.[39]

The career of the above nobles reveals that promotions were fairly well spread and it would not be correct to assume that the sole passport to promotion was the favour of the 'junta'. Many of the persons mentioned above were either hostile to the so-called 'junta' or not connected with it,[40] while the affiliations of many others are not known. Thus, it would not be correct to assume that during this period, the court was divided into two factions, for and against the 'junta'. In a very interesting letter which the Khan-i-A'zam wrote to Jahangir in 1613, he makes his dislike for Qilij Khan, 'Abdullah Khan Firuz Jung, Mahabat Khan, Khan-i-Jahan, and Murtaza Khan obvious. Qilij Khan and Murtaza Khan apparently intrigued against Khan-i-Dauran.[41] Shahjahan's relations with Murtaza Khan were by no means cordial,[42] though the latter was certainly no partisan of Khusrau. Mahabat Khan may or may not have been hostile to Nurjahan, but he was certainly hostile to both Asaf Khan and to Shahjahan.[43] Therefore, there seems to have been an antipathy between Khan-i-Khanan and 'Abdullah Khan.[44] It will thus be seen that there were many factions among the nobles, that they intrigued against each other; but no single group succeeded in ousting the others from positions of power or importance.

If the position of the princes is carefully analysed, it would appear that the 'junta' theory does not offer a satisfactory explanation of the actual situation. Khusrau had not only been put forward as a claimant to the throne against Jahangir himself, but had actually revolted in 1606. In 1608, it was alleged that he had entered into a conspiracy for an attack upon the emperor's life. In 1610, there was an outbreak in Bihar in his name. Under these circumstances, Jahangir's attitude towards Khusrau had become hardened even before his marriage to Nurjahan. He had tried to build up the position of Parvez, but Parvez failed first in the Mewar campaign, and then in the Deccan. Moreover, he could earn a reputation neither as a commander nor as an administrator. Consequently, it was but natural that Khurram was given a chance to lead the Mewar campaign in 1613.[45]

Khurram, it seems, had been nursing ambitions from his early youth. It was he who had discovered the alleged conspiracy of Khusrau in 1608. We cannot judge whether Khusrau was actually guilty of the conspiracy or not, but the discovery of the plot earned for Khurram his father's gratitude.[46] When he was appointed to the Mewar campaign, he accused Khan-i-A'zam of intriguing in the interest of Khusrau. With the suspicion which Jahangir already had regarding both Khusrau and Khan-i-A'zam, he readily believed Khurram and imprisoned Khan-i-A'zam.[47] At the same time, restrictions on Khusrau were reimposed.[48] It is thus easy to see that these actions were taken at the instance of Khurram.

The victory of Khurram in the Mewar campaign not only raised the prestige of the empire, but seems to have convinced Jahangir that Khurram was the ablest among his sons. It was therefore natural that when in 1615–16, the situation in the Deccan continued to remain out of control, he decided to transfer Parvez, who had proved to be a failure, to Allahabad, and send Khurram in overall command of the Deccan. To give Khurram added prestige, his mansab was raised and the title of Shah conferred upon him. It was about this time that the custody of Khusrau was transferred from Ani Rai Singh Dalan to Asaf Khan, presumably to reassure Khurram.[49]

The problem of the Deccan had defied solution since the beginning of Jahangir's reign and had not been solved by many of the renowned generals. The constant bickerings among the commanders and the rumours of bribery and corruption were deemed to be the principal causes of this failure. When Parvez, as the representative of the emperor, was unable to handle the situation, and the Khan-i-Khanan sent urgent appeals for reinforcements, Khurram was the obvious choice. There is no doubt that Khurram's appointment materially contributed to the successful conclusion of the Deccan campaign.[50] The Mughals regained what they had lost; perhaps they did not want anything more. It was hoped that a peace concluded on such a basis would prove to be durable and bring to an end the prolonged warfare which had almost ruined the economy of the Deccan and had caused such a drain on the treasury. The magnificent reception accorded to Khurram must have also impressed the Deccan states. In any case, Khurram became the emperor's favourite, received the unprecedented title of Shahjahan, an extraordinary rise in his mansab, and marked out as the heir designate.[51]

It seems that by 1619, it was being realized that Shahjahan was becoming too powerful and it would not be prudent to allow a situation to develop in which he might consider himself no longer dependent upon the emperor's favour. Consequently, Khusrau was released in 1619, and the mansab of Parvez was raised to 20,000/10,000 in the same year.[52] The release of Khusrau could not have been to the liking of Shahjahan,[53] and when he was asked to proceed to the Deccan for the second time, he insisted on taking Khusrau with him. This insistence suggests that he was perhaps afraid that the court circles might put Khusrau on the throne should anything happen to Jahangir. However, Shahjahan was in such a strong position at that time that his demand for taking Khusrau could not be turned down. But it is very likely that this demand was resented and it was decided at that very time that Shahriyar should be betrothed to Ladli Begum,[54] possibly as a check upon the ambitions of Shahjahan.[55] While the positions of Parvez and Shahriyar were built up to some extent as a safeguard against the possibility of Shahjahan assuming greater airs, nothing was done against him directly. Not only was Khusrau handed over to him, but when he left for the Deccan, a magnificent army and a large number of *mansabdars* and *ahadis* were sent with him.[56]

While a stage did come when the interests of Shahjahan differed from those of the emperor, the interests of Nurjahan were intimately bound up with those of the emperor. She certainly had the wisdom to realize that her own position depended entirely on the life of her husband. Thus it is not possible to find a dichotomy between her interests and those of Jahangir, and this presumably was the reason for whatever influence she exercised. However, till 1620, the decisions, even though influenced by Nurjahan to some extent, were definitely the decisions of Jahangir himself. There seems to be no special motive for Nurjahan to enter into an alliance with Shahjahan in her own selfish interests, as distinct from the interests of Jahangir. Thus, the position of Shahjahan was built up not because of the existence of a 'junta', but as a part of imperial policy; measures against Khusrau were taken at the instance of Shahjahan; and finally, the position of the other princes was sought to be strengthened as a safeguard against the ambitions of Shahjahan.[57]

The reign of Jahangir saw a deepening crisis in the Mughal nobility. The desire of the nobles to have increasingly higher mansabs for themselves and their associates, and the laxity with which Jahangir granted these mansabs, seems to have created a difficult situation. It was not possible to find enough jagirs to keep pace with the increase in the mansabs and the number of mansabdars. In such situation it was only natural that there should be intrigues and factional struggles among the nobles.[58] Jahangir's own temperament was such that he could not handle such a situation with firmness or foresight. He was susceptible to backbiting and was often fickle-minded.[59] At the same time he showed leniency to a remarkable degree and continued to keep in high places many officers in whose integrity and loyalty he had little confidence.[60] This must have contributed even further to factionalism. Naturally, nobles tried to attach themselves either to the princes or to the other influential nobles. But although a close study of these groupings has yet to be undertaken, two observations may be tentatively made: (a) that the groupings and alliances were shifting in character; and (b) that no single group could be considered to have become so powerful as to oust all the other groups from positions of importance. This crisis in the nobility is to be seen from the beginning of Jahangir's reign, and was not a new feature which developed after his marriage to Nurjahan.

While the Amir-ul-Umara lived, he certainly enjoyed a dominant position at the court. After his death, I'timad-ud-Daula gradually rose in the emperor's favour and occupied the position which the Amir-ul-Umara had enjoyed. Jahangir had implicit faith in his wisdom, ability, and loyalty.[61] Perhaps, his affection for Nurjahan contributed to the influence of I'timad-ud-Daula, much in the same way as the matrimonial alliance must have contributed to the remarkable rise of the family of Raja Bharah Mall during the reign of Akbar. But there is overwhelming evidence to show that during the period under review, the main decisions were those of Jahangir himself and that the rise of I'timad-ud-Daula did not mean that the nobles who were not attached to him had lost their influence. But the position of Asaf Khan, even though he became the *wakil*, was certainly much less important than that of his father.[62] The marriage of his daughter with Shahjahan must have led to the belief that he was partial to the interests of that prince. But as soon as occasion arose to provide safeguards against Shahjahan, I'timad-ud-Daula cast his weight against the prince, and hence by implication, against Asaf Khan.[63]

## Conclusions

The above review suggests the inadequacy of the 'junta' theory, for it provides an oversimplified picture of an otherwise complex situation. The assumption that between 1611 and 1620, Nurjahan, I'timad-ud-Daula, Asaf Khan, and Shahjahan formed a single faction, does not conform to facts. During this period, there is little evidence to suggest that Nurjahan was playing an active political role. Her independent political role starts with the decline in the health of Jahangir and the death of I'timad-ud-Daula. However, during this period, it does not seem that she exercised her influence, for factional ends. While I'timad-ud-Daula's position must have been strengthened because of Nurjahan, there is no reason to doubt his implicit loyalty to Jahangir, and evidence of his factionalism is lacking. Asaf Khan's loyalty to Shahjahan however does not suggest that there was also a factional alliance between the prince and I'timud-ud-Daula or Nurjahan. In fact, in his desire to build up his own position, Shahjahan could rely far more upon other nobles than either upon Nurjahan or I'timad-ud-Daula. Finally, there seem to be innumerable groupings among the nobles who were intriguing against each other, but it would not be correct to assume that the groupings revolved principally in favour of or against the 'junta', or that any single group succeeded in ousting the other groups from position of importance. Thus many of the political events of Jahangir's reign as well as the crisis in the nobility would become clear when the role of the different nobles is studied and the working of these groupings and their stresses and strains further analysed.

## Notes and References

1. Though Beni Prasad starts by saying that the 'junta' broke up in 1622 with Itimad-ud-Daula's death and Shahjahan's rebellion, he later suggests that it broke up with Shahriyar's marriage.

2. 'All those who were, or fancied that they were deprived of their due neep of power and left in outer darkness'. 'Abd-ur-Rahim Khan-i-Khanan temporized with the dominant 'junta', but prouder spirits like Mahabat Khan refused to pay them homage'.

3. Beni Prasad, *A History of Jahangir*, 1940, pp. 150–72.

4. Ibid., pp. 160–3.

5. Ibid., p. 168.

6. 'His disgrace was only one more in the game for unquestioned supremacy which the "Nurjahan junta" was now playing with heart and soul.' Ibid., p. 204.

7. Ibid., pp. 16, 65, 230, 242–3.

On his return from the Deccan, where he had achieved nothing significant, he was given the unusual title of Shahjahan and an unprecedented rise in mansab. 'But the "junta" celebrated this performance with high pomp and magnificence which were calculated to enhance their own glory and prestige.' Ibid., p. 243.

8. Ibid., pp. 166, 230.

9. Ibid., pp. 169–72, 283–91.

10. R. P. Tripathi has rejected the 'junta' theory, but has not put forward his arguments in details for doing so. Cf. *Rise and Fall of the Mughal Empire*, Allahabad, 1956, pp. 391–2.

11. *Purchas and his Pilgrims*, Vol. IV, pp. 361–2, 365–6, 377–8.

12. *Letters received by the East India Company from its Servants in the East,* 1896–1902, Vol. V, p. 362.

13. *Purchas,* Vol. IV, p. 383.

14. *The Embassy of Thomas Roe to India,* 1615–19, ed. W. Foster, London, 1926.

15. *Purchas,* Vol. IV, p. 404.

16. Roe, p. 407. Cf. Della Valle (*The Travels of Pietro Della Valle in India,* tr. Edward Grey, Hakluyt Society, 2 vols., London, 1892) that Nurjahan repeatedly offered her daughter in marriage to Khusrau, but he rejected the offer. In despair she gave her daughter to Shahriyar, pp. 56–7.

17. *English Factories in India,* Vol. I, p. 122.

18. Ibid., Vol. I, p. 123.

19. Terry, *Early Travels in India* ed. W. Foster, 1927, pp. 406, 411–12; James Bickford to Sir T. Smith, *Letters Received,* Vol. V, p. 134.

20. *Iqbal Nama-i-Jahangiri* (Bib. Ind.), Vol. III, pp. 74–80.

21. Although the third volume of *Iqbal Nama* gives the impression that it was written during the reign of Jahangir, it is very unlikely that it could have been written when Jahangir was alive and Nurjahan was at the height of her power. In the preface to the earliest known copy of *Iqbal Nama* dated 1635 (Bankipur MS. 560), it is definitely stated that the work was written in two volumes concluding with the death of Akbar. The third volume, dealing with the reign of Jahangir, was therefore written, presumably after 1635 when Mu'tamad Khan was holding the post of the Imperial Bakhshi to Shahjahan. *Ahwal-i-Shahzadagi-i-Shahjahan Padshah* (being the first section of Bankipur MS. 565) was definitely written during Shahjahan's reign (for his criticism of Nurjahan's hostility to Shahjahan, see. ff. 10–17b et seq.).

The historians of Shahjahan's reign were faced with a political dilemma: if they justified Shahjahan's rebellion, they would be supporting a dangerous political theory (cf. Aurangzeb's taunt to Shahjahan in 1638, *Adab-i-Alamgiri*); if, however, they were to condemn the rebellion, it would be a slur on imperial dignity. Shahjahan's rebellion was therefore represented not as a revolt against Jahangir, but as an act of loyalty to him to free him from the undesirable and selfish influence of Nurjahan.

22. Bodleian, Seldon MS. 23 (Cat. No. 231) ff. 389b–421a. The author, Wali Sirhindi, had prepared a dictionary of medical terms, *Farhang-i-Badi'- ul-Lughat-i-Jahangiri*. This sketchy history was included as a sort of a preparatory note to the dictionary.

23. Bibliotheque Nationale, Paris (Blochet iii/1874). A metrical history giving an account of the victory of Nurjahan over Mahabat Khan during the latter's rebellion. Also entitled *Waqai-uz-Zaman*.

24. Elliot and Dowson (hereafter ED), Vol. VI. pp. 446–7. British Museum, Or., 1618 ff. 181b–201b. It appears that a much later writer collected from the *Tuzuk,* the *Iqbal Nama,* and other works (contemporary

or later) a number of disjointed anecdotes and legends regarding
Jahangir's reign (many in the direct form of speech). All of these cannot
be entirely relied upon.

25. B.M. Or. 1618, ff. 195a et. seq. ED, Vol. VI, p. 451.

26. While Jahangir was at Brindaban in 1619, Khusrau was released
from confinement and permitted to come and pay his respects at the court.
*Tuzuk*, p. 280. According to *Iqbal Nama-i-Jahangiri* (hereinafter IN) 'Aziz
Koka had asked Jad Rup Gosain to pray for Khusrau's release (Vol. III,
pp. 129–30). Wali Sirhindi, writing in 1619, praises the sons of the
emperor, starting with Khusrau. His account certainly goes against the
possibility of Khusrau being in confinement at the time (ff. 406a and b).

27. From a statement in *IN*, that Khusrau, Khan-i-Jahan, and Khan-i-
Alam rode one stage behind the emperor during the march to Kashmir
in 1620 (Vol. III, p. 128), it appears possible that Khan-i-Jahan might have
been entrusted with the responsibility of keeping an eye on Khusrau. But
Mu'tamad Khan contradicts himself when he says in *IN*, that when Khusrau
was handed over to Shahjahan he had been in prison for a long time (Vol.
III, p. 176). In *Ahwal*, he says that at that time Khusrau was in prison in
the custody of Khwaja Abul Hasan, (f. 15b).

28. Immediately after leaving Pakli and before reaching Kashmir,
Jahangir ordered that in view of the narrowness of the road, no officer
should ride with him except Asaf Khan and Mu'tamad Khan. *Tuzuk*,
pp. 292–3; *IN*, Vol. III, p. 138.

In view of the points raised in this and the preceding notes, it appears
that the anecdote mentioned in Or. 1618 may have been based on later
legends which grew out of the incidents given in the *Tuzuk* and *IN*.

29. *Tuzuk*, pp. 287–9.

30. E.g., the family of Aziz Koka:

Khan-i-Kalan, 5000; Qutub-ud-Din Muhammad Khan, 5000; Naurang
Khan, 4000; Sharif Muhammad Khan, 3000; Shah Muhammad Khan, 2000;
Shamsud-Din Husain (later Jahangir Quli Khan), 2000; Shadman, 1500;
'Aziz Koka himself reached the mansab of 7000 during Akbar's reign.

The family of Man Singh:

Bhagwan Das, 5000; Man Singh 7000; Jagannath, 5000; Raj Singh,
4000/3000; Askaran, 3000; Madho Singh, 3000/2000; Khangar, 2000, etc.

31. There is no evidence that Khan-i-Khanan temporized with the
dominant 'junta', as Beni Prasad suggests. According to Roe, Shahjahan
was more favourably inclined towards 'Abdullah Khan Firuz Jung than
towards Khan-i-Khanan. Purchas, Vol. IV, p. 359.

32. The account of the mansabs and the appointments is based on the
*Tuzuk*.

33. *Ahwal*, f. 8b.

34. *Tuzuk*, p. 190.

35. Ibid., pp. 126–7.

36. Ibid., p. 196.
37. Ibid., p. 320.
38. Ibid., p. 305.
39. The above information is based on the *Tuzuk*.
40. E.g., Khan-i-Alam, Khan-i-Jahan, Murtaza Khan, Ani Rai Singh, Dalan, Khan-i-Azam, Khwaja Abul Hasan, etc.
41. This letter is included in Jalal Hisari's *Maktabt-i-Khan-i-Jahan Muzaffar Khan wa Gwaliyar Nama waghaira* (British Museum, Add. 16, 859, ff. 17a–19b), apparently by mistake. I am grateful to my colleague, Irfan Habib, for drawing my attention to this letter.
42. *Tuzuk*, p. 254.
43. *Ahwal*, ff. 18b–19b.
44. *Purchas*, Vol. IV, p. 359.
45. Jahangir suggests that Khurram was appointed at the request of Khan-i-A'zam, *Tuzuk*, p. 126. But this is not supported by the account given earlier on p. 125.
46. *Tuzuk*, p. 58.
47. *Tuzuk*, p. 58.
48. *Tuzuk*, p. 128. Restrictions on Khusrau had been relaxed in autumn 1613. Ibid., p. 123.
49. Ibid., p. 164.
50. Cf. Wali Sirhindi, f. 412b; *Ahwal*, ff. 12a and b.
51. *Tuzuk*, p. 259.
52. Ibid., p. 267.
53. The rumours of Khurram's downfall and of the rehabilitation of Khusrau which became current in September 1619 (quoted above) strengthen this assumption.
54. Shahriyar's betrothal, November–December 1620, *Tuzuk*, p. 320; Shahjahan's departure, December 1620. Ibid., p. 322.
55. Mu'tamad Khan clearly says that the betrothal of Ladli Begum to Shahriyar was an act of hostility to Shahjahan. *Ahwal*, f. 17a.
56. *Tuzuk*, p. 323.
57. Among the reasons for the break-up of the 'junta', Beni Prasad mentions the religious factor—Shahjahan was gradually estranged from his Shiite associates and the Persian interest saw itself threatened by the rising Sunni party of Shahjahan. Op. cit., pp. 271, 276. Although there is no evidence to show that Nurjahan was a Shi'ite, whatever might have been her religion, it is likely that her brother, Asaf Khan, also belonged to the same religion. There is certainly no reason to assume that Shahjahan was estranged from Asaf Khan.
58. Cf. Khan-i-Azam's letter, *BM*, Add. 16, 859.
59. Ibid.
60. E.g., Khan-i-Khanan, Khan-i-A'zam, Man Singh, Asaf Khan, Jafar Beg, etc.

61. Cf. his obituary notice written by Jahangir, *Tuzuk*, p. 839; *cf.* also p. 136.

62. For examples of Asaf Khan being admonished, *cf. Purchas*, Vol. IV, pp. 382–3.

63. It appears from the *Tuzuk* that the betrothal of Shahriyar with Ladli Begum was arranged between Jahangir and I'timad-ud-Daula. *Tuzuk*, p. 320. In 1622, Mahabat Khan distinguished between the positions of Nurjahan and Asaf Khan. He responded to the call of the former, but insisted that the latter be removed from the capital. *Ahwal*, ff. 18b–19b.

# 12

# Zamindars Under the Mughals*

The zamindar class played a vital role in the political, economic, and cultural life of medieval India. During the Mughal period, its importance increased, and its position in society became more complex.[1] The surplus of agricultural production, appropriated from the peasants, was shared among the emperor, his nobles, and the zamindars, and the power exercised by the zamindars over the economic life of the country—agricultural production, handicrafts, and trade—was tremendous. In spite of the constant struggle between the imperial government and the zamindars for a greater share of the produce, the two became partners in the process of economic exploitation.

Politically, there was a clash of interests between the Mughal government and the zamindars. Most of the administrative difficulties which the Mughal emperor had to face were the result of the zamindars' activities. At the same time, the administration had to lean heavily on their support. In the cultural sphere, the close links of the zamindars with the imperial court contributed in no small measure to the process of cultural synthesis between the distinctive traditions of the various communities and different regions, and between the urban and rural cultures. At the same time, the separatist, localist, and parochial trends received powerful patronage from the zamindar class. The Mughal

* *Land Control and Social Structure in Indian History*, ed. E. Frykenberg, Wiscosin, 1969, pp. 18–31. First published in *Indian Economic and Social History Review*, Vol. I, No. 4, 1964, pp. 107–14 under the title 'The Position of Zamindars in the Mughal Empire'.

empire achieved its great power largely because it could secure the collaboration of this class; but the inherent contradictions between a centralized empire and the zamindars were too deep to be resolved. These contradictions within the Mughal empire contributed to its downfall even before the Western powers were established in the country.

The word 'zamindar' gained currency during the Mughal period. It was used to denote the various holders of hereditary interests, ranging from powerful, independent, and autonomous chieftains to petty intermediaries at the village level. Before the Mughals, the chieftains were designated as rajas, *rais, thakurs,* and so on, while the small intermediaries would be termed *chaudhuris, khots, muqaddams,* etc. The Mughal practice of using the same generic term for the holders of widely varying types of landed interests is a reflection of the Mughal desire to reduce the chieftains to the status of intermediaries while compensating them in other ways.

The existence of the various types of landed interests was the result of a long process of evolution spread over several centuries. By the close of the twelfth century, a pyramidal structure had already been established in agrarian relations. Even though there were important regional differences, the nature of land rights in most parts of the country was basically similar. During the Sultanate period (1206–1526), significant changes in land rights occurred, but the essential features remained more or less the same. However, the process of change accelerated during the Mughal period.

Zamindars in the Mughal empire may be classified in three broad categories: (a) the autonomous chieftains; (b) the intermediary zamindars; and (c) the primary zamindars. These categories were by no means exclusive. Within the territory held by the autonomous chieftains were to be found not only vassal semi-autonomous chiefs, but also intermediary as well as primary zamindars. While the intermediary zamindars exercised jurisdiction over groups of primary zamindars, most of the intermediary zamindars were also primary zamindars in their own right. A chieftain might exercise primary rights over some lands and intermediary rights over others, while simultaneously enjoying 'sovereign' or 'state' powers over his dominions.

It may be noted that the territories held by the zamindars were not separate from the *khalisa* or *jagir* lands. The distinction between the jagir and the khalisa lay only in the distribution of the state's share of the revenue. If the revenue from a particular area were deposited in the imperial treasury, it would be deemed to be khalisa; if it were to be assigned to an officer in lieu of salary, it could be considered a jagir. Thus, the khalisa as well as the jagir comprised various types of zamindaris. A careful study of the various types reveals that there was hardly a pargana in the Mughal empire in which there were no zamindars.[2]

## The Chieftains

The chieftains were the hereditary autonomous rulers of their territories and enjoyed practically sovereign powers. Since the establishment of the Sultanate, the sultans had tried to obtain from these chieftains the recognition of their overlordship and imposed on them the obligation to pay regular tribute and to render military assistance to the Sultanate whenever called upon. But there were many cases of resistance or rebellions; and the nature of control exercised by the imperial government depended upon the extent of military pressure which it could bring against the chieftains. On a number of occasions, during the course of struggles against the sultan's authority, the ruling houses of the chieftains were altogether overthrown or their territories substantially reduced. Conversely, taking advantage of the weakness of the imperial authority, the chieftains would on occasion assume independence, or extend their territories. In either case, the rights of the vassals of the chieftains and of the intermediary or primary zamindars were not substantially affected. By the time Akbar (1556–1605) came to the throne, such autonomous chieftains held sway over the major portion of the Mughal empire; many who had accepted the overlordship of the Surs had by now become independent.

Akbar and his successors not only continued the policy of the sultans of demanding from the chieftains a recognition of their overlordship, the payment of tribute, and the rendering of military assistance, but also introduced the following ne· elements in their treatment of the chieftains.

1. Akbar was the first emperor who realized the import/ of forging powerful links between the empire and the chie/

by absorbing many of them in the imperial hierarchy and the administrative machinery. This policy was continued by his successors; and it is estimated that during the latter half of Aurangzeb's reign (1658–1707), eighty-one persons belonging to the ruling houses of the chieftains held *mansabs* of a thousand horsemen and above, representing almost 15 per cent of the total number of *mansabdars* of a thousand or more horsemen.[3] When a chieftain received a high mansab (a military rank regulated by the supposed number of horsemen the holder of the title could bring into the field), he also received a substantial jagir for the support of his troops. The revenue from this *jagir* would far exceed that of the chieftain's hereditary dominion; for example, the jagir granted to a mansabdar of five thousand *zat*, five thousand *sawar*, was expected to yield a yearly revenue of 8.3 lakhs of rupees which was several times the income of many of the principal Rajput rulers.[4] This policy resolved to an appreciable degree the basic contradiction between the chieftains and the imperial power and made it more fruitful for them to seek promotion in the imperial service than to cast off the imperial yoke and attempt to expand their territory in defiance of imperial authority. The imperial service also provided to the retainers and clansmen of the chieftains lucrative employment as well as a share in the plunder while conducting campaigns on behalf of the empire. Apart from bringing monetary advantages, imperial service was a source of power to the chieftains and enabled them to strengthen their position by recruiting and maintaining large armies.

2. The Mughals asserted the principle which later came to be known as that of 'paramountcy'. This meant that a chieftain depended for his position on the goodwill of the emperor rather than on his inherent rights. Only such of the chieftains were designated 'rajas' as were given the title by the emperor. While generally conforming to the law of primogeniture and hereditary succession, the Mughals asserted the right of 'recognizing' a younger son or even a distant relative of a deceased raja as his successor. The emperor Jahangir (1605–27) specifically claimed this right when he rejected the nomination of a younger son by Rai Rai Singh of Bikaner and nominated the elder one instead. Similarly, on the death of Raja Man Singh of Amber, the claims of Maha Singh, the son of Man Singh's eldest son, were

overruled, and Bhao Singh, a younger son of Man Singh, 'was given the principality of Amber with the lofty title of Mirza Raja'.[5] When Raja Sangram, the chieftain of Kharakpur in Bihar, incurred the displeasure of the emperor and action was taken against him, he was killed and his territories were taken over in khalisa; but after some time they were restored to his son, Raja Rozafzun. During Shahjahan's reign (1627–58), the claim of Jaswant Singh of Marwar was upheld in preference to that of his elder brother on the grounds that he was the son of the favourite wife of the late raja, a decision the reverse of that made by Jahangir with regard to Bikaner. The assertion of this right of the emperor to decide who would be the ruler of a principality not only strengthened the control of the central government over the chieftains, but also gave the latter a sense of personal obligation to the emperor. The well-known policy of matrimonial alliances with the houses of the leading chieftains further strengthened the sense of attachment of the chiefs to the emperor. The Mughal insistence that the chiefs should remain in attendance at the court of the emperor or a governor, or should be represented there by one of their close relatives if they themselves held posts elsewhere helped to consolidate the imperial hold over the chiefs.

3. Although all the sultans had claimed the right to call upon their vassal chiefs to render military assistance to the Sultanate whenever required to do so, the Mughals were successful in utilizing systematically the military services of even such chieftains as did not hold mansabs. In practically all the major campaigns conducted by the Mughals, the contingents of the vassal chiefs played a prominent part. For example, during the reign of Akbar, a number of the leading chiefs of south Bihar served under Raja Man Singh in the Orissa campaign of 1592. At about the same time in Gujarat, many vassal chiefs were required to provide contingents of sawars, or horsemen, at the call of the governor. The troops supplied by the chieftains contributed appreciably to the military might of the Mughal empire. How greatly valued was this military obligation of the chiefs may be judged from Jahangir's statement describing the importance of Bengal in terms of the obligations of its chiefs to supply fifty thousand troops rather than in terms of the enormous revenue it provided.[6]

4. The Mughal emperors appear to have pursued the policy of entering into direct relationship with the vassals of some of the more important chieftains, thus reducing the power of these chieftains and creating a new class of allies. The most obvious example of this policy may be seen in the case of Garha Katanga where Akbar established direct relations with the vassals of the Garha chief. Sometimes the vassals of the ruling chiefs were directly offered imperial mansabs as in the case of Marwar after Jaswant Singh's death.

5. Of great importance was the Mughal attempt to treat the hereditary dominions of the autonomous chiefs as *watan* jagirs. This meant that theoretically the chiefs were supposed to have the status of *jagirdar*s, and thus were subject to the imperial revenue regulations, but exercised jagirdari rights in hereditary succession over their territories, which were consequently immune from transfer. Even though this theory could be applied mainly to the chiefs who were enrolled as mansabdars, the imperial government made attempts to change the character of the tribute payable by the chiefs into land revenue assessed on the basis of the actual production. It is difficult to estimate the extent to which the Mughals succeeded in this effort as we find that a very large number of chiefs continued to pay tribute on an irregular basis, which was known as *peshkash*.[7] However, even in fixing the amount of the peshkash, the Mughal administrators tried to obtain data regarding the area under cultivation, the crop pattern, and the revenue realized by the chiefs from their vassals or subordinate zamindars. The information in the *Ain-i-Akbari* regarding the states of the chieftains and the account of the revenue settlement of Gujarat conducted by Todar Mal in the sixteenth century provide the most obvious evidence of this effort. In spite of the fact that this policy could be enforced only with partial success, it increased the de jure as well as the de facto control of the empire over the chiefs. It also increased the imperial pressure on their economic resources and compelled many of them to seek imperial service as mansabdars. Administratively it tended to bring the land revenue system of the chiefs in line with the Mughal pattern.

6. The Mughal emperors succeeded to a greater extent than their predecessors in compelling the autonomous chiefs to

conform to imperial regulations, especially in regard to the maintenance of law and order and the freedom of transit. Not only were the emperors able to make the chiefs take vigorous action against rebels, criminals, and fugitives who happened to enter their territory, but they also claimed the right to dispense justice to those who appealed to the imperial government against their chiefs. For example, when Raja Suraj Siṅgh of Bikaner arrested the retainers of his brother Dalpat, Jahangir ordered that they be released.[8] Several *farmans* are in existence directing the chieftains not to harass traders passing through their territory or to levy taxes on them. Even though several instances are recorded of chiefs disobeying the imperial orders and levying unauthorized taxes on transit goods, there is no reason to doubt that such orders were generally respected.

The existence of a large number of independent principalities in the country and its political fragmentation could hardly have contributed to its progress. Internecine warfare, a logical corollary of such fragmentation, could not have been conducive to material progress. It is difficult to accept Francois Bernier's statement that the peasantry was better off under the autonomous rajas than in the rest of the empire,[9] not only because the French doctor's prejudice in favour of feudal rights apparently clouded his judgment, but also because the available original records indicate that the rate of assessment on land and other taxes paid by the peasants in the territories of the chiefs were not lower than those in the contiguous areas outside the chiefs' dominions.[10] Furthermore, if there had been no centralized empire subjecting the chiefs to the payment of tribute, which in the last resort was passed on to the peasants, some other powerful chieftain would have established his overlordship and extracted tribute of a similar type and magnitude.

A centralized empire, by establishing comparatively greater peace and security, by enabling trade and commerce to expand, and by increasing and diversifying the purchasing power of the consuming classes which led to the development of industries, brought about conditions favourable to the growth of a money economy. The emergence of a money economy began to affect agricultural production to a considerable extent, especially because revenue was being realized more and more in cash. It also led to the expansion of cash crops and the extension of the cultivated area, partly as a result of the demand for greater revenue.[11] To the extent that the Mughal empire succeeded in establishing its authority over the numerous chieftains and the considerable measure of success that it achieved in unifying the country politically and administratively, it played a progressive role in the development of Indian society.

There is no doubt that the Mughals were more successful than any of their predecessors in bringing the numerous chieftains within the pale of their empire. As a result of intensive military campaigning, they compelled the chieftains in practically the whole country to accept their suzerainty. In accordance with the tenets of their policy enumerated above, they succeeded in securing loyalty and willing cooperation from the overwhelming majority of the chieftains and conformity with the broad aspects of their administrative policy. To this extent they were able to place curbs on the powers of the chiefs.

However, the policy of firmness coupled with friendship was able to resolve the contradiction between the chieftains and the imperial government only to a limited extent. Not all chiefs could have been granted high mansabs and lucrative jagirs. Furthermore, many of the nobles who were not zamindars envied the security enjoyed by the chiefs in imperial service and brought pressure on the emperor to restrict the grants of mansabs and jagirs to this class. As the pressure on jagirs increased, the emperor was no longer in a position to satisfy the aspirations of the chieftains. In such a situation many of the chiefs enjoying high positions in imperial service attempted to convert the jagirs assigned to them outside their ancestral territories into their hereditary dominions, as in the case of Bir Singh Deo Bundela during the reign of Jahangir and Jai Singh Sawai of Amber during the reign of Muhammad Shah. The imperial policy of demanding the payment of land revenue based on cultivated area could only have reduced the share of the chiefs. Rebellions were therefore inevitable. The chiefs hardly ever missed the opportunity of taking advantage of the difficulties facing the empire. For example, the chieftains of Orissa and Bengal supported Shahjahan when he rebelled against his father, but they quickly deserted the rebel prince when he was defeated by the imperial forces. On the other hand, whenever, because of various difficulties, the imperial government was unable to maintain its military pressure on the zamindars, the revolts became more frequent. Such was the case in the seventeenth century during the reign of Aurangzeb when the chieftains of Maharashtra, Bundelkhand, Mewat, and Rajputana, all took up arms against the Mughal empire and in their struggle drew upon the support of the lower classes of the zamindars, and also sometimes the peasants, especially when they belonged to the same clan or caste. The widespread dissatisfaction of the chiefs with the imperial government seriously weakened the military power of the Mughal empire. The empire depended too much on the support of the chiefs to have been successful in suppressing their power completely.

The frequent revolts of the chieftains, leading to long-drawn-out military campaigns and the inability of the imperial government to prevent the chiefs from expanding their dominions, placed a serious drain on the economy, adversely affected agricultural production in many cases, and weakened administrative unity. Consequently, by the close of the seventeenth century, the economic and administrative advantages of a unified empire had begun to disappear.

### The Intermediary Zamindars

This category comprised the various types of zamindars who collected the revenue from the primary zamindars and paid it to the imperial treasury, or to the jagirdars, or to the chieftains—or in certain cases kept it themselves. Such intermediaries not only formed the backbone of land revenue administration, but were also responsible for the maintenance of law and order. In return for their services they enjoyed various types of perquisites, such as commissions, deductions, revenue-free lands (*nankar* or *banth*), and cesses. Usually their share of the revenue ranged between 2½ and 10 per cent. Most of the zamindars possessed hereditary rights, though in a few cases they held their position on short-term contracts.[12] Among the intermediaries may be included *chaudhuris*, *desmukhs*, *desais*, *deshpandes*, certain types of *muqaddams*, *qanungos* and *ijaradars*, and the class of zamindars who contracted with the state to realize the revenue of a given territory and who began to be known during the second half of the seventeenth century by the generic designation of *taluqdars*. Practically the entire country was under the jurisdiction of one or the other types of intermediary zamindars. The statement in the *Ain-i-Akbari* regarding the caste of zamindars in parganas, other than those under the chieftains seems to refer to this class.[13] The fact that in the majority of the parganas, the zamindars belonged to a single caste and also that persons of the same caste were the zamindars of many contiguous parganas suggests that certain families or clans held zamindari rights over large tracts.

While the rights of the intermediary zamindars were hereditary, the state reserved to itself the authority to interfere with succession and even to partition the jurisdiction among brothers or relations. In the case of imperial displeasure, some of these intermediaries could be dismissed or transferred. An order of Akbar mentions the dismissal of a chaudhuri in Allahabad on the grounds that he had been harassing the pilgrims going to Triveni for holy baths.[14] A *nishan* (order) of Murad Bakhsh conferred the *deshmukhi* of a pargana in *suba* Telingana on one Rama Reddy, rejecting the claim of half the deshmukhi of the pargana put forward by the adopted son of his elder deceased brother.[15] Aurangzeb issued an order that there could not be more than two chaudhuris in a pargana; if there were, they were to be dismissed.[16] In some cases, the Mughal emperors conferred zamindari rights on persons appointed to maintain law and order or to facilitate the assessment and collection of land revenue.[17] Akbar's farman to Gopaldas conferring on him the rights of chaudhuri and qanungo in *sarkar* Tirhut formed the basis of the subsequent rise of the Darbhanga *raj*.[18] To satisfy the desire of the high mansabdars and nobles not belonging to the zamindar class to acquire hereditary territorial rights, the Mughal emperors instituted the practice of conferring *watan* and *altamgha* jagirs. In such cases, the persons concerned were given permanent jagirdari rights. Usually the territories granted in such jagirs were small, comprising a single village or a small number of villages, though in some cases they were larger. The holders of these jagirs tried to acquire proprietary rights and in due course were often called upon to pay land revenue. For instance, the watan jagirs granted by Jahangir to Anirai Singh Dalan developed into large and powerful zamindaris of Anupshahr in Bulandshahr District. A similar case was that of the watan jagir granted during the reign of Jahangir to Miran Sadr Jahan at Pihani in Shahjahanpur District.

Most of the intermediaries were supposed to prepare the details of revenue assessment for the perusal of the state, help in the realization of the land revenue, encourage extension of cultivation, assist the imperial officers in the maintenance of law and order, and supply a fixed number of contingents. However, in actual practice, they were constantly struggling to enhance their rights and to appropriate to themselves a greater share of the revenue if not the whole of it. The extant records are full of references to the *zamindaran-i-zor-talab*, that is, those who paid revenue only when it was demanded forcibly. Similarly, the intermediaries who contracted to collect revenue, either as *ijaradars* or as taluqdars tried to avoid supplying detailed figures of assessment and only paid the stipulated amount. The Mughal custom of frequent transfers of jagirs encouraged the practice of revenue farming, or the letting of contracts to someone else to collect the revenue.

On the one hand, these intermediaries strove to consolidate their rights at the expense of the state; thus, for example, they often appropriated to themselves the state's right to dispose of the uncultivated wastelands. On the other hand, they intensified the exploitation of the rural population and attempted to depress the position of the primary zamindars under their jurisdiction. Since they had the responsibility to pay the land revenue, whether the primary zamindars paid it or not, they were led on occasion to collect the revenue directly from the peasants, in which case they were supposed to leave the primary zamindars the customary 'proprietary' share (*malikana*). But the temptation in such a situation to step into the place of primary zamindars and become proprietors themselves must have been overwhelming.[19]

At the same time, they sought to build up hereditary territorial rights and, whenever the occasion arose, tried to become chieftains. As the Mughal empire became weak and the crisis of the jagirdari system was intensified, these intermediaries enhanced their powers and frequently rose in rebellion along with the other intermediary zamindars of their own clan or joined hands with some of the chieftains who were in revolt against the imperial authority. Apart from the political and administrative

disturbances which resulted from the tussle between such
zamindars and the state, agricultural production and the position of the peasantry also suffered.

While the imperial authorities strove to subjugate the recal-
citrant zamindars and attempted to force them to conform to
the imperial land revenue regulations, they could not afford to
suppress this class as a whole. Under strong administrators the
intermediaries generally performed their duties in accordance
with imperial regulations and exercised their rights within specified limits. But under weak administrators the situation frequently got out of hand. The widespread revolt of these zamindars
deprived the imperial officers of their income and consequently
reduced their military strength. In turn, the officers started
demanding transfers from the turbulent areas and even began
to claim cash salaries instead of jagirs.[20]

## The Primary Zamindars

The primary zamindars were for all practical purposes the
holders of proprietary rights over agricultural as well as
habitational lands. In this class may be included not only the
peasant-proprietors who carried on cultivation themselves, or
with the help of hired labour, but also the proprietors of one or
several villages. All agricultural lands in the empire belonged
to one or the other type of the primary zamindars. The rights
held by the primary zamindars were hereditary and alienable.
Numerous sale deeds of such zamindaris dating back to the
sixteenth century are still available.[21] The Mughal state considered it its duty to protect the rights of these zamindars and
encouraged the registration of transfer deeds at the court of the
qazi so that a proper record of claims could be maintained.

In addition to those who had been enjoying these rights for
generations or had acquired them by purchase, the Mughals
conferred such zamindari rights on a large number of persons.
In pursuance of their policy of extending the cultivated area, the
emperors freely bestowed zamindari rights to those who would
bring forest and wasteland under cultivation. It is also significant
that the majority of the madad maash grants (revenue free grants
given for charitable purposes) related to uncultivated land. The
madad maash grants required confirmation at the accession of

each monarch, but the hereditary succession was not usually interfered with. In due course, the madad maash grants also acquired the character of zamindari, as appears from the sale deeds of madad maash lands in the eighteenth century.

The zamindars, other than the peasant proprietors, generally gave their lands in hereditary lease to their tenants, who enjoyed security of tenure in terms of the *patta* granted to them, on the condition that they paid their land revenue regularly. Even in cases of non-payment the tenant was not usually deprived of his landholding rights, but the arrears were realized by other means. Considering the fact that there was not much pressure on land, the rights of the landholding tenants were generally respected. At the same time, in view of the shortage of cultivators, the zamindars enjoyed the right to restrain the tenants from leaving their lands and to compel them to cultivate all arable land held by them.[22] From the evidence it seems that where the primary zamindars did not pay the land revenue, it was collected directly from the peasants, leaving about 10 per cent as the proprietary share (*malikana*) of the zamindars.[23] It may be inferred that this percentage represents the normal share of the zamindars. In addition to their share in land revenue, the zamindars were also entitled to a large variety of cesses, though a considerable portion of the income from such cesses had to be surrendered by the zamindars along with the land revenue.

The zamindars were deemed to be the malguzars or those on whom land revenue was assessed by the state. They were also expected to collect the revenue from the peasants and to deposit the share of the state with the higher authorites. It was their duty to assist the administration in the maintenance of law and order and in many cases to supply troops under the orders of their superiors.

Sandwiched as most of these zamindars were between the superior zamindars and the state on the one hand and the peasantry on the other, they were constantly struggling to improve their position and thus frequently came into conflict with both sides. Unless these zamindars were able to withstand pressure from above, they passed on the burden of revenue demands to the cultivators and so contributed to the intensification of the economic exploitation of the latter. On such occasions, they played an economically retrogressive role. But on many occasions they led the revolts of the peasantry against the growing exactions of the state, often utilizing the caste and clan appeal to rally support. Where revolts were not possible, many of these zamindars refused to pay the revenue until force was employed. As has been mentioned earlier, the intermediary zamindars often tried to depress the status of the primary zamindars, and where the attempt was successful, a fresh category of sub-proprietary rights emerged. Sometimes the intermediary zamindars created a class of sub-proprietors, such as the *birtias*, in order to strengthen their position in the countryside.

Thus, there emerged not only a variety of land rights but also a kind of a pyramidical structure in agrarian relations wherein rights of various kinds were superimposed upon each other. The burden of the shares of the different categories of zamindars and also of the imperial revenue demand ultimately fell on the cultivator and placed such a strain on the agrarian economy that much progress was hardly possible. The imperial government tried its best to ensure that the peasant was not called upon to pay more than 50 per cent of the produce. But as imperial authority declined and as the pressure on jagirs increased, the agricultural economy had to face a crisis which began to deepen in the eighteenth century.

Politically and administratively, the zamindar class in general rendered loyal cooperation and assistance to the Mughal empire. Yet the conflicts of interest between the zamindars and the state, and between the different classes of zamindars, could not be eliminated. The conflicts led to frequent clashes, disturbed law and order, and seriously weakened the administrative and military power of the state. The numerous measures adopted by the Mughal government to resolve these contradictions worked well, but only for a time. By the middle of the seventeenth century, strains began to appear, and after the death of Aurangzeb in 1707, the central government had become too weak to maintain the equilibrium between conflicting interests. In any case, the dependence of the Mughal empire on the various classes of the zamindars for its revenue resources as well as administration was far too deep for the conflicts of interest between the empire and zamindars to be resolved.

Only a class which was not dependent on the zamindars could have attempted to change the pattern of agrarian relations. Such a class had not emerged by the middle of the eighteenth century.

## Notes and References

1. The following discussion of the zamindars is aimed at focusing the attention of historians on the urgent need for a detailed study of the working of the zamindari system during the Mughal period. The opinions expressed are tentative and are based on only a small fraction of the evidence available.

2. See Irfan Habib, 'The Zamindars in the Ain', *Proceedings of the Indian History Congress*, XXI Session, Trivandrum, 1958, pp. 320–3.

3. M. Athar Ali, *The Mughal Nobility Under Aurangzeb*, Bombay and New York, 1966, p. 13.

4. This figure was calculated on the basis of the eight-month scale. The zat rank was the personal rank of the officer, while the number of his horsemen was indicated by the sawar rank.

5. *Tuzuk-i-Jahangiri*, Aligarh, 1864, pp. 106, 130, 145.

6. Ibid., p. 7.

7. Detailed information on the assessment of peshkash from the zamindar of Trichnopoly from the years AH 1104–17 (AD 1692–1706) may be seen in the Central Records Office, Hyderabad, Reg. no. 83 of Aurangzeb's reign.

8. Farman no. 29, dated 9 October 1614, in the *Descriptive List of Farmans, Manshurs, and Nishans*, Bikaner, 1962, published by the Government of Rajasthan, Directorate of Archives.

9. V. A. Smith (trans.), Francois Bernier's *Travels in the Mughal Empire, 1656–67*, London, 1916, p. 205.

10. Comparing the *arsattas* (monthly accounts of receipts and disbursements) of the parganas of Amber and Sawai Jaipur with those of the parganas of Chatsu and Hindaun reveals a general similarity in the rates of assessment (Rajasthan State Archives).

11. For an excellent discussion of the impact of money economy on agricultural production and for the nature of the agrarian relations existing in the Mughal empire, see Irfan Habib's *Agrarian System of Mughal India*, Bombay, 1963.

12. For a discussion of the various types of land rights, see B. R. Grover, 'Nature of Land Rights in Mughal India', *Indian Economic and Social History Review*, Vol. I, pp. 1–23.

13. 'Account of the Twelve Subas', in H. S. Jarrett (trans.), Abul-Fazl-'Allami's *Ain-i-Akbari*, 2nd ed., Calcutta, 1949.

14. Copies of a number of farmans issued in this connection by Akbar and Jahangir were made available to the writer by M. A. Ansari of Allahabad University.

15. Andhra Pradesh State Archives, Hyderabad, Shahjahani Register, Vol. 40, no. 608, *nishan* dated 15 Ramazan, twenty-third regnal year of Shahjahan. The suba was a division of the empire, like a province.

16. Habib, *Agrarian System*, p. 292.

17. A farman of Shahjahan issued during the fifth regnal year promised zamindari rights to anyone who could bring the turbulent zamindars of the parganas of Kant and Gola under control. He was then to found a town named after the emperor in that region. A photostat of the farman is in the possession of the writer. See also Grover, op. cit., p. 12.

18. Qeyam Uddin Ahmed, 'Origin and Growth of Darbhanga Raj (1574–1666), Based on Some Contemporary and Unpublished Documents', *Proceedings of the Indian Historical Records Commission*, XXXVI Session, pp. 88–98. The *sarkar* was a government administrative district.

19. For example, in 1703, Raja Ibadullah Khan of Muhammadi contracted for the whole of the parganas of Barwar-Anjana and Bhurwara in sarkar Khairabad, suba Awadh, and in course of time acquired proprietary rights over the whole estate.

20. Numerous cases are cited in a number of contemporary documents included in *Durr-ul-Ulum*, a collection of papers arranged by Sahib Rai Surdaj in 1688–9, now in the Bodleian Library, Oxford.

21. Numerous transfer deeds are preserved at the Central Records Office, Allahabad.

22. See N. A. Siddiqi, 'Dasturul Amal-i-Bekas', *Proceedings of the Indian History Congress*, XXIII Session, Aligarh, 1960, pp. 243–7.

23. Grover, op. cit., p. 15.

# 13

# Three Studies of the Zamindari System*

When the East India Company acquired *diwani* rights in Bengal, its officials had to find out the nature of land rights prevalent in India. Inquiries were made from several persons regarding the rights of an individual, family or of a given region, and their replies were considered. Occasionally, an individual had a tract written in order to support his own claims. Many such statements made or tracts written between 1767 and 1795, are fortunately preserved. The writer has come cross a number of manuscripts in Britain and Europe which contain such replies, statements, and tracts. The following list, by no means exhaustive, is of manuscripts seen by the writer.

## Berlin Manuscripts, Now in Marburg[1]

Historical Discourse on the Origin of Zamindari and an account of Sarkar Bhojpur (Pertsch 505).

Ahwal Sarkar Shahabad (Pertsch 503).

Haqiqat Suba Bihar (Pertsch 500).

Haqiqat Mansabdaran-i Bengal (Pertsch 499).

## Berlin Manuscripts, Now in Tubingen

Questions and Answers re: revenue administration (Pertsch 72).

Revenue Papers (Pertsch 81).

* *Medieval Indian: A Miscellany*, Vol. I, 1967, pp. 233–9.

Dastur-ul-'Amal (Pertsch 82).

Revenue Papers Relating to Bihar (Pertsch 501).

Zamindars, Chaudhuris and Ta'alluqadars of Bengal, Bihar, and Orissa (Pertsch 502).

Revenue Papers (Pertsch 517).

Akbar-us Sidq (Pertsch 520).

Makhzan-i Ihtisab (Pertsch 524).

Goshwara Jamadami (Pertsch 527).

Revenue Papers (Pertsch 531).

## Bibliotheque Nationale, Paris MSS[2]

Miscellaneous Collection (Blochet iv/2330).

Miscellaneous Collection (Blochet iv/2331).

## British Museum Manuscripts

Papers Relating to Zamindari (Add. 6586, Rieu i/408).

Miscellany (Add. 19, 504, Rieu i/409).

Miscellany (Add. 19, 503, Rieu i/409).

Some of these manuscripts contain a discourse directly on the nature of land rights, while in the others the information is incidental or indirect. A great deal of statistical data are also contained in these works. These can be analysed and used for drawing conclusions. The aspect of land rights to which most of the information pertains is obviously the zamindari system. A great deal of the information is inaccurate and contradictory. Some of it concerns a given locality and any generalization based upon it would be dangerous. On other occasions, the information regarding the earlier position may have been distorted because of the situation existing in the eighteenth century. Notwithstanding all these difficulties, the information contained in these manuscripts is of very great value for the study of land rights, and specially of zamindari system during the Mughal period.

In the present paper, the information regarding the zamindari system available in the first three manuscript lists above has been summarized.

## Historical Discourse on the Origins of Zamindari and Account of *Sarkar* Bhojpur

The Hindus have divided the ages into four *yugas—satyuga, tretayuga, dwaparyuga,* and *kalyuga.*[3] During satyuga, Suryavanshi Rajputs were the rulers of India. There was no single monarch, and the country was divided among a few rajas. In that period the zamindars paid the *malguzari* according to their capacity. Generally they paid at the rate of 10 per cent, more or less. The same system continued more of less during *treta* and *dwapar* yugas. Gradually the malguzari rate was enhanced, but with the concurrence of the zamindar. But during this entire period, the proprietor of the land was the ruler, while the zamindar paid *kharaj*. During the reign of Akbar, in accordance with the *dastur-ul-'amal* of Raja Todar Mal, most of the zamindars obtained the *sanad*s of zamindari so that they could make the country prosperous (populous). The *chaudhuri*s and *qanungo*s together engaged themselves in the task of serving the government and the welfare of the *ri'aya*. Thus, it appears from the dastur-ul-'amal of Raja Todar Mal and the sanads of that period, that zamindari is a service (an appointment). The proprietor of the land, the king, gave a sanad for *jagir* or *altamgha* to whomsoever he liked. It is not within the power of the zamindar to give even one bigha of malguzari land, nor is he empowered to sell it. But after (paying) malguzari, the zamindar has full authority over his rights, which he can alienate to whomsoever he likes during his lifetime. In case his descendants also have the responsibility of working for prosperity of land (i.e., the zamindari is hereditary), he could alienate the rights hereditary. Since the ancestors of the zamindars had loyally served the government throughout their lives, it had been considered desirable that their descendants should not be displaced till they continued to render proper service.

Perquisites have been attached to zamindari because of the services the zamindar performs and the efforts he makes for populating the country, which cannot be properly accomplished without the zamindar. The example of a village may be taken into account. In a village, the *ri'aya* and the *muzari'an* flock round the zamindar, and he and they are integral parts of the same body. The people serve the zamindar from their adolescence till old age and the zamindar too shares their joys and sorrows. Consequently, without the zamindar, the muzari'an and the labourers (*taraddud karan*) will not be able to toil willingly for populating land. Therefore, zamindari was made hereditary.

It is a well-known saying that zamindari is conditional upon *malguzari*, while *nankar* is conditional upon service, *zamindari ba'iwaz malguzari wa nanker ba shart i khidmatguzari*. Consequently, the *malik* of a single village obtained land for *muqaddami*, while the large zamindars obtained villages or *ta'alluqa* in *nankar*, for which they received sanads. The term *malikana* was not used.

During the reign of Shahjahan most of the zamindaris originated in *bankati* or populating land after clearing forests. Those who did so became zamindars and obtained nankars for their lifetime. After the death of such zamindars, their sons obtained sanads for the rights held by them on condition of continued service. It was not within the competence of the zamindar to sell malguzari land. However, the zamindar is entitled to dispose of the nankar for the duration of his own life-time, with the permission of the sultan. One who renders service is entitled to enjoy the fruits of nankar. Any one deviating from the path of loyalty, or one remiss in service, or one guilty of some crime, is punished and is deprived of his zamindari.

From the reign of Farrukh Siyar, when Abdullah Khan and Husain Ali Khan having killed Mu'izz-ud-Din (Jahandar) Shah raised Farrukh Siyar to the throne, and then having murdered the latter, put Muhammad Shah on the throne, the law was contravened and the empire declined day by day. Many irregularities were committed. The administrators acquired for themselves *nazrana* for increasing state revenue and taxes. In the meanwhile, because of the ignorance of regulations and the decay of the empire, the term nankar disappeared, and the zamindars no longer strove to populate land in terms of the earlier sanads. Without bothering about the possible devastation of the country, they had their claims registered in the offices as *malik*s and called themselves maliks of a tenth of the land.

From the time of Timur to that of Humayun, the Deccan and Bengal were separate kingdoms. Akbar, who adopted the policy of *sulh-i-kul* towards the followers of all the different faiths and became famous as *Jagat Kunwar*, brought Bengal and the south within the empire of Delhi. He had sympathy for all and he wanted to help everybody. According to the *dastur-ul-'amal* of Raja Todar Mal, the *jama dami* (at the rate of 40 dams per rupee) of twenty-two *subas* was fixed at 13,809,279,949 dams. The *raqami*, at the above-mentioned rate was Rs 339,230,498–14 as. The *hal hasil* in the reign of Bahadur Shah was Rs 243,442,351–8–3 pies. The detailed papers regarding *dami, raqami*, and *hal hasil* have been given in the volume, for each reign, suba and sarkar-wise. The author then proceeded to give the details of only one sarkar, that of Bhojpur of Shahabad, suba Bihar, including the position of zamindari therein, from the time of Timur to the thirty-sixth regnal year of Shah Alam.

After giving an account of the foundation of Ujjainiya *raj* of Bhojpur, the author says that Dalpat Sahi did not give proper obedience to the ruler. But he conducted the revenue statement (*bandubast*) in a manner that the rights of the *ri'aya* were not infringed. He did not permit the regulations of the qanungos to be improved. According to his statement, the position was as follows:

Mahals—9, *Jama dami* 37,447,019, dams (cultivated land—9,816,000 bighas), *raqami* Rs 936,175–7–6, hal hasil agreed upon by the Ujjainiyas Rs 967,000). In 1568–9 when Akbar brought Bengal and Bihar in his kingdom, the Raja agreed to pay to the *hakim* the sum of Rs 5 lac per annum as malguzari. Then Narain Mal and his brother Pratap Rudra strove to populate the land and without depriving the *ri'aya* of its share, raised the hal hasil to Rs 1,471,000. He did not permit the administration of the qanungos either. After remaining the chief for many years, Narain Mal rebelled and was killed. The Ujjainiyas then pleaded with the hakim that in view of Pratap Rudra's kind treatment of the ri'aya he should be recognized as the chief. Pratap Rudra also agreed to pay Rs 2 lac per annum as *nazrana* over and above the malguzari. Having regained in 1022H/1613–14 the title of Raja, he settled as follows:

> *jama raqami*—Rs 9.36 lac
>
> *hal hasil*—Rs 14.71 lac
>
> *malguzari*—Rs 5 lac
>
> *nazrana*—Rs 2 lac

After twenty years Pratap Rudra revolted and took to the hills. Finally in 1059H/1649–50, he was defeated and killed. His successor was appointed by the hakim in consultation with the Ujjainiyas, and the revenue settlement continued as before. He died in 1089H/1678–9. During the reign of Farrukh Siyar, there were serious disturbances. Ultimately, during the reign of Muhammad Shah, the Raja repopulated the territory and according to the papers of his *mutasaddis*, the revenue went up to Rs 17 lac. He paid in malguzari Rs 5 lac.

## Ahwal Sarkar Shahabad wa Rohtas

Sarkar Shahabad—12 mahals. *raqba arazi* 12,532,000 bigha. *Jamadami* fixed by Raja Todar Mal during the reign of Akbar, on the basis of *raqba bandi*—49,967,019 dams, *raqami* @ 40 *dams*=1 rupee: Rs 1,248,175–7 annas. The *jama* of *sal-tamam* having been written from the early days inclusive of expenses of *tahsildari* and *malikana* of zamindars, etc., was deposited in official treasury. Enough, however, was left of the produce to cover the expenses of the zamindars who, along with troops retained by them, passed their days in plenitude and the ri'aya received its own dues.

For a long time, the zamindari was of the Bhumiya, Dhikh, etc., Rajputs and Bamnhiyas. In the early days Mana Singh and Shuja Singh, two Ujjainiya brothers came from Ujjain to Shahabad and purchased *tu'alluqa*s. After some years, Mana Singh became Raja of Shahabad and Shuja Singh having purchased the *ta'alluqa* of Bihiya created a zamindari. The Ujjainiyas, after some years, having thought of taking over the zamindaris of the Bhumiyas, Dhikhs, and Bamnhiyas, approached the *Nazim* of the period. During the *subadari* of Nawab Fakhrud Daula, in 1131 *fasli*, there was a fight between the two branches of the Ujjainiyas. During the course of their fight, the *subadar* conducted the settlement with the Bhumiya, Dhikh, and other zamindars in accordance with the *jamadami*. Later, after the departure of Fakhr-ud-Daula, the Ujjainiyas were restored to their old position, but the settlement continued to be in accordance with the jamadami of 45,821,381 dams (raqami Rs 1,145,540). The realization was managed through the zamindars. Later, when Nawab Zainuddin Ahmad Khan became the *naib* of Bihar, the *chaudhuris* of the Bhumiya,

Dhikh, and other reza zamindars approached him to say that because of the partiality of the officials for the Ujjainiyas, they (reza zamindars) were being excluded from their ancestral zamindari. The author has then given the names of the chaudhuris, qanungos, and ta'alluqadars of each pargana in sarkar Bhojpur.

## Haqiqat Suba Bihar

From the time of Shahjahan, it was customary that woodcutters and ploughmen used to accompany his troops, so that forests may be cleared and land cultivated. Ploughs used to be donated by the government. Short-term pattas were given, the government demand was fixed at the rate of I anna per bigha during the first year. Chaudhuris were appointed to keep the ri'aya happy with their considerate behaviour and to populate the country. They were to ensure that the pattas were issued in accordance with imperial orders and the pledged word was kept. These was a general order that whosoever cleared a forest and brought land under cultivation, such land would be his zamindari. Qanungos were instructed to prepare the settlement regulations with the concurrence of the chaudhuris in a manner as to contribute to the populousness of the territory. The revenue demand was to be determined accordingly. They were to prepare the papers from harvest to harvest and to deposit these with the amil at the end of the year. They were to put forward the claims of rozina, dastur, nankar, in'am, etc. before the amil at the time of the settlement of the pargana, keeping in view their devoted service to the state and the welfare of the ra'iyat. The qanungos were required to obtain the qubuliyat in accordance with the regulations, and deposit these with their own signatures, and to secure pattas for them. The state revenue was to be deposited by them in the imperial treasury at each tahsil harvest-wise and instalment-wise.

After giving a detailed account of the manner of assessment and the rate of demand according to the principles of land classifications which had been introduced, and of administrative procedure, the author records the official instruction that after allowing one plough per twenty bighas of well-cultivated land, the other ploughs should be allotted to virgin land or that which had lain fallow for a long time. Ploughs should also be given on behalf of the state. The price of these ploughs should be realized from the zamindars in two to three years. Each *hal mir* (i.e., one who has four or five ploughs) should be found out and given a *dastur* so that he may clear the forests and bring land into cultivation. In this manner, the people and the ri'aya would be attracted by good treatment to come from others regions and subas to bring under cultivation wasteland and land under forests.[4]

## Conclusions

An examination of the above three studies leads to the following main conclusions:

(i) Proprietorship of land vests in the ruler and not in the zamindar.

(ii) Zamindari rights accrue from imperial sanads in lieu of the service of malguzari, of extending cultivation, and making the country prosperous. The zamindar may enjoy nankar for other duties performed by him.

(iii) The zamindar does not possess the right to alienate malguzari land, but he may, with the permission of the ruler, alienate his rights as zamindar and also the land held by him in nankar.

(iv) Even though *jamadami* was fixed by the state and remained unchanged, the hasil could be very much more. The hasil was determined by the zamindar from time to time.

(v) In the case of some of the rajas, the malguzari could be more or less than 50 per cent of the hasil. Further, there was not much change in the malguzari though nazrana could be added.

(vi) The recognition of succession of the zamindars was dependent upon the discretion of the government, though the views of the leading members of the class of the zamindar concerned were invariably taken into account.

(vii) Zamindari rights could also originate from purchase, subject to recognition by the government.

(viii) Powerful chiefs could acquire superior rights over petty zamindars (called reza zamindars). They sometime tried to depress the status of these petty zamindars, but he government preferred to maintain the position of the petty zamindars.

(ix) The government gave every encouragement to the zamindars to clear forest and to being more land under cultivation. From the time of Shahjahan there was a general order that whosoever cleared a forest and brought new land under cultivation, such land would be his zamindari. A very large number of sanads of zamindari were granted in this manner.

(x) Even those owning four to five ploughs were encouraged to extend cultivation and acquire zamindari rights.

(xi) It was the duty of the officials to allot ploughs at the rate of twenty bighas of well-cultivated land for one plough. The other ploughs in the village were to be utilized to cultivate virgin land or land which had been out of cultivation for a long time. In this manner, new zamindaris were sought to be cultivated, even of peasant proprietorships.

(xii) The government assisted the zamindars to extend cultivation by giving new ploughs, the cost of which was recovered from them gradually, and by fixing a nominal government demand which was progressively raised.

As has been stated at the beginning, these conditions may or may not hold good for all regions of the country for the entire medieval period. They represent a particular point of view which is to be taken for whatever it is worth.

## Notes and References

1. I acknowledge with gratitude the gift of xerox copies of the four manuscripts of Marburg to the Aligarh Muslim University.

2. The writer sincerely thanks the German Academic Exchange Service and the Government of France for enabling him to study the manuscripts of the Berlin Collection and the Bibliotheque Nationale. A large number of manuscripts in the British Collections, notably of India Office Library, have not been included in this list.

3. The author is mixed up between *Treta* (the third) and *Dwapar* (the second), yugas.

4. This is a large work and deals with many problems. Here points bearing on zamindars have been summarized.

# 14

## Aspects of the Zamindari System in the Deccan (1695–1707)*

The study of the surviving administrative documents of the seventeenth and eighteenth centuries has made it possible for the students of medieval Indian history to understand in detail the nature of social relationships and the position of the various elements constituting agrarian society. One of the extremely rich collections that is now available for scrutiny is the Inayat Jung Collection of documents acquired by the National Archives of India. These documents, starting from the reign of Aurangzeb, are of great value for the study of the administrative, economic, and social history of the Deccan. The purpose of the present paper is to draw the attention of scholars to some of these documents in the hope that a systematic study of the collection will be undertaken at an early date.

It is well-known that the Mughal empire leaned heavily on the support of the zamindars for revenue administration, military service, and the maintenance of law and order. But the nature, pattern, and extent of the partnership between the empire and the zamindars require fuller investigation. In the Deccan, it is

* *Proceedings of Indian History Congress*, XXXI Session, Varanasi, 1969, pp. 262–6.

I am extremely grateful to S. A. I. Tirmizi, Assistant Director, National Archives of India for the facilities which he was kind enough to extend to me, and to Mr Waqarul Hasan Siddiqui of the Archaeological Survey of India for assisting me in this study.

quite obvious that the Mughals were keen to win over the Maratha *zamindars* to their side. Athar Ali has recorded the names of a number of Maratha zamindars who held a *mansab* of 1000 or above during the period of 1679–1707. He has also brought out the fact that two of these—Jakia and Jagat Rai—were *deshmukhs*, while Ram Chand was a *thanadar*.[1] But these documents provide us with many details of the participation of the Maratha zamindars in the administration of the state.

The most important Maratha leader to enter imperial service in the post-Shivaji period was Satvaji Dafle who was given, in 1698, the mansab of 6000/5000 and kettledrums.[2] In spite of this high mansab, he asked for and received the *deshmukhi* of four parganas in suba Bijapur, namely, Jat, Karjagi, Holwar, and Bardol, on condition of paying to the imperial government a *peshkash* of Rs fifty thousand. He could thus be described as belonging to the category of an intermediary zamindar. Usually the highest ranks of 5000 and above were held either by ruling chiefs or by nobles whose principal source of income was their jagir. The present writer is not aware of any other person holding such a rank who was essentially an intermediary zamindar.[3]

A document of the same year refers to another Maratha zamindar, apparently a deshmukh, Sukhoji, son of Raghoji, who had been given the mansab of 6000 under the three months' rule and was sanctioned jagir worth 5,606,000 dams in pargana Shah Nagar and the adjoining territories.[4] There is no reference to this person in the chronicles and his name is not included in the list given by Athar Ali.

The number of other and smaller intermediary zamindars awarded mansabs and given military duties is, of course, very large. In 1700, Rano Naro, the zamindar of pargana Aundargaon in *sarkar* Parenda having put to death the rebel chief Pratap Rao was given the mansab of 1000/100 on the recommendation of Muttalib Khan. He was given the village of Malegaon in that pargana in *daro-bast* (i.e., right of collecting revenue from the entire village) as *inam*; the *hasil sal tamam* (revenue receipt of a full year) of the village was Rs 7266. Rano Naro was ordered to render service with 100 *sawars*.[5]

Yashwant Rao and his associates, the zamindars of Ankola in the province of Aurangabad were given mansabs, Yashwant Rao himself receiving the mansab of 300. They were ordered to ensure the security of the *chowki*s attached to the fort.[6]

On the recommendation of Ghairat Khan, the *qiladar* and *faujdar* of Parenda, Bharji, the zamindar of Kanti who held the *deshmukhi* of the pargana, was entrusted with the responsibility of maintaining 100 *sawar*s (the *zat* rank is not clear in the text of the document) and ordered to guard the highway and assist the faujdar of Parenda. He was allowed a grant of Rs 5400 for maintaining a *thana* in the *qasba* and for his troopers.[7] Madho Rao and Nilkantha Rao, the zamindars of Bir, who had been rendering military service to the empire for sometime, were granted an increase in their mansab to 300/100 and 200/20, respectively, both on the four-monthly scale, and called upon to continue their military service.[8]

The Inayat Jung Collection contains an almost complete series of documents giving the full list of zamindars, village-wise, in the provinces of the Deccan with whom the state was expected to deal. These were almost exclusively the intermediaries and included *deshmukh*s, *deshpande*s, *muqaddam*s, *chaudhari*s, *qanungo*s, and *patwari*s. Although it had been suggested before that the muqaddams belonged to the zamindar class,[9] the inclusion of muqaddams in the list of zamindars is significant.[10]

Even more interesting is the inclusion of patwaris in the list of zamindars. An equally noteworthy feature is that in some of the parganas, the name of mahajan is also included in the list of zamindars. The purpose here obviously seems to be to include those mahajans who had furnished zamini for the payment of *peshkash*. In some cases, the deshmukh was entrusted with the office of both the *muqaddam* as well as the deshpande. Occasionally, the *muqaddami* was held by chaudharis.[11]

It is clear that the imperial government retained the right to appoint intermediary zamindars of various categories, though it could safely be presumed that generally this would be in accordance with custom and usage. There is an example of a *parwana* being issued sanctioning half *deshmukhi* (*nisf deshmukhi*) in a *pargana* of *sarkar* Ahmadnagar, suba Ahmadnagar.[12] In some cases Asad Khan had given orders that deshmukhi be given to the muqaddam.[13] A document contains the order entrusting the *khidmat* of muqaddami in village Bhalawa in suba Khandesh to one Mohammad Namdar subject to his being accepted by the *riaya.* His claim to muqaddami had been opposed by one of *muzari'* and the deshmukh and deshpande of the place.[14] While generally each village had a single muqaddam, there were many with two. In rare cases there were three or four muqaddams in a single village. There are also references to two chaudharis in one village.

The categories of zamindars mentioned above refer almost exclusively to those who were responsible for assessing and collecting land revenue. There is a serial giving the *peshkash* payable by each such intermediary zamindar in the provinces of Deccan;[15] there is another serial giving a village-wise statement of the instalments of peshkash payable by the zamindars.[16] The instalments were being mentioned against the names of deshmukhs, deshpandes, muqaddams, and *raiyat.* However, in the actual list, the dues from *ijaradars*, patwaris, quanungos, and chaudharis are also mentioned. It is significant that in these lists there is nothing to indicate the revenue due either from the primary zamindars or the cultivators. It also seems that the provinces of the Deccan were being actually assessed on a lump sum basis as peshkash rather than as a regular settlement. In one document the peshkash payable by the deshmukhs, and deshpandes of sarkar Sholapur is categorized as being: *naqd bil maqta* (i.e., ad hoc lump sum dues in cash) and *naqd az riaya* (lit. cash from riaya). It seems that this also refers to some sort of a summary assessment from the actual *malguzar* or primary zamindar.[17]

Interesting light is thrown by these documents on the customary perquisites of the intermediary zamindars. In three parganas, the *rusum* of the deshmukhs and deshpandes are entered thus:[18]

| Rusum from the Riyaya | | *Inam Zamin* |
|---|---|---|
| 1. Rs 5820 | | Bighas 4230 |
| | | Rs 3601-4 as |
| | Bhagat | Rs 148–10 Zira at Zira't Rs 3452 |
| 2. Rs 1500 | | Bighas 1000 |
| | | Rs 558–2 as |
| | Bhagat | Rs 77–8 Zira at Zira't Rs 480–10 |
| 3. Rs 4000 | | Rs 1107 |

At the same time there are instances when *rusum* were not sanctioned. In sarkar Cicacol, three villages were entrusted to a deshpande and the peshkash of these villages amounting to Rs 2080 was payable by him. However, the rusum were not sanctioned and he was expected to undertake cultivation and pay for his own living.[19] There is also the case of a deshmukh being allowed *haqqul tehsil* (i.e., collection charges). In the case of Satvaji Dafle mentioned above, he was permitted a haqqul-tehsil Rs 1251 on a total peshkash of Rs 50,000 which comes to 2.5 per cent.[20]

As has already been observed, every intermediary zamindar was required to furnish surety (*zamini* or *muchalka*).[21] But once surety was furnished, instalments could be paid even over a number of years. A particular muqaddam had accepted to pay in peshkash Rs 350. Out of this Rs 87 being one-fourth had to be deposited in the treasury in cash and for the balance a *muchalka* was submitted stating that the remaining amount would be paid in three years.[22]

Although in this paper only a small number of documents have been used, a researcher would find a careful examination extremely fruitful. There is a wealth of statistical data containing the revenue demand of each village over a period of years (*mawazana yak harifi*), applications for the grant of jagirs and orders granting jagirs, grant of mansabs, and fixation of salary for various categories of mansabdars, and the working of local administration.

## Notes and References

1. M. Athar Ali, *The Mughal Nobility Under Aurangzeb*, Bombay, 1966, pp. 216–71.

2. *Maasir-i Alamgiri*, p. 395.

3. National Archives of India, Inayat Jung Collection, I/573–4, S. Nos 7542, 7543 dated 11 Zil-hijja 43 Julus/AD 1700.

There are, however, examples of chieftains holding very high mansabs securing in *ijara* or *taalluqa* intermediary rights in adjoining parganas. See Satya Prakash Gupta, 'The Expansion of the Territories of the Kachhwahas in Mughal Times', *Proceedings of Indian History Congress*, XXVII Session, Allahabad, 1965, pp. 177–82.

4. I/15/549, S. No. 7518, Zil-hijja 43 Julus.

5. I/16/41/7676, Safar 44 Julus.

6. I/16/5, 33, 49 S. Nos 7640, 7668, 7684, 44 Julus.

7. I/16/2, 90, 91; S. Nos 7636, 7725, 7726, 44 Julus.

8. I/15/619/621, 634; S. Nos 7588–90, 7604, 43 Julus.

9. For example, the present author's paper entitled 'Farid's Administration of His Father's *Jagir*', *Proceedings of Indian History Congress*, XXVI Session, Ranchi, 1964.

10. For a discussion of the position of the chieftains, intermediary zamindars and primary zamindars, see the present author's article on 'Zamindars Under the Mughals', in *Land Control and Social Structure in Indian History*, Wisconsin, 1969, pp. 17–31.

11. The series is entitled '*Ism navisi Zamindaran*', I/3/1–50, 59–85, 201–55, 301–32; S. Nos 302–51, 360–80, 502–56, 602–33; 1106 Fasli I/ 15/463–81, 491, 493–512, 551; S. No. 7432–50, 7460, 7462–81, 7520; 1108 Fasli. This list is by no means exhaustive.

12. I/19/456; S. No. 8491; 47 Julus.

13. I/3/1–50; S. No. 302–51; 1106 Fasli.

14. I/19/435; S. No. 8470; 47 Julus.

15. For example, I/19/301–42; S. No. 8336–77; 1099 to 1108 Fasli, entitled *Peshkash Zamindaran*.

16. For example, I/19/344–50; S. No. 8379–85; 43 and 44 Julus, entitled *Talab Aqsat Peshkash Zamindaran*.

17. I/3/98; S. No. 399; 1106 Fasli.

18. I/3/86–9; S. No. 387–90; 1106 Fasli.

19. I/3/52; S. No. 353; 1106 Fasli.

20. I/15/573–4; S. No. 7542–3; 43 Julus.

21. For example, I/15/433–5; S. No. 7402–4; 42 Julus; I/19/342/S. No. 8377.

22. I/19/435; S. No. 8470, 47 Julus.

# 15

<!-- decorative flourish -->

## Further Light on Zamindars Under the Mughals
### A Case Study of (Mirza) Raja Jai Singh Under Shahjahan*

Many years ago, this writer attempted a study of the position of the zamindars under the Mughals (Chapter 12 in this volume).[1] In that study it was pointed out that Akbar had made a conscious attempt to absorb many of the leading chieftains into the Mughal nobility as *amirs*. While they continued to hold their ancestral domains as *watan*, they were assigned high *mansabs*, their relations were also granted mansabs, and they received extensive *jagirs* on a personal basis. They were given important commands, participated in military campaigns, and held administrative posts, like those of governors and *faujdars*. In subsequent studies, the writer attempted to point out that while there were inherent conflicts between the state and zamindars, as well as between the zamindars of different categories themselves, the Mughal state could not have survived without the support of the zamindars, and, as such, the zamindars became integral part of the Mughal ruling class.[2]

In this brief paper, as a case study, a number of *farmans* (including *nishans* of the princes) issued by Shahjahan to (Mirza) Raja Jai Singh of Amber have been discussed.[3] These deal with affairs other than the military campaigns undertaken by Jai Singh

* *Proceedings of Indian History Congress*, XXXIX Session, Hyderabad, 1978, pp. 497–502.

under the orders of the emperor, and throw light on the various types of duty that Shahjahan expected Jai Singh to perform.

Even during the period of his rebellion, Shahjahan in a *farman* addressed to Jai Singh (dated 23 April 1626) had sought the latter's support, emphasizing that he was descended from Shahjahan's maternal uncle (his stepmother's brother), Raja Man Singh, who had enjoyed the favours of Akbar and promising that he would be looked after by Shahjahan in the same way as Akbar has looked after Man Singh.[4] Shortly after Jahangir's death, and before he had formally ascended the throne, Shahjahan in a farman (dated 30 November 1627) had assured Jai Singh of his favours and instructed him to remain loyal to his (Shahjahan's) cause.[5]

Jai Singh served Shahjahan with distinction in many important campaigns. Right from 1629, when he was sent to pursue Khan Jahan Lodi, he served intermittently in the Deccan in the campaigns against Ahmadnagar and Bijapur up to 1647, (1629–32, 1634–5, 1636–7, and 1646–7). He served at the court in Lahore in 1637, and then in the north-west during 1639–40. He participated in the campaign against Mau and Mirpur in 1641–2; in the Kabul, Balkh, and Qandahar campaigns in 1647–8, 1651–2, 1653, respectively; and the Chittor campaign in 1654. He was not only confirmed in his mansab, watan, and jagirs, but also rewarded from time to time. In 1630, he was given additional jagir worth 3,748,820, dams in pargana Deoti Sanchari, near his watan, and many of his relations received increases in mansab and additional jagirs, both near their homes as well as in the Deccan.[6] A grant was given, in 1639, in pargana Baikunthpur, *sarkar* and *suba* Bihar, of two hundred bighas of cultivable land which was not included in *jama*, for the maintenance of the *chhatri* of Raja Man Singh's mother.[7] From 1640, he is referred to as Mirza (Prince) Raja Jai Singh, which was an act of special favour.[8] His eldest son, Ram Singh, was given the mansab of 1000/1000 and jagir worth 10,000,000 dams in the Deccan in 1646.[9] In 1650, he held, according to S. P. Gupta, jagirs worth 82,000,000 dams in parganas of Amber, Chatsu, Phagi, Mauzabad, Jhag, Bohrana, Pachwara, Khori, Deoti Sanchari, Bharkol, Jalalpur, Umran, Sakras, Bawal, and Jat Kalewa, all fairly close to his watan. To crush the rebels of Kaman and Pahari, he got the pargana of Hal Kaliyana (Chal Kalanah) worth 7,000,000 dams.[10] A little later, in 1661, the *faujdari* of Mewat parganas was given to his other son Kirat Singh[11] (Kesri Singh of Khafikhan). Jai Singh made no attempts to convert his jagirs into his watan.[12] Practically all the jagirs assigned to Jai Singh were in parganas in which many villages were in *khalisa* or jagirs of other princes or *mansabdars*.

According to the *A'in*, the principal responsibility for ensuring that the realization of revenue from khalisa territories was not obstructed, that turbulence and truculence were suppressed, and that jagirdars were not prevented from realizing revenue which was assigned to them, was entrusted to the *sipahsalar* (governor) or the *faujdar* of the territory concerned.[13] All these duties were frequently given to Jai Singh, even though he neither held the office of sipahsalar or faujdar in the territories now comprising Rajasthan (except for the faujdari of Mewat given to Kirat Singh, in 1650).

## Assistance in the Relation of Revenue of Khalisa Mahals

| | |
|---|---|
| 14 June 1637 | Some of the ryots of the *mahals* of pargana Hindaun, which is khalisa, are remiss in payment of revenue. Since this is near your jagirs, you should help the Karori in realizing revenue and in giving exemplary punishment to truculent elements (No. 45). |
| 27 February 1640 | Since the undermentioned parganas have been taken in khalisa with effect from July 1639, you should look after these and ensure that no one oppresses the ryots of these parganas. The *Karoris* of these *mahals* should be assisted in realizing imperial revenues (No. 55). Parganas: Khandar in Sarkar Ranthambore, Silawa, and Toda in pargana Bijwara. |
| 4 May 1640 | Report has reached that ryots in some khalisa areas of pargana Hindaun are procrastinating in the payment of revenue. This should be looked into and Sagar Mal Karori should be assisted in realizing the revenue (No. 55). |

3 November 1640     It has been reported that in pargana Jalalpur, in which Jai Singh also has jagir, the realization of revenue from khalisa has fallen in arrears and the ryots are avoiding to make payment. He should make urgent efforts to realize the arrears of revenue, otherwise these would be deducted from the jagirs of Jai Singh (No. 63).

17 December 1643     It is reported that in pargana Mu'izzabad and in other mahals of Jai Singh's jagir salt is being manufactured. As a result of this, the khalisa revenue from the salt of Sambhar has fallen by more than rupees 1 lac. Jai Singh was ordered to ensure that all manufacturers of salt should be stopped forthwith, failing which these parganas would be transferred from him (No. 68).

## Assistance to Princes and Other Jagirdars in the Realization of Revenue

3 September 1637     The imperial servant Yazdani has reported that Hriday Ram Kachwaha and Sardul Kachwaha, former jagirdars of Kala Khoh and other villages of pargana Sahar, are preventing Yazdani from realizing revenue of these villages now assigned to him. Hriday Ram is trying to bring back the turbulent Chauhans who had been expelled. Further, the jagir assigned to Yazdani in pargana Gujjarh is being occupied by Jai Singh's men from Bhabra.

    Jai Singh should ensure that Yazdani is not troubled (No. 47).

26 March 1640     Narhar Sanghi, the *mustajir* of pargana Sambhar, has reported that he is facing difficulty in realizing imperial revenues. He should be assisted (No. 56).

| | |
|---|---|
| 16 April 1640 | Khan-i-Khanan should be assisted in realizing revenues from his jagir in *sarkar* Alwar; Audchi and Mandawar in *sarkar* and *suba* Agra; and Kirki in sarkar Ranthambore *suba* Ajmer (No. 57). |
| 10 December 1650 | *Nishan* of Dara Shikoh asking Jai Singh to assist Izzat Khan in realizing the revenues of (Dara's?) jagir in pargana Sambar (?) (No. 78). |

## Suppression of Turbulent Elements

| | |
|---|---|
| 13 November 1632 | Ratan Singh Kachwaha has reported that in parganas of Roshanpur and Naraina, which he holds in jagir, some Rajput zamindars are unnecessarily interfering and have killed some innocent people. Jai Singh should look into the matter and obtain assurance that they should not do such a thing again. If they resist and show turbulence, they should be expelled from their zamindari so that there is no further oppression (No. 39). |
| 12 May 1638 | Some Chauhan and Jadon zamindars of pargana Deoti Sanchari have joined hands with Sabal Singh, Parasram, etc., *Badgujars*, who are turbulent and troublemakers, and have been brought to the pargana by Jai Singh. These should be expelled so that no one in the pargana is oppressed. If any one gives shelter to these troublemakers, he should be punished (No. 49). |
| 16 July 1650 | The territories of Kaman and Pahari should be cleared of troublemakers and rebels and they should be suppressed and killed (No. 76). |
| 28 September 1650 | Action should immediately be taken against the troublemakers of Kaman and Pahari so that they may not oppress the people. Kirat |

Singh, Jai Singh's son, is being appointed
*faujdar-i-mustaqil* (substantive faujdar) for
this purpose. Under his jurisdiction would
be 44 mahals: Khalisa—7 mahals in Suker
Tijara; Jagirs—37 mahals in *sarkars* Rewari,
Alwar, Tijara, Rewari, and Narnaul. These
included the jagirs of Jai Singh (No. 77).

3 October 1651      *Nishan* (presumably of Dara Shikoh).
Troublemaker of Kaman and Pahari should
be replaced by Rajputs.

## Assistance in Safe Transit of Imperial Treasures

27 December 1647  Jai Singh to collect Rupees 10,000,000 from
the *tahsil* of Jawahar Khan and 280,000
*ashrafis* from the tahsil of Khwaja Rozbahan
and carry it from Agra to the court in Lahore
(No. 71).

26 May 1654       Jai Singh to arrange for the safe transport
of 2 crore of dams from pargana Mirat (?)
to the court (No. 83).

## Regarding Despatch of Marbles and Stone-cutters to Agra

20 September 1632  Muluk Shah is being sent to Amber to
arrange for the transport of marble from
new quarries. Jai Singh should arrange for
*arabas*, assist Muluk Shah, and reimburse
the cost from imperial exchequer (No. 38).

31 January 1633   A large number of arabas are needed for
bringing marble from Makrana for the
buildings of Agra. Jai Singh should procure
these from his own and from the jagirs of
his relatives (No. 33).

30 June 1637      A number of stone-cutters have been assembled by Jai Singh in Amber and Raj
Nagar. This has caused shortage in

Makrana. These should all be sent to
Makrana (No. 46).[14]

Another interesting document[15] throws light on mutual jealousy among the zamindars. Raja Jai Singh had proposed to visit Hardwar to bathe in the Ganges and had intended to visit the court on his way back in 1657. In a *nishan*, Dara Shikoh asked him that in view of his enmity with Raja Bithaldas, who was then at the court, Jai Singh need not come to the court, but return to Amber.

## Notes and References

1. 'Position of the Zamindars Under the Mughals', first presented to the International Congress of Orientalists, New Delhi, later printed in *Social and Economic History Review*, Vol. I, Delhi, 1964, and in, Frykenburg, *Land Control and Social Structure in Indian History*, Wisconsin, 1969. Many studies have subsequently been undertaken where various aspects of the problem have been examined. Among these, mention may be made of A. R. Khan, *Position of Chieftains Under Akbar*, Shimla, 1977; G. D. Sharma, *Rajput Polity*, Delhi, 1977; and S. P. Gupta, *Land Revenue System in Eastern Rajasthan*, c. 1650–1750 (to be published shortly), and some articles of the present author.

2. Cf. S. Nurul Hasan, *Thoughts on Agrarian Relations in the Mughal Empire*, Delhi, 1972. (No. 21 in this collection)

3. Mughal *farmans* to the rulers of Amber, preserved in the Rajasthan State Archives, Bikaner. The documents are referred to by their serial number in the Archives.

4. Farman no. 19.

5. Farman no. 22.

6. Farman no. 30 dated 8 July 1630.

7. Farman no. 53 dated 17 August 1639.

8. Farman no. 55 dated 27 February 1640.

9. Farman no. 69 dated 13 April 1646.

10. S. P. Gupta, op. cit., p. 9.

11. Farman no. 77 dated 28 September 1650.

12. S. P. Gupta, op. cit., p. 10.

13. *A'in-i-Akbari*, Nawal Kishore Press, Vol. I, pp. 343–7.

14. A similar document of 1658 (dated 17 January) No. 88 has been left out because conditions had already become unsettled.

15. Farman no. 87.

# PART III

# RURAL ECONOMY AND TOWNS

# 16

# Revenue Administration of the Jagir of Sahsaram by Farid (Sher Shah)*

The account of Farid's revenue administration in his father's *jagir* given by Abbas Khan has led many scholars to express an opinion regarding the agrarian relations existing during the early years of the sixteenth century. Even though this account cannot be wholly relied upon since it was written more than half a century later, its importance is undeniable. The purpose of the present paper is to raise doubts regarding the veracity of some of the existing interpretations and to draw the attention of the scholars to the importance of some of the passages which have not received adequate notice.

The first problem which requires reconsideration is whether Farid entered into a direct revenue settlement with the peasants. Elliot has translated the passage thus:

When he had finished exhorting the soldiery, he turned to the peasantry, and said: 'This day I give you your choice as to your mode of payment. Do whatever is most advantageous to your own interest in every possible way.'[1]

In this passage Elliot has translated the word *ra'iyat* as peasantry. In the preceding paragraph, Abbas Khan states that on reaching the pargana, Farid had called the *muqaddams* and the *muzarian*, on whom depended the prosperity of cultivation, as also the

* *Proceedings of Indian History Congress*, XXVI Session, Ranchi, 1964, pp. 102–7.

*patwari*s and soldiers, each category being then addressed by him. Elliot has translated the word muzarian as cultivators.

The interpretation of ra'iyat as peasantry and of muzarian as cultivators has been accepted by most scholars. Qanungo has argued that Farid wanted to protect the peasants against the violence of the soldiers and extortion of the muqaddams and then goes on to say that he turned to the peasants and told them to make their choice as to whether they should pay rent in cash or kind, 'He meant to make a settlement direct with ra'iyat and not through the muqaddams.'[2] Moreland accepts the same theory with a minor modification. He states that Farid found the land held partly by peasants and partly by chiefs, (Moreland translates zamindars as chiefs). The former were regarded as the true source of prosperity and the latter as dangerous nuisances. Farid's first step was to give the peasants their choice as to the system on which the demand should be assessed.[3] The same view has been accepted by Tripathi who states that, 'The cultivator had the option to choose whichever method he liked and give his acceptance in writing.'[4]

A careful examination of Abbas Khan's text reveals that the author has used two terms distinct from each other, viz. ra'iyat and *reza-i ra'iyat*. The latter term has obviously been used in the sense of cultivators who were to be protected from the oppression of the muqaddams and the *amils*.[5] It is therefore reasonable to infer that the term ra'iyat would denote another class of persons. *Tarikh-i Daudi*, which is an early paraphrase of Abbas Khan, contains significant variations which help clarify the meaning of the term ra'iyat. Where Abbas Khan has written, 'certain zamindars who have been behaving contumaciously, who did not attend upon the *hakim*, who do not pay their full revenue and who harass the villages in their neighbourhood' were to be chastised, *Tarikh-i Daudi* has the following statement: 'The muqaddams of Farid decided to chastise the muqaddams of some of the villages who had become contumacious and rebellious and who had not attended upon him.' Later, Abbas Khan writes that Farid 'called for horses from the ra'iyat.' The same statement is given in *Tarikh-i Daudi* as 'from the muqaddam of each village he called for a horse on loan'.[6] It would thus appear that the term ra'iyat has been used in the sense of muqaddam and the latter in the sense of zamindar. In fact, Abbas Khan has himself used the word muqaddam in the sense of zamindar and ra'iyat in the sense of muqaddam. Describing the action against contumacious zamindars Abbas states that Farid having laid waste the villages of the rebels and plundered their property refused to accept their terms of surrender. He was determined to kill and uproot them and decided that money would not be accepted from such people. After they had been killed, their property confiscated, and their women and children sold, Farid 'rehabilitated on their lands other ra'iyat'. Farid then stated that 'if from such contumacious persons the hakim agrees to accept money and let them off they would oppress the other people. It was, therefore, incumbent upon the hakim that he should not spare the lives of such troublesome muqaddams.'[7]

The word *muzarian* also requires a word of explanation. Technically it means the tenant cultivator who holds his land on lease under certain specified terms and conditions which indicate that it could not be used in the sense of an ordinary cultivator or tenant.[8] However, *Waqiat-i Mushtaqi* has at one place used the term in the sense of an ordinary cultivator.[9] But we have some definite evidence to suggest that a muqaddam could also be a *muzari*.[10] The famous *farman* of Aurangzeb issued to Rasik Das Karori states inter alia that the muzaris were classified as mustajir and *riaya*.[11] Furthermore, Abbas Khan having stated that Farid having called the muqaddams, *muzarian*, patwaris, and soldiers, goes on to mention the conversation he had with each category of persons called. The actual conversation described is with only two categories: (a) the soldiers and amils; and, (b) the ra'iyat and muqaddams. There is no reference in this context to the *muzarian*. The latter, were, therefore, included by Abbas in the category of ra'iyat and muqaddam. An anecdote regarding the reign of Sikandar Lodi relates to the sultan's calling the muqaddams, patwaris, and ria'ayan of the villages comprising a sizeable jagir in order to ascertain the *hasil* of those villages.[12] It seems unlikely that the sultan could have called the ordinary cultivators; the ria'yan, presumably refers here to the petty zamindars.

From our study of the relevant passages, it would appear that the term ra'iyat has been used here in the sense of such petty zamindars as had accepted the authority of the ruling power. We may recall the term *zamindaran-i ra'iyati*, contrasted to rebellious (*zor-talab*) zamindars, used in Mughal documents precisely for this class of persons.[13] Generally speaking, the muqaddam would be one of the zamindars, being obliged to collect the land revenue from his peers. The revenue, then, might conceivably be assessed either on the individual zamindars directly, or on the village as a whole with the muqaddam engaging for it. It is not denied that the zamindars were not always intermediaries and that they might have lands, later styled *khud-kashta*, which they got cultivated through labourers or tenants; nor that the muqaddams sometimes took lands on lease from other zamindars, and so appear as their 'tenants'.[14] The greatest variety could, indeed, prevail. Our present purpose is only to show that the assumption that Farid entered into direct relations with ordinary cultivators, mainly and primarily, is not plausible and is not sustained by the evidence from which it was first deduced. On the contrary, the far more logical interpretation would be that he dealt generally with the petty zamindars.

The next problem concerns the mode of assessment. According to the *Ain*, the prevailing systems of assessment before the reign of Sher Shah were *ghalla-bakhshi* and *muqtai*.[15] Moreland was unable to explain the significance of muqtai but suggested that it might be 'farming' or 'assignment'.[16] Irfan Habib has however described it as fixed revenue demand.[17] As suggested by him, it is presumably the system mentioned in *Daulat-i Sher Shahi* in the following words:

Sher Shah said: we may make one person from the village responsible for the payment of Government dues. He is expected to collect the dues from the various pieces of land and farms, and to pay a fixed sum. But (in such cases) some power of coercion shall have to be conceded inevitably. Therefore it is necessary that the Government officials should be instructed to look to the protection and security of the people, so that none of the *malguzars* should stretch his hand to oppress the subject in any place.[18]

The system of *kankut*, which involved measurement, is included by Abul Fazl in ghalla-bakhshi,[19] implying that before the introduction of the *zabt* system, the revenue assessed on the basis of measurement was in kind. Taking into consideration the statement of Abbas Khan that the major revenue reform of Sher Shah was the introduction of the 'year-by-year *jarib*' (*sal ba sal jarib*),[20] it may be inferred that even where the revenue was assessed on the basis of measurement, the demand was fixed for many years. The incident in *Waqiat-i Mushtaqi* mentioned above indicates that where there was a dispute regarding the actual amount of the revenue yield of a territory an officer would be appointed to undertake measurement (*masahat*).[21] From the foregoing it would appear that the real significance of Farid's revenue administration lies in the fact that he ordered that the revenue demand be fixed either in relation to the actual produce or on the basis of the area under each crop. This impression is further strengthened by the instruction he gave that at the time of *jarib*, the *bud* and *nabud* were to be taken into account.[22]

From a statement in *Tarikh-i Daudi* that Ibrahim Lodi issued definite orders for revenue to be realized in grain only,[23] Moreland has drawn the conclusion that Farid must have collected it in kind. However, the instruction to the muqaddams given by Farid, as quoted by Abbas Khan, was that the amount of money due as land revenue (*arz-i wajibi-i diyuni*) be paid from harvest to harvest.[24] This would suggest that while the basis of assessment was grain, the actual payment of the revenue was in cash.

The account of Abbas Khan also throws some light on the system of assignment. Apparently the *jagir* of an *amir* was assigned on the basis of the number of troopers that he brought for muster at the time of the fixation of his salary. The assignee was then expected to sub-assign one part of his jagir to the troopers and to appoint whomsoever he liked as the hakim and *shiqqdar* of the remainder. In fact, however, the officers seldom carried out the sub-assignment properly and did not maintain the requisite number of troopers. Farid, on the other hand, seems to have enforced the system of sub-assignment among the troopers that he enrolled.[25] Sub-assignment of this type appears to have been continued during the reign of Sher Shah.[26] But *Waqiat-i Mushtaqi* contains the statement that 'during the reign of Sher Shah, people were given salaries, while (Islam Shah) gave them *wilayat* and parganas.'[27] We may infer from this evidence that in his father's jagir Farid enforced the system of sub-assignment to individual troopers according to the then current theory, that afterwards difficulties were felt by him in continuing the system when he wanted to raise a large army during his rule in Bihar (when the territories at his disposal were small but he had adequate treasures), and that on ascending the throne he made an attempt, though not entirely successfully, to follow the practice of cash payment to soldiers.

A comment may, finally, be made on the veracity of Abbas Khan's statements. Since he is the only author who has described in detail the administration of a pargana by an assignee, considerable importance has been rightly attached to his account. However, it may be recalled that Abbas Khan wrote his work during the middle of Akbar's reign. It is thus quite possible that he uses terms which were not used in the Lodi period, and is influenced in his description by the institutions of his own time. His father was a native of Roh and the family came to India only during the time of the Surs. It is unlikely that Abbas Khan could have gathered accurate information from his family regarding the technicalities of the Indian revenue administration at local levels, or could have been personally familiar with the conditions in Bihar. Any attempt to make generalizations regarding agrarian relations on the basis of such an account should therefore be made only with great caution.

## Notes and References

1. Elliot and Dowson, Vol. IV, p. 313.

2. K. R. Qanungo, *Sher Shah*, 1929, pp. 16–18.

3. W. H. Moreland, *The Agrarian Systems of Moslem India*, Allahabad, 1929, p. 69; cf. Moreland, 'Sher Shah's Revenue System', *JRAS*, 1926.

4. R. P. Tripathi, *Some Aspects of Muslim Administration*, 1959, p. 299.

5. *Tarikh-i Sher Shahi*, Aligarh Text, pp. 20, 246.

6. Abbas, *op. cit.*, pp. 22–3; *Tarikh-i-Daudi*, Aligarh, p. 10.

7. Ibid., pp. 28–9. Daudi's account is as follows: 'Having suitably punished such people he made them *ra'iyati*', pp. 108–9.

8. *Dastur-ul-Albab*, Raza Library, MS, f. 39a. Cf. *Medieval India Quarterly*, Vol. I, nos 3–4, pp. 72–3.

9. B. M. Ms. f. 22b.

10. Allahabad Documents, no. 329, dated 1088 AH 1677.

11. *Nigar Nama-i Munshi*, Lucknow, pp. 129–31.

12. *Waqiat-i Mushtaqi*, f. 27a.

13. N. A. Siddiqi, 'Classification of Villages Under the Mughals', *Indian Economic and Social History Review*, Vol. I, No. 3, 1964, pp. 73–38.

14. Irfan Habib, *The Agrarian System of Mughal India*, Asia, 1963, p. 130.

15. *Ain-i Akbari*, ed. Blochmann, Vol. I, p. 296.

16. Moreland, op. cit., pp. 73–4, 275.

17. *Agrarian System of Mughal India*, pp. 233–4. The present writer is

unable to agree with P. Saran, 'Revenue System of Sher Shah', *JBORS*, Patna, xviii, 1930–1, and his *Provincial Government of the Mughals*, 1941, p. 276 & n.

18. Tripathi's translation of fragment of the *Tawarikh-i Daulat-i Sher-Shahi*, in *Medieval India Quarterly*, Vol. I, No. 1, July 1950, p. 62. Unfortunately, the original text of this fragment has disappeared.

19. *Ain-i Akbari*, ex. Blochmann, Vol. I, pp. 285–6.

20. Abbas Khan, op. cit., p. 246.

21. *Waqiat-i Mushtaqi*, f. 27a.

22. *Abbas Khan*, op. cit., p. 21.

23. *Tarikh-i Daudi*, pp. 104–5.

24. Abbas Khan, op. cit., p. 20.

25. Ibid., pp. 23 ff.

26. As is indicated by Shujaat Khan's attempt to expand his own *khalisa* at the expense of his troopers' *jagirs*, see Abbas Khan, op. cit., pp. 266 ff.

27. *Mushtaqi*, f. 71b. But Badauni, *Muntakhabut Tawarikh*, I, p. 384, followed by *Tarikh-i Daudi*, p. 65, says that Islam Shah made the whole of his dominions his own *khasa* and continued to pay his soldiers in cash.

# 17

The Pattern of Agricultural
Production in the Territories
of Amber (c.1650–1750)*

Till now it has not been possible to study the pattern of agricultural production as it existed in the medieval period because of
the paucity of data. No definite estimate could be made regarding the percentage of the various crops and consequently no
worthwhile study was made about changes in the crop pattern.
Fortunately, the *arhsatta*s of the territories held by the rulers of
Amber enable us to fill partly this gap in our knowledge. The
present study is based on the examination of the arhsattas of the
contiguous parganas of Amber (Sawai Jaipur), Malarna, Bahatri,
and Chatsu. The period covered in these documents is 1664–
1750. However, the continuous series is not available and the
gaps are considerable. The arhsattas contain information, among
other things, on the following points:

Total revenue demand:

Proportion of the demand from *kharif* and *rabi* harvests;

Cash demand of areas given in *ijara* (for which no particulars are
available). Area under each crop assessed according to the *zabti*
system, the rate of payment per bigha and the total revenue assessed
per crop;

* Written in collaboration with Mrs. Khursheed Nurul Hasan and S. P.
Gupta, *Proceedings of Indian History Congress*, XXVIII Session, Mysore, 1966,
pp. 244–64.

Total revenue realized in kind according to the *batai jinsi* system and the sale price of the revenue realized in kind per crop. Sometime the total produce is also mentioned along with the share of the produce left with the ryot and the share realized by the state in kind.

Although information contained in the arhsattas is extremely valuable yet its analysis is fraught with serious difficulties. First of all, the size of the parganas does not remain constant. For example, the number of villages in pargana Amber, later designated as Sawai Jaipur, increases from 541 in 1677 to 611 in 1690, 700 in 1715, 780 in 1723, 874 in 1725, 998 in 1737, and 1140 in 1744. This enormous increase was due to the absorption of many contiguous tracts into the pargana. In pargana Chatsu, the number of villages increases from 256 in 1708 to 399 in 1737. In pargana Bahatri the number increases from 261 in 1665 to 339 in 1716. In Malarna, however, the size of the pargana remains on the whole fairly steady. Apart from the fluctuation in size, another difficulty is that detailed information is available only in respect of the villages held by the ruling family in *khalisa* and excluding those areas of the khalisa whose revenue was farmed out for a fixed sum. The territory held in khalisa as well as that given in *ijara* increased or decreased from season to season and year to year. However, it may be assumed that the crop pattern in the khalisa areas would represent the crop pattern of the territory as a whole.

The most serious difficulty in utilizing the statistical information in the arhsattas is that the figures are given in two distinct sets which are, strictly speaking, not comparable with each other, namely the jinsi and the zabti. As a general rule the crops which are assessed according to the batai jinsi system continue to be assessed in the same system throughout the period under review. Similarly, those assessed according to the zabti system continue to be so assessed during the period. The figures for the zabti system do not give any indication of either the produce per bigha or the price of the crop or the incidence of taxation. In so far as the crops assessed according to the batai jinsi system are concerned, occasionally the total produce is given alongside the quantity demanded as revenue, but generally only the quantity demanded as revenue is given alongside the sale price of the portion sold. The area sown and the rate of demand per bigha in kind is not given. Thus it is not easy to make the two sets of figures comparable.

To study the relative position of crops, the one obvious common denominator has been used, namely to examine the revenue realized from each crop (Table 1). Although this method gives a rough indication, there are too many variable factors involved to permit us to judge the crop pattern exclusively by comparing the revenue derived from different crops. Under the zabti assessment different rates per bigha were applicable even in individual villages. And there were changes in the rate of demand from year to year. Apparently, the rate depended on the quality of the produce, the productivity of the soil, and prices. However, an examination of the rate of revenue demand per bigha for zabti crops shows a remarkable continuity (Table 2). Since during the period under review there is apparently a general rise in prices (Table 3), the zabti system tended to be more advantageous to the ryot than to the state. It was perhaps for this reason that there is a tendency for an increase in the cultivation of zabti crops.

For the jinsi crops too, the revenue figures do not necessarily provide a safe guide to the crop pattern. The fluctuation in price is of course an obvious difficulty. At the same time, we know from these documents that the share of the state in respect of the different crops varied even within each pargana and quite frequently from year to year. However, the average remains fairly steady. The following gives the average of the share of the total produce for each of the principal crops taken by the state in the four parganas:

State Share of Total Produce
(in percentage)
*Kharif*

| Pargana | Bajra | Jowar | Moth | Urd | Mung | Til | Chola |
|---|---|---|---|---|---|---|---|
| Jaipur | 39.6 | 46.8 | 40.0 | 41.0 | 39.0 | 42.0 | – |
| Malarna | 42.0 | 44.5 | 41.0 | 44.0 | 43.0 | 44.0 | – |
| Bahatri (Baswa)* | 45.0 | 46.0 | 44.0 | 44.0 | 43.0 | 42.0 | 50.0 |
| Chatsu | 35.0 | 36.0 | 36.0 | 38.0 | 39.0 | 33.0 | – |

* This pargana contained the *qasba* of Baswa, which has now given its name to the whole pargana.

*Rabi*

| Pargana | Barley | Wheat | Gram |
|---------|--------|-------|------|
| Jaipur | 31.8 | 32.6 | 36.1 |
| Malarna | 34.0 | 34.6 | 38.0 |
| Bahatri | 33.0 | 32.0 | 41.0 |
| Chatsu | 32.0 | 33.0 | 37.7 |

A perusal of the above mentioned figures reveals that the incidence of demand for the principal jinsi crops of the rabi harvest was more or less the same as that of the zabti crops while for the kharif harvest, the incidence of the revenue demand of the jinsi crops would tend to be 10–15 per cent higher than that of zabti crops.

Fortunately, some of the jinsi crops were occasionally, in part, assessed according to the zabti system and therefore the zabti rates as well as the demand in kind and price for the same crop in the same pargana are available. It is consequently possible to convert the cash demand per bigha into kind demand per bigha (on the basis of the prevailing price). It is also possible, by assuming that zabti rates were calculated on the basis of one-third of the average produce, to work out the average yield per bigha. By examining the average yield per bigha and the average demand in kind per bigha it is possible to work out the area under each crop where the state demand in kind is given. Although this method is not entirely accurate, and it is based on assumptions which are not always correct, it provides a possible method of estimating the total number of bighas under each crop. Such an estimate has of course to be moderated on the basis of the differences in the weight of the *maund* (ranging from 28 to 40, and even 42) and the size of bigha (which was generally a square of 75 *haths* or cubits).

By this method, the proportion of area under different crops has been estimated (Table 5). Although the proportion of the different crops estimated according to revenue yield and according to the area (Tables 1 and 5) is different in many respects, the overall picture of the crop pattern as well as of the major changes during the period under review appears to be the same according to both the estimates.

## The Principal Crops

### Kharif

*Bajra, jawar,* and the pulses *moth, urd,* and *mung* were the most important *jinsi* crops while *chola,* sugar cane, cotton and *makka* were the most important zabti crops. In Malarna, Bahatri, and Chatsu, *kodon* was also a very important crop. The other significant crops were *til* (*jinsi*), vegetables, indigo, *barti, marhwa,* tobacco, and paddy (zabti).

### Rabi

The most important rabi crops were assessed according to the batai jinsi system and the zabti crops were only of marginal significance. The principal jinsi crops were barley, wheat, and gram with mixed crops such as *baijhri, gojai* and *gochani* occupying a significant place. The other jinsi rabi crop was *sarson* but its cultivation appears to have been fairly restricted. Among rabi zabti crops mention may be made of vegetables, *china,* tobacco, and *ajawain.* But none of these occupied a significant place in the scheme of agriculture. In pargana Chatsu, however, *chomli* was an important crop.

The most important changes in the pattern of agricultural production were an increase in the zabti crops of the kharif harvest. These were apparently cash crops. The increase is most marked in the following crops: sugarcane—in parganas Jaipur and Bahatri, cotton—in Malarna and Chatsu; makka—in Jaipur, Bahatri, and Chatsu; and chola and kodon—in all the four parganas.

There is a corresponding decrease in the percentage of the bajra and the pulses. The increase in these cash crops, accompanied as it was with a general rise in prices and a comparatively stable cash demand per bigha, was not without significance for the economic life of the region. It reflects a comparative decrease in local self-sufficiency, a greater use of money economy and commodity production and indicates that at least in this region, capital was available to some extent for developing agricultural production. This indication is also available from the fact that the proportion of production during the rabi harvest increases in comparison to kharif harvest. The geographical condition of the region is such that rabi production can only be increased if there is a reasonable investment in agriculture.

Table 1
Table Showing the Percentage of Revenue
Derived from Different Crops
*Kharif*
Pargana Jaipur (Amber)

| Year | Bajra | Jowar | Moth | Urd | Mung | Chola | Sugar cane | Cotton | Makka |
|------|-------|-------|------|-----|------|-------|------------|--------|-------|
| 1666 | 31.0 | 17.0 | 27.0 | – | 1.0 | – | 1.0 | 13.0 | – |
| 1677 | 32.0 | 3.0 | 35.0 | 1.0 | 1.0 | – | 3.0 | 16.0 | 1.0 |
| 1688 | 18.0 | 1.8 | 27.0 | 1.0 | 3.0 | – | 1.3 | 18.0 | – |
| 1689 | 18.0 | – | 37.0 | – | 3.0 | – | – | 11.0 | 5.4 |
| 1690 | 11.0 | 1.4 | 41.0 | 1.0 | 3.0 | – | – | 24.0 | 2.5 |
| 1712 | 31.0 | 1.2 | 32.0 | – | 2.5 | – | 2.7 | 14.0 | 5.0 |
| 1715 | 15.0 | 4.6 | 18.0 | 1.0 | 1.0 | – | 12.0 | 19.0 | 12.0 |
| 1716 | 5.7 | 25.0 | 18.0 | 1.0 | 1.5 | 5.0 | – | 19.0 | 15.0 |
| 1718 | 30.0 | 5.0 | 13.0 | – | – | 2.5 | 3.0 | 15.6 | 12.6 |
| 1720 | 25.0 | 1.8 | 15.4 | 1.0 | 1.8 | 5.6 | 3.0 | 16.0 | 16.0 |
| 1723 | 22.0 | 3.0 | 20.0 | – | – | 6.0 | 1.4 | 20.0 | 12.0 |
| 1724 | 8.0 | 2.0 | 27.0 | – | 2.0 | 8.0 | 3.0 | 15.0 | 15.0 |
| 1725 | 13.0 | 1.0 | 7.0 | – | – | 8.0 | 5.6 | 25.0 | 20.0 |
| 1733 | 3.6 | 1.0 | 10.0 | 1.0 | 1.4 | 1.0 | 3.0 | 46.0 | 12.4 |
| 1734 | 4.3 | 1.7 | 26.0 | 1.9 | 2.3 | 9.1 | 6.0 | 19.8 | 16.0 |
| 1737 | 6.3 | 1.7 | 23.0 | 1.9 | 1.8 | 11.0 | 4.0 | 20.0 | 18.0 |
| 1744 | 7.7 | 8.0 | 20.0 | – | 1.0 | 6.0 | 10.0 | 9.8 | 17.0 |

Pargana Malarna

| Year | Bajra | Jowar | Moth | Urd | Kodon | Sugar cane | Cotton | Makka |
|------|-------|-------|------|-----|-------|------------|--------|-------|
| 1690 | 13.2 | 26.8 | 19.6 | – | 1.0 | 23.6 | 9.0 | – |
| 1699 | 29.0 | 20.0 | 6.2 | 1.5 | – | 16.0 | 7.8 | – |
| 1711 | 40.0 | 26.0 | 9.8 | – | – | 10.0 | 1.5 | – |
| 1712 | 32.0 | 15.0 | 14.0 | – | – | – | – | – |
| 1713 | 35.6 | 9.3 | 26.9 | 5.0 | 1.0 | 5.9 | 2.0 | – |
| 1714 | 41.8 | 11.0 | 6.8 | 2.7 | 1.9 | 15.3 | 3.9 | – |
| 1715 | 34.0 | 15.5 | 14.2 | 3.7 | 1.8 | 14.9 | 6.2 | – |
| 1716 | 26.0 | 5.2 | 17.7 | 7.7 | 1.7 | 14.0 | 7.4 | – |
| 1717 | 37.3 | 11.2 | 14.7 | 9.2 | 1.0 | 7.0 | 7.5 | |
| 1718 | 42.6 | 16.9 | 6.3 | 2.0 | 3.3 | 9.0 | 10.0 | – |
| 1719 | 24.9 | 29.3 | 18.0 | 2.2 | 2.7 | 8.0 | – | – |
| 1720 | 32.0 | 29.3 | 7.3 | 1.6 | 1.3 | 10.6 | 4.2 | – |
| 1722 | 36.8 | 26.6 | 8.0 | 1.6 | – | 7.0 | 4.2 | – |

(Table 1 contd.)

Table 1 contd.

| Year | Bajra | Jowar | Moth | Urd | Kodon | Sugar cane | Cotton | Makka |
|---|---|---|---|---|---|---|---|---|
| 1723 | 34.3 | 33.8 | 8.8 | 1.0 | 1.0 | 5.4 | 5.2 | – |
| 1726 | 21.6 | 29.6 | 3.8 | 2.3 | 3.2 | 20.0 | 9.7 | – |
| 1727 | 27.0 | 30.0 | 6.6 | 3.0 | 2.7 | 10.2 | 6.9 | – |
| 1728 | 21.8 | 24.4 | 11.8 | 1.9 | 2.3 | 4.3 | 8.8 | – |
| 1729 | 22.8 | 26.0 | 9.3 | 2.6 | 2.0 | 9.0 | 13.7 | – |
| 1732 | 16.5 | 26.0 | 3.3 | 1.0 | 6.3 | 12.8 | 22.2 | – |
| 1736 | 15.0 | 25.3 | 5.5 | 3.9 | 1.7 | 20.4 | 22.0 | – |
| 1737 | 19.5 | 30.0 | 9.0 | 1.5 | 3.7 | 11.6 | 12.3 | – |
| 1738 | 28.0 | 31.6 | 14.2 | 2.3 | 1.6 | 3.0 | 2.5 | – |
| 1743 | 30.3 | 38.2 | 3.0 | – | – | 5.3 | 5.7 | – |
| 1744 | 21.7 | 26.5 | 15.0 | – | 2.0 | 14.6 | 2.0 | – |
| 1745 | 29.2 | 25.2 | 10.2 | 2.0 | – | 7.0 | 5.0 | – |
| 1748 | 26.8 | 27.8 | 12.6 | 2.5 | – | 5.5 | 4.0 | – |
| 1749 | 19.4 | 34.8 | 10.2 | 2.4 | – | 6.4 | 2.8 | – |

| | | | | Pargana Bahatri | | | | |
|---|---|---|---|---|---|---|---|---|
| Year | Bajra | Jowar | Moth | Urd | Mung | Sugar cane | Cotton | Makka |
| 1665 | 14.8 | 15.0 | 13.7 | 2.0 | 1.3 | – | 17.0 | – |
| 1669 | 16.0 | 21.4 | 15.3 | 4.8 | 2.5 | 2.0 | 27.0 | – |
| 1684 | 11.0 | 15.0 | 18.4 | 8.0 | 2.0 | 5.0 | 30.0 | – |
| 1685 | 11.0 | 18.0 | 9.6 | 4.0 | – | 7.8 | 44.0 | – |
| 1686 | 15.0 | 15.0 | 15.0 | 4.0 | – | 6.0 | 27.0 | 1.0 |
| 1688 | 4.7 | 14.0 | 13.0 | 5.0 | – | 8.0 | 28.0 | 2.0 |
| 1689 | – | 17.0 | 22.0 | 6.0 | – | 21.0 | 16.0 | – |
| 1691 | 4.0 | 16.0 | 20.0 | 5.0 | – | 9.0 | 30.0 | – |
| 1696 | 10.0 | 13.0 | 2.0 | – | – | 9.0 | 33.0 | 7.0 |
| 1706 | 24.0 | 23.0 | 17.0 | – | – | 5.0 | 19.0 | 1.0 |
| 1708 | 27.0 | 25.0 | 12.0 | 1.0 | – | 5.0 | 16.0 | 3.0 |
| 1710 | 12.0 | 13.0 | 32.0 | 7.0 | 4.0 | 3.0 | 18.0 | 2.0 |
| 1716 | 5.3 | 10.7 | 13.8 | 9.9 | 11.0 | 12.8 | 33.0 | 2.4 |
| 1717 | 18.4 | 5.6 | 3.4 | – | – | 29.8 | 29.9 | 2.8 |
| 1718 | 24.4 | 18.0 | 12.7 | 2.5 | – | 2.7 | 17.2 | 4.6 |
| 1720 | 12.2 | 6.7 | 13.0 | 4.1 | 2.0 | 14.4 | 23.0 | 9.9 |
| 1721 | 14.6 | 15.9 | 15.7 | 5.8 | 1.6 | 8.1 | 15.3 | 6.2 |
| 1723 | 17.0 | 17.6 | 13.8 | 27.0 | – | 5.1 | 23.0 | 6.2 |
| 1724 | 10.0 | 10.0 | 18.9 | 4.5 | 1.2 | 6.0 | 13.1 | 5.6 |
| 1725 | 8.6 | 5.9 | 16.4 | 10.3 | 1.2 | 10.5 | 25.4 | 6.8 |

(Table 1 contd.)

Table 1 contd.

### Pargana Chatsu

| Year | Bajra | Jowar | Moth | Urd | Kodon | Chola | Sugar cane | Cotton | Makka |
|------|-------|-------|------|-----|-------|-------|------------|--------|-------|
| 1664 | 54.0 | 8.4 | 13.0 | – | 1.6 | – | – | 7.0 | – |
| 1708 | 55.0 | 5.0 | 1.0 | 1.0 | – | – | – | – | – |
| 1710 | 40.0 | 7.6 | 26.0 | – | 3.0 | –. | – | 5.5 | 1.2 |
| 1711 | 51.0 | 3.4 | 16.0 | – | 4.3 | – | – | 10.0 | 1.8 |
| 1712 | 56.0 | 3.8 | 15.0 | – | 3.0 | – | – | 10.0 | 2.3 |
| 1713 | 11.0 | 12.0 | 35.0 | 4.0 | – | – | 5.2 | 6.2 | 4.4 |
| 1714 | 35.0 | 8.0 | 28.0 | – | 9.0 | – | – | 9.0 | 4.5 |
| 1715 | 41.0 | 7.0 | 26.0 | 1.9 | 4.5 | – | 2.0 | 7.0 | – |
| 1716 | 24.0 | – | 22.0 | 5.2 | 9.0 | – | – | 19.0 | – |
| 1721 | 35.0 | 9.0 | 21.0 | 2.0 | 4.8 | 1.8 | 1.8 | 10.0 | 5.5 |
| 1723 | 36.0 | 12.0 | 10.0 | – | 4.2 | 1.2 | – | 18.0 | 7.0 |
| 1724 | 15.0 | 11.0 | 37.0 | 1.2 | 3.7 | 3.3 | 1.0 | 9.0 | 2.8 |
| 1726 | 11.4 | 7.8 | 10.0 | 2.7 | 1.7 | 4.0 | 6.4 | 42.0 | 3.4 |
| 1730 | 10.0 | 1.8 | 13.0 | 3.0 | 10.0 | 1.8 | 6.3 | 32.0 | 6.5 |
| 1731 | 5.7 | 1.8 | – | – | – | – | 8.3 | 56.0 | 14.0 |
| 1733 | 7.8 | 2.3 | 19.0 | 3.4 | 9.8 | 2.7 | 4.2 | 24.0 | 8.6 |
| 1735 | 3.3 | – | 28.0 | 7.4 | 6.6 | 5.2 | 4.6 | 19.0 | 2.2 |
| 1736 | 14.0 | 7.5 | 6.8 | 2.0 | 5.8 | 5.5 | 4.5 | 31.0 | 12.0 |
| 1737 | 6.0 | 4.0 | 27.0 | 2.5 | 7.0 | 5.0 | 3.0 | 28.5 | 9.5 |
| 1740 | 7.7 | 4.8 | 19.0 | 3.7 | 9.0 | 4.0 | 2.4 | 20.0 | 11.0 |
| 1741 | 5.4 | 1.5 | 12.4 | 3.2 | 9.4 | 1.9 | 6.3 | 29.5 | 12.2 |
| 1742 | 11.0 | 10.0 | 3.2 | – | 4.7 | – | 8.9 | 40.4 | 11.3 |
| 1744 | 10.3 | 13.5 | 25.6 | 2.4 | 7.0 | 2.7 | 3.4 | 5.7 | 3.5 |
| 1745 | 14.1 | 10.3 | 16.2 | 3.0 | 7.3 | 2.9 | 3.0 | 11.0 | 12.8 |
| 1748 | 19.0 | 2.9 | 13.8 | 1.4 | 4.9 | 2.2 | – | 21.6 | 14.7 |
| 1749 | 11.5 | 4.5 | 14.4 | 2.8 | 5.0 | 2.1 | 1.7 | 18.8 | 19.2 |
| 1750 | 4.6 | 3.0 | 7.4 | – | – | – | 3.3 | 28.3 | 25.6 |

### Rabi

| Year | Pargana Jaipur | | | Pargana Malarna | | |
|------|-------|--------|------|-------|--------|------|
| | Wheat | Barley | Gram | Wheat | Barley | Gram |
| 1665 | – | – | – | 39.0 | 29.0 | 21.0 |
| 1677 | 5.1 | 49.6 | 40.0 | – | – | – |
| 1688 | 15.8 | 52.9 | 27.0 | – | – | – |
| 1689 | 10.0 | 57.0 | 23.9 | – | – | – |
| 1690 | 7.0 | 47.5 | 33.0 | 39.4 | 29.0 | 21.0 |
| 1711 | – | – | – | 1.0 | 14.0 | 40.0 |

(Table 1 contd.)

Table 1 contd.

| Year | Pargana Jaipur | | | Pargana Malarna | | |
|---|---|---|---|---|---|---|
| | Wheat | Barley | Gram | Wheat | Barley | Gram |
| 1712 | 21.7 | 58.0 | 12.0 | – | – | – |
| 1713 | – | – | – | 13.0 | 54.7 | 18.6 |
| 1714 | – | – | – | 19.9 | 66.0 | 9.7 |
| 1715 | 23.7 | 57.0 | 15.0 | 14.0 | 48.0 | – |
| 1716 | 31.4 | 50.6 | 17.0 | – | 53.0 | 23.0 |
| 1717 | – | – | – | 15.0 | 71.0 | 9.0 |
| 1718 | 29.0 | – | 1.2 | 17.0 | 69.0 | 11.0 |
| 1719 | – | – | – | 17.0 | 53.0 | 16.0 |
| 1720 | 17.4 | 72.0 | 4.0 | 25.0 | 38.0 | 8.0 |
| 1722 | – | – | – | 15.0 | 62.0 | 17.0 |
| 1723 | 16.0 | 77.8 | – | 17.0 | 65.0 | 10.0 |
| 1724 | 17.0 | 29.0 | 9.0 | – | – | – |
| 1725 | 10.5 | 50.0 | 29.5 | – | – | – |
| 1726 | – | – | – | 9.7 | 43.0 | 27.9 |
| 1727 | – | – | – | 18.6 | 41.0 | 28.9 |
| 1728 | – | 70.0 | 16.0 | 21.5 | 25.0 | 38.0 |
| 1729 | 12.6 | 61.5 | 6.0 | 13.8 | – | 35.7 |
| 1730 | – | – | – | 10.8 | 38.0 | 35.4 |
| 1732 | – | – | – | 8.5 | 67.0 | 20.0 |
| 1733 | 9.6 | 52.3 | 3.2 | – | – | – |
| 1734 | 15.3 | 73.4 | 1.0 | – | – | – |
| 1736 | – | – | – | 1.5 | 70.0 | – |
| 1737 | 11.7 | 82.0 | 1.6 | 17.9 | 68.0 | 7.5 |
| 1738 | – | – | – | 24.8 | 26.0 | 21.0 |
| 1743 | – | – | – | 37.6 | 45.8 | 8.5 |
| 1744 | 12.8 | 73.8 | 5.9 | 25.7 | 47.0 | 17.0 |
| 1745 | – | – | – | 21.8 | 36.9 | 19.7 |
| 1748 | – | – | – | 36.4 | 45.0 | 12.0 |
| 1749 | – | – | – | 34.5 | – | 25.0 |
| 1750 | – | – | – | 42.6 | 38.0 | 13.5 |

| Year | Pargana Bahatri | | | Pargana Chatsu | | | |
|---|---|---|---|---|---|---|---|
| | Wheat | Barley | Gram | Wheat | Barley | Gram | Chombli |
| 1665 | 14.5 | 61.8 | 17.0 | – | – | – | – |
| 1669 | 7.7 | 60.8 | 21.7 | – | – | – | – |
| 1686 | 11.7 | 61.5 | 11.7 | – | – | – | – |
| 1688 | 20.7 | 48.0 | 9.5 | – | – | – | – |
| 1689 | 24.4 | 45.0 | 8.6 | – | – | – | – |
| 1696 | 13.0 | 78.6 | – | – | – | – | – |

(Table 1 contd.)

Table 1 contd.

| Year | Pargana Bahatri | | | Pargana Chatsu | | | |
|------|-------|--------|------|-------|--------|------|---------|
|      | Wheat | Barley | Gram | Wheat | Barley | Gram | Chombli |
| 1697 | 14.7 | 72.4 | 4.3 | – | – | – | – |
| 1706 | 22.0 | 60.7 | 11.6 | – | – | – | – |
| 1708 | 21.0 | 63.0 | 7.8 | – | – | – | – |
| 1710 | 24.8 | 39.0 | 27.4 | 10.0 | 48.0 | 31.0 | 2.0 |
| 1711 | 30.0 | 34.0 | 28.0 | 16.0 | 41.0 | – | 2.0 |
| 1712 | – | – | – | 15.0 | 60.0 | 7.0 | 9.0 |
| 1713 | – | – | – | 30.0 | 49.0 | 14.0 | – |
| 1714 | – | – | – | 14.0 | 49.0 | 24.0 | 8.6 |
| 1716 | 32.0 | 42.0 | 18.0 | 13.0 | 37.0 | 27.0 | 10.0 |
| 1717 | 18.0 | 73.0 | – | 10.0 | 78.0 | – | 6.7 |
| 1718 | 17.0 | 70.0 | 3.0 | – | – | – | – |
| 1720 | 28.0 | 67.0 | – | – | – | – | – |
| 1721 | 25.0 | 58.0 | 9.0 | 15.0 | 57.0 | 18.0 | 2.8 |
| 1723 | 29.0 | 79.0 | 5.0 | 13.0 | 75.0 | – | 5.4 |
| 1724 | 28.0 | 52.0 | 11.0 | 17.0 | 52.0 | 14.0 | 4.0 |
| 1725 | 20.0 | 47.0 | 19.0 | – | – | – | – |
| 1726 | – | – | – | 10.0 | 57.0 | 9.0 | 12.5 |
| 1730 | – | – | – | 10.0 | 59.0 | 18.0 | 4.5 |
| 1731 | – | – | – | 8.0 | 77.0 | – | 7.9 |
| 1733 | – | – | – | 14.0 | 60.0 | 6.0 | 11.0 |
| 1735 | – | – | – | 13.0 | 56.0 | 12.0 | 3.5 |
| 1737 | – | – | – | 10.0 | 70.0 | 7.0 | 3.4 |
| 1738 | – | – | – | 8.0 | 63.0 | 13.0 | 9.8 |
| 1740 | – | – | – | 12.0 | 57.0 | 9.0 | 5.5 |
| 1741 | – | – | – | 13.0 | 60.0 | 13.0 | 4.7 |
| 1742 | – | – | – | 3.2 | 79.6 | 1.4 | 5.0 |
| 1743 | – | – | – | 8.0 | 74.0 | 4.0 | 6.4 |
| 1744 | – | – | – | 13.0 | 66.0 | 5.0 | 5.0 |
| 1745 | – | – | – | 13.0 | 63.0 | 5.0 | 11.9 |
| 1748 | – | – | – | 17.0 | 65.0 | 2.0 | 9.6 |
| 1749 | – | – | – | 11.0 | 64.0 | 7.0 | 10.0 |

Table 2
Rate of Revenue Demand per Bigha
(in Rupees)
Pargana Jaipur

| Year | Cotton | Sugarcane | Kodon | Makka | Chola |
|------|--------|-----------|-------|-------|-------|
| 1666 | 1.28 | 4.73 | 1.17 | 1.87 | 0.94 |
| 1677 | 1.35 | 4.64 | 1.17 | 1.61 | 0.61 |

(Table 2 contd.)

Table 2 contd.

| Year | Cotton | Sugarcane | Kodon | Makka | Chola |
|------|--------|-----------|-------|-------|-------|
| 1688 | 1.28 | 3.70 | 1.14 | 1.57 | 0.62 |
| 1689 | 1.33 | – | – | – | 0.60 |
| 1690 | 1.36 | 3.75 | 1.16 | 1.50 | 0.61 |
| 1712 | 1.13 | 2.62 | 1.08 | 1.28 | 0.49 |
| 1715 | 1.23 | 3.31 | 1.10 | 1.42 | 0.48 |
| 1716 | 1.18 | – | 1.07 | 1.34 | 0.49 |
| 1718 | 1.21 | 3.19 | 1.12 | 1.37 | 0.49 |
| 1720 | 1.20 | 3.22 | 1.03 | 1.28 | 0.50 |
| 1723 | 1.23 | 3.30 | 1.08 | 1.31 | 0.51 |
| 1724 | – | – | 1.08 | – | 0.50 |
| 1725 | 1.27 | 3.32 | 1.09 | 1.36 | 0.52 |
| 1728 | 1.23 | – | 1.00 | 2.00 | 0.64 |
| 1729 | 1.16 | 3.91 | 1.00 | 1.69 | 0.60 |
| 1733 | 1.18 | 3.74 | 1.11 | 1.46 | 0.57 |
| 1734 | 1.29 | 3.68 | 1.12 | 1.45 | 0.56 |
| 1736 | 1.29 | 3.69 | 1.11 | 1.42 | 0.57 |
| 1737 | 1.30 | 3.77 | 1.11 | 1.41 | 0.55 |
| 1744 | 1.36 | 3.68 | 1.11 | 1.41 | 0.56 |

Pargana Malarna

| Year | Cotton | Sugarcane | Kodon | Makka |
|------|--------|-----------|-------|-------|
| 1690 | 1.24 | 3.24 | 0.97 | – |
| 1699 | 1.09 | 2.69 | 1.00 | 0.87 |
| 1711 | 1.22 | 3.15 | 0.99 | 1.00 |
| 1713 | 1.21 | 3.11 | 0.96 | 0.94 |
| 1714 | 1.21 | 3.06 | 0.98 | 0.98 |
| 1715 | 1.15 | 3.01 | 0.95 | 1.00 |
| 1716 | 1.22 | 2.96 | 0.98 | 1.00 |
| 1717 | 1.19 | 7.89 | 1.00 | – |
| 1718 | 1.18 | 3.06 | 0.93 | 0.88 |
| 1719 | 1.18 | 2.86 | 0.88 | 0.91 |
| 1720 | 1.19 | 3.07 | 0.98 | 1.00 |
| 1721 | 1.21 | 3.15 | 0.97 | 1.00 |
| 1722 | 1.22 | 3.13 | 0.97 | 1.00 |
| 1723 | 1.20 | 3.19 | 0.97 | 0.97 |
| 1726 | 1.21 | 3.18 | 0.99 | 1.00 |
| 1727 | 1.24 | 3.24 | 0.99 | 1.00 |
| 1728 | 1.22 | 3.25 | 0.99 | 1.00 |
| 1729 | 1.23 | 3.22 | 0.99 | 1.00 |
| 1730 | 1.24 | 3.16 | 0.99 | 1.00 |

(Table 2 contd.)

Table 2 contd.

| Year | Cotton | Sugarcane | Kodon | Makka |
|------|--------|-----------|-------|-------|
| 1731 | 1.23 | 3.19 | 1.00 | 0.97 |
| 1732 | 1.22 | 3.21 | 0.96 | 0.94 |
| 1736 | 1.23 | 3.18 | 0.99 | 0.99 |
| 1737 | 1.23 | 3.16 | 0.99 | 0.98 |
| 1738 | 1.23 | 3.17 | 1.00 | 0.99 |
| 1743 | 1.21 | 3.02 | – | 0.98 |
| 1744 | 1.21 | 3.14 | 0.99 | 0.98 |
| 1745 | 1.15 | 3.09 | 0.97 | 0.98 |
| 1748 | 1.17 | 3.09 | 0.99 | 0.98 |
| 1749 | 1.17 | 3.11 | 0.96 | 0.98 |
| 1750 | 1.09 | 3.97 | 0.99 | 0.99 |

Pargana Bahatri

| Year | Cotton | Sugarcane | Kodon | Makka |
|------|--------|-----------|-------|-------|
| 1665 | 1.41 | 2.00 | – | 1.74 |
| 1669 | 1.44 | 2.00 | – | 1.79 |
| 1684 | 1.45 | 2.00 | – | – |
| 1685 | 1.40 | 2.00 | 1.60 | 1.60 |
| 1686 | 1.44 | 2.00 | 1.40 | 1.23 |
| 1688 | 1.30 | 1.80 | – | 1.25 |
| 1689 | 1.39 | 2.00 | 1.50 | 1.74 |
| 1691 | 1.25 | 2.00 | 1.25 | 1.80 |
| 1696 | 1.25 | 1.75 | 1.25 | 1.33 |
| 1706 | 1.30 | 1.90 | 1.40 | 1.30 |
| 1708 | 1.36 | 1.83 | 1.33 | 1.25 |
| 1710 | 1.34 | 1.87 | 1.44 | 1.25 |
| 1716 | 1.30 | 2.00 | 1.50 | 1.20 |
| 1717 | 1.25 | 1.91 | 1.46 | 1.21 |
| 1718 | 1.37 | 1.96 | 1.46 | 1.19 |
| 1720 | 1.34 | 2.00 | 1.40 | 1.23 |
| 1721 | 1.33 | 1.94 | 1.39 | 1.24 |
| 1723 | 1.35 | 1.96 | 1.40 | 1.24 |
| 1724 | 1.42 | 1.95 | 1.47 | 1.24 |

*Pargana* Chatsu

| Year | Cotton | Sugarcane | Kodon | Makka |
|------|--------|-----------|-------|-------|
| 1664 | 0.82 | 2.00 | 0.83 | 1.09 |
| 1708 | 1.24 | – | 1.12 | 1.36 |
| 1709 | 1.23 | – | 0.96 | 1.41 |
| 1710 | 1.12 | – | 1.03 | 0.95 |

(Table 2 contd.)

Table 2 contd.

| Year | Cotton | Sugarcane | Kodon | Makka |
|------|--------|-----------|-------|-------|
| 1711 | 1.11 | 2.02 | 1.00 | 1.07 |
| 1712 | 1.11 | 2.30 | 0.98 | 1.08 |
| 1713 | 1.14 | 1.06 | 1.41 | 1.24 |
| 1714 | 1.10 | 2.20 | 0.95 | 1.05 |
| 1715 | 1.11 | 2.45 | 0.97 | 1.10 |
| 1716 | 1.11 | 2.71 | 0.94 | 1.08 |
| 1717 | 1.10 | 2.59 | 0.90 | 0.93 |
| 1721 | 1.11 | 2.75 | 0.97 | 1.10 |
| 1723 | 1.08 | 2.74 | 0.95 | 1.08 |
| 1724 | 1.11 | 2.91 | 0.98 | 1.10 |
| 1726 | 1.12 | 2.97 | 1.08 | 1.10 |
| 1730 | 1.10 | 2.91 | 0.98 | 1.08 |
| 1731 | 1.08 | 2.82 | – | 1.07 |
| 1733 | 1.11 | 2.97 | 0.98 | 1.09 |
| 1735 | 1.11 | 2.97 | 0.98 | 1.05 |
| 1736 | 1.07 | 2.92 | 0.96 | 1.05 |
| 1737 | 1.09 | 2.93 | 0.92 | 1.06 |
| 1740 | 1.09 | 2.94 | 0.95 | 1.09 |
| 1741 | 1.10 | 2.88 | 0.96 | 1.09 |
| 1742 | 1.10 | 2.91 | 0.97 | 1.09 |
| 1744 | 1.10 | 2.73 | 0.97 | 1.07 |
| 1745 | 1.09 | 2.86 | 0.97 | 1.06 |
| 1748 | 1.07 | 2.44 | 0.94 | 1.04 |
| 1749 | 1.08 | 2.59 | 0.96 | 1.06 |
| 1750 | 1.10 | 2.91 | – | 1.07 |

Table 3
Average Price of Principal *Jinsi* Crops
(in Maunds per Rupee)

| Year | Kharif | | | | | Rabi | | | |
|------|--------|-------|------|------|------|-------|-------|--------|------|
|      | Bajra | Jowar | Moth | Urd | Mung | Chola | Wheat | Barley | Gram |
| 1666 | 2.25 | 2.48 | 2.43 | 2.26 | 1.98 | 2.46 | – | – | – |
| 1677 | 1.41 | 1.42 | 1.43 | 1.21 | 1.11 | 1.40 | 1.02 | 1.53 | – |
| 1688 | 1.35 | 1.35 | – | 1.21 | 1.31 | 1.47 | 1.33 | 1.71 | 1.69 |
| 1690 | 1.85 | 2.23 | 2.50 | 1.86 | 1.77 | 2.33 | 1.46 | 2.11 | 2.14 |
| 1708 | 1.42 | 1.59 | 1.37 | 0.98 | 1.02 | – | 0.85 | 1.26 | 1.05 |
| 1712 | 0.65 | 0.79 | 0.56 | 0.44 | 0.41 | 0.39 | 0.41 | 0.52 | 1.35 |
| 1715 | 0.78 | 0.80 | 0.75 | 0.69 | 0.57 | 0.71 | 0.83 | 1.07 | 1.07 |
| 1716 | 0.88 | 0.71 | 0.91 | 0.73 | 0.67 | 0.96 | – | 1.30 | 1.34 |

(Table 3 contd.)

Table 3 contd.

| | Kharif | | | | Rabi | | | |
|---|---|---|---|---|---|---|---|---|
| Year | Bajra | Jowar | Moth | Urd | Mung | Chola | Wheat | Barley | Gram |
| 1718 | 0.59 | 0.63 | 0.55 | 0.51 | 0.42 | 0.53 | 0.58 | 0.78 | – |
| 1720 | 1.01 | 1.14 | 1.08 | 0.99 | 0.86 | 1.11 | 0.68 | 0.88 | 0.82 |
| 1723 | 0.91 | 1.00 | 0.91 | 0.86 | 0.79 | 0.91 | 0.76 | 0.94 | 0.80 |
| 1725 | 1.13 | 1.41 | 1.18 | 0.83 | 0.80 | 0.97 | 0.99 | 1.42 | 1.41 |
| 1728 | 1.08 | 2.24 | 1.14 | 1.57 | 0.24 | 1.36 | 1.58 | 2.04 | 1.58 |
| 1729 | 0.80 | 0.96 | 0.92 | 0.96 | 0.85 | – | 0.75 | 0.99 | 0.91 |
| 1733 | 0.99 | 1.23 | 0.99 | 0.87 | 0.81 | 0.93 | 0.76 | 1.02 | 0.90 |
| 1734 | 0.83 | 1,13 | 0.95 | 0.92 | 0.80 | 1.02 | 0.74 | 0.98 | 0.87 |
| 1737 | 0.59 | 0.73 | 0.66 | 0.77 | 0.53 | 0.70 | 0.56 | 0.75 | 0.58 |
| 1744 | 0.88 | 1.11 | 0.95 | 0.75 | 0.75 | 0.84 | 0.91 | 1.36 | 1.05 |
| 1748 | 0.68 | 0.69 | 0.72 | 0.65 | 0.62 | – | 0.55 | 0.75 | 0.62 |
| 1750 | 0.90 | 0.93 | 0.84 | 0.78 | 0.76 | – | 0.55 | 0.75 | 0.62 |

Table 4

Proportion of Revenue from Kharif and
Rabi Harvests

Pargana Jaipur

| | % of Total Revenue | | % of Kharif Revenue | | % of Rabi Revenue | |
|---|---|---|---|---|---|---|
| Year | Kharif | Rabi | Zabti | Jinsi | Zabti | Jinsi |
| 1667 | 49.0 | 51.0 | 24.0 | 76.0 | 1.0 | 99.0 |
| 1688 | 18.0 | 82.0 | 41.0 | 59.0 | 2.0 | 98.0 |
| 1689 | 38.0 | 62.0 | 32.0 | 68.0 | 1.0 | 99.0 |
| 1690 | 46.0 | 54.0 | 37.0 | 63.0 | 3.0 | 97.0 |
| 1712 | 42.0 | 58.0 | 29.0 | 71.0 | 1.0 | 99.0 |
| 1715 | 47.0 | 53.0 | 58.0 | 42.0 | 2.0 | 98.0 |
| 1716 | 33.0 | 67.0 | 62.0 | 38.0 | 3.0 | 97.0 |
| 1718 | 55.0 | 45.0 | 49.0 | 51.0 | 4.0 | 96.0 |
| 1720 | 37.0 | 63.0 | 55.0 | 45.0 | 2.0 | 98.0 |
| 1723 | 48.0 | 52.0 | 50.0 | 50.0 | 2.0 | 98.0 |
| 1724 | 89.0 | 11.0 | 60.0 | 40.0 | 30.0 | 70.0 |
| 1725 | 19.0 | 81.0 | 76.0 | 24.0 | 1.0 | 99.0 |
| 1733 | 34.0 | 66.0 | 72.0 | 28.0 | 1.0 | 99.0 |
| 1734 | 38.0 | 62.0 | 58.0 | 42.0 | 2.0 | 98.0 |
| 1737 | 39.0 | 61.0 | 57.0 | 43.0 | 1.0 | 99.0 |
| 1744 | 30.0 | 70.0 | 63.0 | 37.0 | 2.0 | 98.0 |

(Table 4 contd.)

Table 4 contd.

## Pargana Malarna

| Year | % of Total Revenue | | % of Kharif Revenue | | % of Rabi Revenue | |
|---|---|---|---|---|---|---|
| | Kharif | Rabi | Zabti | Jinsi | Zabti | Jinsi |
| 1690 | 70.0 | 30.0 | 29.0 | 71.0 | 2.0 | 98.0 |
| 1711 | 50.0 | 50.0 | 50.0 | 50.0 | 2.0 | 98.0 |
| 1712 | 96.0 | 4.0 | 92.0 | 8.0 | 1.0 | 99.0 |
| 1713 | 63.0 | 37.0 | 11.0 | 89.0 | 60.0 | 40.0 |
| 1714 | 56.0 | 44.0 | 23.0 | 77.0 | – | 100.0 |
| 1715 | 55.0 | 45.0 | 24.0 | 76.0 | – | 100.0 |
| 1716 | 83.0 | 17.0 | 27.0 | 73.0 | – | 100.0 |
| 1717 | 20.0 | 80.0 | 15.0 | 85.0 | – | 100.0 |
| 1718 | 79.0 | 21.0 | 23.0 | 77.0 | – | 100.0 |
| 1719 | 30.0 | 70.0 | 13.0 | 87.0 | – | 100.0 |
| 1720 | 70.0 | 30.0 | 17.0 | 83.0 | – | 100.0 |
| 1722 | 81.0 | 19.0 | 13.0 | 87.0 | – | 100.0 |
| 1723 | 86.0 | 14.0 | 13.0 | 87.0 | 5.0 | 100.0 |
| 1726 | 72.0 | 28.0 | 34.0 | 66.0 | – | 95.0 |
| 1727 | 70.0 | 30.0 | 22.0 | 78.0 | 5.0 | 100.0 |
| 1728 | 79.0 | 21.0 | 18.0 | 82.0 | – | 95.0 |
| 1729 | 58.0 | 42.0 | 26.0 | 74.0 | 5.0 | 95.0 |
| 1732 | 62.0 | 38.0 | 50.0 | 50.0 | 5.0 | 95.0 |
| 1736 | 59.0 | 41.0 | 45.0 | 55.0 | – | 95.0 |
| 1737 | 52.0 | 48.0 | 31.0 | 69.0 | 5.0 | 95.0 |
| 1738 | 33.0 | 67.0 | 15.0 | 85.0 | 5.0 | 95.0 |
| 1743 | 36.0 | 64.0 | 23.0 | 87.0 | 5.0 | 95.0 |
| 1744 | 31.0 | 69.0 | 27.0 | 73.0 | 5.0 | 95.0 |
| 1745 | 61.0 | 39.0 | 20.0 | 80.0 | – | 100.0 |

## Pargana Bahatri

| Year | % of Total Revenue | | % of Kharif Revenue | | % of Rabi Revenue | |
|---|---|---|---|---|---|---|
| | Kharif | Rabi | Zabti | Jinsi | Zabti | Jinsi |
| 1665 | 73.3 | 26.6 | 27.8 | 72.1 | 3.00 | 97.0 |
| 1669 | 63.3 | 36.6 | 30.0 | 70.0 | 2.0 | 98.0 |
| 1684 | 48.1 | 51.8 | 40.0 | 60.0 | 2.0 | 98.0 |
| 1685 | 63.4 | 36.5 | 57.0 | 43.0 | – | – |
| 1686 | 64.8 | 35.1 | 47.0 | 53.0 | 4.0 | 96.0 |
| 1688 | 35.8 | 64.1 | 56.0 | 44.0 | 8.0 | 94.0 |
| 1689 | 53.9 | 46.1 | 60.0 | 40.0 | 8.0 | 92.0 |
| 1691 | 55.2 | 44.7 | 52.0 | 48.0 | 4.0 | 96.0 |

(Table 4 contd.)

Table 4 contd.

| Year | % of Total Revenue | | % of Kharif Revenue | | % of Rabi Revenue | |
|------|--------|------|-------|-------|-------|-------|
|      | Kharif | Rabi | Zabti | Jinsi | Zabti | Jinsi |
| 1696 | 24.1 | 75.8 | 73.0 | 27.0 | 96.4 | 4.0 |
| 1706 | 66.3 | 33.6 | 32.0 | 68.0 | 4.0 | 96.0 |
| 1708 | 74.0 | 25.9 | 31.0 | 69.0 | 4.0 | 96.0 |
| 1710 | 48.0 | 51.9 | 28.0 | 72.0 | 35.0 | 65.0 |
| 1716 | 23.7 | 76.2 | 58.0 | 42.0 | 2.0 | 98.0 |
| 1717 | 21.3 | 78.6 | 73.0 | 27.0 | 8.0 | 92.0 |
| 1718 | 71.5 | 28.4 | 39.0 | 61.0 | 7.0 | 93.0 |
| 1720 | 41.1 | 58.8 | 59.0 | 41.0 | 3.0 | 97.0 |
| 1721 | 49.0 | 50.0 | 42.0 | 58.0 | 3.0 | 97.0 |
| 1723 | 65.7 | 34.2 | 45.0 | 55.0 | 4.0 | 96.0 |
| 1724 | 55.1 | 44.8 | 36.0 | 64.0 | 3.0 | 97.0 |
| 1725 | 42.2 | 55.7 | 54.0 | 46.0 | 3.0 | 97.0 |

Pargana Chatsu

| Year | % of Total Revenue | | % of Kharif Revenue | | % of Rabi Revenue | |
|------|--------|------|-------|-------|-------|-------|
|      | Kharif | Rabi | Zabti | Jinsi | Zabti | Jinsi |
| 1708 | 82.0 | 18.0 | 66.0 | 34.0 | 41.0 | 59.0 |
| 1709 | 53.0 | 47.0 | 19.0 | 81.0 | 68.0 | 32.0 |
| 1710 | 53.0 | 47.0 | 13.0 | 87.0 | 40.0 | 60.0 |
| 1711 | 55.0 | 45.0 | 20.0 | 80.0 | 6.0 | 94.0 |
| 1712 | 52.0 | 48.0 | 19.0 | 81.0 | 10.0 | 90.0 |
| 1713 | 66.0 | 34.0 | 27.0 | 73.0 | 3.0 | 97.0 |
| 1714 | 58.0 | 42.0 | 33.0 | 67.0 | 10.0 | 90.0 |
| 1716 | 54.0 | 46.0 | 42.0 | 58.0 | 13.0 | 87.0 |
| 1717 | 22.0 | 78.0 | 27.0 | 73.0 | 9.0 | 91.0 |
| 1721 | 63.0 | 37.0 | 26.0 | 74.0 | 4.0 | 96.0 |
| 1723 | 74.0 | 26.0 | 37.0 | 63.0 | 7.0 | 93.0 |
| 1724 | 58.0 | 42.0 | 26.0 | 74.0 | 6.0 | 94.0 |
| 1726 | 46.0 | 54.0 | 61.0 | 39.0 | 2.0 | 98.0 |
| 1730 | 33.0 | 67.0 | 66.0 | 34.0 | – | 100.00 |
| 1731 | 44.0 | 56.0 | 91.0 | 9.0 | 11.0 | 89.0 |
| 1733 | 53.0 | 47.0 | 49.0 | 51.0 | 13.0 | 87.0 |
| 1735 | 51.0 | 49.0 | 14.0 | 86.0 | 4.0 | 96.0 |
| 1737 | 39.0 | 61.0 | 51.0 | 49.0 | 4.0 | 96.0 |
| 1744 | 26.0 | 74.0 | 33.0 | 67.0 | 7.0 | 93.0 |
| 1748 | 45.0 | 55.0 | 52.0 | 48.0 | 12.0 | 88.0 |
| 1749 | 37.0 | 63.0 | 57.0 | 43.0 | 11.0 | 89.0 |

## Table 5
### Table Showing the Percentage of Area under Different Crops
#### Pargana Jaipur

| Year | Bajra | Jowar | Moth | Chola | Sugarcane | Cotton | Makka |
|------|-------|-------|------|-------|-----------|--------|-------|
| 1677 | 25.0  | 1.5   | 64.0 | 0.4   | 0.3       | 6.2    | 0.35  |
| 1744 | 5.0   | 4.7   | 41.0 | 9.1   | 2.3       | 4.8    | 10.7  |

#### Pargana Malarna

| Year | Bajra | Jowar | Moth | Kodon | Sugarcane | Cotton | Makka |
|------|-------|-------|------|-------|-----------|--------|-------|
| 1690 | 12.6  | 16.6  | 50.0 | –     | 4.0       | 4.0    | –     |
| 1749 | 19.8  | 28.0  | 25.0 | 0.78  | 1.8       | 2.1    | 1.7   |

#### Pargana Bahatri

| Year | Bajra | Jowar | Moth | Urd  | Kodon | Chola | Sugar cane | Cotton | Makka |
|------|-------|-------|------|------|-------|-------|-----------|--------|-------|
| 1665 | 20.0  | 14.0  | 45.0 | –    | –     | –     | –         | 9.0    |       |
| 1725 | 5.7   | 2.6   | 36.0 | 20.0 | 1.2   | 1.3   | 4.0       | 14.0   | 5.0   |

#### Pargana Chatsu

| Year | Bajra | Jowar | Moth | Kodon | Chola | Sugar cane | Cotton | Makka |
|------|-------|-------|------|-------|-------|-----------|--------|-------|
| 1708 | 55.0  | 0.5   | 0.9  | –     | 1.8   | –         | 0.3    | –     |
| 1710 | 32.0  | 3.7   | 51.0 | 2.0   | 0.7   | –         | 3.0    | 0.9   |
| 1749 | 10.9  | 2.6   | 33.0 | 5.5   | 4.0   | 0.7       | 18.6   | 19.7  |

#### *Rabi*
#### Pargana Jaipur

| Year | Wheat | Barley | Gram |
|------|-------|--------|------|
| 1677 | 3.0   | 55.0   | 40.0 |
| 1744 | 6.5   | 79.0   | 5.0  |

#### Pargana Malarna

| Year | Wheat | Barley | Gram |
|------|-------|--------|------|
| 1690 | 32.0  | 34.0   | 25.0 |
| 1749 | 27.0  | 42.0   | 25.0 |

(Table 5 contd.)

Table 5 contd.

### Pargana Bahatri

| | | | |
|---|---|---|---|
| 1665 | 9.0 | 71.0 | 16.0 |
| 1725 | 12.0 | 52.0 | 19.0 |

### Pargana Chatsu

| | | | | Chomli |
|---|---|---|---|---|
| 1708 | 8.0 | 35.0 | 2.0 | 44.0 |
| 1710 | 8.0 | 55.0 | 28.0 | 2.6 |
| 1749 | 10.0 | 70.0 | 6.0 | 8.0 |

# 18

❦❧

## Prices of Food Grains in the Territories of Amber (c.1650–1750)*

An attempt has been made in the present paper to present the prices of principal food grains in the territories of the state of Amber from the middle of the seventeenth to the middle of the eighteenth century (Table 5).[1] The figures are taken from the *arhsattas* preserved in the Rajasthan State Archives, Bikaner. The arhsattas are not available for the entire period continuously and the gaps are considerable. The prices are based on either the actual sale price of grain collected as revenue or the national price of the revenue realized in grain. Consequently the price of commodities for which revenue was charged by measurement (*zabti*) is given in the arhsattas only occasionally and the figures are inadequate for any detailed examination. In this category, mention may be made of *chola, kodon, makka,* sugar cane, and cotton. Thus excluding these crops, the prices of all the important food grains[2] have been discussed, viz. *kharif*: bajra, jowar, moth, urd, and *mung*; and *rabi*: wheat, barley, gram.

The area selected for the study comprises the contiguous parganas of Amber (later Sawai Jaipur) Chatsu, Dausa, Lalsot, Bahatri (Baswa), and Malarna. In order to make comparison possible, all prices have been given in rupees (fraction being calculated in terms of decimals) per *maund*. In the original, the

* In collaboration with S. P. Gupta, *Proceedings of Indian History Congress,* XXIX Session, Patiala, 1967, pp. 345–67.

figures are, of course, given in terms of quantity per rupee. But in view of the fluctuations in the number of *seers* per maund, which were observed not only in terms of different parganas but also in different years in the same pargana and sometime in terms of different commodities, the prices have been calculated in terms of the maund of 40 seers. It has been assumed, of course, that the weight of a seer has remained constant. This assumption may not be true; but at present there is not enough evidence to verify this assumption.

The study also suffers from the inadequacy of data in another important respect. No account is taken of seasonal variation of prices. When comparative prices are given, it is not known whether they relate to the same or to different periods. Similarly, the differences in quality have not been taken into account. Nevertheless, it has been assumed that the prices given represent the average in terms of quality, which were prevailing soon after the realization of revenue, roughly at the same time of the year after each harvest. A sample check conducted on the basis of a few of the table of rates (*nirakh jamabandi* and *nirkh bazar*) conveys the impression that the assumption is probably valid.[3]

## Pargana-wise Comparison of Prices

An examination of the table of prices reveals considerable variations in prices prevailing in different parganas. The variation is less marked in the case of rabi crops than in the case of the kharif crops. Further, the variation tends to be less during the reign of Aurangzeb than in the period 1710–50. It may also be observed that the relative position of the different food grains differs from pargana to pargana and the changes in the comparative value of the different grains over the years do not follow a uniform pattern either.

Notwithstanding the above observations, it may be noticed that in the years of a sharp rise in prices as well as in years of sharp decline, these tendencies are noticeable in all parganas. In other words, while sharp price rise or acute depression affected the prices in all the parganas, there remained a considerable divergence in the prices prevailing in the different parganas as well as in the relative value of the commodities.

This may partly be explained due to differences in productivity and the geographical condition of even adjoining parganas. For example, during the reign of Akbar, Amber had one *dastur* while Chatsu and Malarna had another. The difference in the standard revenue per bigha was considerable, as may be seen from Table 1.

Table 1
Standard Demand per Bigha in Dam and Jital[4]

|  | Kharif | | | |
|  | Amber | | Chatsu & Malarna | |
|  | D. | J. | D. | J. |
| --- | --- | --- | --- | --- |
| Jowar | 11 | 16 | 32 | 22 |
| Moth | 15 | 16 | 22 | 9 |
| Urd | 39 | 2 | 39 | 3 |
| Mung | 15 | 16 | 36 | 22 |
|  | Rabi | | | |
| Wheat | 31 | 8 | 53 | 18 |
| Barley | 20 | 3 | 38 | 0 |
| Gram | 20 | 3 | 38 | 0 |

The difference is also due to a variety of other factors. Food grain which are consumed locally and are not generally exported to other areas would naturally show a greater variation. This may be noticed in the case of jowar and bajra. In the case of wheat, gram, and barley, the difference in the price is not as marked. Another important factor would be the increase or decrease of area under cultivation under a particular crop. It has been observed that the increase or decrease in the percentage of area under different crops differs from pargana to pargana.[5] The inadequacy of transport would of course contribute materially to the variation in prices even in contiguous parganas. The overall picture, however, does indicate that although the impact of money economy was felt in the countryside, the process had not unfolded itself fully, as may be seen also in the differences in the value of the *taka* from pargana to pargana (Table 6).

A sample study of the prices prevailing in the different villages of the same pargana reveals that the range of variation in prices as between different villages was small, suggesting that the self-sufficiency of the village had been appreciably reduced, as would appear from Table 2.

Table 2
Variation in the Prices of Food Grains as Between
Villages of the same Pargana
(in rupees per *maund*)

|  | Kharif | | |
|---|---|---|---|
|  | Chatsu 1684 | Chatsu 1730 | Malarna 1730 |
| Bajra | 0.55 to 0.68 | 1.66 to 2.00 | 2.00 to 2.31 |
| Jowar | 0.59 to 0.69 | 1.66 to 1.90 | 2.00 to 2.28 |
| Moth | 0.73 to 0.85 | 1.48 to 1.90 | 1.74 to 2.10 |
| Urd | 1.00 to 1.14 | 1.55 to 1.90 | 1.85 to 2.10 |
| Mung | 1.21 to 1.29 | 1.66 to 2.10 | 1.81 to 2.10 |
|  | Rabi | | |
| Wheat | Not available | 1.66 to 1.78 | 1.79 to 2.00 |
| Barley | Not available | 1.29 to 1.43 | 1.37 to 1.50 |
| Gram | Not available | 1.42 to 1.55 | 1.37 to 1.54 |

## Crop-wise Comparison of Prices

The changes in the prices of different food grains relative to wheat may be observed from Table 3 for selected representative years.

Table 3
Relative Price of Different Food Grains
(Index: Wheat being 100 in each Pargana in each year)

| | Amber | | | | | | | |
|---|---|---|---|---|---|---|---|---|
| Year | Wheat | Barley | Gram | Bajra | Jowar | Moth | Urd | Mung |
| 1677 | 100 | 67 | 67 | 45 | 74 | 71 | 84 | 92 |
| 1715 | 100 | 70 | 72 | 100 | 98 | 103 | 110 | 131 |
| 1725 | 100 | 67 | 72 | 85 | 67 | 80 | 115 | 118 |
| 1734 | 100 | 76 | 86 | 88 | 66 | 80 | 115 | 92 |
| 1744 | 100 | – | 94 | 116 | 88 | 104 | 131 | 130 |

Table 3 contd.

Chatsu

| 1714 | 100 | 71 | 94 | 79 | 68 | 86 | 124 | 151 |
|---|---|---|---|---|---|---|---|---|
| 1726 | 100 | 74 | 78 | 87 | 77 | 100 | 111 | 133 |
| 1735 | 100 | 79 | 84 | 108 | 96 | 83 | 85 | 97 |
| 1744 | 100 | 67 | 85 | 101 | 84 | 94 | 126 | 133 |

Dausa

| 1700 | 100 | 72 | 84 | 58 | 55 | 69 | 85 | 88 |
|---|---|---|---|---|---|---|---|---|
| 1715 | 100 | 76 | 77 | 99 | 86 | 106 | 114 | 124 |
| 1736 | 100 | 79 | 104 | 108 | 95 | 110 | 118 | 140 |
| 1744 | 100 | 66 | 85 | 96 | 81 | 84 | 110 | 100 |
| 1750 | 100 | 74 | 90 | 72 | 72 | 86 | 108 | 93 |

Lalsot

| 1715 | 100 | 73 | 75 | 150 | – | 151 | 184 | 191 |
|---|---|---|---|---|---|---|---|---|
| 1734 | 100 | 73 | 82 | 110 | 100 | 94 | 100 | 112 |
| 1741 | 100 | 97 | 106 | 116 | – | 100 | 115 | 134 |
| 1745 | 100 | 58 | 67 | 58 | 88 | 57 | 90 | 90 |

Bahatri

| 1665 | 100 | 66 | 70 | 62 | 56 | 59 | 72 | 59 |
|---|---|---|---|---|---|---|---|---|
| 1689 | 100 | 71 | 70 | 82 | 67 | 65 | 72 | 87 |
| 1716 | 100 | 68 | 69 | 114 | 96 | 87 | 81 | 111 |
| 1725 | 100 | 70 | 67 | 75 | 73 | 57 | 63 | 68 |

Malarna

| 1690 | 100 | 79 | 73 | 82 | 81 | 70 | 75 | 84 |
|---|---|---|---|---|---|---|---|---|
| 1715 | 100 | 68 | 70 | 106 | 118 | 123 | 145 | 151 |
| 1726 | 100 | 76 | 76 | 88 | 74 | 89 | 104 | 100 |
| 1732 | 100 | 80 | 81 | 77 | 66 | 78 | 91 | 88 |
| 1744 | 100 | 77 | 87 | 85 | 71 | 95 | 144 | 120 |

## *Pargana Amber*

Among the kharif crops, a remarkable increase in the absolute
and relative price of bajra may be observed. Between 1666 and
1690, bajra was selling at between 0.44 and 0.54 rupee per
maund at approximately half the price of wheat. In the second
decade of the eighteenth century, the price of bajra shoots up

and becomes level with wheat. Compared to wheat, the price falls by 12 per cent to 15 per cent during the next twenty years but again rises in the mid-forties. This was perhaps the result of a decline in the area under bajra from 25 per cent in 1667 to only 5 per cent in 1744.

In the case of jowar on the other hand, the index of price in terms of wheat rises from 74 in 1667 to 98 in 1715, declines to around 66 for the next twenty years, and then again rises to 88. The area under jowar increases from 1.5 per cent to 4.7 per cent. Although in 1744, the area under jowar and bajra is about the same, the price of jowar is appreciably less (0.89 per maund) than that of bajra (1.18 per maund), whereas in 1666 the price of the two commodities was about the same. Since jowar and bajra constitute the staple diet of the population, and since under 10 per cent of the cultivated area was under these crops, it appears quite possible that either the peasants had started consuming makka and barley in a greater measure or that jowar and bajra were being imported from the neighbouring parganas.

Among the pulses, the most important was moth although its cultivated area declined from 64 per cent in 1657 to 41 per cent in 1744. The index of the relative price of moth, urd, and mung rises from 71, 84 and 92 in 1677 to 104, 131, and 130 in 1744 respectively. This remarkable increase however is not continuous and the position in the twenties and the thirties is not much different from the earlier date. However, relative to moth, urd has become particularly expensive, which may be due to a decrease in the area under cotton with which it is generally grown.

Among the rabi crops, there is a decline in the relative position of wheat between 1677 and 1744. Compared to the general increase in the price of food grains, the increase in the price of wheat is not particularly sharp, although there was very probably an average increase of 30 per cent to 40 per cent. This may have been due to an increase in the area under wheat cultivation from 0.3 per cent to 6.5 per cent.

Although the area under barley increases from 55 per cent to 79 per cent between 1667 and 1744, it more or less retains its distance from wheat. Gram on the other hand becomes more expensive compared to wheat because of the sharp decline in the cultivated area from 40 per cent to 50 per cent.

## Pargana Chatsu

Although the general level of prices in pargana Chatsu is higher than in pargana Amber, the trend in the change of relative prices in Chatsu is more or less the same as in Amber. There is a marked increase in the price of bajra between 1664 and 1749, and compared to 1708 the price of bajra relative to wheat increases by about the middle of the century. Until about 1744, the index is almost level with wheat though in the subsequent years, the index tends to revert to 80. During the period 1719 to 1749, the percentage of area under bajra falls from 30 to 10.9.

Although jowar fetched about the same price as bajra in 1664, its price compared to bajra was definitely less in the subsequent years. During the period 1710 and 1749, the percentage of area under jowar falls from 3.6 to 2.7, but relative to bajra the area under jowar increases considerably. So far as the pulses are concerned, these prices relative to wheat remain more or less the same with moth selling for less than wheat and urd and mung at appreciably more. The area under moth declines from 51 per cent in 1717 to 33 per cent in 1749. The position of barley relative to wheat does not change materially during the period 1701–18, but in 1749 there is a sudden increase. The figure for 1749 may not be taken into account as it probably was an exceptional year for barley. The cultivated area increases from 55 per cent in 1710 to 70 per cent in 1719. The price of gram ranges from 20 per cent less than wheat to about 5 per cent more than wheat. The area under gram falls from 28 per cent in 1710 to 6 per cent in 1749.

## Pargana Malarna

In pargana Malarna, the price of bajra relative to wheat remains more or less the same between 1699 and 1744, but it tends to fall in 1749 and 1750. In fact, compared to 1690, there is no significant increase in the price of bajra in 1749 and 1750. This may have been due to an increase in the area under bajra from 12.6 per cent in 1690 to 19.8 per cent in 1749. The index of the relative price of jowar on the other hand shows a fall from 81 in 1690 to 71 in 1744. The actual price of jowar in 1719 is only very slightly more than what it was in 1690. Notwithstanding the relative fall in the power of jowar, the area under its cultivation rises from 16.6 per cent in 1690 to 28 per cent in 1749.

The index of the price of pulses, on the other hand, reveals a significant increase between the period 1690 and 1741, with the rise in index being more significant in the case of urd. This may have been due to a sharp decrease in the area under moth from 50 per cent in 1690 to 25 per cent in 1749. The reduction by half in the percentage of area under cotton between 1690 and 1749 was perhaps responsible for a proportionate decrease in the area under urd.

The relative position of wheat, barley, and gram remains practically the same throughout the period between 1690 and 1749. During this period, the percentage of area under the different crops does not undergo much change, as would appear from the following figures:

Percentage of Area Under Different Rabi Crops

|      | Wheat | Barley | Gram |
|------|-------|--------|------|
| 1690 | 32    | 34     | 25   |
| 1749 | 27    | 42     | 25   |

## Pargana Bahatri (Baswa)

In pargana Bahatri, the price of bajra and jowar compared to wheat undergoes some increase (the index moving from 62 and 56 in 1665 to 75 and 78 respectively in 1725). During this period, there is a marked decrease in proportion of area under the two crops which falls from 20 and 14 per cent in 1665 to 5.7 and 2.6 per cent respectively in 1725. Among the pulses, the relative price of moth does not change very much but that of urd decreases and of mung increases. The area under moth is reduced from 45 per cent in 1665 to 30 per cent in 1725. During the same period, the area under urd shows a remarkable increase and goes up to 20 per cent (area under cotton going up to 14 per cent during the same period).

The relative position of the three rabi crops viz. wheat, barley, and gram remains more or less constant between 1665 and 1725. The percentage of area under each of these crops however undergoes a change as may be observed from the following figures:

Percentage of Area Under Different Rabi Crops

|      | Wheat | Barley | Gram |
|------|-------|--------|------|
| 1665 | 9     | 71     | 16   |
| 1725 | 12    | 52     | 19   |

## Pargana Dausa and Lalsot

Since the earliest figures available for Dausa are for 1709 and
for Lalsot for 1713, and since as a result of the remarkable
increase in the general level of prices in 1712, the price level
remained disturbed for sometime, the trend can only be studied
inadequately. However, in Dausa, the index of the price of bajra
and jowar in terms of wheat rose from 58 and 55 in 1709 to 71
and 72 respectively in 1750. In Lalsot, the prices of these food
grains appreciably fall during the period, the fall being particularly marked in the case of bajra. The index for pulses rises
somewhat between 1709 and 1750; but compared to 1715 there
is a sharp decline in the index of pulses in terms of wheat in
1745. However, the prices of barley and grain relative to wheat
remained more or less constant in both the parganas.

On an overall basis, it appears that the increase in the case
of the kharif food grains is more marked than in the case of
the three principal rabi food grains, viz. wheat, barley, and
gram. Perhaps the relative increase in the production of rabi
crops compared to kharif, may explain this phenomenon.[6]

## Changes in the Level of Prices

Leaving aside the differences in the position of the different
crops and in different parganas, a few observations may be
made regarding the general level of prices. There is a considerable fluctuation in the price of the different commodities from
year to year, the fluctuation varying from commodity to commodity and from pargana to pargana. But, except for unusual years,
the range of fluctuation of prices over a decade is not very much.
The most unusual year of increase is, of course, 1712; after which
prices never came down to the level prevailing during the reign
of Aurangzeb. The other years of significant rise are 1717–18,
1731 and 1737. In the forties, however, the prices tend to decline.
It may be pointed out that during the reign of Aurangzeb, the

price of wheat generally remains under a rupee per maund with that of the other food grains being considerably less. By the middle of the eighteenth century, these prices tend to be over one rupee per maund.

This broad picture of increase in the price level may be exemplified by the price of indigo prevailing in the pargana of Amber (later Sawai Jaipur) as appears from Table 4.

Table 4
Price of Indigo in Pargana Amber
(in Rupee per Maund)

| 1666 | – | 25.28 | 1720 | – | 41.72 |
|------|---|-------|------|---|-------|
| 1677 | – | 23.33 | 1723 | – | 52.00 |
| 1680 | – | 28.29 | 1724 | – | 37.40 |
| 1688 | – | 25.98 | 1725 | – | 44.50 |
| 1690 | – | 28.58 | 1726 | – | 40.00 |
| 1712 | – | 38.68 | 1729 | – | 38.50 |
| 1715 | – | 51.66 | 1733 | – | 59.60 |
| 1716 | – | 45.61 | 1737 | – | 47.00 |
| 1718 | – | 45.30 |      |   |       |

Although there is no direct correspondence between the fluctuation in the price of food grains and of the bullion, to some extent, a broad conformity may be observed. Assuming that the changes in the value of *takas* per rupee reflect a change in the relative price of copper and silver, Table 6 would indicate the trend in the price of bullion. The value of the rupee which was 17 takas in 1661 and rose to 20 takas subsequently registers a fall after 1725 and in the forties came down to 14 and 15. This fall in the value of silver is reflected, to some extent, in the increase in the price of food grains per rupee. However, the value of gold in terms of silver as reflected in the price of the *muhr* does not seem to change as appears from the following figure:

Price of *Muhr* in Pargana Amber

| 1688 | – | Rs 12 |
|------|---|-------|
| 1720 | – | Rs 12 |
| 1723 | – | Rs 12 |

It may nevertheless be observed that the changing value of the taka does not conform essentially to the changes in the price of

food grains. It is possible that the value of the taka in terms of
the rupee fell partly as a result of the import of copper (possibly
from Japan) and rose when the import appears to have declined.

Table 5
Price of Food Grains in Different Parganas
(in Rupees per maund)
1. Wheat

| Year | Amber | Chatsu | Dausa | Lalsot | Bahatri (Baswa) | Malarna |
|------|-------|--------|-------|--------|---------|---------|
| 1665 | – | – | – | – | 0.99 | – |
| 1669 | – | – | – | – | 0.94 | – |
| 1677 | 0.97 | – | – | – | – | – |
| 1684 | – | – | – | – | 0.73 | – |
| 1686 | – | – | – | – | 1.10 | – |
| 1688 | 0.74 | – | – | – | 1.01 | – |
| 1689 | 0.59 | – | – | – | 0.79 | – |
| 1690 | 0.68 | – | – | – | – | 0.84 |
| 1696 | – | – | – | – | 1.32 | – |
| 1697 | – | – | – | – | 0.87 | – |
| 1706 | – | – | – | – | 0.95 | – |
| 1708 | – | 1.53 | – | – | 1.67 | – |
| 1709 | – | 1.10 | 0.99 | – | – | – |
| 1710 | – | 1.10 | – | – | 1.17 | – |
| 1711 | – | 1.48 | – | – | 1.83 | 1.64 |
| 1712 | 2.40 | 2.98 | 3.75 | – | – | 3.42 |
| 1713 | – | 1.07 | 1.41 | 1.55 | – | 1.61 |
| 1714 | – | 1.47 | – | 1.40 | – | 1.55 |
| 1715 | 1.27 | – | 1.50 | 1.35 | – | 1.34 |
| 1716 | – | 1.24 | – | – | 1.78 | – |
| 1717 | – | 3.18 | – | 3.55 | 3.68 | 2.76 |
| 1718 | 1.75 | – | – | 2.33 | 2.65 | 2.21 |
| 1719 | – | – | – | 1.53 | – | 1.59 |
| 1720 | 1.46 | – | – | 1.87 | 2.56 | 1.91 |
| 1721 | – | 1.99 | – | 2.11 | 2.58 | – |
| 1722 | – | – | – | 2.33 | – | 1.79 |
| 1723 | 1.27 | 1.84 | – | – | 1.66 | 1.68 |
| 1724 | 1.08 | 0.74 | – | – | 1.38 | – |
| 1725 | 1.04 | – | – | – | 1.69 | – |
| 1726 | – | 1.74 | – | – | – | 1.58 |

(Table 5 contd.)

Table 5 contd.

| Year | Amber | Chatsu | Dausa | Lalsot | Bahatri (Baswa) | Malarna |
|------|-------|--------|-------|--------|------------------|---------|
| 1727 | – | – | – | – | – | 1.12 |
| 1728 | 0.87 | – | – | – | – | 1.44 |
| 1729 | 1.38 | – | – | – | – | 1.86 |
| 1730 | – | 1.79 | – | – | – | 1.92 |
| 1731 | – | 3.06 | – | 3.18 | – | – |
| 1732 | – | – | – | – | – | 1.35 |
| 1733 | 1.48 | 2.17 | – | 1.57 | – | – |
| 1734 | 1.34 | – | – | 1.66 | – | – |
| 1735 | – | 1.79 | – | – | – | – |
| 1736 | – | – | 1.89 | – | – | 2.12 |
| 1737 | 1.74 | 2.51 | 2.61 | 2.37 | – | 2.46 |
| 1738 | – | 1.98 | 1.75 | – | – | 1.67 |
| 1739 | – | – | 1.40 | 1.66 | – | – |
| 1740 | – | 1.27 | – | 1.22 | – | – |
| 1741 | – | 1.16 | 1.39 | 1.17 | – | – |
| 1742 | – | 2.02 | 1.95 | – | – | – |
| 1743 | – | 1.66 | – | – | – | 1.26 |
| 1744 | 1.01 | 1.64 | 1.57 | – | – | 1.37 |
| 1745 | – | 1.27 | 1.04 | 1.51 | – | 1.08 |
| 1746 | – | – | 1.35 | 1.91 | – | – |
| 1747 | – | – | 1.65 | 2.13 | – | – |
| 1748 | – | 1.82 | – | 2.01 | – | – |
| 1749 | – | 1.49 | – | – | – | 1.38 |
| 1750 | – | – | 1.35 | – | – | 1.15 |

2. Barley

| Year | Amber | Chatsu | Dausa | Lalsot | Bahatri (Baswa) | Malarna |
|------|-------|--------|-------|--------|------------------|---------|
| 1665 | – | – | – | – | 0.65 | – |
| 1669 | – | – | – | – | 0.60 | – |
| 1677 | 0.65 | – | – | – | – | – |
| 1684 | – | – | – | – | 0.55 | – |
| 1686 | – | – | – | – | 0.76 | – |
| 1687 | – | – | – | 0.73 | – | – |
| 1688 | 0.58 | – | – | – | 0.76 | – |
| 1689 | 0.42 | – | – | – | 0.55 | – |
| 1690 | 0.47 | – | – | – | – | 0.67 |
| 1691 | – | – | – | – | 0.73 | – |
| 1696 | – | – | – | – | 1.03 | – |

(Table 5 contd.)

Table 5 contd.

| Year | Amber | Chatsu | Dausa | Lalsot | Bahatri (Baswa) | Malarna |
|------|-------|--------|-------|--------|-----------------|---------|
| 1697 | – | – | – | – | 0.60 | – |
| 1706 | – | – | – | – | 0.64 | – |
| 1708 | – | 1.12 | – | – | 1.13 | – |
| 1709 | – | 0.79 | 0.71 | – | – | – |
| 1710 | – | 0.81 | – | – | 0.72 | – |
| 1711 | – | 1.10 | – | – | 1.41 | 1.27 |
| 1712 | 1.91 | 2.66 | 2.92 | – | – | – |
| 1713 | – | 0.79 | 1.07 | 1.21 | – | 1.17 |
| 1714 | – | 1.04 | – | 0.98 | – | 1.08 |
| 1715 | 0.89 | – | 1.14 | 0.99 | – | 0.91 |
| 1716 | 0.72 | 0.91 | – | – | 1.22 | 1.00 |
| 1717 | – | 2.73 | – | 2.95 | 2.82 | 2.21 |
| 1718 | 1.17 | – | – | 1.69 | 1.91 | 1.42 |
| 1719 | – | – | – | 1.05 | – | 0.93 |
| 1720 | 1.12 | – | – | 1.28 | 1.27 | 1.18 |
| 1721 | – | 1.50 | – | 1.57 | 1.96 | – |
| 1722 | – | – | – | 1.44 | – | 1.28 |
| 1723 | 1.06 | 1.33 | – | – | 1.15 | 1.00 |
| 1724 | 0.84 | 1.05 | – | – | 1.08 | – |
| 1725 | 0.70 | – | – | – | 1.21 | – |
| 1726 | – | 1.28 | – | – | – | 1.20 |
| 1727 | – | – | – | – | – | 0.76 |
| 1728 | 0.50 | – | – | – | – | 0.90 |
| 1729 | 1.01 | – | – | – | – | 1.42 |
| 1730 | – | 1.42 | – | – | – | 1.46 |
| 1731 | – | 2.39 | – | 2.59 | – | – |
| 1732 | – | – | – | – | – | 1.08 |
| 1733 | 0.98 | 1.64 | – | 1.05 | – | – |
| 1734 | 1.02 | – | – | 1.20 | – | – |
| 1735 | – | 1.41 | – | – | – | – |
| 1736 | – | – | 1.50 | – | – | 1.65 |
| 1737 | 1.33 | 1.74 | 2.01 | 1.79 | – | 1.88 |
| 1738 | – | 1.47 | 1.51 | – | – | 1.22 |
| 1739 | – | – | 0.95 | 1.08 | – | – |
| 1740 | – | 0.85 | – | 0.78 | – | – |
| 1741 | – | 0.94 | 0.98 | 1.14 | – | – |
| 1742 | – | 1.50 | 1.52 | – | – | – |

(Table 5 contd.)

Table 5 contd.

| Year | Amber | Chatsu | Dausa | Lalsot | Bahatri (Baswa) | Malarna |
|------|-------|--------|-------|--------|-----------------|---------|
| 1743 | – | 1.21 | 1.23 | – | – | 0.86 |
| 1744 | – | 1.11 | 1.04 | – | – | 1.06 |
| 1745 | – | 0.78 | 0.67 | 0.88 | – | 0.61 |
| 1746 | – | – | 0.95 | 1.21 | – | – |
| 1747 | – | – | 1.23 | 1.24 | – | – |
| 1748 | – | 1.31 | – | 1.42 | – | 1.41 |
| 1749 | – | 2.00 | – | – | – | 1.07 |
| 1750 | – | – | 1.00 | – | – | 0.82 |

3. Gram

| Year | Amber | Chatsu | Dausa | Lalsot | Bahatri (Baswa) | Malarna |
|------|-------|--------|-------|--------|-----------------|---------|
| 1665 | – | – | – | – | 0.69 | – |
| 1669 | – | – | – | – | 0.63 | – |
| 1677 | 0.65 | – | – | – | ,– | – |
| 1686 | – | – | – | – | 0.81 | – |
| 1687 | – | – | – | 0.78 | – | – |
| 1688 | 0.59 | – | – | – | 0.79 | – |
| 1689 | 0.42 | – | – | – | 0.56 | – |
| 1690 | 0.47 | – | – | – | – | 0.62 |
| 1691 | – | – | – | – | 0.79 | – |
| 1697 | – | – | – | – | 0.73 | – |
| 1706 | – | – | – | – | 0.69 | – |
| 1708 | – | 1.62 | – | – | 1.36 | – |
| 1709 | – | 1.00 | 0.83 | – | – | – |
| 1710 | – | 0.81 | – | – | 0.66 | – |
| 1711 | – | 1.22 | – | – | 1.13 | 1.32 |
| 1712 | 2.43 | 2.83 | 3.79 | – | – | 3.48 |
| 1713 | – | 0.75 | 1.05 | 1.43 | – | 1.40 |
| 1714 | – | 1.38 | – | 1.33 | – | 1.58 |
| 1715 | 0.91 | – | 1.16 | 1.02 | – | 0.94 |
| 1716 | 0.69 | 0.84 | – | – | 1.23 | 0.95 |
| 1717 | – | 3.20 | – | 3.49 | 3.77 | 2.59 |
| 1718 | 1.69 | – | – | 2.31 | 2.98 | 1.77 |
| 1719 | – | – | – | 1.15 | – | 1.08 |
| 1720 | 1.23 | – | – | 1.60 | 2.47 | 1.36 |
| 1721 | – | 1.69 | – | 1.66 | 1.88 | – |
| 1722 | – | – | – | 1.06 | – | 1.31 |

(Table 5 contd.)

Table 5 contd.

| Year | Amber | Chatsu | Dausa | Lalsot | Bahatri (Baswa) | Malarna |
|------|-------|--------|-------|--------|-----------------|---------|
| 1723 | 1.24 | 1.64 | – | – | 1.30 | 1.25 |
| 1724 | 0.94 | 0.74 | – | – | 0.99 | – |
| 1725 | 0.75 | – | – | – | 1.13 | – |
| 1726 | – | 1.36 | – | – | – | 1.19 |
| 1727 | – | – | – | – | – | 0.74 |
| 1728 | 0.82 | – | – | – | – | 0.90 |
| 1729 | 1.08 | – | – | – | – | 1.45· |
| 1730 | 1.54 | – | – | – | – | 1.44 |
| 1731 | – | 3.25 | – | 3.28 | – | – |
| 1732 | – | – | – | – | – | 1.13 |
| 1733 | 1.10 | 1.96 | – | 1.20 | – | – |
| 1734 | 1.15 | – | – | 1.36 | – | – |
| 1735 | – | 1.51 | – | – | – | – |
| 1736 | – | – | 1.97 | – | – | 1.84 |
| 1737 | 1.97 | 2.46 | 2.95 | 2.66 | – | 2.42 |
| 1738 | – | 1.87 | 0.83 | – | – | 1.48 |
| 1739 | – | – | 1.34 | 1.29 | – | – |
| 1740 | – | 0.98 | – | 0.88 | – | – |
| 1741 | – | 1.16 | 1.14 | 1.24 | – | – |
| 1742 | – | 2.19 | 2.14 | – | – | – |
| 1743 | – | 1.66 | 1.26 | – | – | 1.11 |
| 1744 | 0.95 | 1.40 | 1.34 | – | – | 1.19 |
| 1745 | – | 1.00 | 0.87 | 1.01 | – | 1.19 |
| 1746 | – | – | 1.46 | 1.67 | – | – |
| 1747 | – | – | 1.63 | 1.40 | – | – |
| 1748 | – | 1.62 | – | 1.56 | – | 1.46 |
| 1749 | – | – | – | – | – | 1.14 |
| 1750 | – | 1.29 | 1.22 | – | – | 0.95 |

4. Bajra

| 1664 | – | 0.64 | – | – | – | – |
| 1665 | – | – | 0.57 | – | 0.61 | – |
| 1666 | 0.44 | – | – | – | – | – |
| 1669 | – | – | – | – | 0.72 | – |
| 1677 | 0.44 | – | – | – | – | – |

(Table 5 contd.)

Table 5 contd.

| Year | Amber | Chatsu | Dausa | Lalsot | Bahatri (Baswa) | Malarna |
|------|-------|--------|-------|--------|------------------|---------|
| 1684 | – | – | – | – | 0.85 | – |
| 1685 | – | – | – | – | 1.09 | – |
| 1686 | – | – | – | – | 0.79 | – |
| 1687 | – | – | – | 0.82 | – | – |
| 1688 | 0.73 | – | – | – | 0.87 | – |
| 1689 | 0.50 | – | – | – | 0.65 | – |
| 1690 | 0.54 | – | – | – | – | 0.69 |
| 1691 | – | – | – | – | 0.73 | – |
| 1696 | – | – | – | – | 1.87 | – |
| 1699 | – | – | – | – | – | 0.38 |
| 1706 | – | – | – | – | 0.53 | – |
| 1708 | – | 0.88 | – | – | 0.26 | – |
| 1709 | – | 0.75 | 0.57 | – | – | – |
| 1710 | – | 0.87 | – | – | 0.74 | – |
| 1711 | – | 0.90 | – | – | – | – |
| 1712 | 1.52 | 1.95 | 1.91 | – | – | 2.04 |
| 1713 | – | 2.02 | 2.52 | 2.79 | – | 2.43 |
| 1714 | – | 1.16 | – | 1.21 | – | 1.05 |
| 1715 | 1.27 | 1.54 | 1.48 | 2.03 | – | 1.42 |
| 1716 | 1.13 | 1.28 | – | – | 2.06 | 1.31 |
| 1717 | – | 2.72 | – | 3.32 | 4.19 | 2.59 |
| 1718 | 1.67 | – | 2.29 | 1.87 | 2.30 | 1.73 |
| 1719 | – | – | – | 1.66 | – | 1.44 |
| 1720 | 0.96 | – | – | 1.66 | 1.96 | 1.29 |
| 1721 | – | 1.28 | – | 1.61 | 1.35 | 1.17 |
| 1722 | – | – | – | 1.56 | – | 1.27 |
| 1723 | 1.08 | 1.16 | – | – | 1.37 | 1.16 |
| 1724 | 0.86 | 0.99 | – | – | 1.25 | – |
| 1725 | 0.88 | – | – | – | 1.27 | – |
| 1726 | – | 1.52 | – | – | – | 1.39 |
| 1727 | – | – | – | – | – | 0.72 |
| 1728 | 0.92 | – | – | – | – | 0.76 |
| 1729 | 1.24 | – | – | – | – | 1.35 |
| 1730 | – | 1.74 | – | 2.07 | – | 2.00 |
| 1731 | – | 3.73 | – | 4.08 | – | 3.60 |
| 1732 | – | – | – | – | – | 1.04 |
| 1733 | 1.02 | 1.23 | – | 1.36 | – | – |

(Table 5 contd.)

Table 5 contd.

| Year | Amber | Chatsu | Dausa | Lalsot | Bahatri (Baswa) | Malarna |
|---|---|---|---|---|---|---|
| 1734 | 1.18 | – | – | 1.83 | – | – |
| 1735 | – | 1.95 | – | – | – | – |
| 1736 | – | 1.94 | 2.06 | – | – | 1.70 |
| 1737 | 1.68 | 2.18 | 2.37 | 2.31 | – | 1.70 |
| 1738 | – | 2.09 | 2.19 | – | – | 1.59 |
| 1739 | – | 0.98 | 1.07 | 1.22 | – | – |
| 1740 | – | – | – | 1.17 | – | – |
| 1741 | – | 1.30 | 1.25 | 1.36 | – | – |
| 1742 | – | 1.71 | 1.90 | – | – | – |
| 1743 | – | – | 1.02 | – | – | 0.77 |
| 1744 | 1.18 | 1.66 | 1.51 | – | – | 1.16 |
| 1745 | – | 1.03 | 0.89 | 0.88 | – | 0.72 |
| 1746 | – | – | 1.41 | 1.56 | – | – |
| 1747 | – | – | 1.09 | 1.19 | – | – |
| 1748 | – | 1.46 | – | 1.41 | – | 1.18 |
| 1749 | – | 1.20 | – | – | – | 0.75 |
| 1750 | – | 1.10 | 0.97 | – | – | 0.53 |

5. Jowar

| Year | Amber | Chatsu | Dausa | Lalsot | Bahatri (Baswa) | Malarna |
|---|---|---|---|---|---|---|
| 1664 | – | 0.63 | – | – | – | – |
| 1665 | – | – | 0.56 | – | 0.55 | – |
| 1666 | 0.42 | – | – | – | – | – |
| 1669 | – | – | – | – | 0.63 | – |
| 1677 | 0.72 | – | – | – | – | – |
| 1684 | – | – | – | – | 0.55 | – |
| 1685 | – | – | – | – | 1.01 | – |
| 1686 | – | – | – | – | 0.76 | – |
| 1687 | – | – | – | 0.74 | – | – |
| 1688 | 0.74 | – | – | – | 0.81 | – |
| 1689 | 0.44 | – | – | – | 0.53 | – |
| 1690 | 0.44 | – | – | – | – | 0.68 |
| 1691 | – | – | – | – | 0.64 | – |
| 1696 | – | – | – | – | 1.70 | – |
| 1699 | – | – | – | – | – | 0.38 |
| 1706 | – | – | – | – | 0.45 | – |
| 1708 | – | 0.84 | – | – | 0.89 | – |
| 1709 | – | 0.64 | 0.54 | – | – | – |
| 1710 | – | 0.83 | – | – | 0.64 | – |
| 1711 | – | 0.80 | – | – | – | – |

(Table 5 contd.)

Table 5 contd.

| Year | Amber | Chatsu | Dausa | Lalsot | Bahatri (Baswa) | Malarna |
|------|-------|--------|-------|--------|------------------|---------|
| 1712 | 1.21 | 1.29 | 1.81 | – | – | 1.97 |
| 1713 | – | 2.23 | 2.62 | 2.99 | – | 2.50 |
| 1714 | – | 1.01 | – | – | – | 1.00 |
| 1715 | 1.24 | 1.43 | 1.30 | – | – | 1.58 |
| 1716 | – | 1.06 | – | – | 1.70 | 1.37 |
| 1717 | – | – | – | – | 4.10 | 2.21 |
| 1718 | 1.55 | – | 2.06 | 2.66 | 2.08 | 1.78 |
| 1719 | – | – | – | 1.52 | – | 1.19 |
| 1720 | 0.87 | – | – | 1.44 | 1.70 | 1.17 |
| 1721 | – | 1.09. | – | 1.60 | 1.23 | 1.08 |
| 1722 | – | – | – | 1.41 | – | 1.11 |
| 1723 | 0.98 | 1.25 | – | – | 1.22 | 0.96 |
| 1724 | 0.75 | 0.98 | – | – | 1.17 | – |
| 1725 | 0.70 | – | – | – | 1.23 | – |
| 1726 | – | 1.34 | – | – | – | 1.14 |
| 1727 | – | – | – | – | – | 0.65 |
| 1728 | – | – | – | – | – | 0.63 |
| 1729 | – | – | – | – | – | 1.34 |
| 1730 | – | 1.86 | – | – | – | 2.14 |
| 1731 | – | 3.25 | – | 3.99 | – | 3.74 |
| 1732 | – | – | – | – | – | 0.89 |
| 1733 | 0.81 | 1.00 | – | 1.09 | – | – |
| 1734 | 0.88 | – | – | 0.66 | – | – |
| 1735 | – | 1.73 | – | – | – | – |
| 1736 | – | 1.63 | 1.79 | – | – | 1.58 |
| 1737 | 1.30 | 1.81 | 2.05 | 2.39 | – | 1.50 |
| 1738 | – | 1.82 | 2.00 | – | – | 1.45 |
| 1739 | – | – | 0.96 | – | – | – |
| 1740 | – | 0.81 | – | – | – | – |
| 1741 | – | 1.02 | 1.00 | – | – | – |
| 1742 | – | 1.44 | 1.27 | – | – | – |
| 1743 | – | – | 0.94 | – | – | – |
| 1744 | 0.89 | 1.37 | 1.28 | – | – | 0.98 |
| 1745 | – | 0.76 | 0.79 | 1.33 | – | 0.55 |
| 1746 | – | – | 1.16 | 1.34 | – | – |
| 1747 | – | – | 0.89 | 1.06 | – | – |
| 1748 | – | 1.44 | – | 1.19 | – | 1.27 |
| 1749 | – | 1.06 | – | – | – | 0.77 |
| 1750 | – | 1.06 | 0.97 | – | – | – |

(Table 5 contd.)

Table 5 contd.

| Year | Amber | Chatsu | Dausa | Lalsot | Bahatri (Baswa) | Malarna |
|------|-------|--------|-------|--------|-----------------|---------|
| | | | 6. *Moth* | | | |
| 1664 | – | 0.74 | – | – | – | – |
| 1665 | – | – | 0.57 | – | 0.58 | – |
| 1666 | 0.40 | – | – | – | – | – |
| 1669 | – | – | – | – | 0.62 | – |
| 1677 | 0.69 | – | – | – | – | – |
| 1684 | – | – | – | – | 0.46 | – |
| 1685 | – | – | – | – | 1.02 | – |
| 1686 | – | – | – | – | 0.77 | – |
| 1687 | – | – | – | 0.74 | – | – |
| 1688 | 0.39 | – | – | – | 0.74 | – |
| 1689 | 0.40 | – | – | – | 0.51 | – |
| 1690 | 0.39 | – | – | – | – | 0.59 |
| 1691 | – | – | – | – | 0.63 | – |
| 1696 | – | – | – | – | 2.12 | – |
| 1706 | – | – | – | – | 0.53 | – |
| 1708 | – | 1.07 | – | – | 1.03 | – |
| 1709 | – | 0.76 | 0.68 | – | – | – |
| 1710 | – | 0.88 | – | – | 0.68 | – |
| 1711 | – | 0.90 | – | – | – | – |
| 1712 | 1.77 | 2.04 | 1.81 | – | – | 1.98 |
| 1713 | – | 1.98 | 2.48 | 2.51 | – | 2.53 |
| 1714 | – | 1.27 | – | 1.56 | – | 1.16 |
| 1715 | 1.31 | 1.52 | 1.59 | 2.04 | – | 1.65 |
| 1716 | 1.08 | 1.03 | – | – | 1.55 | 1.32 |
| 1717 | – | 3.00 | – | 3.03 | 4.37 | 2.54 |
| 1718 | 0.99 | – | 2.28 | 2.16 | 2.36 | 1.99 |
| 1719 | – | – | – | 1.17 | – | 1.08 |
| 1720 | 0.92 | – | – | 1.40 | 1.76 | 2.29 |
| 1721 | – | 1.29 | – | 1.49 | 1.26 | 1.13 |
| 1722 | – | – | – | 1.40 | – | 1.16 |
| 1723 | 1.09 | 1.63 | – | – | 1.22 | 1.15 |
| 1724 | 0.64 | 0.81 | – | – | 0.94 | – |
| 1725 | 0.84 | – | – | – | 0.94 | – |
| 1726 | – | 1.75 | – | – | – | 1.40 |
| 1727 | – | – | – | – | – | 0.71 |
| 1728 | 0.87 | – | – | – | – | 0.64 |
| 1729 | 1.08 | – | – | – | – | 1.43 |

(Table 5 contd.)

Table 5 contd.

| Year | Amber | Chatsu | Dausa | Lalsot | Bahatri (Baswa) | Malarna |
|------|-------|--------|-------|--------|-----------------|---------|
| 1730 | – | 1.66 | – | 1.77 | – | 1.92 |
| 1731 | – | 4.41 | – | 4.08 | – | 4.50 |
| 1732 | – | – | – | – | – | 1.06 |
| 1733 | 1.00 | 1.14 | – | 1.08 | – | – |
| 1734 | 1.06 | – | – | 1.56 | – | – |
| 1735 | – | 1.50 | – | – | – | – |
| 1736 | – | 2.17 | 2.08 | – | – | 1.82 |
| 1737 | 1.49 | 1.86 | 2.09 | 1.97 | – | 1.65 |
| 1738 | – | 1.95 | 2.11 | – | – | 1.72 |
| 1739 | – | – | 1.00 | 1.07 | – | – |
| 1740 | – | 0.85 | – | 1.06 | – | – |
| 1741 | – | 1.10 | 1.01 | 1.17 | – | – |
| 1742 | – | 2.16 | 2.08 | – | – | – |
| 1743 | – | – | 1.28 | – | – | 1.07 |
| 1744 | 1.05 | 1.55 | 1.32 | – | – | 1.31 |
| 1745 | – | 0.93 | 0.80 | 0.86 | – | 0.69 |
| 1746 | – | – | 1.48 | 1.56 | – | – |
| 1747 | – | – | 0.97 | 1.17 | – | – |
| 1748 | – | 1.38 | – | 1.25 | – | 1.10 |
| 1749 | – | 1.14 | – | – | – | 0.94 |
| 1750 | – | 1.18 | 1.16 | – | – | – |

7. Urd

| Year | Amber | Chatsu | Dausa | Lalsot | Bahatri (Baswa) | Malarna |
|------|-------|--------|-------|--------|-----------------|---------|
| 1664 | – | 1.02 | – | – | – | – |
| 1665 | – | – | 0.68 | – | 0.71 | – |
| 1666 | 0.48 | – | – | – | – | – |
| 1669 | – | – | – | – | 0.76 | – |
| 1677 | 0.82 | – | – | – | – | – |
| 1684 | – | – | – | – | 0.48 | – |
| 1685 | – | – | – | – | 1.06 | – |
| 1687 | – | – | – | 0.85 | 0.86 | – |
| 1688 | 0.83 | – | – | – | 0.79 | – |
| 1689 | 0.53 | – | – | – | 0.57 | – |
| 1690 | 0.53 | – | – | – | – | 0.63 |
| 1691 | – | – | – | – | 0.69 | – |
| 1696 | – | – | – | – | 2.14 | – |
| 1699 | – | – | – | – | – | 0.60 |

(Table 5 contd.)

Table 5 contd.

| Year | Amber | Chatsu | Dausa | Lalsot | Bahatri (Baswa) | Malarna |
|------|-------|--------|-------|--------|-----------------|---------|
| 1706 | – | – | – | – | 0.86 | – |
| 1708 | – | 1.05 | – | – | 1.45 | – |
| 1709 | – | 1.00 | 0.84 | – | – | – |
| 1710 | – | 1.21 | – | – | 0.95 | – |
| 1711 | – | 1.08 | – | – | – | – |
| 1712 | 2.20 | 2.01 | 1.93 | – | – | – |
| 1713 | – | 2.24 | 2.33 | 3.33 | – | 2.74 |
| 1714 | – | 1.82 | – | 1.85 | – | 1.49 |
| 1715 | 1.40 | 2.01 | 1.71 | 2.49 | – | 1.95 |
| 1716 | 1.25 | 2.17 | – | – | 1.01 | 1.50 |
| 1717 | – | 2.66 | – | 3.32 | – | 2.61 |
| 1718 | 1.92 | – | 2.68 | 2.37 | 2.67 | 2.26 |
| 1719 | – | – | – | 1.53 | – | 1.32 |
| 1720 | 1.00 | – | – | 1.66 | 1.88 | 1.51 |
| 1721 | – | 1.51 | – | 1.52 | 1.35 | 1.37 |
| 1722 | – | – | – | 1.66 | – | 1.35 |
| 1723 | 1.13 | 1.93 | – | – | 1.44 | 1.60 |
| 1724 | 0.92 | 1.09 | – | – | 1.10 | – |
| 1725 | 1.20 | – | – | – | 1.06 | – |
| 1726 | – | 2.03 | – | – | – | 1.64 |
| 1727 | – | – | – | – | – | 0.97 |
| 1728 | – | – | – | – | – | 0.90 |
| 1729 | – | – | – | – | – | 1.76 |
| 1730 | – | 1.72 | – | 1.78 | – | 1.95 |
| 1731 | – | – | – | 4.52 | – | 5.14 |
| 1732 | – | – | – | – | – | 1.23 |
| 1733 | 1.14 | 1.20 | – | 1.36 | – | – |
| 1734 | 1.55 | – | – | 1.65 | – | – |
| 1735 | – | 1.52 | – | – | – | – |
| 1736 | – | 2.41 | 2.23 | – | – | 2.28 |
| 1737 | – | 2.23 | 2.55 | 2.54 | – | 1.70 |
| 1738 | – | 2.24 | 2.19 | – | – | 1.80 |
| 1739 | – | – | 1.16 | 1.46 | – | – |
| 1740 | – | 0.96 | – | 1.38 | – | – |
| 1741 | – | 1.25 | 1.29 | 1.35 | – | – |
| 1742 | – | 2.40 | 2.60 | – | – | – |
| 1743 | – | – | 2.07 | – | – | 1.82 |
| 1744 | 1.33 | 2.06 | 1.73 | – | – | 1.98 |

(Table 5 contd.)

Table 5 contd.

| Year | Amber | Chatsu | Dausa | Lalsot | Bahatri (Baswa) | Malarna |
|------|-------|--------|-------|--------|------------------|---------|
| 1745 | – | 1.33 | 1.12 | 1.35 | – | 1.17 |
| 1746 | – | – | 2.04 | 1.97 | – | – |
| 1747 | – | – | 1.37 | 1.56 | – | – |
| 1748 | – | 1.53 | – | 1.56 | – | 1.21 |
| 1749 | – | 1.52 | – | – | – | 1.01 |
| 1750 | – | 1.26 | 1.46 | – | – | – |

8. Mung

| Year | Amber | Chatsu | Dausa | Lalsot | Bahatri (Baswa) | Malarna |
|------|-------|--------|-------|--------|------------------|---------|
| 1664 | – | 1.23 | – | – | – | – |
| 1665 | – | – | 0.79 | – | 0.58 | – |
| 1666 | 0.50 | – | – | – | – | – |
| 1669 | – | – | – | – | 1.03 | – |
| 1677 | 0.89 | – | – | – | – | – |
| 1684 | – | – | – | – | 0.59 | – |
| 1685 | – | – | – | – | 1.21 | – |
| 1686 | – | – | – | – | 0.88 | – |
| 1687 | – | – | – | 0.88 | – | – |
| 1688 | 0.76 | – | – | – | 0.81 | – |
| 1689 | 0.63 | – | – | – | 0.69 | – |
| 1690 | 0.56 | – | – | – | – | 0.71 |
| 1691 | – | – | – | – | 0.68 | – |
| 1699 | – | – | – | – | – | 0.73 |
| 1706 | – | – | – | – | 0.72 | – |
| 1708 | – | 1.58 | – | – | 1.39 | – |
| 1709 | – | – | 0.87 | – | – | – |
| 1710 | – | 1.11 | – | – | 0.90 | – |
| 1711 | – | 1.18 | – | – | – | – |
| 1712 | 2.42 | 2.34 | 1.84 | – | – | – |
| 1713 | – | 2.22 | 2.69 | 3.61 | – | 2.66 |
| 1714 | – | 2.22 | – | 1.96 | – | 1.51 |
| 1715 | 1.67 | 2.52 | 1.86 | 2.59 | – | 2.03 |
| 1716 | 1.40 | 1.63 | – | – | 1.98 | 1.49 |
| 1717 | – | 4.66 | – | 3.07 | – | 3.14 |
| 1718 | 2.36 | – | 2.74 | 2.86 | 2.80 | 2.40 |
| 1719 | – | – | – | 1.57 | – | 1.16 |
| 1720 | 1.15 | – | – | 1.83 | 2.01 | 1.46 |
| 1721 | – | 1.71 | – | 1.71 | 1.32 | 1.33 |
| 1722 | – | – | – | 1.70 | – | 1.31 |

(Table 5 contd.)

Table 5 contd.

| Year | Amber | Chatsu | Dausa | Lalsot | Bahatri (Baswa) | Malarna |
|------|-------|--------|-------|--------|-----------------|---------|
| 1723 | 1.26 | 2.01 | – | – | 1.43 | 1.42 |
| 1724 | 0.97 | 1.28 | – | – | 1.11 | – |
| 1725 | 1.23 | – | – | – | 1.¹2 | – |
| 1726 | – | 2.32 | – | – | – | 1.59 |
| 1727 | – | – | – | – | – | 0.95 |
| 1728 | – | – | – | – | – | 0.75 |
| 1729 | 1.16 | – | – | – | – | 1.59 |
| 1730 | – | 1.82 | – | 1.79 | – | 1.97 |
| 1731 | – | – | – | 4.72 | – | 5.14 |
| 1732 | – | – | – | – | – | 1.18 |
| 1733 | 1.24 | 1.48 | – | 1.44 | – | – |
| 1734 | 1.23 | – | – | 1.86 | – | – |
| 1735 | – | 1.74 | – | – | – | – |
| 1736 | – | 2.65 | 2.66 | – | – | 2.29 |
| 1737 | 1.81 | 2.50 | 2.69 | 3.12 | – | 1.87 |
| 1738 | – | 2.54 | 2.82 | – | – | 1.77 |
| 1739 | – | – | 1.16 | 1.48 | – | – |
| 1740 | – | 1.33 | – | 1.57 | – | – |
| 1741 | – | 1.60 | 1.25 | 1.57 | – | – |
| 1742 | – | 3.10 | 2.60 | – | – | – |
| 1743 | – | – | 1.69 | – | – | 1.36 |
| 1744 | 1.32 | 2.18 | 1.57 | – | – | 1.77 |
| 1745 | – | 1.31 | 0.95 | 1.36 | – | 1.13 |
| 1746 | – | – | 1.94 | 2.33 | – | – |
| 1747 | – | – | 1.27 | 1.66 | – | – |
| 1748 | – | 1.58 | – | 1.61 | – | 1.23 |
| 1749 | – | 1.58 | – | – | – | 1.05 |
| 1750 | – | 1.31 | 1.26 | – | – | – |

Table 6

Value of Taka per Rupee in Different Parganas

| 1664 | 17 | 17 | – | – | – | – |
|------|-----|-----|---------|---|---------------|---|
| 1665 | – | – | 16 1/2 | – | 15 3/4 | – |
| 1666 | 16 1/2 | – | – | – | – | – |
| 1677 | 17 1/2 | – | – | – | – | – |
| 1684 | – | – | – | – | 18 1/2 | – |
| 1685 | – | – | – | – | 18 1/2 to 19 | – |
| 1686 | – | – | – | – | 20 | – |

(Table 6 contd.)

Table 6 contd

| | | | | | | |
|---|---|---|---|---|---|---|
| 1687 | – | – | – | 20 1/4 | – | – |
| 1688 | 19 | – | – | – | – | – |
| 1689 | 19 | – | – | – | 18 to 18 1/2 | – |
| 1690 | 18 1/2 | – | – | – | – | 18 1/2 |
| 1694 | – | 19 | – | – | 20 | – |
| 1696 | – | – | 20 | – | 19 | – |
| 1697 | – | – | – | – | 19 1/2 | – |
| 1706 | – | – | – | – | 19 | – |
| 1708 | – | 18 1/2 to 19 | – | – | 18 | |
| 1709 | – | 18 | 17 | – | – | – |
| 1710 | – | 17 | – | – | 17 | |
| 1711 | – | – | – | – | 18 | 17 1/2 to 18 |
| 1712 | 18 | – | 16 1/2 | – | – | 18 |
| 1713 | – | – | 16 1/2 | – | 18 | 17 1/2 to 18 |
| 1714 | – | 18 | – | – | – | 18 |
| 1715 | – | 18 | 16 1/2 | – | – | – |
| 1716 | 18 | 18 | – | – | 17 1/2 | 17 1/2 to 17 3/4 |
| 1717 | – | 19 | – | 18 | 18 1/2 | 17 3/4 to 18 |
| 1718 | 18 1/2 | – | 16 1/2 | 19 | 17 1/2 | 18 |
| 1719 | – | – | – | 18 | – | 18 |
| 1720 | 17 1/2 | – | – | 17 1/2 | 17 | 17 3/4 |
| 1721 | – | 18 | – | 17 1/2 | 16 1/2 | 18 |
| 1722 | – | – | – | 17 | – | 17 |
| 1723 | 16 | 17 | – | – | 16 | 16 |
| 1724 | – | 16 1/2 | – | 16 1/2 | 17 | – |
| 1725 | – | – | – | – | 16 | – |
| 1726 | – | 16 | – | 16 | – | 16 |
| 1727 | – | – | – | – | – | 16 |
| 1728 | 15 1/4 to 15 1/2 | – | – | – | – | 15 1/2 |
| 1729 | 15 | – | – | – | – | – |
| 1730 | – | 16 | – | 16 | – | 16 |
| 1731 | – | 16 | – | 16 | – | 16 |
| 1732 | – | – | – | – | – | 15 |
| 1733 | 15 | 14 1/4 to 15 | – | 15 | – | 15 |
| 1734 | – | – | – | 15 | – | – |
| 1735 | – | 15 | – | – | – | – |
| 1736 | – | 14 1/2 | – | – | – | 14 1/2 |
| 1737 | 15 | 15 | 15 | 15 3/4 | – | 15 1/2 |

(Table 6 contd.)

Table 6 contd.

| 1738 | – | 16 | 15 | – | – | 15 |
|------|---|------|----|------|----|--------|
| 1739 | – | – | 15 | 15 | – | – |
| 1740 | – | 16 | – | 15 | 15 | – |
| 1741 | – | 16 | 15 | 14 | – | – |
| 1742 | – | 15 1/2 | 15 | – | – | – |
| 1743 | – | 15 | – | – | – | 15 |
| 1744 | – | 15 3/4 | – | – | – | 15 |
| 1745 | – | 14 3/4 | 15 | 15 1/2 | – | 14 1/2 |
| 1746 | – | – | 15 | 14 1/2 | – | – |
| 1747 | – | – | 15 | 15 | – | – |
| 1748 | – | 15 | – | 15 | – | 14 1/2 |
| 1749 | – | – | – | – | – | 14 |
| 1750 | – | – | – | – | – | 14 |

## Notes and References

1. The authors wish to pay their homage to the memory of the late Mrs Khursheed Nurul Hasan who had undertaken, along with the present authors, the study of the economic history and the historical geography of the territories of Amber. As a result of this study, she had presented, jointly with the present authors, the paper entitled, 'The Pattern of Agricultural Production in the Territories of Amber (c. 1650–1750)', at the XXVIII Session of the Indian History Congress. This paper is a continuation of earlier paper and incorporates many of the ideas of the late Mrs Hasan.

Grateful thanks are due also to N. R. Khadgawat, Director, Rajasthan State Archives, Bikaner, for providing facilities in the collection of material.

2. Cf. S. Nurul Hasan, K. N. Hasan, S. P. Gupta, 'The Pattern of Agricultural Production in the Territories of Amber (c. 1650–1750)', *Proceedings, Ind. Hist. Cong.*, XXVIII, Mysore, 1966.

3. Cf. *nirkh Jamabandi* for Pargana Bahatri date-wise and village-wise for two months of the year 1656 and *nirkh bazar* of pargana Amber for one month of the year 1688 preserved in R.A., Bikaner.

4. Abul Fazl, *Ain*, H. S. Jarrett, Vol. II, Delhi, 1978, pp. 103–4.

5. Cf. 'The Pattern of Agricultural Production, in the Territories of Amber (c. 1650–1750)'.

6. This point has been suggested in 'The Pattern of Agricultural Production, in the Territories of Amber (c. 1650–1750)'.

# 19

## Agra*

Agra, town, headquarters of a division, and district of the name in the state of Uttar Pradesh, is situated on the banks of river Yamunā, 27° 1´ N, 77° 50´ E, population (1951) 375,665, of whom 15.6 per cent are Muslims. The city was for a long time the seat of residence of the Mughal emperors, and is renowned especially for its remarkable monuments of Mughal architecture.

## History

Little is known about the early history of Āgra, but there is no doubt that it was founded long before the Muslim invasions of India. The first reference to the city, and to an ancient fortress in it, is contained in a *kaṣīda* written in praise of the Ghaznawid prince Maḥmūd b. Ibrāhīm by the poet Masʿūd b. Saʿd b. Salmān (d. 515/1121 or 526/1131), wherein the conquest of the fortress (presumably during the reign of Sulṭān Masʿūd III, 493–508/ 1099–1155) is mentioned. The town was ruled by Rājpūt chiefs, who, upon making their submission to the Sultanate of Delhi, were allowed to keep their control over it, under the overall command of the governor of Biyāna province. It remained unnoticed until Sultan Sikandar Lōdi (894–923/1489–1517) rebuilt the city in 911/1505 and made it the seat of his government. The place quickly gained in importance and attracted scholars

* H. A. R. Gibbs and others, eds, *Encyclopaedia of Islam*, Vol. I, New Edition, E. J. Brill, Leiden, 1979, pp. 252–4.

and learned men from many parts of the Muslim world. Commanding routes to Gwalior and Mālwa in the south, Rājpūtāna in the west, Delhi and the Panjāb in the north-west, and the plain of the Ganges in the east, it soon became a strategic and trading centre. It continued to be the capital of Ibrāhim Lōdi (923–32/ 1517–26) and, on his defeat in 932/1526, it became the capital of Bābur. In addition to building his palace of Charbāgh, Bābur laid out a number of gardens in the city and constructed many baths. His nobles followed his example, and a considerable portion of the old city was levelled down. The city remained Humāyūn's and Shīr Shāh's capital, but neither Humāyūn, nor Shīr Shāh or his successors were able to spend much time there. It again became the seat of government in the third year of Akbar's reign (965/1558), when he took up residence in the citadel formerly known as Badal Gadh, and his nobles built their homes on both banks of the river. In 972/1565, the construction of the fort on the site of Badal Gadh was undertaken, but before it could be completed, the building of Fathpūr Sikrī (q.v.) was commenced. From 982/1574 to 994/1586, Akbar lived mostly in the new city, and later, till 1006/1598, his headquarters were generally at Lahore. In the latter year, he returned to Āgra. On his death in 1014/1605, Jahāngīr ascended the throne in that city and lived there almost continuously from 1016/1607 to 1022/ 1613. He spent another year at Āgra in 1027/1618, but later, until his death in 1037/1628, he spent most of his time in Kashmīr and Lahore. Like his father, Shāhjahān also ascended the throne at Āgra, but had to leave for the Deccan in the following year. From 1040/1631 to 1042/1633 he again resided in the city, but after that, except for brief visits, he did not stay there for long. Thereafter, he lived mostly at Delhi, where he built the new city of Shāhjahānabād. (The name of Āgra was also changed to Akbarabad, but the latter name was never widely used.) In 1067–1657 he fell seriously ill and was brought to Āgra by his eldest son, Dārā Shikūh. In the war of succession that broke out, Aurangzeb was victorious and ascended the throne in 1068/1658. Shāhjahān was imprisoned in the Fort, where he died in 1076–1666. On hearing the news, Aurangzeb returned to Āgra and held court there for some time. Later, he again stayed in Āgra from 1079/1669 to 1081/1671. However, Aurangzeb's usual place of residence was, first, Delhi, and then, in the

Deccan. Though, in the seventeenth century, the court did not remain at Āgra for long, the place was nevertheless regarded as one of the capital cities of the empire. Most of the European travellers who visited India considered it to be one of the largest cities they had seen, comparable in size to Paris, London, and Constantinople. It was a centre of trade and commerce and was well-known for its textile industry, gold inlay work, stone and marble work, and crystal. However, the population as well as the trade diminished considerably when the court was away.

The successors of Aurangzeb lived mostly in Delhi, though Āgra continued to be important politically. During the second half of the eighteenth century, it suffered much from the depredations of the Jāts, the Mahrattās, and the Rohillāhs. Though nominal Mughal sovereignty over the town continued till it was annexed by the British in 1803, except for the years 1774 to 1785 when Nadjaf Khān (d. 1782) and his successors were its governors, Āgra was under the occupation of the Jāts (1761–70 and 1773–4) and the Mahrattās (1758–61, 1770–3, and 1785–1803).

## Monuments

### The Fort

The present fort of Āgra was built by Akbar on the site of the Lōdi fortress of Badal Gadh on the right bank of the Yamunā. It was constructed in about eight years (1565–73) under the superintendence of Muhammad Ķāsim Khān Mīr-i Baḥr at a cost of 15 lakhs of rupees. It is in the shape of an irregular semicircle with its base along the river. The fort is surrounded by a double wall, loopholed for musketry, the distance between the walls being 40 ft. The outer wall, just under 70 ft high and faced with red sandstone, is about 1½ miles in circuit and represents the first conception of dressed stone on such a large scale. The principal gateway, the Delhi Gate, is one of the most impressive portals in India. Within the fort, according to Abu'l Faḍl, Akbar built 'upward of 500 edifices of red stone in the fine styles of Bengal and Gujrāt'. Most of these buildings were demolished by Shāhjahān to make room for his marble structures, among those that still stand Akbari and Bangālī Mahalls are the earliest. Akbar's buildings are characterized by carved stone brackets which support the stone beams, wide eaves, and flat ceilings, the arch being used sparingly. Similar in design is the Jahāngīrī Mahall, a double-storeyed construction, 261 ft by 288 ft supposed to have been built by Akbar for prince Salim (later Jahāngīr) but very probably built by Jahāngīr himself for the Rājpūt princesses of the harem, though Cunningham thinks it was built by Ibrāhīm Lōdī. After the accession of Shāhjahān, architectural style underwent a radical change. With the discovery of marble quarries, red sandstone was practically eliminated and large-scale use of marble made carved line and flowing rhythm of style possible. Instead of the beam and brackets, foliated or cusped arches became common and marble meads of engrailed arches distinguished the buildings of Shāhjahān. Among the most important of his buildings in the fort are the Khāṣṣ Mahall and its adjoining north and south pavilions; the Shish Mahall, a bath whose walls and ceilings are spangled over with tiny mirrors of irregular shape set in stucco relief; the *Muthamman Burj* built for the empress Mumtāz Mahall (in which building Shāhjahān breathed his last); the Diwān-i Khāṣṣ (or private assembly chamber); the Diwān-i 'Amm (or public audience chamber) having a court 500 ft by 73 ft, and a pillared hall 201 ft by 67 ft with an alcove of inlaid marble being the throne gallery (built of red sandstone plastered with white marble stucco which is artistically gilded); the Moti Masjid (or Pearl Mosque), a magnificent structure of white marble standing on a plinth of red sandstone.

## Jami Masjid

Not far from the fort stands the Jami' Masjid, built by Jahān Ārā Begam, the eldest daughter of Shāhjahān, in 1058/1648, a red sandstone building having three domes and five gracefully proportioned arches, the central archway being a semi-domed double portal.

## Tomb of Akbar

The tomb of Akbar at Sikandara, constructed in Jahāngīr's reign on a site selected by Akbar himself, stands in the middle of a well-laid garden about five miles from Āgra. Very probably some idea of the design was settled by Akbar, but the building lacks that correctness which is characteristic of the construction undertaken by that monarch. The building is 140 ft square, consisting of five terraces diminishing as they ascend. The lowest storey is arcaded and in the centre of each side is inserted a large portico with a deeply recessed archway. The next three storeys consist of superimposed tiers of pillared arcades and kiosks built mainly of red sandstone. The topmost storey is of white marble and is screened with perforated lattices. Each corner of this storey is surmounted by a slender kiosk.

## Tomb of I'timād al-Dawla

The tomb of Jahāngīr's minister, Mirzā Ghiāth Bēg entitled I'timād al-Dawla (d. 1622), constructed by his daughter, the empress Nūrjahān and completed in 1628, stands in the middle of a well-laid garden on the left bank of the river. The mausoleum consists of a square lower storey 69 ft wide with a gracefully proportioned octagonal turret, like a dwarfed minaret, thrown out from each corner; while the second storey rises in the form of a traceried pavilion covered by a canopy-shaped vaulted roof sending out broad stooping eaves surmounted by two golden pinnacles. It is the first large building in India built entirely of marble and is remarkable for the richness of its decoration and profuse pietra dura work.

## Tāj Mahal

The most famous building at Āgra is the Tāj Mahal, the beautiful mausoleum erected by Shāhjahān for his dearly loved wife, Ardumand Bānū Bēgam, entitled Mumtāz Mahall, popularly known to her contemporaries as Tāj Mahal. She was the daughter of Āsaf Khān, son of I'timād al-Dawla, and was married to Shāhjahān in 1612 at the age of nineteen. She bore him fourteen children and died in June 1631 at Burhānpur after giving birth to a daughter. Work on the mausoleum was started almost immediately after her death and was completed in about twelve years at a cost of five million rupees, though some later writers have put the figure at 30 million rupees. According to the contemporary European traveller, Tavernier, the structure, together with its subsidiary buildings, was completed in about twenty-two years during which period twenty thousand workmen were continuously employed on it. The best architects and craftsmen, each a specialist in his own field, available in the empire as well as in the neighbouring countries were engaged for the work, which was carried on under the general supervision of Makramat Khān and Mīr 'Abd al Karīm. The tradition that the architect of the Tāj Mahal was a Venetian, Geronimo Veroneo, based on a statement made by Father Manrique, finds no corroboration either in the Mughal chronicles or in the writings of the other contemporary European travellers like Tavernier, Bernier, and Thevenot, who regarded the building as a purely oriental work. Its close resemblance with the tomb of Humāyūn at Delhi, and an analysis of its architectural as well as decorative features, suggest that it was undoubtedly the culminating point in the evolution of the Indo-Muslim style of architecture, though no other building in India is quite as exquisite, elegant or beautiful.

The tomb, built of white marble from Jodhpur, stands on a raised platform, 18 ft high and 313 ft square, faced with foliated arches. At each corner of this platform, there is a beautifully proportioned cylindrical minaret, 133 ft high girt with three galleries and finished with an open domed *čatr* throwing out broad eaves. In the centre of the platform stands the mausoleum, a square of 186 ft, with angles canted to the extent of 33 ft 9 in, the facade rising 92 ft 3 in from the platform. In each face of the building is a high arched recessed porch. On either side of each porch, and at the canted angles, there are arched recesses of uniform size arranged in two storeys. These recesses and the porches are vaulted. Above each of the canted angles stands a domed pillared kiosk, while the centre is occupied by a beautiful bulbous dome, rising from a high circular drum, and surmounted by a gilt pinnacle finished with a crescent. The central dome, 58 ft in diameter and rising 74 ft above the roof or 191 ft from the platform, is one of the finest in the world. Beneath the dome is the central chamber, octagonal within, buttressed at each angle by small octagonal rooms of two storeys, with the great porches in between each pair. In the middle of the central chamber is the cenotaph of Mumtāz Mahall, and beside it that of her husband. Immediately beneath these, in the crypt, are the two graves. The cenotaphs are enclosed by a remarkable screen of trellis-work of white marble. The porches are framed in ornamental inscriptions from the

Kur'ān and the beauty of the whole is enhanced by copious and graceful ornamentation in *pietra dura*. All the spandrels, angles, and important architectural details are inlaid with semi-precious stones combined in wreaths, scrolls, and frets, as exquisite in design as beautiful in colour. The tomb is surrounded by a formal garden of great beauty, with long lily ponds, also of marble, containing a row of fountains, leading from the principal entrance to the mausoleum. The river, which bounds the garden on the north, provides marvellous reflections of the building.

## Bibliography

*Bābur-nāma* (tr. Beveridge). ii; *Akbar-nāma* (Bib. Ind.), esp. ii, 246–7; 'Alā-al-Dawla Kazwini, *Najāis al-Ma'athir* (Aligarh Univ. Ms.), ff. 266a–268b; *Tuzuk-i Jahāngiri* (tr. Rogers and Beveridge), esp. i, 3–7, 152; 'Abd al Hamid Lāhawri, *Pādshāh-nama* (Bib. Ind.), esp. 384, 402–3, 1/2, 235–41, II, 322–31; Muhammad Sālih, *'Amal-i Sālih* (Bib. Ind.), esp. ii, 380–5; *Hālāt-i Tāj Mahall* (Aligarh Univ. Ms.); De Laet, *The Empire of the Great Mogol,* Bombay, 1928, 36–44; *Tavernier's Travels in India,* (ed. V. Ball, 1889), i, 105–12; *Bernier's Travels,* London, 1881, 284–99; *Indian Travels of Thevenot and Careri* (ed. Sen, 1949), 46–57; S. M. Latif, *Agra, Historical Descriptive,* 1896; Duncan, *Keene's Hand Book for Visitors to Agra,* 1909; *Imperial Gazetteer of India* (1905); *Report, Arch. Survey of India,* 1874, and 1904–5, pp. 1–3; E. B. Havell, *A Handbook to Agra and the Taj,* 1912; J. Fergusson, *History of Indian and Eastern Architecture,* 1910; *Camb. History of India,* vol. iv, chap. xviii; Havell, *Indian Architecture,* 1913; *idem, Ancient and Medieval Architecture of India,* 1913; E. W. Smith, *Akbar's Tomb at Sikandara,* 1909; M. Moinuddin Ahmad, *The Taj and its Environments,* 1924; M. Ashraf Husain, *An Historical Guide to the Agra Fort,* 1937; Stuart, *The Gardens of the Great Mughals,* 1913; Hosten, 'Who Planned the Taj?', *Jour. As. Soc. Bengal,* June 1910; V. Smith, *History of Fine Arts in India,* 183–5; Mahdi Husain, 'Agra before the Mughals', *Jour. U.P. Hist. Soc.,* xx, pt. ii, 80–7; Sarkar, *Studies in Mughal India,* 1919, 27–32.

# 20

# The Morphology of a Medieval Indian City
## A Case Study of Shahjahanabad in the Eighteenth and Early Nineteenth Century*

It is a welcome sign that Indian historians have turned their serious attention to urban history, at a time when the fast changing landscape of cities, has left many of the old recognizable features still intact. Sooner, rather than later, many of these would also disappear, leaving behind a few important monuments. It would, however, be difficult then, to appreciate fully the meaning of the written record or to fill up the gaps on the basis of surviving features.

As is well known, Delhi was populated several times; each time a new part was populated, the earlier part lost its glory, though was never depopulated. The ancient Indraprastha (Inderpat) was repopulated when Humayun rebuilt its old fort and the township (*Din Panah*). The cities of the Tomars survived as three suburban villages, the fort of Prithviraj Chauhan; was never fully depopulated as it retained a part of its importance due to Qutb Minar, Quwwat-ul-Islam Mosque, and the Alai Darwaza. Hauz Khas and the tomb of Shaikh Qutb-u-Din Bakhtiyar Kaki in Mehrauli, Ghiyaspur (which acquired fame due to the tomb of Shaikh Nizamud-Din Auliya), Kilokheri, Siri, Mubarakpur,

* *Proceedings of Indian History Congress*, XLIII Session, Kurukshetra, 1982, pp. 307–17.

Tughlaqabad, Firozabad, Khizrabad, Sher Mandal, Salimgarh, etc., have all survived through the centuries in one form or the other. The last Mughal capital was, of course, Shahjahanabad, whose foundation stone was laid by Shahjahan on 9 Muharram . 1049H/12 May 1639. The construction of the main buildings of the fort was completed in nine years. Where the city of Shahjahanabad now stands, some monuments of the Sultanate period have survived, such as the dargah of Shah Turkman Biyabani (d. 632H/1234–5) or the Kalan Masjid, now called Kali Masjid, built by Khan-i-Jahan Maqbul in 789H/1387. Another important landmark is the Khari Bawri (Baoli as it is called today which bears two inscriptions of Islam Shah's reign 952H/ 1545) and another of 958H/1551 (being the date of the completion of the Baoli).

This paper, however, deals only with Shahjahanabad. Apart from the still existing old names, and some early eighteenth and nineteenth century works, extensive use has been made of two early Persian works, both of which are published but not used in the present context.

One is *Muraqqa-i-Delhi* by Dargah Quli Khan, who wrote the work as a travelogue when he visited Delhi in 1151 H/1738–9 along with Nizam-ul Mulk Asaf Jah.[1] This work deals with shrines, monuments, important men and women in the arts, especially music, etc. Its principal value is for the study of social life in Delhi and for the monuments of the city and its suburbs, but it has also been found to be valuable for the study of the layout of the city and the functional features of the different landmarks.

The other work which has been used is the *Sair-ul-Manazil*[2] of Sangin Beg, son of Ali Akbar Beg, which was written at the instance of Charles Metcalf, who was the Resident at Delhi in 1811–19 and again from 1825–7 and completed around the year 1827. The name of William Frazer, Deputy Superintendent, was also added to that of Metcalf, though perhaps later. This work seeks to describe the various localities, districts, layout, streets, and some of the monuments. Written about twenty years before Sir Syed Ahmed Khan's famous work *Asar-us-Sanadid*, it has attracted much less attention of scholars.

It is beyond the scope of this brief paper to give a description of the city of Shahjahanabad during the period under study.

However, certain broad functional features may be pointed out. The number of streets and *mohallas* which have continued to exist under the same name is remakably large. Some of these have retained their traditional features, while in many other cases though the names have survived, the type of activity and the character of the population have undergone a complete change. For example, in Paiwalan near Jami Masjid, one can still buy fireworks; similarly, in Chawri Bazar, shops selling copper or brass utensils are still to be found.[3]

One of the most significant features of Shahjahanabad is that there is no segregation of the houses of the rich and poor, or of residential parts and the commercial parts, a feature that developed under the British. While many localities were perdominantly inhabited by a single community, the localities where people of the other communities lived in close proximity were interspersed. This was as true of religious communities as of caste or professional groups. For example, the following description may be seen:

From the south of Hauz-i-Qazi till Turkman Gate, along with streets on the both sides are: On one side, the shop of a *halwai* (sweetmeat seller), Kucha Bazar Imli Mohalla, and Kucha of Pati Ram, Bangla of Hafiz Fida, Kucha Murghian (birds and fowl), residences of ryots (*Maskan-i-riya*), houses of Kashmiri pandits, Haveli of Dudhadhari, house of Lala Gulab Rai Pandit, the Tahsildar of Palam proper, Kucha of Mai Das, Than of Panj Piram, Kucha of Shidi Qasim, which leads to Kucha of Pati Ram. In the latter Kucha (Shidi Qasim) there is the residence of Govardhan Kashmiri and of Mir Khan Tunda, who is unsurpassable in singing and dancing, the house of Mirza Fathullah Beg Chela, haveli of Maulavi Fath Ali Sahib *Jagirdar*, houses of other ryots (*riaya*), the well of Naurang Rai, havelis of banias (bagga-i-an). And in the Kucha going, towards the city wall, there is the property (*riyasat*) of *khatiks* who work with leather (*chirm sazan*), the small garden of Tansukh Rai Kaghazi, the hauz (tank) of Nawab Muzaffar Khan and the residences of ryots (*riaya*). From the Than of Panj Piran, may be found *havelis* of Lala Basanti Ram and Sadasukh Pandit, and Bazar Sita Ram, the Katra of Jani Khan and the riyasat (properties) of the ryots. On the opposite side there is a Kucha going towards the Chhatta of Shah Haji. Before that there is a *doraha* (bifurcated road): one goes towards mohalla of *Churigaran* (bangle-makers) and the other towards the *hammam* (public bath) of Sital Das, who lived at the time of Shah Alam. Further down is the haveli of Rai Shambhu Nath, the stables (*tavela*) of Murtaza Khan, haveli of Raja Kedar Nath and the katra of *gari-banan* (cart drivers). One road is adjacent to the above-mentioned well with saline water, and the other is towards the *bangla* of Shidi Faulad Khan, the kucha of Imam and the houses of the ryots.[4]

It has been mentioned above that though sometime the localities where Hindus and Muslims lived were separated, there was nevertheless a great deal of intermixture between the two communities. Only some examples of joint celebrations of festivals and the absence of distinction between Shias and .Sunnis in the observance of Muharram may be quoted here. Although the tomb of Shaikh Nasir-ud Din Chiragh-i-Delhi was situated at the distance of 3 *krohs* from Shahjahanabad, it was considered sacred by both Hindus and Muslims (presumably of the city as well) who celebrated in large number the festival of 'light' every year at the tomb during the month of Diwali. Muhammad Shah had built a *pucca* enclosure, and musical preformances were of great importance.[5] The other example is that of a person who was held in great veneration by Hindus and Muslims alike, namely, Majnun Nanak Shahi.[6] Similarly the celebration of Basant (*Basant Panchmi*) was started from the shrine of the footprint of the Prophet and joined in by musicians and public of both the communities.[7]

About the celebration of Muharram, similarly, there is no indication that its observance was confined only to one sect. For example, the followers of the saint Majnun Nanak Shahi observed in their own way the tenth of Muhrram where every one participated.[8] In the *Ashur Khana* managed by Jawed Khan, the famous *Marsia Khawn* (reciter of elegies on Imam Husain), every one assembled.[9] The popularity of the *marsias*, written in *rekhta* (early Urdu) by three brothers, Miskin, Hazin, and Ghamgin was considerable. *Tazia* keeping was fairly common and people from all walks of life came to *Taziakhana* of Imam Husain.[10] Although the word Imambara is not used in *Muraqqa* in Delhi it is used in *Sair-ul-Manazil*, for example, Imambara of Mir Askari.[11]

The city of Shahjahanabad centred basically round the fort (which was the Imperial Palace) and the Jami Masjid. It was surrounded by the city walls, many parts of which still survive along with the city gates, for example, Delhi darwaza, Ajmeri darwaza, Turkman darwaza, Kashmiri darwaza, Lahori darwaza, Mori darwaza. The famous Chandni Chowk going from west to east, (starting by the side of Jami Masjid towards the west and

going towards the fort in the east) was for all purposes what a
'down town' or city 'centrum' would be called in the West. A
chowk is a 'square' though in many cases it would be a
rectangle. It is a central marketing place with many streets
joining it. It also serves as a meeting place, as well as a centre
of professional entertainment. The most important place in
Shahjahanabad was Chandni Chowk, still retaining its importance, but much changed during the last fifty years. A description given by Dargah Quli Khan in 1737, is quite interesting.

## Chandni Chowk

'Chandni Chowk' is most pleasant and entertaining than the
other chowks, and compared to other streets and roads, much
more decorated. It is a place where important people come for
entertainment and pleasure, and sight seeing for beauty and
elegance. Articles of every description are found in its adjoining
streets, and goods from every locality are available here in
plenty. In the middle of it is a beautiful canal. On one street are
jewellers where rubies and pearls and all the gems are available
in plenty. On another side are the perfumeries, oils, and apoth-
ecaries. On yet another side are arms and daggers. Chinaware
is also readily available along with glassware of different shapes
and sizes, whose decoration defies all description. They have
arranged such attractive (wine) glasses that an austere and
pious man, hundred years old, would feel tempted to drink wine.
Several other articles of common use are sold here which would
probably never be available even in the *karkhana*s of the nobles.

Apart from the merchandise, it is a place which is extremely
pleasant for an evening stroll. It is attractive to the eye and its
fragrance provides great freshness, so much so that going
through a pleasure garden would not be so enjoyable. In its many
coffee houses, literary personalities gather every day and recite
their pieces to each other. It is such a pleasure resort that the
great amirs, in spite of their elevated status, enjoy the sight of
this chowk, and if they wish to purchase its novelties, even the
great wealth of Qarun would disappear. If the son of an amir
wishes to visit this chowk for enjoying life, his mother would
secretly give him a lakh of rupees out of the monies left by his
father, even though she would offer the excuse that she did not

have enough money, hoping that the son would buy novelties from the chowk, but the pleasure loving young man would blow up the money in things that attract his fancy.[12]

## Sacred Places

Of the sacred places, largest number was, naturally, that of mosques, of which apart from Jami Masjid and Kalan Masjid (Kali Masjid) there were many. The next, in numbers, were the tombs, variously referred to as just *qabr* or if the superstructure was imposing, as *maqbara*, or *Rauza* (as of Shah Turkman Biyabani). Other names for tombs were *Turbat Kada*, dargah (as Qudam Sharif) *astana*, *taklya*, and *mazar*. *Kashana* could be used for a place where *quwwali* was recited, while for places connected with the observance of Muharram, the names used were Chauki Khana, Aza Khana, Tazia Khana, Ashur Khana, and presumably latter, *Imambara* and *Panja*.[13] Karbala was naturally not mentioned within the city walls of Shahjahanabad, though it existed outside. Majlis Khana are also mentioned.

Among the charitable places were madrasas, of which quite a few have been mentioned in Shahjahanabad. There is only one hospital mentioned, the *darush-shafa*, founded by Shahjahan. No temples are recorded, in either of the two works, within the city walls of Shahjahanabad, though there are references to Rajghat, Nigambodh Ghat, and Ghat Kela, as well as to *mandirs* of Paras Nath, Jogmayaji, Kalkaji, Hanumanji, and Makan Shitla.[14] In the *Chhatta* of Nigambodh Ghat there were houses of Gosains, *Thakurdwaras*, *chhatris*, and places held sacred by the Hindus.

## Streets, Lanes, and Roads

The most common word for streets was *kucha* which, quite frequently, is used along with the word bazar. It could be named after a person or of the dominant community residing there, or a profession. Examples would be kucha-i-Bulaqi Begum or kucha-i-Pati Ram, Kucha-i-Balli Maran, kucha-i-Jogiwara, etc. *Sarak* is not mentioned in either of the two works. In common parlance, some of the *kuchas* are now called *gali*, such as kucha Samosa[15] is called *Samose wali gali* or *kucha batasha walah* is popularly called Batashe wali gali. *Gandhi gali* (not *gaandhi*)[16] is mentioned by that name. Where a road bifurcates, it is called *sihraha,* such as Sihraha Bairam Khan.[17]

## Localities, Districts, and Market

The most commonly used term for a locality is *mohalla.* It could be named after an individual, such as Mohalla Hakim Muhsin Khan or Mohalla Muhammad Ali Khan, but the commonest are those named after artisans, such as Mohalla churigaran (mentioned above), Mohalla Dhobiwala (quarters of washermen) or Mohalla Kashtibanan (boatmen). Some of the mohallas bear the name of some characteristic feature of the place such as mohalla *imli* (tamarind) or mohalla *chah-i-rahat* (well with a Persian wheel). In the case of Matia Mahal, mohalla changes its form.

In the same way, the markets were generally known as *bazar,* though the largest ones, as mentioned before, were chowks, such as Chandni Chowk or chowk Saadullah Khan. Bazar is hardly ever used in the context of Shahajahanabad as a covered market, but there are shops on both sides of a street and behind the shops are residential houses. Most derive their names from persons, such as Bazar Sita Ram or Bazar Nawab Mir (Amir?) Khan Chaghta or Faiz Bazar or from crafts, such as *Jauhari* (jewellers) Bazar or Bazar Mazid Parcha.

Marketplaces which were specially built for retail or wholesale shops were referred to as *Ganj,* but their names were not necessarily associated with any particular feature, such as Daryaganj, Paharganj, Jahangirganj, and Rakabganj. Shops were sometimes collectively referred to as *dakakin* such as *dakakin-bisatiyan* (general merchants), *dakakin-chirimaran* (bird catchers), *dakakin-halwaiyan* (sweetmeat sellers); or, where an individual shop gave its name to many adjoining shops, as *dukan* as in the case of dukan Thande Baqqal or dukan Tek Chand or dukan Kishan Chand Sarraf. Yet another name for a market would be *mandi* or *mandvi,* usually a wholesale market of a commodity, as in the case of Sabzimandi (vegetable market) or Mandvi pan or Mandvi gul-faroshan (market for flower sellers).

Two interesting names are *chhatta* and *katra. Chhatta* literally means a covered lane or a bazar, but it frequently refers to the locality where artisans practising a particular craft lived and/or worked, such as Chhatta mimaran (masons), or Chhatta momgaran (wax makers). In many cases, a *chhatta* would be named after the person who built it, or with a place with which it may otherwise have been associated, such as Chhatta Lala Tansukh Rai or Chhatta Jan Nisar Khan, or Chhatta Nigambodh Ghat or Chhatta Lahori darwaza. *Katra* literally means a small square bazar, but quite often it refers to a wholesale market or where stocks were kept. There is a *nishan* of Nurjahan Begum ordering officers not to interfere with the merchants stocking their merchandise in a *katra*.[18] Some of these were named after merchants of a particulars commodity, such as Katra bazzazan (cloth merchants) Katra Raghav Zard or Ghi ka-katra (clarified butter), Katra nil (indigo) but quite often it was named after the builder or the owner, such as Katra Adina Beg Khan, or Katra Munshi Kanwal Nain.

Tripolia (literally three gates) was also used as a term denoting a locality. In *tripolia* were the *makan* of Shagunchand Sahu, *mandvi gul faroshan*, a *sharab-khana* (wine house), Mumtazganj, the habitation of *garibanan* (cart owners or drivers), later the royal artillery, going up to Kauriapul (bridge over Faiz canal).

## Nagar Seth

Unfortunately, not much is known about the institution of the Nagar Seth in Shahjahanabad, but that the institution existed here may be deduced from the reference to Haveli Nagar Seth in *Sair-ul-Manazil*.[19] Presumably his duties and privileges were the same as those of the famous Nagar Seth of Ahmedabad. We may also assume that what has been described in *Ain-i-Kotwal*[20] as the appointment of a notable of each community of artisans and a headman of each mohalla, must have existed in Shahjahanabad, though its form may have changed. An indication may be had from the fact that even now there is supposed to be only one entrance to a mohalla or katra bazar.

## Residences

It seems that the residences were generally named according to the plan, size, and the status of the person who built/owned it. First would come the *haveli*, such as haveli Ibrahim Ali Khan, or haveli Azam Khan or haveli Bakhshi Shanker. But there are

certain obvious exceptions which the present writer is unable
to explain, like haveli Puran Khaiyat (tailor) or haveli Zeenat
Tawaif (dancing girl and/or prostitute), or haveli *mimaran*
(masons) or *haveliyat baqqalan* (banias). A haveli was a house
complex with its *deorhi* (entrance), Sahn (courtyard), mahal
*saras* (living quarters), *balakhana* (the upper story), jilawkhana
(upper storey with a projecting balcony and external access),
and *diwan-khana* (office room). *Bala-khana* Shaikh Badrul-Din
Muhr-kun or *Bala-khana* Nawab Fathulla Beg Khan are mentioned. Similarly, Diwan-khana Hakim Qudrat-ullah Khan and
Diwan-khana Nawab Faizullah Khan are also mentioned, while
a *Jilaw-khana* in Chowk Sadullah Khan is mentioned in *Muraqqa-
i-Dihli*[21] A *burj* (engaged quoin or tower with rooms) was also
an important feature of many havelis; for various reasons it
occasionally acquired an independent position.[22]

Other names, lower in the hierarchy were just *makan* as those
of Bajne *tawaif*, or of Bag Singh. As in the case of haveli, makan
would also be sometimes used for important people, as in the
case of makan Raja Jai Singh, or makan Nawwab Fathullah Beg
Khan. *Makanat* (pl. of makan) was a collection of houses, used
either for a social entity or for houses owned by an individual.
Makanat-i–Panditan-i-Kashmiri, makanat Qaum Khattri or
makanat-Murshidzadaha (princes) would be examples of the
former, while makanat-i-Mahammad Amin Khan, makanat-i-
Nawwab Faiz Muhammad Khan, and makanat-i-Nawwab Qamar-
ud-Din would be examples of the latter.

*Manzil*, so common among Urdu-speaking people today, was
rarely used; the only example we have is in the plural—*manazil*
Nawab Jahan Ara Begum. *Kothi*, which literally is a diminutive
of fort, and was commonly used in the sense of 'factories' owned
by the European companies, or kothars used in the same period
as godown (for example, kothar of Hathras or of Marchra[23]) has
not been used in either of the two works, nor is it used today in
the walled city except in its dimunitive form *kothri* (for a very
small room or even a cell). *Kothi*, however, is frequently used as
denoting an upper class residence, whether of Indians or the
Europeans. Examples would be Kothi Nawab Ahmad Baksh
Khan, Kothi Nawab Faiz Muhammad Khan Bahadur, Kothi Lala
Saudagar Mal, Kothi Lala Mangat Rai. In the case of the Europeans, though most of these residences were outside the city

walls, they were a part of the city, such as *Kothi Daktar* Ludlow Saheb (Ludlow Castle), and *Kothi* Col. James Skinner etc. The term *bangla* seems to have come from Bengal. Its use in *Muraqqa-i-Dihli* where it is stated that there were *bangla*s in every locality,[24] suggests that it had been used for long, though the term and the type of the houses it denoted appear to have been popularized by the British. Among the many names mentioned in *Sair-ul-Manazil*, Bangla Saiyid Firoz, Bangla Shidi Faulad Khan, and Bangla Sukunat-i-Angrez (residences of Englishmen may be mentioned here). In contrast to a *haveli*, a *bangla* (bungalow) was essentially a detached house.

## Parks and Gardens

Gardens were presumably laid by individuals, as pleasure resorts, but in course of time became public gardens, such as Bagh Begum Saheba. Bagh of Begum Sumroo was just outside the city walls. Smaller gardens or parks were Baghicha Tansukh Rai Kaghazi (paper manufacturer or dealer), Baghicha Guruji Pandit, Baghicha Muhammad Karora, Zeenat Bari, etc.

## Water Bodies

There were mainly *hauz* or *talab* (tanks), *nahr* (canal), *chah* (wells), and *Bari* or *Baoli* (step-wells) in Shahjahanabad, for these provided water to the city. Some of these were fitted with Persian wheels (*rahat*).

## Conclusion

When we look at the eighteenth century, we find Shahjahanabad as a vibrant city with artisans, trade, and commerce with residences of wealthy *jagirdar*s and merchants, a city of pleasure and sin, as well as of sacred edifices and monuments. Then came the catastrophes: Nadir Shah's invasion, Ahmad Shah Durrani's invasions, the domination of the Marathas and the Afghans, virtual independences of the Governors and, finally, the establishment of the British domination in 1803. This was the time of which the poets expressed their grief, such as Sauda, who wrote his *Shahr Ashok*, or the migration of Mir Taqi Mir to Lucknow and his famous lines, written in anguish.

Dehli, which was a city Select of the World
Where the elite of the Times lived;
It has been robbed and destroyed by circumstances;
I belong to that very desolate city.

The evidence of decline cannot be overlooked; the loss of source of power and wealth of the landed aristocracy and the impoverishment of the king took their toll in terms of the city's prosperity. And yet it remained a well populated city marked by its graces and culture.

## Notes and References

1. The printed version in the library of Anjuman Taraqqi-i-Urdu, Hind, New Delhi, has been used.
2. The text edited by Sharif Husain Qasimi of Delhi University and published by Ghalib Institute, New Delhi in 1982 has been used.
3. *Sair-ul-Manazil,* Editors' introduction.
4. *Sair-ul-Manazil,* p. 23.
5. *Muraqqa-i-Dihli,* pp. 7–8.
6. Ibid., p. 23.
7. Ibid., p. 30.
8. Ibid., p. 25.
9. Ibid., p. 50.
10. Ibid., pp. 51–2.
11. *Sair-ul-Manazil,* p. 35.
12. *Muraqqa-i-Dihli,* pp. 17–19.
13. Both *Muraqqa-i-Dihli* and *Sair-ul-Manazil* mention all the places, except Imambara and Panja which are mentioned by the latter only.
14. *Sair-ul-Manazil,* pp. 43, 52, 62, 88, 93, 107.
15. *Sair-ul-Manazil,* p. 21.
16. Ibid., p. 36.
17. Ibid., pp. 28, 33.
18. S.A.I. Tirmizi, *Edicts from the Mughal Harem,* Delhi, 1979, p. 29.
19. *Sair-ul-Manazil,* p. 29.
20. *Ain-i-Akbari,* tr. Jarrett, Vol. II, Delhi, 1978, p. 44.
21. *Muraqqa-i-Dihli,* p. 14.
22. Ibid.
23. Ibid.
24. Ibid., pp. 12–13.

# 21

## Thoughts on Agrarian Relations in Mughal India*

### Problems, Sources, and Method

I am happy to have the privilege of addressing a distinguished gathering on the problems of agrarian history of medieval India with special reference to agrarian relations. To a learned audience like this I need hardly spell out the problems of agrarian history which are worrying the students of medieval India. Briefly, I shall indicate what appears to me to be some of the most baffling problems.

First of all—I am saying this not in order of importance—is the question whether the relationships in India could be considered to be feudal in character and, if so, what was the nature of this feudalism? In what ways was it different from the type of feudalism that had existed in India in the earlier phase? And what are the changes, if any, that were taking place in this feudal structure?

There is no doubt that in medieval India the surplus produce was controlled by the intermediaries and also a part of it was appropriated by them. By all accounts the major share of the surplus went to the *amirs*, although the process of cultivation and the rural life was certainly controlled by the zamindar. The amir could not exist independently of the zamindar. This is a system which can only be described as feudal if we accept a totally

* U.G.C. National Lectures, Patna University, Peoples' Publishing House, Delhi, 1973.

modified definition of feudalism. It is mainly a system (1) in which the major source of production is agricultural production, (2) in which a substantial share of the surplus produce is appropriated by a class which holds power militarily, (3) in which the economic power of the class which appropriates surplus is based not only on the military strength of that class but also on the role that class is playing in the production process, whether of agricultural production or the subsidiary handicrafts production, and (4) in which this dominating class in spite of changes within its fold is by and large a fairly closed group. We notice that there is very little chance of this class being overthrown by those who are actually cultivating or engaged in the process of cultivation, that it is dominant socially, politically and militarily, that even the revolts against the imperial government are dominated by this class, and finally that, while this class is dependent on the emperor or the king for its position in many ways, the imperial system itself is dependent on the support of this particular class. It is only in this sense that we can call this system a feudal system.

But if you use the word feudal in the western European sense of the term, then quite obviously we do not have any of the characteristics of the western European feudalism. I would go along with Professor R. S. Sharma that the word feudalism should be used. It should be used because it helps us to understand certain vital characteristics of a phase of social development which undergo a change subsequently. This is my reason for rejecting the formulation of the Asiatic mode of production. It appears to me that there is very little evidence of the existence of what was deemed to be communal ownership. What was the village community? It was really the community of the proprietors in a village, especially where the village happened to be a *bhayyāchāra* village or a village of co-parcenaries. But otherwise, in the sense of the village commune or the village community holding rights over land as a whole, we have hardly any evidence.

The medieval system has been regarded as 'oriental despotism', which, I think, is a very much overworked word. The most interesting refutation of the theory of oriental despotism is in the writings of the Britishers who came to India between 1743 and 1793. In that fifty-year period they had discussed this question at great length. If you compare the concept of property as defined by Blackstone in the pre-Adam Smith period—

Blackstone's commentaries as you know were written before Adam Smith—then you will find that the concept of property is very similar to the concept of property that was in existence here. So in that sense it is basically a feudal relationship, that is to say, the property is not an exclusive property. The capitalist definition of property is the absolute right to use, to abuse, and to dispose of; the word *abuse* is the vital word. This term actually originated after Ricardo's theories began to influence the British jurists, because the right to abuse property was never recognized in the pre-capitalist phase. In medieval India, the zamindar had absolute rights in terms of property. But he had simultaneously the obligation to ensure that cultivation was continued, and that good quality crops (*jins-i-kamil*) were sown. This system of overlapping and overriding rights undergoes a change in the capitalist system, where taxation acquires a meaning totally different from the pre-capitalist relationship. Since I find a great deal of similarity between the concept of property in Mughal times and the concept defined by Blackstone in the pre-physiocratic and pre-Adam Smith phase, I suggest that the Mughal system was feudal and pre-capitalist in character.

Coming to the concrete aspect of the agrarian relations in medieval India, the problem has become particularly acute because we notice two very distinct elements in the ruling class, by which I mean the class that was enjoying the benefits of surplus agricultural production. From the time of the Sultanate in particular—I am not denying the existence of this class earlier—we observe that there are two entirely different elements, the elements which the medieval historians have started calling the nobility or the *umara* (pl. of amir), to use the contemporary Persian term, and the hereditary landed classes, be they chieftains, or the various types of intermediaries or the proprietors of land of other descriptions. These two mutually exclusive classes subsequently began to merge with each other or established overlapping relationships with each other, and yet retained their distinct identity, and this poses a number of problems which I shall not attempt to answer in this very short time. Nor do I have the competence to answer these questions even to my own satisfaction, leave alone to your satisfaction.

The questions that arise are: did this constitute double exploitation? Or if there was no double exploitation, what was the fundamental relationship between these two distinct elements of society, and in what way did it affect the organization of Indian polity and society? And this naturally takes us to the next problem of agrarian history. What was the nature of the medieval state in terms of social relationships? Was this state dominated by one section or the other? Was it fundamentally assisting one group of the agrarian ruling class or the other? What was the nature of contradictions between these various classes? And what was the overall and net impact of these contradictions on the social situation prevailing during the medieval period?

Sometime ago it was treated as axiomatic that basically the social relationships in India remained constant, and that there was no change. This was a view which was first put forward by various British authors, and in a way it was accepted by the late K. M. Ashraf. But while this statement can be accepted as true in a very, very broad sense, the question still arises: how broad is the sense in which we can accept it? Because we do find numerous changes taking place in the position of various elements of the ruling class or the nobility from the lower to the higher, from the higher back to the lower, constant struggles and strifes frequently expressing themselves in military struggles, sometimes remaining basically and fundamentally economic struggles, with the state or the state apparatus, if you prefer to use that term, playing a definite part in this struggle. And these changes are there for us to see if we care to do so. Therefore we are not able to accept any longer the old hypothesis of a static medieval society; it was a changing society. But we still do not know what was the nature of this change, what was the direction of this change, and what factors caused this change. However, the broad outline seems to be discernible, and this takes us to our next problem.

Was this society capable of transforming itself? This question has been posed by different scholars in different ways. But basically the problem remains the same. Some people have asked: could India or Indian society have developed into a capitalist society or a modern industrial society if the British had not intervened? As students of history we are all allergic to playing the game of 'ifs' of history. It is fruitless to speculate on the 'ifs' of history; it is even unprofessional and unhistorian-like to do so.

Having said so, I still want to pose the question: could our society have been transformed into an industrial society or into a capitalist society or into a modern society if the British and the other Europeans had not intervened? Whether it would have happened or not is a different matter. The question is: was our society capable of doing so? Did it have within itself the germs of social change or was it too static?

Once we come to discuss this issue, several matters deserve our consideration. For example, the problem which was posed rather sharply in the nineteenth century by diverse writers was: was there a village community in India? And if so, what was its nature? What did it mean? Did it mean communal ownership of land during the medieval period, or was land basically individually owned? Did agricultural self-sufficiency, and self-sufficiency of the village or a group of small villages in fact exist? Or was trade, internal as well as overseas, carried on a large scale? Was the economy developing into a monetary economy? And if there was the growth of monetary economy, how fundamental was this growth? After all, the use of money has been in existence from the fifth century BC, but this does not necessarily mean that the country in general, and especially agrarian society in general, had developed a full-fledged monetary economy. And what was the role of money? Was it merely an instrument of exchange? Was the exchange carried on fundamentally through the barter system or was money economy in its modern sense playing a significant part? In this connection we cannot ignore the fact: was production increasing and expanding? Was the technique of agricultural production undergoing any change? Was there any factor contributing to change? Was there an agrarian crisis? And if there was an agrarian crisis, what do we mean by it? Did it mean the collapse of agriculture? Did it mean the collapse of agrarian relationships?

In this connection I need hardly emphasize, before an audience like this, the importance of village industries. I think that one of the major points which we should consider is this: why was it that Gandhiji came to the conclusion that the uplift of Indian rural society was linked up with the revival of village industries? Does it mean that when Gandhiji was born, the memory of village industries was still so vivid and its collapse still so apparent that he concluded that if the countryside in India is to be put back on its feet, the village industries must be revived? If so, are we conscious of the extent and the magnitude of village industries which existed in India before India was drawn into the vortex of modern industrial economy? It is obvious that no study of agrarian relationships will be adequate unless simultaneously we investigate the nature and extent of village handicrafts.

This takes us back to an earlier question but in a slightly modified form: what was the overall impact of the state system and of the changing state policies on all these different facets of agrarian relationships? Quite obviously, the economy of our country had been in medieval times, as it still is, primarily an agrarian economy. We were not facing the type of difficulty which was being faced in the West, that is to say, agricultural production had apparently reached the plateau which made further expansion virtually impossible. We in India until about six years ago were so firmly convinced of the capacity of our land to yield more agricultural produce by extending and expanding cultivation that even during the Second World War and afterwards, the slogan of 'grow more food' meant digging up your lawns! If there was any lawn in a university or elsewhere, wheat was sown and grown therein. And this was the theme which you can find throughout the medieval period. In most of the Mughal documents that have survived, instructions are continuously given for expanding the area under cultivation. The exact wordings were 'populate more land', which obviously meant bringing more areas under cultivation. In pursuance of their policy of extending the cultivated area, the emperors freely bestowed zamindari rights on those who would bring forest and wasteland under cultivation. It is also significant that the majority of the *madad-i-ma'āsh* grants (revenue-free grants given for charitable purposes) related to uncultivated land. So the overall impact of the state on agrarian relations is another problem which must concern us and to which, I confess, we do not know any satisfactory answer.

These are some of the major problems of agrarian relationships which we have to tackle, but we are not fully in a position to do so. The principal cause of our failure to do so lies in the nature of the source material that we have. As everybody knows, these were not the problems that really exercised the minds of the medieval intelligentsia, and therefore the writers of the medieval period in general did not expound their views on these questions. Even where there are references to agrarian relationships, they are in the nature of broad comments—rather like those one hears in Parliament today wherein the prejudices of an individual based on limited observation are sought to be put across as a generalized fact covering the entire Indian situation. Such statements and comments, and the type of comments we ourselves make every day, are certainly not based either on any empirical assessment or on any statistical analysis.

Let me give you another example. Some of us may believe that there has been no change in the Indian agrarian situation for the last five hundred years. But really the Indian situation has radically changed. There has been a complete revolution; old values have disappeared and a totally new society has been born. The nature of the change is described in various ways depending upon the class to which the speaker may belong. If he belongs to the zamindar class which is tending to lose its power, the generalizations will be of this type: what has happened? These illiterate and uneducated people have come into power, there is no law and order in the countryside. On the other hand, if he belongs to the newly emerging rich peasant class then he will remark: oh, what a social change there has been! If he belongs to the class of landless peasantry, he will express his total dissatisfaction with this change, and so on. Such attitudes can be observed even today when we have the means of securing statistical information, when we can go and make empirical observations, when social sciences have developed so much, and when we have advanced means of communication, mass media.

Therefore, for a medieval observer to make comments with any sense of proportion, I think, would be impossible. I am emphasizing this point because many of us have tended to write books on history on the basis of the observations of contemporaries or on the basis of the generalizations made by contemporaries, especially of the foreign travellers. Is there any reason to assume that Bernier was more competent than Katherine Mayo for example? It is difficult to accept Bernier's statement that the peasantry was better off under the autonomous rajas than in the rest of the empire, not only because the French doctor's prejudice in favour of feudal rights apparently clouded his judgement, but also because the available original records indicate that the rate of assessment of land revenue and other taxes charged from the peasants in the territories of the chiefs was not lower than that in the contiguous areas outside the chief's dominions.[1] But whereas Katherine Mayo's observations are rejected out of hand, Bernier's are regarded as sacred.

Can we really understand such a complex problem as that of agrarian relations on the basis of these comments whether by Indians or by foreigners who came and visited India? I have had the occasion to read, and, I am sure, historians of modern India must have seen numerous examples, the reporting by officials from the districts. If we look carefully into them we find how absurd many of these reports have been and how factually incorrect they tend to be. This is the case with the reports of people who were actively engaged in tackling administrative problems. We will therefore be justified in saying that a casual comment made by any one must be scrutinized in order to see to what extent it is true. You can see my difficulty in accepting general comments and observations, whether by Indians or by foreigners. Take statements like this: in the reign in such and such a king, everything was good, but in the reign of so and so, everything was bad. We know that whatever happened before our times appears to be good to most of us; that old days are always 'good old days', and the present is always the 'bad present'. Why should we really waste so much of our time and energy in attempting to understand the agrarian relationship of medieval India in terms of such observations and comments? If this method is to be totally rejected for understanding the present social situation in India, why does it become a valid method for understanding the social situation in the medieval period? And yet what are we to do? If we do not accept them, where do we go?

We can take the view that we will keep on studying history in the exact manner our forefathers did. We will keep on filling the 'gaps' of medieval Indian history which means one mono-graph for each king, and what has not been written on is the 'gap' which is easily identified. The chapters are ready-made: the first is ancestry, birth, and early childhood; the second is accession and the problems of accession; the third is wars and conquests; the fourth is minor wars and rebellions; the fifth is administration; and the sixth is society and culture during the age. I am not attempting to denigrate the importance of such studies. If that work had not been done, we would not be sitting together and talking of newer problems. Today we can talk, and I am saying it with all humility, of a radically new way of research because of the excellent work already done by our predecessors. But are we for ever and ever going to write history on the old pattern and filling the gaps of this type? Because if we are not going to fill the gaps of this type, then what is the type of source material that we have? We cannot manufacture the source material; I wish we could. Only we cease to be historians if we do that. Then what do we do?

The nature of the source material is going to condition partly the nature of our research, and yet we have to break through and evolve newer methods so that with the same type of source material we are able to answer the type of questions that are worrying us. This means having a second look at our source material and attempting new methods of investigation. Now one of the methods is that you subject your chronicles to a quantitative analysis so that the qualitative statements can then be checked up with the actual quantitative data. I know that in this audience perhaps I am disrespectfully quoting the example of Sher Shah, but I will remind you that if you take the principal source of the reign of Sher Shah, namely Abbas Sarwani's book, in the last few pages there is an account of the administration of Sher Shah, an account which led the late K. R. Qanungo in 1921 to describe exactly how Sher Shah administered his kingdom. There is a statement that Sher Shah divided his kingdom into a number of *sarkār*s. In each of the *sarkār*s he appointed a *shiqdar-i-shiqdārān* and a *munṣif-i-munṣifān* on the basis of which the more sophisticated among our scholars draw very nice charts and diagrams how Sher Shah administered his kingdom. I started by accepting this. Then I thought, let us see how many individuals were appointed shiqdār-i-shiqdārān. In the whole of Sarwani's book, barring these last four pages, there is no reference to any single individual having been appointed shiqdār-i-shiqdārān of such and such a sarkār. There is a variety of titles which are used: *walī, ḥākim, amīn*, etc. All these terms are used, but what is never used is the term shiqdār-i-shiqdārān. This is just to illustrate how we take things for granted without carefully consulting the original sources.

We cannot understand anything about Sher Shah's reign unless we study Abbas Sarwani's book with great care. And yet this observation of Abbas Sarwani when subjected to a quantitative analysis creates doubts in our minds. Now I am not going into the controversy why he used these terms. For example, a chronicler may write that in the reign of so and so this happened to the nobles, but such an observation has to be supported by facts and figures. For example, my colleague Athar Ali decided to make out a list of all the nobles of the reign of Aurangzeb, and establish the pattern of their promotion and the grade of the *manṣab* they attained. It is hard work, but once such a list is prepared it enables us to discard faulty generalizations.

Exaggeration is not a virtue which we have acquired only lately. We have the experience of it for centuries. All of us like to generalize, and it depends on what the mood of the author is at a given moment, what his historical prejudices are, and what he sincerely believes to be true although his contemporaries may not be accepting those things to be true. And then there is that wonderful institution, the bāzār gossip, which many of the westerners tended to believe in and to reproduce. And yet even when we know that a particular person could have no other access to information except the bāzār gossip, we still tend to accept his statement. Therefore, every statement becomes in a sense subject to scrutiny and confirmation. I am not saying that every statement is to be disbelieved. All that I am submitting is that we have to evolve new methods of subjecting these generalized statements to rigorous criticism on the basis of (a) quantitative analysis, and (b) the statement of facts which are narrated as first-hand observations. We must see whether the generalizations which have been made are borne out by the actual narratives. We have to put the question in such a manner that the narrative is made to yield at least some information on the types of problems that are worrying us. For example, let us concretely examine the incidents mentioned by the chroniclers having a bearing on the relationships between any of the nobles and any of the ruling chiefs. Let us collect all these facts, analyse them and sift them, maybe the picture that begins to emerge is more reliable than the one that has been commonly made. If we come across the statements of the chroniclers that on such and such an occasion, the zamindars were for the king or against the king, then we can test them with the present sophisticated techniques of analysis, which will enable us to define the type of relationship, the nature of relationship, the regional variations, if any, the changes in terms of time that were taking place. The question of revenue administration, on which there is a great deal of information, can also be subjected to this type of investigation.

If we change our focus from revenue administration to agrarian relations, then a close study of the revenue administration in itself will give us some worthwhile information about this subject. Fortunately in regard to revenue administration, we have two types of material apart from the chronicles. First, there are the innumerable administrative manuals, *dastūrul 'amals*. Dasturul 'amal has its limitations. Like all manuals, we can assume, it must have been observed more in its breach. And yet these manuals, if scrutinized properly, can yield a great deal of information. I am giving you as an instance the classification of land by Akbar for the purposes of assessment of revenue, a classification which was based not on fertility but on continuity of production. I am referring to the *polaj, parautī, chachar,* and *banjar* form of classification. But there is, on the other hand, a general statement in the *Ain-i-Akbarī* that land was classified into three categories, the good, the middling, and the bad, although nothing further is said about the good, the middling, and the bad. However, there is considerable detailed description of what is *polaj*, what is *chāchar*, what is *banjar*, and what is *parautī*. If we link it up with the other instructions that are given in that text, the instruction to bring more and more land under cultivation and to take various steps if a particular village becomes deserted, then we have a fairly clear picture of the basic policy of the state.

It appears that one of the most serious problems that the administration encountered at that time was how to bring under cultivation land which had either never been brought under cultivation or which had gone out of cultivation. And therefore concessional rates of revenue and such other things as the grant of zamindari rights were given so that this could be implemented. The administrative manuals also define various types of rights and other institutions. I have a feeling that if we continue the investigations which we are making in many of our universities by analysing these administrative manuals more carefully, we will be able to get considerable information on the problems of agrarian relations.

The other type of revenue documents is the original revenue records which fortunately for us have survived in various places. The two biggest collections are, as you know, in Bikaner and in Hyderabad. In Bikaner, for the seventeenth and eighteenth centuries we have the most complete records of the former princely house of Jaipur. We know that many *parganas* were held by the rulers of Amber, either as their *waṭan jāgīr* or as *jāgīr* or in any other form, and the detailed abstract of each pargana with the details of each village were maintained; many of these have fortunately survived. I am referring to the *arsattas*. Several papers have been written on the nature of the arsatta records. I have myself done some work in relation to the information contained in these records. For example, if we get information regarding the detailed revenue collected village-wise or pargana-wise, one of the things we can do is to detect the changing proportion as between the *kharīf* and the *rabī'* harvests. Is the revenue collected from kharīf growing in proportion to the revenue collected from rabī' over a period of years in a fairly large area? We may find this tendency in 5–6 parganas or perhaps even more. I have made an analysis of six parganas. It seems that between 1663 and 1743, the proportion of revenue from the rabī' crops increases compared to that from the kharīf crops. Now this region is situated in eastern Rajasthan between Jaipur, and Delhi and Agra, and we know that this area depends for irrigation almost entirely on rainfall. Therefore, traditionally the kharīf harvest has been the principal harvest. Hence if the relative position of the rabī' harvest has been increasing, it means that more inputs have been going into cultivation. Without more inputs we cannot have more rabī' production in that part of our country. This poses newer problems. Where is this investment coming from?

Let us take another aspect of the same problem which I attempted to investigate—that is to say, let us find out the mode of assessment and the amount of revenue assessed. In attempting to bring the two sets of figures on the same scale, a serious difficulty arises. You will either get the quantity where it is *ghalla-bakhshi* or the area where it is *zabt*. Now the two cannot always be put on the same scale because some of the crops were assessed on the basis of crop sharing where the total production is given in terms of quantity whereas some were assessed on the basis of bighas, and you get the total area under cultivation.

I posed this problem before the late D. D. Kosambi, and the brilliant mathematician that he was, he suggested a formula which to his mind was very simple, but it is very, very complex. The original intention was that we would take all the data to him and request him to work it out, but as bad luck would have it he died. He was the only statistician who said how the two types of evidence could be put on the same scale. After his death I proceeded on the basis of whatever little I could understand of his suggestion. It was possible to work out the area under each crop in the two harvests as also the yield in terms of quantity per bigha. The picture that emerged more or less confirmed the impression gained from a comparison of the amount of revenue realized from the two harvests.

Further, if changes in the cropping pattern are taking place, then coupled with this change in the relative position of the kharīf and rabī' harvests and changes in cropping production, we can start examining (a) whether any extension of cultivation is taking place or (b) whether the yield or productivity of land is going up. Another problem which we could tackle by utilizing these revenue statistics is to find out the changes in the price level.

Changes in the price level present an interesting feature. If there is a sharp fall in the price of one commodity in one part of Rajasthan, it is very soon reflected in a similar fall in the price of the same commodity in a very different part of Rajasthan, and if this change in the price situation also corresponds to the change in price situation as available from the European Company records, then it is quite clear that there is no self-sufficiency of the village economy. If there was a self-sufficient village system, how is it that the products of different parts of the country were being made available to the villager? Some statistics from Bengal bearing on this subject have survived. If we take those along with the information contained in the arsattas of Rajasthan, we can see that the system in East Bengal was not so totally different from the system in eastern Rajasthan. We come across the *nirkh bāzār* where fluctuations in prices were well reported in terms of different types of currency, and so on.

What is significantly absent in these records is a document which is also found in Bihar but which is more common in UP and in the other parts of our country and which is a traditional document, that is to say the field book. It provides all the relevant details about the field under cultivation. It tells us: who is its cultivator? Who is its owner? What is cultivated? Unfortunately this particular document has not survived in good numbers for the different parts of the country. Had it been so, many of the problems on which we are speculating today would have been conclusively solved.

The earliest revenue documents prepared by the British administrators in the second half of the eighteenth century have not yet been given sufficient attention. As you know, when the British first came to Bengal and acquired *dīwanī* rights, they had to offer their comments on what the land system was. They had to answer these questions: who was the proprietor of the soil? What were the rights of the different categories of zamindars? There were sharp differences of opinion amongst extremely knowledgeable British administrators such as Warren Hastings, Philip Francis, James Grant, Sir John Shore, and Boughton Rouse, to quote only a few. Each one of them put forward his own theory. There is no doubt that these people made actual observations. Assuming that they were influenced by their own prejudices and predilections, as Ranajit Guha has rightly pointed out in *Rule of Property in Bengal*, assuming that they were trying to understand the Indian situation in terms of their own experience, the question that arise is: how is it that the information given by the Indians is equally contradictory? And because of this I started examining the nature of information supplied by the Indians.

Fortunately the bulk of this material has survived in the various libraries of Britain and Europe, but most of it is preserved in the India Office, all in Persian. I have ventured to give my own hypothesis regarding the sharp differences of opinion among these Indians who were writing. I consider it to be symptomatic of social change that each person described one aspect of land rights at a given point of time, and this naturally resulted in the confusion we notice. However, that is neither here nor there. For the first time in these documents, the questions were posed and answers given as to the identity of the proprietor. There were several other issues. How did proprietary rights emerge? What were the details of these proprietary rights? How was succession sanctioned? What happened if a person went away and left his land? What happened if someone else acquired the right of collection, and so on?

These questions were put particularly on four occasions, in 1772, in 1775, in 1787, and finally in 1788. One questionnaire had fourteen questions, another had fifty-two questions which is the most detailed, and then there were two with four questions each. These questions and answers have survived, and are very important for understanding the views of individuals. But at the same time what has survived is a detailed account in over fifty-two volumes of the revenue administration of Bengal, Bihar, and Orissa and of the revenue administration of the whole of the Mughal empire. Figures are available. There is one series which gives the changes in jāgīr holdings. We can subject such statements to a quantitative check. For instance, we have a statement that during the Mughal empire after Akbar, the transfers of jāgīrs were very frequent. Now here the jāgīrs are arranged subah-wise, sarkār-wise so that we can check such observations. We can detect these changes and answer a number of questions. How frequent these changes were? Is this tendency to be observed everywhere? Or is it confined to a few areas? Are there any differences between the outlying provinces and the central provinces?

Again, the details about the zamindars, the *jotdārs* are available at least so far as Bengal, Bihar, and Orissa are concerned. This could be subjected to further analysis. There are some other documents which I have not found in Persian except by way of examples, but the translations of these documents are to be found in the revenue consultations of Bengal; these are the pattas (documents stating assessed revenue demand). The patta is of every type, the patta as well as the *muchalka* (undertaking to pay) and the *qabūliat* (document recording acceptance of revenue demand). These have been translated, and a fairly good cross-section of the pattas is to be found in the revenue records of the East India Company so far as Bengal is concerned for the period 1765 to 1793. I am a little doubtful about depending entirely on this type of material because the examples may not be typical. It may not be a fair sample. But if we use this sample together with the sample which has survived in the original Persian, perhaps some sort of a generalization would become valid. This is roughly the nature of the source material for agrarian history which is available to us.

I have not deliberately referred to the very important source which we have to use constantly and to which I have made reference, that is to say, the records left by the trading companies. The trading company records are very important, but they are not directly important for this purpose. I have also not referred to another mine of information because my study of these documents has been much too inadequate; I have in mind the Portuguese records. I learnt a little bit of Portuguese about three years ago. Although it was not enough for me to be able to use this, it was enough to be able to understand the nature of these records. The Portuguese records should throw a great deal of light on many of the problems of the economic history of the period. Some of my friends in England were good enough to translate copies of Portuguese documents that are available in the India Office. With the help of these translations and with the help of some other translations which have been made in the India Office, I have been able to get a general idea of the type of information that is contained in the Portuguese records. But I am sorry to say that I have not used the records of Goa. I hope that someone who knows medieval history and Portuguese as well will take the trouble of going through the available records at Goa and try to see what light can be thrown on agrarian relations by them.

## Organization of Agrarian Economy

Earlier, I attempted to focus attention on some of the most important problems of agrarian relations and the difficulty in answering the questions relating to the agrarian history of the period because of the nature of the source material. I also indicated some of the methods which might by usefully employed in studying agrarian relations.

I shall now touch very briefly on those aspects which I think are now more or less accepted, and hazard a few hypotheses in relation to the changes that were taking place. From what I have said earlier, it will be apparent that what I am submitting for your consideration here can only be a tentative hypothesis; much more work has to be done before we can say anything with certainty. Then there is another important consideration. Our country is so vast and its geography so varied, that its economy cannot be exactly the same at any time. And yet, as a result of the establishment of the Mughal empire, some uniformity was introduced into the institutions. Therefore, although it is possible for us to make generalizations for the country as a whole, we must remember that in many cases these generalizations would be oversimplified.

Broadly speaking, the bulk of agricultural economy in India during the medieval period was of two types—the free peasant economy and the tenant-cultivator economy. I think, it is now accepted that the most important form of rural organization was the free peasant economy. I would first like to indicate the type of evidence on the basis of which it can be said that the free peasant economy was the dominant form of rural organization.

It was the constant endeavour of the Mughal state to ensure that cultivation was extended; the extension of cultivation could not naturally be carried out by an average agricultural labourer who did not have the resources to do so. In one of the eighteenth century documents relating to the present state of Bihar, we have come across a term which may be peculiar only to this part but which nevertheless does indicate a general type. The word used is *halmir*, that is to say, a person who had at his disposal four or more ploughs, and usually the extension of cultivation was undertaken by persons who could command four or more ploughs. And a person who brought new land under cultivation was, in accordance with the Hindu as well as the Mohammedan law as it was then understood, entitled to be recognized as the proprietor of that soil. In Mughal terminology he would be recognized as the zamindar and also as the *mālik* of that particular piece of land. There is definite evidence from the sixteenth, seventeenth, and eighteenth centuries that persons who brought new areas under cultivation were recognized as the mālik or the proprietors of the land.[2] The India Office series of documents, which I mentioned earlier, also contain frequent references to *jotdārs*. For any land, the following questions were asked: who is its proprietor or in whose *jotdārī* does it lie? In whose *ta'lluqdārī* is it? And in whose zamindari is it situated?

The jotdār can have only one meaning, and that is a free peasant cultivator. He may or may not do the cultivation himself but nevertheless he would be responsible for carrying on the cultivation. We also come across in medieval documents the words *kṛṣaka* and *kisān* used in much the same sense. The term kisān is used in the eighteenth century, but kṛṣaka occurs even earlier. The term *ra'iyyat*, which is most commonly used in the Mughal documents, is, as I attempted to show, mainly used for a zamindar. But, in the manner the word ra'īyyat is used in different chronicles, it seems that these were large peasant proprietors. The word *muzāra'* is also used and is supposed to be distinct from the term ra'īyyat. Muzāra' would include not merely the peasant proprietor but also the tenant-cultivator, and this, I think, is the only justification for using two distinct terms, the ri'āya and the muzāra'. However, literally ri'āya means subject, and muzāra', one who lives on cultivation.

When the British came here, they were a little worried about these terms, and so they asked some of the knowledgeable persons to define the word muzāra'. We have some very interesting definitions of the term muzāra'. In spite of the confusion in these definitions, it is absolutely clear that the term muzāra' is used almost invariably for the person who is undertaking cultivation himself. Muzāra' incidentally is also used in the sense of a revenue farmer, but from the manner the word muzāra' is used in the Mughal documents, it is clear that it does not refer to revenue farmer. The term ra'īyyat would be used for both the zamindars who would be conducting cultivaton through tenant-cultivators as well as for free peasant cultivators. In the Rajasthani documents, the term riā'ya is almost always used in a sense that approximates more or less to the free peasant cultivator.

Irfan Habib has discussed the term khudkāsht at some length, and it has also been discussed by Moreland. We should not get confused by the definition which is given by the earlier British administrators; the definition of khudkāsht which is rather unusual is given in the introduction to the *Amini Commission Report*. *Khudkāsht*, according to that definition and also according to a minute of Warren Hastings and Boughton Rouse, is the land of the cultivator who cultivates it in the village where he stays; it is different from the *pāhīkāsht*, that is to say, the land which a person cultivates in a village other than the one to which he belongs. Now this is in my opinion a confusing definition of the word khudkāsht.

The word khudkāsht is well understood even now; at least before 1947 it was very well understood as a person who himself organizes cultivation, and that is the sense in which Jahāngīr had used so that his 'āmils were instructed not to make the lands of the ri'āya their own khudkāsht. Khudkāsht land therefore, according to this early British definition, would indicate the land where the bulk of the people were cultivating lands or living. This is really an indication of the special type of proprietary rights.

From the date of the *Amini Commission Report*, it will be clear that after that, the word 'zamindar' began to be used for revenue farmers by the British; quite obviously they could not use the term zamindar in the sense it was intended to be used in the earlier period. Again, from the manner in which the *madad-i-ma'āsh* documents were drafted, it will be noticed that in most of these grants, the land given was described as *zamīn-i-uftādah qābil-i-zirā't*, that is to say, the land which is uncultivated but which is cultivable and which is not included in the revenue rolls. Evidently the person to whom madad-i-ma'āsh is granted would be a religious person; he could be a Hindu or a Muslim. The Mughal *farmāns* published by K. K. Datta contain a number of madad-i-ma'āsh grants that were given as donations to non-Muslims or to retired officials; it could be given as a pension sometimes. I have come across two such madad-i-ma'āsh grants whose copies exist in the Khudabakhsh Library; these were granted to persons who had been rendering service. One is in a collection which I have not been able to identify; the other is in the well-known collection, *Insha-i-Harkaran*.

The madad-i-ma'āsh grants required confirmation at the accession of each monarch, but the hereditary succession was not interfered with usually. In due course, the madad-i-ma'āsh grants also acquired the character of zamindari, as appears from the sale deeds of madad-i-ma'āsh lands in the eighteenth century. As the British administrators make out, most of these madad-i-ma'āsh holders or revenue-free grantees acquired proprietary rights or almost semi-proprietary rights. But this could only be possible if this was the dominant form of making revenue-free grants. I mean unless there was a large number of persons holding two to three hundred bighas of land which they were cultivating themselves, this particular form of giving revenue-free grant would not have been so common. This is the standard form which obtained in almost the whole country from Gujarat to Bengal, and from Kashmir to the Deccan. If you also see the list of concessional landholders in the arsattas of Rajasthan, there again you get a similar picture that there are persons who are holding 50–100–200 bighas of land; they are either exempted from payment of revenue or required to pay only concessional revenue.

What I am trying to make out is that we find a very large number of persons holding 50–200–300 bighas of land, many of whom were also doing cultivation themselves. But at the same time, they were organizing cultivation in other ways also. Only a few documents of the actual field book called the *khatauni* belonging to the late eighteenth century have survived, but I have no doubt that the examples they give would be typical. I have not come across the khatauni of any village having more than ten names in the field book—ten names as proprietors. So, broadly speaking, one could say what these were; they could not be large zamindars, but they would be, by and large, free peasants. Place names also throw some light on the system. A careful study of these would be rewarding.

The organization of cultivation was roughly as follows: some of these were self-cultivating peasants who were carrying on cultivation with the help of their collaborators, especially in the *bhayyāchāra* system, of which there is plenty of evidence right from the *Aīn-i-Akbarī* onwards. Members of a clan group utilized the services of what seems to be known a little later in the Mughal period as the *khidmatīpraja*. The khidmatīpraja almost always consists of what we now call the Scheduled Castes, who were not permitted to hold land themselves, who were expected to render labour services of different types, and who in return for this were either given strips of land at the very borders of the village or a share of the produce for having rendered customary services. It is therefore very clear that in this organization, caste was playing a very important role. Not enough work has been done by us on the role of caste in the organization of agriculture at the grass roots level. The taboo regarding ploughing by higher caste people made it necessary that there should be a considerable body of agricultural labourers for ploughing and performing other agricultural services, leaving the rest of the process of cultivation to the peasant proprietors.

Many of the peasant proprietors, there is evidence to show, gave out their land on a sharecropping basis, a system which survives even today in many parts of the country. In Bengal, the whole of the *tebhāgā* movement in the forties of the present century was based on the demand for two-thirds of the crop for the sharecroppers, leaving one-third to the owner of the land. We come across the customary one-third rate in medieval times also, which may have continued from the ancient period. In the medieval period, evidence suggests that where the seed and other inputs were provided by the landholder, in whose name the field stood, the actual agricultural labourer got one-third; on the other hand, where the inputs were provided by the labourer himself he took two-thirds and gave the landholder one-third of the produce. I do not think that any substantial percentage of these peasant proprietors was engaged in the actual cultivation almost entirely with their own labour, though the available evidence on this point is totally inadequate. It is necessary to go deeper into the evidence, but my overall impression is that very few of these peasant proprietors were carrying on cultivation entirely by themselves.

These peasant proprietors were holding the *milkīyat* rights, and as such they were recognized as zamindars unless, for other reasons which we shall discuss a little later, their zamindari rights were suppressed. These persons also enjoyed the right to sell their property. Hereditary succession among the males was recognized. Why the females were excluded we can only guess. The personal law of succession of the Muslims was not applicable. In this case, all the evidence points to that. It was considered necessary, however, that either with the change of proprietary rights or of succession, there will be a renewal of the patta. And in the case of large owners, which we shall discuss a little later, a formal sanad from the higher officers was needed. The patta meant that it was the responsibility of the new proprietor to pay the stipulated revenue for which he submitted a *muchalka* (undertaking) and a *ẓāminī* (surety). Since the surety had to be provided in all such cases, the practice operated as one of the major factors leading to the rise of the moneylender in the village. As cash payment became more and more common, the local moneylender accepted whatever currency the landholder paid and charged the *batta* (commission) for converting it into the standard currency. The landholder was responsible for maintaining the continuity of cultivation and ensuring that the land did not go out of cultivation so that the revenue did not suffer. He was also responsible for ensuring the continuous cultivation of superior crops or *jins-i-kamil*, a term which is still used in revenue terminology in many of our villages. If such a peasant proprietor left the land it would be temporarily given to somebody else. But the proprietor would still be entitled to receive the *malikāna*, and to get back the land whenever he was in a position to take it back; the malikāna rights in this case were usually 10 per cent of the gross produce. The principal obligation of such a person was to render or to submit revenue, *mālguzārī*. Whosoever happened to be the primary proprietor was held responsible for payment of the imperial revenue, but he would be entitled to hold back 10 per cent out of the imperial revenue as his malikāna share.

Now that sufficient documentary evidence is available, we can say that all that the actual cultivator paid was deemed to be the imperial revenue, and that the share of all intermediaries or all proprietors was a lawful deduction from this imperial revenue. Once upon a time there was a confusion that the imperial revenue was over and above whatever was supposed to have been collected from the actual cultivator. But now it is very clear that any type of expenditure or any type of concession or any type of tax to which any functionary or proprietor or intermediary was entitled had to go out of the imperial share, and it was the duty of the authorities concerned to submit to the imperial government a full statement of the total amount that was collected whether by way of *māl* (regular revenue) or *jihāt* (cesses). In addition to the two items, there was a third called *sa'ir-jihāt* or taxes other than land revenue. Collectively all this came to be known as *abwāb*s, and the early British documents take care to demarcate the revenue from the cess. It is also discussed at some length by Sir John Shore. It is found in the *Amini Commission Report*, in three/four minutes of Warren Hastings which are published as appendices to the *Annals of Rural Bengal*, and so on.

The two systems which were fairly common before the time of Akbar and Sher Shah, namely the *muqta'ī* system or the *nasaq* system, are translated by Moreland as group assessment. I do not agree with this interpretation. Moreland is correct up to the point that the revenue of a village was assessed in a lump sum on the basis of earlier records. Once the revenue was determined, the responsibility of its payment devolved on the village headman, who had to distribute this amount among the individual proprietors. But a statement of the amount collected from the proprietors had to be submitted to the imperial government right from the time of Sher Shah. I do not think that it could have become the common practice in the short time that Sher Shah had at his disposal. But from the time of Akbar onwards, it did become the common practice. Again, it is possible to infer on the basis of the arsattas which I quoted that perhaps the revenue statements were not given individually. It was not stated how much revenue was due from an individual; on the other hand, the total revenue under each crop was given, the total area under cultivation or the total quantity produced was mentioned, and the state share that was due was almost always specified.

So the main function of the peasant proprietor, so far as the state was concerned, was to keep up cultivation, to cultivate superior crops, and to give the revenue to the imperial authority or to the local functionary, whichever was the case.

In the organization of cultivation tenant economy also played an important part. One can see very clearly that between the free peasant economy and the tenant-cultivator economy, there is a basic relationship. As a result of political factors, a free peasant can easily become a tenant, and similarly a tenant can easily become a free peasant depending on the military and the class situation in any given village or locality or the type of administration that we have. I am particularly struck by two/three examples. The Minās were the dominant free peasant groups in eastern Rajasthan, and were looked upon as zamindars of that region until the time of Babur. Then gradually the Rajputs and in a few places the Jats depressed the status of the Minās to that of tenants, and in some places they ceased to be even tenants but were reduced to the position of landless labourers; many of them became vagabonds, and till lately they were classified as one of the criminal tribes. This is within a period of four hundred years or so, and we can easily work out and trace their history. There are on the other hand other groups such as the Jats, who, once they become politically or militarily strong, not only rise to be zamindars but also come to acquire intermediary rights as zamindars depressing the other sections, especially the Ahirs, to a position lower than that of the tenants. The tenants had certain rights, of which these people were deprived.

So the tenant economy grew quite obviously out of the free peasant economy as a result of political, social, and economic factors. Political factors are quite obvious. Among the social factors I attach the greatest importance to the caste system. As the dominant group in any locality rose in the *varṇāśrama* ladder, it sought the status of the previously dominant group in that region. The whole process worked as a sort of chain reaction. Because the peasants lost politically, they were sought to be depressed socially, and their social depression was adduced as a justification for depriving them of the rights they had been enjoying.

We cannot ignore several economic factors that led to the emergence of the tenant economy. One such factor was lack of investment where more investment was needed. I referred to the growth of the relative importance of the rabī economy in portions of eastern Rajasthan requiring more and more inputs. Now wherefrom would more and more inputs come? In my opinion, the free peasant belonging to this region was not economically strong enough to bring those inputs in. These could only be brought in by socially stronger groups, which in the process would naturally seek to reduce the free peasants to tenant farmers.

However in many respects, the rights of the tenant-farmers were similar to those of the peasant proprietor, especially so in the matter of security of tenure. The lack of pressure on land, of which there is ample evidence, guaranteed to the tenants an absolute security of tenure. There are examples to show that where a tenant wished to leave his land, he could be forced or induced to stay on his own land. There are not many instances of force being used in this respect. I have come across precisely three examples in original documents, although observations to this effect have been made by several other contemporaries; there may be many more documents. One of the three documents relates to Bihar wherein a zamindar asks another zamindar to send his forces to bring back his tenant to his own soil.

But the other examples in which the tenants were induced and persuaded to stick to the soil are numerous. Such cases are found in the time of Shahjahan, and we have come across about fifteen/twenty documents of Aurangzeb's reign, and many of the eighteenth century which all speak of inducements offered to the tenants to come back to their lands. In the case of Banaras incident, one rupee in cash was sent to each person to come back in addition to the expenses of his return. Now one rupee in those days had far more purchasing value than it has today; perhaps twenty-eight times would be a fair guess.

Here I would like to digress a little and say that on the basis of the records that I have seen I do not find many examples of the desertion of villages. In fact, there is a remarkable continuity of the villages as they existed in the seventeenth century. I have found the village list of a number of provinces of the seventeenth century, and I have been able to identify more than 75 per cent of those villages in the modern village maps on one-inch sheets. If my identification is correct then this is truly a remarkable continuity. Again, many arsattas mention the number of villages. Accounting for the changes in the boundaries of parganas the number of villages that are deserted is really very small.

Taking all these things into consideration I would put forward the view that the tenant economy was a fairly stable economy. However, the fragmentation of holdings in settled areas frequently led to the migration from the villages to the towns and to other places in different ways. Where fragmentation was considerable and where the upper caste was not in a position to colonize new areas or to clear forests—for that is a very difficult business—they would almost invariably go into the professional army. I can cite the example of the Rajputs of Buxar. We have the other types of instances concerning the menial castes. The menial castes were not permitted to hold land anywhere, and therefore if there was a surplus of population, that is to say, if they could not survive the hardships of their environment, then quite obviously they would go to the cities or to the towns to seek employment there unless they were invited to go and settle down in another village in the same capacity in which they were living in their original settlements.

I am now putting forward a very tentative hypothesis. How is it that while there was very little pressure of population on the land, while the state was making continuous efforts to expand cultivation, tremendous expansion of crafts and towns took place simultaneously? We notice a lack of pressure of population on land on the one hand and growing urban population and growing handicrafts and industry on the other. There is no doubt that from the middle of the sixteenth century until the middle of the eighteenth century, handicraft production increased tremendously. The numerical strength of the purely agricultural labourers could not have been very large, confined as they were to the khidmatīprajā or sections of *pāhīkāsht.* These are the only two major forms of agricultural labourers that we find in addition to, of course, certain categories of sharecroppers, especially in the adjoining tribal areas. There is a lot of evidence to suggest that the tribals living in the neighbouring areas were invited to undertake labour on a sharing basis. They would do the cultivation, and then they would go back after having taken their share of the produce; in fact, they did not settle down. This implied that their status remained inferior to that of the tenant-cultivators.

The tenant-cultivators did not have the right to sell or alienate their holdings. This was the most important difference between them and the peasant proprietors. But there is plenty of evidence to suggest that, in case a tenant-cultivator left his field, the other cultivators in the village would be invited to cultivate the land and give to this tenant-cultivator, when he came back, his share. It was obligatory for the other cultivators of the village to cultivate the land left by a tenant-cultivator. But the tenant-cultivator on his return, and sometimes, as I have found in one document—a person returning even after about three years—was entitled to get back his field and his share of the produce. The actual share is not mentioned in the documents. I do not know what was the share of a tenant-cultivator who, in fact, did not cultivate his land.

## Fluctuating Landed Classes vis-à-vis the State

It is reasonable to postulate that where there is large scale tenant cultivation, there would also be a large number of non-cultivating primary zamindars. I am deliberately using the term primary zamindar and avoiding the use of the word proprietary zamindar. As I submitted earlier, the rights were fluctuating all the time, and therefore a person who is a proprietary zamindar at one time may cease to be holding proprietary rights, and somebody else who is an intermediary may acquire direct rights over land. Therefore I would use the word primary zamindar in preference to the word proprietary zamindar; that is to say, the primary zamindar is not necessarily a small zamindar, he can also be a big zamindar. It means a zamindar who is directly exercising proprietary rights over land either as a peasant proprietor or as a person who is doing khudkāsht (cultivating his lands) or as a person who has given out his land to his tenant farmers. The primary zamindars were for all practical purposes the holders of proprietary rights over agricultural as well as habitational lands. In this class may be included not only the peasant proprietors who carried on cultivation themselves or with the help of hired labour but also the proprietors of one or several villages. All agricultural lands in the empire belonged to one or the other type of the primary zamindars. The rights held by the primary zamindars were hereditary and alienable. Numerous sale deeds of such zamindaris dating back to the sixteenth century are still available, and some of the transfer deeds are preserved at the Central Records Office, Allahabad. The Mughal state considered it its duty to protect the rights of these zamindars, and encouraged the registration of transfer deeds at the court of the qāzī, so that a proper record of claims could be maintained.

Some of these non-cultivating primary zamindars were exercising their authority simultaneously as ruling chiefs in relation to the other areas or over various categories of intermediaries. Throughout this period we find a continuous shift in the position of the primary zamindars. Sandwiched as most of these zamindars were between superior zamindars and the state on the one hand and the peasantry on the other, they were constantly struggling to improve their position and thus came frequently into clash with both sides. Unless these zamindars were able to withstand pressure from above, they passed on the burden of revenue demands to the cultivators and so contributed to the intensification of the economic exploitation of the latter. On such occasions they played an economically retrogressive role. But on many occasions they led the revolts of the peasantry against the heavy exactions of the state, often utilizing the caste and clan appeal to rally support. Where revolts were not possible, many of these zamindars refused to pay the revenue until force was employed. The second category of zamindari right was the intermediary right, which is not a proprietary right. It is the right of service, a service obligation. In medieval documents it is described as *khidmat*. Zamindari could be both mālguzārī as well as khidmat-guzārī. Where it is mālguzārī it is a primary right, where it is khidmatguzārī it is an intermediary right or an intermediary obligation. There are innumerable types of intermediaries. We may take the case of the *muqaddam* or the *mukhiyā*, who was usually chosen from among the primary zamindars of the village, sometimes the most important among them, and who was paid differently. A very common mode of payment to the muqaddam for the services rendered by him was that he was taxed at a concessional rate. But sometimes he was also entitled to various types of discounts commonly called in medieval terminology as *rusūmāt muqaddamī*. The practice can be traced back to pre-Sultanate times when we hear of *pratihāra-prastha, akṣapatal-ādāya*, etc. meant for various types of royal officers.

Then there was a *chaudharī*, usually of a pargana. He belonged to the class of the primary zamindars but was a leading zamindar. Chaudharāī was hereditary, although it was an office. The main duty of the chaudharī was to assist in the collection of land revenue. He was entitled to various types of perquisites and a percentage of the total revenue. In his own individual territory holding, the chaudharī would be a primary zamindar, but in relation to a number of other zamindars, he would exercise the powers of the chaudharī, collecting revenues from them on behalf of the state.

An important intermediary was the *ta'lluqdār*, who performed duties very similar to that of the chaudharī. The class of zamindars who contracted with the state to collect the revenue of a given territory began to be known during the second half of the seventeenth century by the generic designation of ta'lluqdārs. The word ta'lluqdār does not carry the same connotation in Bengal as it does in Avadh. In Avadh, ta'lluqdār is usually a very big man who is assigned the responsibility of collecting revenue from a whole lot of other fairly big zamindars. In Bengal where large zamindaris were established, the large zamindars farmed out their own zamindari rights to inferior intermediaries who were called the ta'lluqdārs. Therefore, the ta'lluqdār in Bengal is usually a small intermediary, but in Avadh he is a very big intermediary. The same is the position in Hyderabad. The equivalent of the term collector of a district in Hyderabad as late as 1946–7 was ta'lluqdār, head of a *ta'lluq*, thus indicating the territory which lay under the control of this officer.

Then there was the *qānūngō*, who was supposed to be responsible for maintaining complete records of production, of land rights, and of the revenues paid, and the crops sown. When the term qānūngō first appeared I do not know. But from the time of Sher Shah, the qānūngō certainly became one of the most important of the intermediaries.

I am indebted to Qeyamuddin Ahmad for his paper[3] on the origin of the Darbhanga *rāj* wherein he has pointed out that this *rāj* really developed out of *chaudharāī* and *qānūngōī* of the *sarkār* of Tirhut. So this would give you an idea also of the process of change that was taking place. In other words, a person who was given the *chaudharāī* and the *qānūngōī* would, if he became powerful and if he enjoyed the support of the superior authority, try to acquire primary zamindari rights over all the zamindars, which would result in the depression of the status of the free peasant or of the small zamindars under his jurisdiction. Sometimes these people attempted to become chieftains.

Then we come across the *khuṭ*, another revenue functionary who served as an intermediary. I do not know the origin of this term; it may have been derived from the Sanskrit word *kūṭa* (as in *grāma-kūṭa* and *rāṣṭra-kūṭa*) which is Persianized into khuṭ, or it may have been of Arab origin. But it is one of the terms which appears fairly early in the period of the Turkish Sultanate[4] and continues to be in use right up to the time of the British occupation of Bengal.

*Ijāra* again is a different term for contract or revenue farming. It is very clear that ijāra could be given for a lump sum although it was not very common. It could be also assigned as a right to collect revenue sometimes of a particular harvest and sometimes of particular types of crop. *Ijāradārī* meant that the *ijāradār* would collect the revenue according to imperial regulations and submit detailed accounts to the imperial exchequer, in lieu of which he would get his own percentage or perquisites.

Ijāra contracted for a fixed sum is rather rare. It has been assumed that ijāra was almost always made for a fixed amount, but as far as I know the actual *ijāra* documents do not prove this assumption.

Then pattadār is used in a general sense. As you know, *patta* is given for everything, but sometimes pattadār is also used in the broad sense of a person who was given the right to collect revenue without necessarily specifying what his status would be, and pattadār as such is used in certain parts of the country as a substitute either for ta'lluqdār or ijāradār. But it is used in conjunction with the word '*ilāqa* or *pattadār-i-ilāqa*, which is specified in the document. Normally the other term ta'lluqdār should have been used in relation to '*ilāqa*, but why it is not used I do not know.

We have not exhausted the list of the intermediaries, which also included deshmukhs, desais, deshpandes, etc. Practically the entire country was under the jurisdiction of the one or the other type of intermediary zamindars. The statement in the *Ain-i-Akbari* regarding the caste of zamindars in the parganas other than those under the chieftains seems to refer to this class. The fact that in the majority of the parganas, the zamindars belonged to a single caste suggests that certain families or clans held zamindari rights over large tracts.

The intermediaries played a very important political, administrative, and economic role in the Mughal empire. Their principal duty was to submit the full revenue returns, to maintain law and order through their troops, to keep ferries and irrigation works in good order, and to ensure that assessments were reasonably made and complaints properly looked into.

What did the intermediaries get in return for their services? They enjoyed the right to various types of perquisites, such as commissions, deductions, revenue-free lands, and cesses. *Muḥaṣṣilāna* or *jarībāna*, the measurement tax or the tax for the collection of revenue, are also the type of cesses to which the intermediaries were entitled. But in lieu of these gains it was their duty to satisfy the primary zamindar, who was the basic revenue payer in the Mughal empire. Naturally muḥaṣṣilāna would have to be paid to the agents of the intermediary though sometimes an appeal would be made to the amīn where there was a great deal of dissatisfaction among the primary zamindars.

A number of registers giving the particulars of the deductions made in favour of intermediaries has become available now. These deductions got mixed up with other revenue-free grants, and when the British had the assessments made, these deductions were explained at some length. Qeyamuddin Ahmed has referred to the detailed deduction registers that are still extant in Bihar. This was quite clearly a *khidmat* (service) for which apart from all the other deductions, the intermediary was paid either a percentage which varied from office to office and from situation to situation. Usually their share of revenue ranged between 2½ per cent and 10 per cent. They were granted revenue-free lands (*nānkār* or *banth*), or a lower rate of assessment of revenue, sometimes all the concessions together. Their appointment was always subject to official sanction, but usually the principle of hereditary succession was maintained. Although occasionally the imperial government considered it desirable to bifurcate or to divide the *chaudharāī* or the *muqaddamī* of the village among two brothers or two cousins or other twins, usually the eldest son would succeed to the office; sometimes if the elders of the village suggested that the eldest was not suitable, then somebody else succeeded.

An extremely interesting example from Bihar reveals the relationship between the intermediaries and the primary zamindars. In Shahabad district and in parts of Palamau district, the Ujjainiyas acquired, in addition to primary zamindari rights, intermediary rights in respect of a fairly vast tract, and then they rose to be chieftains. At that stage they came into clash with the imperial government with the result that they were reduced back to the status of intermediaries but with a difference. The difference lay in the fact that while the actual revenue collected by them (*taḥṣīl*) went on increasing, the gross revenue (*jamadāmī*) they had to pay to the imperial exchequer remained constant, and so the balance was appropriated by the Ujjainiya family over a fairly long period. Then again they became turbulent and sought to acquire the rights of a chieftain. Ultimately in the eighteenth century, the local governor in Patna decided that these people deserved to be treated with some severity. And what he did was to establish direct relationship with the small, insignificant zamindars (*zamīndārān-reza*) over whom the Ujjainiyas had acquired intermediary rights. That meant not only loss of income but also a tremendous blow to their prestige, although they later succeeded in winning back the favour of the governors. Eventually in many areas where the Ujjainiyas exercised zamindari rights as intermediaries they reduced the original zamindars to the position of their tenant-farmers. Thus they began to exercise primary zamindari rights in areas where they once functioned as intermediaries. We find that the intermediary zamindars often tried to depress the status of the primary zamindars, and where the attempt was successful, a fresh category of sub-proprietary rights emerged. Sometimes the intermediary zamindars created a class of sub-proprietors such as the *birtya*s in order to strengthen their position in the countryside.

This process had been going on all the time. The various elements such as the peasant proprietors or the small primary zamindars wanted to acquire a higher status and thus become intermediaries; on the other hand, the intermediaries tried to reduce the primary zamindars to the status of tenant-farmers or tried to go up the ladder and become chieftains, and so on; this struggle was constantly going on. In this overall struggle, what was the role of the Mughal empire?

Although I cannot give a satisfactory answer to this question, I could indicate the lines on which my mind is working. Basically it appears to me that whereas the Mughal empire was fundamentally dependent on the cooperation and support of the zamindars of each of these three categories, namely the chieftain, the intermediary, and the primary zamindar, there was at the same time a fundamental contradiction between the interests of the Mughal empire on the one hand and those of each of these three classes of zamindars on the other. The Mughal empire sought to resolve this contradiction by attempting to absorb the ruling chiefs into the imperial nobility and the administrative hierarchy. Akbar was the first emperor to clearly realize the importance of forging powerful links between the empire and the chieftains by absorbing them in the imperial hierarchy and the administrative machinery. Even the highest *mansab*s, important governorships, and military commands were given to them. This policy was continued by his successors; and during the later half of Aurangzeb's reign, eighty persons, belonging to the ruling houses of the chieftains, held mansabs of 1000 and above (representing almost 15 per cent of the total number of *manṣabdārs* of 1000 and above).[5] When the chieftains received high manṣabs and important appointments, they received substantial *jāgīr*s which far exceeded in revenue their hereditary dominions. The Mughals asserted the principle which later came to be known as that of 'paramountcy'. This meant that a chieftain depended for his position on the goodwill of the emperor rather than on his inherent rights. Only such chieftains were designated 'rajas' as were given the title by the emperor. While generally conforming to the law of primogeniture and the customary law of hereditary succession, the Mughals asserted the right of 'recognizing' a younger son or even a distant relation of a deceased raja as his successor. Although the right to call upon their vassal chiefs to render military assistance when needed by the emperor had been claimed by the sultans, the Mughals systematically utilized the military services of even such chieftains as did not hold manṣabs. Further, the Mughal emperors appear to have pursued the policy of entering into direct relationship with the vassals of some of the bigger chiftains, thus reducing the power of these chieftains and creating a new class of allies.

Of great importance was the Mughal attempt to treat the hereditary dominions of the autonomous chiefs as *watan jāgīr*s. This meant that theoretically they were supposed to have the status of *jāgīrdār*s and to be subjected to the imperial revenue regulations, but in practice they exercised *jāgīrdārī* rights in hereditary succession over their territories, which were consequently immune from transfer. Even though this theory could be applied mainly to the chiefs who were enrolled as manṣabdārs, the imperial government tried to change the character of the tribute (*pēshkash*) payable by the chief into land-revenue assessed on the basis of the actual production. The Mughal emperors also compelled the autonomous chiefs to conform to imperial regulations, especially in regard to the maintenance of law and order and the freedom of transit. Several farmāns are in existence directing the chieftains not to harass traders passing through their territory or to levy taxes from them.

As a result of these measures, the ruling chief found it more profitable and advantageous to join the imperial service than to attempt to retain his status as a big ruler; this process conferred on many of the rulers intermediary rights over large tracts, wherein they performed various kinds of services. Instead of giving all these rulers lump sums, the emperor tried to placate them by granting intermediary rights over large tracts of land. At the same time he tried to ensure that the rights of the free peasant were protected; and where for some historical reasons, the free peasant had been reduced to the status of a tenant-farmer, the rights of the tenant-farmer were also protected. The Mughals were shrewd enough to realize that on the continuation of superior cultivation depended the stability of the actual cultivator. Therefore, conditions should be created in which the exactions of different types should never exceed a certain limit. This would mean that sufficient check would be exercised by the imperial authority, and so uniform revenue regulations were introduced. The cultivators had to be given a great deal of protection by way of maintenance of law and order, maintenance of communications, and so on, and as a result of the existence of an overall centralized empire, the impetus given to economy in some ways percolated down to the cultivating class. There was also an attempt to ensure that the intermediaries, while their interests were protected, did not exceed the norms that were prescribed for them. This was the net objective of the Mughal policy.

The Mughal empire had in a way provided conditions for the 'protection', if I may use the word within quotes, of the fundamental interests of these different classes of agrarian society, and as a result of the establishment of this empire, its economic condition improved in many respects. A centralized empire by establishing comparatively greater peace and security, by enabling trade and commerce to expand, by increasing and diversifying the purchasing power of the consuming classes and thus helping the development of industries and manufactures, brought about conditions favourable to the growth of money economy. The emergence of money economy began to affect considerably agricultural production, especially because revenue was being collected more and more in cash. It also led to the expansion of cash crops and the extension of the cultivated area, partly as a result of the demand for greater revenue.[6] To the extent that the Mughal empire succeeded in establishing its authority over the numerous chieftains and the considerable measure of success that it achieved in unifying the country politically and administratively, it played a progressive role in the development of Indian society.

Yet at the same time, the whole system was so full of contradictions that conflicts were inevitable, and these could not have been resolved within the four corners of the Mughal imperial system. Therefore, while this system provided a great deal of stability for about two centuries, nevertheless it generated more and more conflicts. There was conflict of interests between the various groups of landed classes. Again, quite frequently, especially where relationship based on kinship, clan, tribe, or caste proved to be strong, whenever the local intermediary or a local chieftain rose in rebellion, he was able to muster behind him a very large section of primary zamindars as well as of the tenant-farmers against the imperial government. These rebellions were inevitable because not all chiefs could have been granted high manṣabs and lucrative jāgīrs. Many of the nobles who were not zamindars envied the security enjoyed by the chiefs in imperial service and pressed the emperor to restrict the grants of manṣabs and jāgīrs to this class. As the pressure on jāgīrs increased, the emperor was no longer in a position to satisfy the aspirations of the chieftains. Furthermore, towards the close of the Mughal rule, the burden of the share of the different categories of zamindars as also of the imperial revenue demand ultimately fell on the cultivator and placed a strain on agrarian economy in which much progress was hardly possible. The imperial government tried its best to ensure that the peasant was not called upon to pay more than fifty per cent of the produce. But as imperial authority declined and as the pressure on jāgīrs increased, the agricultural economy had to face a crisis which began to deepen in the eighteenth century.

All these factors ultimately led to the collapse of the whole system. When I use the phrase collapse of the whole system, I am not really referring to the collapse at the village level. The collapse came at the level of the imperial government. But at the level of various small provinces which continued to owe their allegiance to the imperial government and in parts of provinces, this system continued. Although this system survived at the provincial level or at a level lower, it maintained many of the weaknesses of the imperial system without bringing the advantages of a centralized empire, and therefore gradually disintegration started even at this lower level although at a later period. The most marked example of this is the collapse of the village industry. As the village handicrafts begin to collapse, whatever 'prosperity' the village had—I am using prosperity again within quotes in a purely relative sense—begins to disappear more and more.

I do not think I have answered the main question: Could this system have created conditions for its own regeneration? I do not think that my answer would be based on sound logic or on a great deal of facts. But if one is permitted to make an observation in the nature of an *obiter dictum*, then I would say: 'Yes, it was capable.' But that capability was not within the framework of the system as it had existed. It appears to me that the decay of the system had already started, and the process of this decline would have necessarily led to the overthrow of the system and to the emergence of something different. It is not essential that it could have only been overthrown by an external power.

## Notes and References

1. The arsattas of parganas Amber and Sawai Jaipur, when compared with those of parganas Chatsu and Hindaun, reveal a general similarity in the rate of assessment.

2. In an article presented by Satish Chandra and Dilbagh Singh to the Indian History Congress session held in December 1972, 'Stratification and Structure in Rural Society in Eastern Rajasthan', evidence is cited of peasants coming from outside the village, with their ploughs, to cultivate *banjar* land. Such peasants, termed *pahi*, had *mālikī* rights.

3. *Indian Historical Records Commission Proceedings*, Vol. XXXVI, pt. II, 1961, pp. 89–98.

4. S. H. Askari informs me that the term *khuṭ-i-khalj* occurs in the *Maktūbāt-i-Muzaffar Shams Balkhi*, a fourteenth-century work preserved in Khudabakhsh Library, Patna. Of course, it is frequently used by Barani.

5. Cf. M. Athar Ali, *The Mughal Nobility Under Aurangzeb*, Asia, Bombay, 1966.

6. For an excellent discussion of the impact of money economy on agricultural production and for the nature of the agrarian relations existing in the Mughal empire, reference may be made to Irfan Habib's *Agrarian System of Mughal India*, Bombay, 1963. For a discussion on the nature of the agrarian crisis in the closing years of the seventeenth century, see Satish Chandra, *Parties and Politics at the Mughal Court*, Aligarh, 1959, second edition, PPH, Delhi, 1972.

# PART IV

# TRACES FROM THE PAST

# 22

# Lataif-i-Quddusi

## A Contemporary Afghan Source for the Study of Afghan–Mughal Conflict*

## Introduction

A proper study of the Afghan rule in India and of the conflict between the Afghans and Mughals is hampered by the absence of contemporary Afghan sources. Our knowledge of the Lodi period and of the early Mughal and Sur periods is based almost entirely either on Mughal works, or on the works of Afghans which were written during the reigns of Akbar and Jahangir. The fragments of *Daulat-i-Sher Shah*[1] which contain copies of seventeen *farmans* of Sher Shah, form the only known contemporary source giving the Afghan point of view. In view of this, any eye-witness account of events which has a pro-Afghan bias, however fragmentary, is a welcome addition to our meagre knowledge of the period.

*Lataif-i-Quddusi* is not a chronicle of events. It is a book describing anecdotes regarding the well-known Chisthi saint, Shaikh Abd-ul-Quddus of Gangoh.[2] The object of the work is to familiarize the readers with an account of the life and the spiritual excellence of the saint. The reference to historical events is only incidental; the events themselves have been arbitrarily selected. The author appears to be more anxious to prove the supernatural powers of the saint than to be accurate in his

* *Medieval India Quarterly*, Vol. 1, no. i, Aligarh, 1950.

statement of facts. Nevertheless, the book contains many facts which would be extremely useful to a student of history. Below we have given a summary with extracts of all the historical material occurring in the book.[3]

The author of the work is Shaikh Rukn-ud-Din, the second son and *Sajjadanashin* of the saint. He was taken into the service of the Sarwānis and remained with them or with their allies for a time, accompanying the Afghan armies to Bihar, Bengal, Malwa, and Gujarat. He writes about incidents which he saw for himself. In the text, he states that he started writing the book in Jamāda I, 944, H. and completed it in Shaabān of the same year (1537). But from a reference to the battle of Qanauj between Humayun and Sher Shah, it appears that the book was not completed till 1540.

## Summary and Extracts

### Story of Shaikh 'Abdul Quddus' Departure from Rudauli

The services of Umar Khān Sarwāni had been placed at the disposal of Sultan Sikandar, then Miyan Nizam, by Sultan Bablūl Lodi. However, Umar Khan's relations with Nizam became strained and he left for Jaunpur to join Barbak Shah. En route he stopped at Rudauli and asked for the blessings of local saints. Among those he met was Shaikh 'Abd-ul-Quddūs. In the meanwhile, emissaries from Nizam came restoring 'Umar Khan back to favour. Soon Sultan Bahlūl died and Nizam succeeded him as Sikandar Lodi

Shortly afterwards, the *'kafirs'* established themselves in Hindustan and their rule was established over Rudauli. The laws of Islam were disregarded and pork began to be sold in bazars. 'Abd-ul-Quddūs being concerned at the state of affairs left the place and went to Nakhna[4] where Sultan Sikandar was camping.

'Abd-ul-Quddūs met Umar Khan and explained to him the situation in Rudauli. 'Umar Khan thereupon invited him to his pargana in Shahabad. 'Abd-ul-Quddūs' eldest son was then twelve years old. After one year's stay in Shahabad, Shaikh Rukn-ud-Din was born, that is, on 5th Jamada I, 897, H. 'Abd-ul-Quddūs stayed in Shahabad for almost thirty-eight years. When, however, the rule of the Afghans came to an end and Bābur came to the throne, Shahabad was destroyed and depopulated. Thereupon he went to Gangoh and died there. Malik Mubārak Khizrabādi got a house built for Shaikh 'Abd-ul-Quddūs, the beams for which were especially brought from the hills. The house was subsequently destroyed during the 'Mughal incident' (*hadisa-i-Mughlan*).

## Relations with the Children of 'Umar Khān

Once Shaikh 'Abd-ul-Quddūs decided to leave Shahabad and to renounce the world, giving his *sajjada* to his eldest son, Shaikh Hamid, who was then fourteen to fifteen years of age. As he went out of the village, the sons of 'Umar Khān went after him and begged him to return, which he did.

Bībī Islam Khanum, the daughter of 'Umar Khan' was a pious lady and a firm disciple of Shaikh 'Abd-ul-Quddūs. Her brothers, Haibat Khan and Saīd Khan, were displeased with her for some reason. The Sarwānis were then with Sultan Sikandar in Jaunpur and decided that on returning to Shahabad they would turn out Shaikh 'Abd-ul-Quddūs. However, as a result of the curse of the Shaikh, Sultan Sikandar became annoyed with the Sarwānis and threw them out of their kingdom. They thereupon went to Gujarat.

Malik 'Usmān Karrāni, the *Wajihdar* of pargana Gangoh, was Shaikh 'Abd-ul-Quddūs' disciple and requested him to send one of his sons to go and stay in his village. Accordingly, Rukn-ud-Din was sent there. After a few days, however, he returned to Shahabad for which Shaikh 'Abd-ul-Quddūs admonished him.

## Destruction During Mughal Invasions

The destruction caused by Mughal invasions have been described thus,

Ultimately Mughal inroads and plunder started. Each time Muhammed Bābur Bādshah came, (the people of) the whole country fled, and suffered destruction. We found refuge in this same village of Gangoh....
When the pargana of Dipalpur was plundered, many religious scholars and pious men were killed and libraries were destroyed. Shaikh Abd-ul-Shakur, son of Shaikh Muhammad 'Arif, was present and asked Shaikh 'Abd-ul-Quddūs to pray to the Almighty as religious scholars and pious men were being killed and the land of Islam was being destroyed.

## The Battle of Panipat

'When Muhammad Babur Badshah fought against Sultan Ibrahim at Panipat, the entire *wilayat* started fleeing and became depopulated. No place of refuge was left'. Consequently, Shaikh 'Abd-ul-Quddūs went with all his dependents to Kutana,[5] hoping that if he stayed behind the Afghan armies, he would be safe, and would get time to escape. His camp was to the east of the river and the Afghan armies were to its west. Many people from the Afghan armies crossed the river and came to seek his blessings. When the report reached Sultan Ibrahim, he made an effort to get Shaikh 'Abd-ul-Quddūs to join his army. Shaikh 'Abd-ul-Quddūs however was not hopeful of Afghan victory and consequently he asked Rukn-ud-Din to take the family and the belongings towards Hindustan while he himself went to the Afghan camp with his eldest son Hamid. On the morning of the battle, as orders were given on both sides for mobilization and the two armies had not yet been engaged, Shaikh 'Abd-ul-Quddūs decided to escape. However, hardly one watch of the day had passed when Ibrahim's defeat became known to all. This was on Friday, 7th Rajab, 932 H. Soon after, the (Mughal) horsemen reached where he was standing and confiscated his horse and belongings and arrested his son and servant. With difficulty he walked back to Delhi.

## Relations with Mughal Officials

Mir Yunus Ali Beg came to visit Shaikh 'Abd-ul-Quddūs in Gangoh. During the Mughal regime, Mir Hasan Ali, the Amir of the locality started terrorizing the population. Shaikh 'Abd-ul-Quddūs cursed him and soon news came that he had been assassinated.

## Rukn-ud-Din Taken in Afghan Service

Shaikh Rukn-ud-Din was in worldly employment for a long time, and went (with Afghan troops) to Gujarat and Mandu.

## Quarrel Between Sarwanis and Farmulis

Masnad-i-Ali Kamal Khan, son of Isa Khan Sarwani was in the village of Thanesar. A battle took place between him and Miyan Sulaiman Farmuli in village Indri, in which the Sarwanis were defeated. Rukn-ud-Din was with the Sarwanis and had no hopes of escaping death. However, owing to the blessings of Shaikh 'Abd-ul-Quddūs, he remained safe.

## Flight of the Afghans After Panipat

After the defeat of Ibrahim, the Afghans started running towards the east. A large number collected at a ferry on the river Sarju. The number of boats being small, there was great confusion and when some Afghans loaded a boat, others would come and snatch it. However, Masnad-i-Ali, Isa Khan Sarwani and Said Khan, with whom was Rukn-ud-Din, crossed the river after waiting for four nights, due to the blessings of Shaikh 'Abd-ul-Quddūs. After crossing the Gogra, the Afghans were in a state of complete confusion and went wherever they liked. The Sarwanis went to Bihar. After sometime Sultan Mahmud, son of Sultan Sikandar, appeared and his appearance filled the Afghans, left leaderless, with good cheer. They all assembled under his banner and agreed to fight against Babur. From Bihar they proceeded to Benares. Between the two armies flowed the river Ganges. There was great anxiety in the hearts of the Afghans regarding the outcome of the battle. The same night Rukn-ud-Din saw Shaikh 'Abd-ul-Quddūs in a dream telling him that 'Although Afghans have assembled for the battle in large numbers yet they are still suffering from selfishness and have not yet been tested. Victory is for Babur Badshah'.[6] The next morning he told Isa Khan about this dream.

On the third night after this dream, Sultan Mahmud fled to Bihar and the Afghans were scattered in all directions. Many of the Sarwanis and some other Afghans went to Balapath where Raja Bir Singh Deva gave villages to many Afghans. When Sultan Mahmud came to Bihar, a *sanyasi*, by the name of Anant Kar (Guru?) came to the tent of Isa Khan and told him that a *jogi* named Bal Nath, of Tilh (Tilhar or Tilpat?), had helped Babur, whereas he (Anant Kar) wanted to help the Afghans. He was taken to Sultan Mahmud. However, nobody paid any heed to what he said. After sometime he fell into the hands of the Mughals who put him to death. From Balapath, Rukn-ud-Din and Malik Rup Chand marched along with Miyan Babban to Mandu.

## The Afghans and the War Between Humayun and Bahadur Shah of Gujarat

When Bahadur Shah surrounded the fort of Chittor which had never been conquered by a Muslim before, the inmates of the fort, despairing of their escape, sent messengers to Humayun appealing for his help and said that in return for freeing them, they would give him one lac of *tanka*s for each stage of the journey to Chittor.[7] Thereupon, Humayun Badshah marched from the Agra fort and sent word to Chittor about his movement, and of his determination to relieve Chittor. By the time he reached Sarangpur, Sultan Bahadur, by the will of God, conquered the said fort and massacred the unbelievers. When Humayun heard of Bahadur's conquest of the fort and the massacre of unbelievers, he marched towards Sultan Bahadur. The latter, having heard that Humayun was approaching posted his men in the fort of Chittor and established Islamic administration there,[8] and himself proceeded to meet Humayun. He reached the fort of Mandasor[9] and entrenched his troops[10] inside the fort; but he did not collect enough food grains. Humayun camped near the defence line of Bahadur and prevented supplies reaching the troops of the latter. Food became scarce and extremely expensive, to the extent that even for a *Muzaffari* one could not purchase a seer of grain. For a few days they slaughtered horses and other animals and ate them. Ultimately the endurance of the troops was sorely tried and they could not stand it any longer. The same night I (Rukn-ud-Din) dreamt of Shaikh 'Abd-ul-Quddūs (who said) that Humayun would win and Bahadur would be defeated.... The same evening it became known that Sultan Bahadur and his troops had fled and each one took his own route of escape.

I also came out of the tent and proceeded alongside the *sawar*s of Gujarat. It was a dark night and my men and luggage went in some other direction and I was separated even from Malik Rup Chand.

After undergoing great hardship, with the blessings of Shaikh 'Abd-ul-Quddūs they reached Burhanpur. Each night the villagers would raid their camp and caused much damage. In Burhanpur, the Afghans again gathered together. Malik Rup Chand had brought Miyan Babban Lodi there. Rup Chand told Rukn-ud-Din that they were with the fleeing Gujarat forces and after an all night chase, the Mughals attacked them and killed many of their companions and secured much booty. However, with Shaikh 'Abd-ul-Quddūs' blessings they were saved. A number of Afghan families in the Deccan decided to stay in the town of Jalgaon, whose commander was Saiyid Umar. Miyan Babban Lodi used to send the author to Saiyid Umar quite frequently and hence Saiyid Umar became most kind to him.

One day a person named Badli Baqqal (the grocer) hatched a conspiracy with Saiyid Umar to bring false claim against Miyan Babban Lodi for 1 lac *tanka* for allegedly taking a loan.

The grocer suggested that if the amount could be recovered, Umar would get half the share. Umar being fond of silver (*sim dost*) readily became an accomplice and asked Rukn-ud-Din to get a lac from Miyan Babban. When Rukn-ud-Din refused to get the money, Umar arrested him and kept him as a hostage for three months. The Afghans several times thought of securing his release by force, but he dissuaded them from causing a commotion in a foreign land. However, after a stratagem he escaped and joined Miyan Babban again. The next morning all the Afghans left Jalgaon and went to Burhanpur.

Humayun went to Gujarat and established himself in Ahmedabad. Sultan Bahadur was in Diu. Sultan Ala-ud-Din, son of Sultan Bahlul, proceeded from Burhanpur to meet the (Gujrati) Sultan. Myself and Malik Rup Chand were with Sultan 'Ala-ud-Din. As we reached (Nadarba?) I dreamt of Shaikh Abd-ul-Quddūs, who asked me to go forward to Gujarat ahead of my companions, greet saints of Gujarat on his behalf and tell them that Humayun Badshah was destroying Islam and did not distinguish between Unbelief (*kufr*) and Islam, and was destroying everything alike. I have come here to assist Islam and yourselves. If you are agreeable I shall come and you and I together will throw Humayun Badshah out of Gujarat. If, however, you wish, I shall go to Mandu and expel Humayun from there, while you expel him from Gujarat so that peace may be brought to Islam; he asked me to tell them on his behalf.

While still in dream, Rukn-ud-Din felt that he had reached Ahmedabad in the vicinity of Shah Munjhan Bokhari.[11] There all the *pir*s of Gujarat had assembled and there was such a crowd that it was difficult to find a place to stand. Rukn-ud-Din conveyed the message of Shaikh 'Abd-ul-Quddūs to Shah Manjhan who asked him to visit Shaikh Ahmad Khatto[12] and to him also Rukn-ud-Din conveyed the message of Shaikh 'Abd-ul-Quddūs, and the latter replied: 'You should first come to us so that you and we should together drive Humayun out of Gujarat and Mandu so that Islam might be strengthened.'

In an instant he was back with Shaikh Abd-ul-Quddūs. Shaikh 'Abd-ul-Quddūs thereupon disappeared and Rukn-ud-Din woke up. The next morning he told the dream to Malik Rup Chand who conveyed it to Sultan Ala-ud-Din. Everyone in the Afghan army felt cheered up with this story and felt confident of victory over Humayun. Fifteen days after this news came that Bahadur having marched from Diu, went to the tomb of Ahmad Khatto and fought a battle against Humayun in which he was victorious. The Mughals having suffered great losses, retired to Agra.

## In Gujarat

When Ala-ud-Din reached the fort of Champanir, he heard that Sultan Bahadur had gone to Cambay. Sultan Ala-ud-Din therefore sent Rukn-ud-Din with four elephants, seven camels and 700 gold *mohur*s to Sultan Bahadur to convey his felicitations, which he took. Then news came that the *firangi*s, having filled a number of ships with firearms, were approaching to conquer Diu. Bahadur rushed toward Diu and Sultan Ala-ud-Din followed him. Then Sultan Ala-ud-Din sent Rukn-ud–Din to his pargana of Dholka and appointed him as the head of his establishment and asked him to carry out his instructions.

Rukn-ud-Din had stayed in Dholka for a few days when he dreamt again of Shaikh 'Abd-ul-Quddūs who asked him to escape from Gujarat as there was likely to be trouble there. The next morning he sought leave to depart from the staff but they would not give it and reported the matter to Sultan Ala-ud-Din who despatched two persons to see to it that he did not leave, and, if need be, put him in chains. One of the two persons was a friend and warned Rukn-ud-Din of the danger ahead. 'However with the help of a camel dealer from Thatta I escaped to the fort of Champanir. There I found 300 of my friends and companions with whom I started marching home. After a couple of nights, the Bhils attacked, killed many persons, and damaged much property. However, I reached Mandu safely. After fifteen days news came that the *firangi*s killed Sultan Bahadur in the river. Great confusion followed in Gujarat.'

## Battle of Qanauj Between Humayun and Sher Shah

'When Sher Shah Sur and Humayun Badshah came face to face with each other on the banks of the river Ganges, Humayun Badshah was on the side of Bhojpur, while Sher Shah was on the opposite bank. Humayun Badshah publicly stated that if he were to win that time and the Afghans were to be defeated, he would not leave the names of Afghans alive, even of children.' When Rukn-ud-Din heard of this, he was much perturbed, but the same night he saw Shaikh 'Abd-ul-Quddūs in dream who told him that Sher Shah would win. On the 4th day the battle took place and Humayun was defeated.

## Rukn-ud-Din as Amil Under Isa Khan

When Sher Shah appointed Isa Khan at the Sambal, the latter went to that area. He had the parganas of Kanth (or Khria?) and Tilhar in his *Wajihdari*[13] 'Masand-i Ali called me and asked me to administer that pargana.' Rukn-ud-Din did not want to go, but that night Shaikh 'Abd-ul-Quddūs appeared in a dream and said that he should make it up as in pargana Kanth there was an old Saiyid woman whose *imlak* had lapsed for some time. He should restore to her *imlak*. The next day he went and became the *Amil* of Kanth and did as Shaikh 'Abd-ul-Quddūs had told him. After sometime he went to Sambhal along with that Saiyid woman and some other women and persuaded Isa Khan to grant them some land.[14]

## Sher Shah Orders Afghan Families to Go to Gawalior

When Sher Shah ordered that the families[15] of Afghans should be brought to the fort of Gwalior, eunuchs were appointed to go to the pargana and send the families, and if they refused, set the houses on fire and send them forcibly with disgrace.... When this news became known, our families were much concerned as they did not have the strength to march. That night Shaikh 'Abd-ul-Quddūs appeared in dream and said that he would remain with the family, and by the will of God no one would come. From the neighbouring parganas they dragged away the families of the Afghans, but no one came to our family, and we remained safe. After some time there was again the rumour that eunuchs had been appointed to take away the families of the Sarwanis, and that they were coming. In our family there was great anxiety and I was also worried.... However, Shaikh 'Abd-ul-Quddūs told me in a dream that 'I will look after your house, why are you worried?' and further stated 'I will keep watch over the entire family, and those who have gone away will realize their mistake and will come back, and no eunuch will enter this place'. And so it did happen that no eunuch came to our family.

## Notes and References

1. The work was discovered by L. Rushbrook Williams and reported to the Indian Historical Records Commission, III Session. It has been

translated by R. P. Tripathi of the Allahabad University. For a short description of the work, see P. Saran, *The Provincial Government of the Mughals*, 1941.

2. Shaikh 'Abd-ul-Quddus, son of Shaikh Ismail, was a native of Rudauli (district Bara Banki, UP). He married the daughter of Shaikh Arif, son of the famous saint of the Chishti-Sabiri order, Shaikh Ahmad Abd-ul-Haq. He was a disciple of Shaikh Muhammad, son of Shaikh Arif. For a long time he wandered in the neighbourhood of Rudauli, but hardly anybody took him seriously. Shortly before the accession of Sultan Sikandar Lodi, one of his nobles, Umar Khan Sarwani fell into disfavour and went towards Jaunpur to join Malik Barbak. On the way he stopped at Rudauli and inquired if there were any saints in the locality. Among others, the name of Shaikh 'Ahd-ul-Quddus was mentioned, and Umar Khan met him. Soon after this meeting, Umar Khan's quarrel with Sikandar Lodi was patched up, and this was regarded as the result of the saint's blessings. A few years later, political disturbances broke out in Rudauli and Shaikh 'Abd-ul-Quddus decided to leave the town. About the year 1490, Umar Khan invited him to live in Shahabad. He stayed there until 1525–6, and was supported and maintained by Umar Khan's family. While he was there, his influence grew rapidly and he gained a large following among the Afghans. After the defeat of Ibrahim Lodi, Shaikh 'Abd-ul-Quddus went to Gangoh (district Saharanpur) where he died in 1537. His disciples include Shaikh 'Abd-ul-Kabir, Shaikh Nizam-ud-Din of Thanesar, and Shaikh Abd-ul-Ahad, all of whom became famous. His grandson, Shaikh Abd-ul-Nabi, was Akbar's *Sadr-us-Sadur*.

3. The text used for the article is the Mujtabai Press, Delhi, Edition of 1311 Hijrah.

4. I have not been able to trace the situation of this village.

5. Or Kuhtana.

6. I have rendered a free translation of the text which is as follows: *Afghānān agarchih bisyār jama' shudah- and wa lekin bā-ishārat (bāsharāt?) i- nifs-i-khud giraftār-and wa hinoz sābit nā-shudah fath Bābar Bādshāh ast.*

7. *Rasūlān-i-khud bar Bādshāh Humāyūn firastādand wa 'ahd kardand ki chun mā rā az madad-i-shumā makhlaṣī shawad ba-muqāblah har manzil yak lakh tanka khāham dād.*

8. The Text is: *Bālā'i qila' Chittor ādmiyān-i-khud nishāndah tarbiyat-i-Islām kardah khud ba-muqāblah-i-Humāyūn Bādshāh rawān shud.*

9. The name in the text as given is obviously a mistake.

10. *katghar kardah wa lashkari-khud miyān-i-katghar kardah.*

11. Shah Alam Bokhari was one of the most famous saints of Gujarat. He was a descendent of the famous Suhrawardi saint Jalal-ud-Din Bokhari, commonly known as Makhdum Jahanian. He was a friend and contemporary of Sultan Mahmud Begarah of Gujarat.

12. One of the patron saints of the ruling dynasty of Gujarat. He died in the early years of the fifteenth century and is buried at Sarkhej, a few miles away from Ahmedabad.

13. *Azdo hifz āmad... kāuth pargana wa Tilhar wa Masnad-i-'Alī farmūdand ki tū* (Ruknuddin) *do pargana barai....*

14. *zamin-i-tū ba-māndah wa pā-badam.*

15. I have translated *basābthai* or *basabatahi* as family, particularly the women.

# 23

〰〰

# *Abu 'l Faḍl* *

Abu'l Faḍl (Fazl) 'Allami (Shaykh), author, liberal thinker, and
informal secretary of the emperor Akbar, was the younger brother
of the poet Faydi and the second son of Shaykh Mubarak Nagawri
(d. 1593), one of the most distinguished scholars of his age in
India, and the author of a commentary on the Kur'an, Mamba'i
*Nafā'is al-'Uyān*. He was born on 6 Muharram 958/14 January
1551 at Agra, where his father had settled, in 1543, as a teacher.
Abu'l Faḍl was a pupil of his father, and owed his profound
scholarship and liberality of outlook largely to the training given
him by the latter. By his fifteenth year he had studied religious
sciences, Greek thought and mysticism; but formal education
did not satisfy the yearnings of his soul nor did the orthodox faith
bring him spiritual solace. While studying in his father's school,
he spent his time in extensive reading, deep meditation, and
frequent discussions of religious questions.

Abu'l Faḍl was presented at the court by his brother, Faydi,
in 1574. He soon gained high favour with Akbar by his scholarly
criticism of the narrow-mindedness of the '*ulama*' in the religious discussions which were started in the '*Ibādat Khāna* in
1575. He helped in freeing the emperor from the domination of
the '*ulama*', and was instrumental in bringing about their ultimate political downfall by the promulgation, in 1579, of the
decree (*mahḍar*), drafted by him in collaboration with his father,

* H. A. R. Gibbs & others, *Encyclopaedia of Islam*, Vol. I, New edition, eds.
E. J. Brill, Leiden, 1979, pp. 117–18.

which invested Akbar with the authority of deciding points of difference between the theologians.

A firm believer in God, whom he regarded as transcendental and the Creator, Abu'l-Faḍl considered that there could be no relationship between man and God except that of servitude (*'abdullahī*) on the part of the former. Servitude required sincerity, suppression of the ego (*nafs*), and devotion to Him, resignation to His will, and faith in His Mercifulness. Though he regarded formal worship as mere hypocrisy, he believed that there were many ways of serving the Lord, but only divine blessing could reveal the Truth. 'In the main', he wrote, 'every sect may be placed in one of two categories—either, it is in possession of the Truth, in which case one should seek direction from it; or, it is in the wrong, in which it is an object of pity and deserving of sympathy, not of reproach' (*Akbar Nama*, ii, 660). His faith in being at 'peace with all' (*sulh-i-kull*) involved not only toleration of all religions but also love for all human beings.

In political affairs, Abu'l-Faḍl sought to emphasize the divine character of Akbar's kingship. Royalty, he claimed, was light emanating from God (*farr-i-īzadī*), communicated to kings without the intermediate assistance of anyone. Though the existence of kings was necessary at all times, it was only after many ages that there appeared, by divine blessing, a monarch who could not only rule effectively, but could also guide the world spiritually. Since Akbar could ensure the material as well as the spiritual well-being of his subjects, he could be truly regarded as the 'Perfect Man' (*insān-i-kāmil*). It was the duty of all to give Akbar complete loyalty and to seek his spiritual guidance by becoming his disciples. The chosen among the disciples would be those who attained the 'four degrees of devotion' (*chahār martaba-i ikhās*), that is, preparedness to place at Akbar's disposal their property, life, honour, and faith.

Though Abu'l Faḍl's religio-political views earned for him the enmity of the '*ulama*', the policy of religious toleration which he helped Akbar in evolving, the non-denominational yet spiritual character of obedience to the emperor which he advocated, his justification, on ethical grounds, of every imperial action, and his persistent efforts to inculcate, especially among the nobles, a sense of mystical loyalty to Akbar, contributed greatly to the political consolidation of the Mughal empire.

In spite of Abu'l Faḍl's immense influence over Akbar and the numerous duties which he performed at court (especially in drafting letters to nobles and foreign potentates), his progress in the official hierarchy was slow. It was only in 1585 that he was promoted to the *manṣab* of 1000, which was doubled in 1592. Six years later it was raised to 2500. Except when he was associated, for a short time in 1586, with Shah Kuli Khān Mahram in the joint government of Delhi, Abu'l Faḍl never held any office untill 1599, when he was posted to the Deccan, at the instance of hostile elements at the court. He distinguished himself there as an able administrator and military commander. In recognition of his services, he was promoted, in 1600, to the rank of 4000, and two years later, to that of 5000. The same year he was hastily summoned to the court when Akbar's son Salīm (afterwards the emperor Jahāngīr) rebelled. On his way back, he was waylaid and assassinated by Rājā Bir Singh Deva, the disaffected Bundela chieftain of Orchha, on 4 Rabi' I 1011/22 August 1602. His head was severed and sent to Salīm, at whose instance the crime had been committed, while the body was buried at Antarī (near Gwalior). The news came as a great shock to Akbar, who mourned the loss deeply and never forgave Salīm for instigating the murder. Abu'l-Faḍl was survived by his son, 'Abddal-Raḥmān Afdal Khān (d. 1613), who rose to be governor of Bihār.

Abul'l Faḍl's principal title to fame as an author rests upon his monumental work, *Akbar Nāma*, a history of Akbar (down to the 46th regnal year) and of his ancestors, compiled in three *daftar*s (first two *daftar*s published in *Bibl. Ind.*, 3 vols). The third *daftar*, *Ā'in-i-Akbari* (*Bibl. Ind.*, 3 vols.), dealing with imperial regulations and containing detailed information on Indian geography, administration, and social and religious life, was the first work of its kind in India. Abu'l-Faḍl's compositions, characterized by an individual literary style, served as a model for many generations, though none was able to imitate him successfully. His numerous works include a Persian translation of the Bible; *Iyār-i-Danish* (a recension of *Anwār-i-Suhayli*); prefaces to *Tarikh-i-Alfi* (unfortunately lost); to the Persian translation of *Mahābhārata*, and to many other works: and a *Munādjāt* (ed. by Rizvi, *Medieval India Quarterly*, Aligarh, I/iii). His letters, perfaces, and other compositions were compiled by his nephew fl

Abu'l Faḍl 295

under the title *Inshā-i-Abu'l Faḍl* (3 vols). Another collection of his private letters is entitled *Ruk'āt-i-Abu'l Faḍl.*

*Bibliography.* Autobiographical accounts: *A'in-i-Akbari*, iii (at end); *Inshā-i-Abu'l Faḍl.* Biographies: *Ma'āthir al-Umard'* (*Bib.*, Ind., ii, 608–22, Eliot and Dowson, vi, iff, Blochman, Introduction to his translation of *A'in-i-Akbari*; Storey, ii/3, 541–51 (detailed reference on 554).

# 24

# Nigar Nama-i-Munshi

## A Valuable Collection of Documents of
## Aurangzeb's Reign*

The study of the history of medieval India is handicapped by the
meagreness of official records. The *Ain,* and the few known
*Dasturul Amal* provide information on the administrative laws,
but enough information is still not available on the working of the
administrative institutions. The *farman*s, though existing in large
numbers, are still too widely scattered, while the few collections
of official correspondence have not been properly analysed. It
is hoped that the record offices of the older Indian princely
states will yield much useful material when they are scrutinized
by historians. But apart from the important volume relating to
*Daftar-i-Diwani* records, not much material has appeared in
print. The present paper is, therefore, intended to introduce to
the historians a rich and important collection of documents and
records of the reign of Aurangzeb—the *Nigar Nama-i-Munshi.*
Two copies of the work are preserved in the manuscript library
of the Aligarh Muslim University.[1] The work was compiled as
a model of letter-writing, and its arrangement is therefore, in
accord with that object. But the letters and documents, though
arranged for a different purpose, are drafts of actual letters sent
or documents issued. Consequently, they are of great value.

* *Proceedings of Indian History Congress,* XV Session, Gwalior, 1952, pp. 258–
63

The author calls himself 'Munshi, known as Malikzada'. From the preface it appears that he served on the staff of Lashkar Khan, who was Mir Bakhshi from July 1670 to January 1671. Some time after the latter's death, he entered the service of Prince Mu'azzam, Shah 'Alam. When the prince was proceeding on his expedition to Afghanistan (in 1677), he was attached to the secretariat of Prince Mu'izz-ud-Din. Due to infirmity, however, the author could not proceed beyond Peshawar. From an incidental reference in the text, we gather that he was given a *mansab* of 200 and was made a *sadr* and *darogha 'adalat* at Multan (f. 110B). Later he joined the staff of Mirza Badiuz-Zaman, Rashid Khan, who held the office of Diwan. Then for sometime he served under Rahmat Khan, the *Diwan-i-Buyutat,* and later, under Mirza Muhammad Irani, entitled Basharat Khan who held the office of the Imperial Diwan. When the Imperial Camp moved from Aurangabad, Munshi did not accompany his master but stayed behind. He had reached the age of seventy years, and decided to devote his time to the compilation of his own drafts, as well as those of other well-known *munshis.* The compilation was done in the year 1095/1684.

## Plan of the Work

The work begins with an introduction on the art of drafting (*insha*), in which the styles of the prominent munshis, from the time of Abul Fazl, are reviewed. The work is divided into two parts, called *Daftar.* The first includes the letters or documents drafted by the author himself, while the second comprises documents drafted by other well-known munshis.

## Daftar I

The first *Daftar* is divided into four *Safha,* each of these being further subdivided into several *Babs.*

## Safha I

Letters drafted for, or on behalf of, the princes of the royal blood.

## Bab i

Petitions, or letters written to elders and superiors. Most of the letters included here were written for Prince Mu'izz-ud-Din, the eldest son of Prince Mu'azzam. There are some letters written for Princess Daulat-Afza and Khujista Akhtar and for Princess Dahr-afruz Banu Begum (10b–22a).

### Bab ii

Letters written to youngers of equal status. This section includes the correspondence of Mu'izza-ud-Din, Daulat-afza Dahr-afruz (22a–23b).

### Bab iii

Letters written for Mu'izz-ud-Din to notables, including Maharaja Jaswant Singh, A'izz Khan,[2] Sheikh 'Abd-ul-Khaliq, the Imperial Vakil, and Mir Mohammad Ma'sum, the Diwan (23b–25b).

Most of these letters are of a personal nature, though some, especially in the *Bab* iii, throw some light on administrative affairs.

### Safha II

Letters written for the nobles, divided into two *bab*s.

### Bab i

Correspondence between the nobles. Most of these letters were written for Lashkar Khan. Three letters are of condolence at the death of Ja'far Khan, in 1670, while two others were also written in condolence. Two letters of congratulations, written to Mukhtar Khan on his appointment as *Subedar* of Kashmir, and to Wizarat Khan on his appointment as Darogha of Imperial *Ghusl-Khana*, are interesting from the administrative point of view. There are a few other letters of a personal nature.

### Bab ii

Contains two letters to inferiors, the second being addressed to Mulla Mushiri of Kashmir, the poet, who was assigned 100 *Kharwar Shali*, from the revenues of the *'amil* of the *jagir* in Kashmir, as stipend (30b–31b).

## Safha III: Letters of Diwans
### Bab i

Petitions, to the emperor and to Prince Mu'azzam. It is difficult to ascertain the name of the *Diwan* on whose behalf these letters were written. Some were written for one Imad, who was probably attached to Prince Mu'izz-ud-Din. These letters deal principally with revenue administration. There are reports that local officials, particularly those entrusted with the maintenance of law and order, like *faujdars*, were tyrannizing over the peasantry. The trouble became acute because the *faujdar* was not subordinate to the diwan of jagirdars. There is considerable information regarding the assignment of the revenues of specified territories to nobles as jagirs in lieu of cash salary. Sometime only part of the revenues of villages had to be sent to the government treasury, or the treasury of some high noble. There are references to the difficulties in the payment of cash salaries to minor officials and troops regularly. Information is also given regarding the difficulties of transferring treasure from one place to the other, and on the widely prevalent system of bills of exchange (*Hundi* or *Hindui* 31b–51a).

### Bab ii

Letters of Diwans to other distinguished nobles. The addresses include Asad Khan, Muhsin Khan, Bahramand Khan, Abdur Rahim Khan, Amanat Khan, Khan-i-Khanan, Anas Khan, Mir Mahdi, Afrasiyab Khan, Amir Khan, and Rashid Khan. These letters, some of which are personal in nature, throw light on the relations of nobles with one another, and also on the working of the administrative machinery. Some letters indicate the difficulties arising out of dual control in jagir areas, as also in the matter of appointments. There is also information on the combining of the offices of amin with *krori* or *thanadar* or faujdar. The rate of revenue was prescribed as half of the produce. Efforts were made to extend the cultivated area, and to stop all extra cesses and taxes even in jagir lands. The accounts were not always kept properly and there were defalcations. The letters describe the efforts to bring the system of accounting in jagirs in conformity with imperial regulations. These letters also show that jagirs were very frequently transferred, and revenue of a territory assigned to one person was sometime transferred in times of emergency to another. There is also some information on the mode of payment of excess revenue by jagirdars to the Imperial Treasury (51a–81b).

## Bab iii

Orders sent to officers. Much of the information regarding revenue administration referred to above is elucidated in these orders. There is criticism of subordinate officials who either tyrannized over the people or neglected their duty. Cooperation between faujdar and amin is urged, and slackness in collecting revenue is disapproved. Some light is thrown on the position of the zamindars. These orders reveal that although the administrative machinery was showing signs of a breakdown, yet the control of the higher authorities was still quite effective. While the realization of revenue in cash had become almost the rule, nevertheless crop sharing system also continued in some places.

There is an interesting order regarding the collection of jaziya. This tax, levied on persons living in jagirs as well, presumably went to the Imperial Treasury. In the absence of classified nominal rolls of Hindus, the imperial tax-collectors demanded from jagirdars large amounts. Consequently, efforts were made to prepare a list of Hindus falling under the three prescribed categories (81b–90a).

## Bab iv

Letters of appointment and other orders. This constitutes the most important section of the work. It includes the actual letters of appointment of various officials and instructions issued to them. There are letters of appointments to the following posts: *faujdar, diwan, amin, krori, qanungo, karkun, thanadar, kotwal, qazi, darogha* of *'adalat, sadr, fotadar, darogha* of treasury, *mushrif,* superintendent of records, *baramad nawis, waqia-nawis, bakhshi,* and *chaudhri.* These orders not only state the duties of the above officials but also reveal the character of administrative machinery. Copies of sanads issued for the grant or resumption of jagirs and grant of madad-i-mu'ash are also given. It is worth noting that grants of madad-i-mu'ash were small, 100 or 200 bighas of arable but uncultivated land. Usually revenue of villages was not assigned for this purpose. Some sanads deal with special duties, such as inquiry into accounts. It appears from these letters as stated above that many posts were frequently combined. For example, *Mir Bahri* with *Kotwali, Wikalat-i-Shava'i* with *Daroghgi-i-baitulmal, Bakshigiri* or *Daroghgi-i-khazana* with *Waqia-nowisi.* The *waqia-nawis* was expected to report not only on general administration but also on the working of the revenue administration (90a–106a. A is incomplete, B gives copies of many more sanads).

## Bab v

Orders of the army department, regarding the appointment of diwan of an expeditionary army, and the inspection of *dagh* and weapons (106a–106b), and miscellaneous orders dealing with farming of revenue (*mustajiri*), taxes on groves, in which a lower rate was prescribed for groves belonging to Muslims. Some letters of appointment of officials are also given. This section concludes with an interesting dastur-ul-amal for *Diwans* (in Ms. B only).

## *Safha IV*

Letters written by the author in his personal capacity to Prince Mu'izz-ud-Din and to many friends, including a letter addressed to the famous historian, Muhammad Salih Kambuh. These letters are personal in nature, though they contain incidental references to political events, administration, and the day-to-day life of the people (106b–125a).

## Daftar II: Letters drafted by other *munshis*

### *Safha I*

Royal farmans and sanads. Correspondence of Shahjahan with Nazr Muhammad Khan of Turan and Shah Abbas II of Iran, drafted by Sa'dullah Khan. These letters are well-known (131a–137b). Correspondence of Aurangzeb with Mirza Raja Jai Singh (125a–128a; 128b–129b). In Safhas IV and V below, more letters of Jai Singh to Aurangzeb are quoted. This chapter includes a large number of letters of appointment, issued by the

Imperial Secretariat, for most of the offices mentioned in Bab iv of Safha III of the first Daftar. There are drafts of public notifications of some of these appointments in which the duties of other officials and the public towards these officers are also stated. Among the more interesting of these documents is an order issued to Rasik Das, in which the entire land revenue administration is reviewed, its defects pointed out, and reforms ordered (129b–131a). Another order grants remission of *jaziya* to peasants on grounds of their poverty and in the interest of the extension of cultivation (B. 231a–232b). It is not clear whether this order was of general application, or was intended for some particular locality (125a–137b. A is incomplete. The rest of the letters are given in B 225b–255a).

## Safha II

Orders issued by Prince Muazzam. These include letters of appointment and instructions to *faujdar*s, *amin*s, and *diwan*. There is a grant of *madad-i-mu'ash* and *parwana*s of safe travel (*rahdari*). This section concludes with copies of letters written mostly by Mu'izz-ud-Din, and contains only incidental information (B. 255b–263a).

## Safha III

Letters and reports written by nobles. These letters were either written by or addressed to the following nobles: Amanat Khan, Hamid Khan, Qasim Khan, Himmat Khan, Lashkar Khan, Adil Khan, Rahmat Khan, Amir Khan, Qiwam-ud-Din. These letters are of great value, in so far as they contain reports on general and revenue administration. These are important from the point of political as well as administrative history (147a–160a).

## Safha IV

Petitions and letters written by the well-known munshi, Udai Raj Rustam Khani. Petitions or letters written to the Emperor (160a–182a) and to Ja'far Khan, to the *Sadr-us-Sudur* to Adil Shah of Bijapur and Qutbul-Mulk of Golconda, and the correspondence of Mirza Raja Jai Singh. These letters contain valuable information on the political history of the earlier part of Aurangzeb's reign (160a–188a).

## *Safha* V

Specimens of drafts of well-known munshis like Sheikh Abdus-Samad Jaunpuri, Mir Muhammad Raza, Sa'dullah Khan, and Sadiqi. Apart from the letters of Jai Singh to Aurangzeb (190a–191b), other letters do not contain much information on administrative or political affairs (188a–206a).

It is not possible, in the course of this short paper, to examine in detail and assess the value of the information contained in the work, or even to give its analytical summary. If this paper draws the attention of the scholars to the need of subjecting this work to a close scrutiny, it would have more than served its purpose.

### Notes and References

1. The first manuscript (A) is in Sir Shah Sulaiman Collection, no. *Farsiya*, 152. Transcribed in 1195 H/1781. Written in stylish *shikast*, with the headings in red. Ff. 206. Size: 8.5" x 5"; 6.7" x 3.2". Ll. to page 15. Slightly moth-eaten and water-stained. Binding defective.

The second manuscript (B) is in Nawab Abdus-Salam Collection, no. 362/132. Transcribed in 1227H/1812–13. Written in bold *nasta'liq*, with the headings in red. Ff. 304. Size: 9.7" x 5.7" Ll. to page 13.

The transcription of A is accurate, while that of B is defective. Both the manuscripts have long gaps, but taken together they are complete.

All references, unless otherwise specified, are to Ms. A.

2. The general who was sent to the Afghanistan expedition, and who has been incorrectly mentioned by Sarkar as Aghar Khan, *History of Aurangzeb*, III, pp. 237 *et seq.*

# 25

# *Du Jardin Papers*+
## A Valuable Source for the Economic
## History of Northern India, 1778–87*

The Bibliotheque Nationale, Paris, contains a valuable collection of papers, belonging presumably to a Frenchman, Daniel
du Jardin, which throw valuable light on the economic history
of northern India during the period 1778 to 1787. The principal
documents so far discovered are as follows:

+ The author acknowledges with thanks the invitation first extended to him
by the French government in 1965 which enabled him to 'discover' the
series, supplément Persan (hereinafter SP) 1594–1604, somewhat mis-
leadingly catalogued in Blochet's famous catalogue. However, the hospi-
tality offered by Maison des Sciences de l'Homme of Paris in 1979,
enabled him to examine, somewhat closely, these documents and some
other important related documents which have been referred to above. The
list of other manuscripts mentioned above, also inadequately catalogued,
is not necessarily exhaustive—there may be more related manuscripts
which have not yet come to light. The Indian Council of Historical Research
has obtained microfilm copies of MSS SP 1594–1604, which are now being
enlarged and chronologically rearranged.

    The paper was presented at the Indian History Congress session in
Waltair in December 1979.

    The map in this paper has been prepared under the supervision of
Professor Moonis Raza of the Centre for the Study of Regional Development, School of Social Sciences, Jawaharlal Nehru University, New Delhi,
for which the author expresses his sincere gratitude.

* *Indian Historical Review*, Vol. V, Nos 1–2, 1978–9.

MS Indien 812: A collection of sixteen documents, written in Modi script with occasional inscriptions in French, English or Persian. These are mostly *hundis*, issued in 1787, either by du Jardin himself, or by his business partners.

MS Indien 813: (Catalogue of Indian MSS no. 175): A collection of thirty-nine documents (mostly of *taqavi*) issued in Persian, with marginal notes in Modi script.

MS Supplement Persan no. 1581: A collection of forty-seven documents, mostly in Persian, with occasional remarks in the margin or elsewhere in French or English.

MS Supplement Persan no. 1582: A collection of seven documents in Persian, the last page of which bears the following inscription in English: Copy of Persian Papers about the affairs of Mr Willes.

The tradition whereof having been made by Mr Lambert and are registered in Calcutta.

MS Supplement Persan nos 1594–1604: These eleven volumes form the Account Books of Daniel du Jardin and of his partner. Although there are references to the year 1778, but the bulk of accounts are for the years 1779 to 1787 (with a brief reference to 1788). These are all in Persian, written in *shikasta* style usual in *siyaq* (accountancy). The pages are disarranged and no chronological order has been maintained.

It is not known how these documents happened to reach Paris and found safe custody in Bibliotheque Nationale. We know very little about Daniel du Jardin, or how he came to India and for how long he lived in this country. We know that he was a Frenchman, partly because of his name, but mainly because of his occasional inscriptions which are in French. Beyond that we know nothing of his family or the place of his origin. It is, however, possible to say that he had established himself in the neighbourhood of what is now Aligarh (UP) long before de Boigne made it his headquarters (1788) or became the commander of Mahadaji Sindhia's army (1784). It is believed that during the administration of de Boigne, several planters, especially of indigo, settled in the district. Among these is mentioned one M. Jourdan at Khair, but it has not been possible to establish any connection between du Jardin and M. Jourdan.

Apart from his Account Books, we get an autobiographical reference to him in a few documents when he pleaded with the respectable people of Sikandarpur and Marehra (both in Etah district) and other places in the neighbourhood of Kol (Aligarh) to give evidence that he was not conspiring against the British, who were then trying to establish their domination over Farrukhabad and Awadh. In this document he says that he came alone, without kith and kin to this land to which he was a total stranger. Here he became a merchant and engaged in the cultivation of indigo. He had taken in *ijara*, a number of villages, such as Pilwa, Nidhauli, and Pora, from Raja Himmat Singh of Etah (1780–1812). He categorically disclaimed any intention of regarding himself as a zamindar, though he also held in ijara several other *ta'alluqa*s, such as one of Jarara in *tappa* Khair of Aligarh district, had acquired a house in Marehra and had indigo factories at least in Pora, Pilwa, Marehra, and Farrukhabad. At the request of Nawab Muzaffar Jung, an English Resident had been appointed at Farrukhabad in 1780, and on 25 February 1784, John Willes was appointed to that post. Even though Willes was recalled sixteen months later, he sent his subordinate, Duke, to squeeze du Jardin out of that region. Duke partially succeeded, the indigo factory at Pilwa was forced to close down temporarily, and a number of documents of du Jardin, including his appeal for evidence, dated 12 April 1786, fell into the hands of Willes.[1] Du Jardin was also forced to surrender the house that he had taken in mortgage at Marehra. The fact that there are no accounts for the period after January 1788 leads to the suspicion that someone, possibly some Englishman, had caused his downfall, or at least forced him to withdraw from trading activity; the coincidence is worthy of note that we get no account of him when de Boigne established his headquarters at Aligarh in 1788.

It would not be correct to get the impression that du Jardin had only enmity with the English or the other Europeans of the period. In fact, very soon after he started his business in 1778–9, he acquired a partner, Louis Perry (it is not possible to decipher the name correctly from the *shikasta* Persian script), who remained with him till the end of his business career in

India. He also seems to have collaborated on a large scale with a Louis Purcerrel, Major Pollier (a Swiss engineer and military adventurer), M. (Chevalier?) Dudrenec, and a host of other well established merchants, like James Grant and Robert Grant[2] (who were enjoying the patronage of the East India Company), Stewart, etc.

Du Jardin's principal activities were both agricultural and commercial. Agriculturally he had acquired many villages in *ijara*, the principal ones being ta'alluqa Jarara in tappa Khair of Aligarh district, Nidhauli, Pilwa, Pora, Tatarpur, Jaisingpur; Dehgawan, Dharawi, and other villages of ta'alluqa Marehra. Some of the ijaras, received from Raja Himmat Singh, were for four years (though they seem to have been terminated earlier),[3] but the others appear to have been with him for a much longer time. Apart from the duties normally associated with ijara, namely to keep the ryot satisfied and to increase cultivation especially by the grant of *taqavi* loans (agricultural credit), the main agricultural activity undertaken by du Jardin was the plantation of indigo, which, it seems, he had done on a very big scale, as well as the processing of indigo in factories. Among his trading activities, special mention needs to be made of food grains, textiles, indigo, saltpetre, salt, and tobacco. It seems that du Jardin kept his stocks of food grains, in depots called *kothar*, at a number of places, such as Pilwa, Pora, Marehra, Farrukhabad, Jarara, Kasganj, Kol, and Etah.

The present author has not yet succeeded in analysing the enormous evidence contained in these volumes, which throw a great deal of light on the cropping pattern, the cost of cultivating indigo, prices, wages, profits on various articles, means and cost of transport, etc.

In the present districts of Aligarh, Etah, and Farrukhabad, where du Jardin's activities appear to have been concentrated, great political turbulence prevailed during the period. One gets some idea of the type of problems faced by private individuals like du Jardin in such times; he was neither a zamindar, nor was he associated with administration. These documents, incidentally, reveal that Muzaffar Jung's authority was respected in the territories of Farrukhabad,[4] while a *parwana* of *rahdari* issued by the Nawab Wazir, Asaf-ud-Daula, at Lucknow, virtually ensured safe conduct for goods from Anupshahr, in Bulundshahr, to Calcutta at least up to the end of 1786. One may also notice the fact that the most economical way of moving cargo in bulk was by boats plying on the Kali Nadi and the Ganga *via* Kanpur, Varanasi, and Patna.

In the present paper, translations of a few original documents are given so that scholars may get an idea of how they were worded. (The author is not aware of any of these documents having been reported earlier.)

## Ijara (Revenue Farms)

Ijaras were of many types and may be noticed from the very beginning of the Sultanate period. These could be given on many terms, such as for one particular crop for one harvest only.[5] The text of an ijara issued by Raja Himmat Singh to Du Jardin, for the *fasli* years 1192 to 1194 (1784–7) is given below:[6]

Seal of Raja Himmat Singh[7]

### *Do Nafar*

In the name of Munshi Tek Chand, *gumashta* of Daniel du Jardin Saheb, Louis Saheb Bahadur, and Purcerrel Saheb Bahadur,[8] to the effect that since village Pilwa, etc. and other villages have been given in ijara in lieu of fifteen thousand six hundred and seventy-five rupees *sicca* Farrukhabad, with all their resources including revenue and cesses (*mal-o-jihat wa sair jihat*), for three years, from the very beginning of the year 1192 *fasli* till 1194 *fasli*,[9] in accordance with the acceptance (*qubuliyat*) of the above-mentioned persons, it is incumbent (upon the lessees) that with single-mindedness they should keep the *ri'aya* satisfied with their good behaviour and, having done that, deposit the stipulated amount year by year, harvest by harvest, as per (prescribed) instalments, in the treasury of the *sarkar*. They should exert themselves to bring about increase in cultivation and prosperity of the villages, so that year after year the revenue (*mal*) may increase and prosperity may become visible. If, God forbid, there is a natural or other calamity (*afat-i-arzi wa samavi*),[10] action be taken as per Regulations, in accordance with the consent (*qubuliyat*).

| 9 villages:<br>*Asli-*7;<br>*Dakhili-*2 | *Jama* of<br>3 years<br>Rs 15,675 | 1192 F—Rs 4525<br>1193 F—Rs 5225 (15.4% increase)<br>1194 F—Rs 5925 (13.4% increase) |
|---|---|---|
| Pilwa. etc.:<br>3 villages | *Jama*<br>Rs 6725 | 1192 F—Rs 2000<br>1193 F—Rs 2225 (11.25% increase)<br>1194 F—Rs 2500 (10.1% increase) |
| Baragaon:<br>3 villages | *Jama*<br>Rs 4800 | 1192 F—Rs 1,400<br>1103 F—Rs. 1600 (14.2% increase)<br>1194 F—Rs 1800 (12.5% increase) |
| Tatarpur:<br>2 villages | *Jama*<br>Rs 3000 | 1192 F—Rs 800<br>1193 F—Rs 1000 (25% increase)<br>1194 F—Rs 1200 (20% increase) |
| Jasinghpur | *Jama*<br>Rs 1125 | 1192 F—Rs 325<br>1193 F—Rs 375 (15.3% increase)<br>1194 F—Rs 425 (13.3% increase) |

Written on 14 *Ramazan* 1198 *Hijri*/1 August 1784.

The most striking feature is the yearly increase in the revenues of the villages, ranging from 10 per cent per annum in the villages of Pilwa to 20 per cent in the villages of Tatarpur—the overall average for the nine villages being 15.4 per cent in the first year and 13.4 per cent in the next year. This sizeable increase could partly be explained by the extension in the cultivation of indigo, which was undertaken on a large scale at the instance of du Jardin,[11] and partly by the severe famine in the area in 1783–4 after which the revenue jumped from Rs 2479 to Rs 4525 (or 75 per cent). It may be recalled that the Mughal state had always insisted on extension of cultivation and thus increase of *mal,* but the order of increase which was considered normal was generally smaller.[12] Isolated examples are available of a more intensified exaction; for example, in *ta'alluqa* Dehgawan in 1195 *fasli* (1787–8), the *kankut* rate had risen to under 2/3 for the *ijaradar,*[13] while the usual rates do not show any increase in the ijara taken from Raja Himmat Singh. The kankut rate in Pilwa, Baragaon, Tatarpur, and Jaisinghpur is half of the produce, while the *zabti* rate for the main cash crops, such as cotton and sugarcane, does not show any unusual rise either.[14]

| | Cotton | Suger cane |
|---|---|---|
| | | Rate per bigha in rupees |
| Pilwa | 4–8–0 | – |
| Baragaon | 4–8–0 | 6–0–0 |
| Tatarpur | 4–8–0 | 6–0–0 |
| Jaisinghpur | 4–8–0 | 6–0–0 |

## Discharge Certificate

It seems that at the end of each *fasli* year (or at the end of a harvest), a discharge certificate was issued, absolving the ijaradar of any further obligation in respect of that year. This was, usually, the culmination of several instalments of receipts paid from time to time.[15] Two such documents, issued by Raja Himmat Singh, are quoted below:

(a) *For 1783–4*[16]

In the name of Munshi Tek Chand, *gumashta* of Daniel du Jardin Saheb Bahadur and Purcerrel Saheb Bahadur, to the effect that the entire amount for the year 1191 *fasli* (1783–4) in respect of villages Pilwa, Baragaon, Tatarpur, and Jaisinghpur has been totally and fully deposited in the treasury of the *sarkar*. Consequently, these few lines have been written in complete discharge of all claims.

| Seal of Raja | Rs 2799–3–1 | For 1191 *fasli* (for *mal* |
|---|---|---|
| Himmat Singh | Arrears of 1190 | as well as *sa'ir*) |
| Bahadur | *fasli* Rs 220–3–1 | Rs 2579–0–0 |

Written on 12 *Rajab*, 14 *Jeth Sudi*, 3 June 1191 F (3 June 1784)

(b) *For 1784–5*[17] (in Hindi) *Sa. Si*

Seal of Raja Himmat Singh Bahadur

In the name of Munshi Tek Chand, gumashta of Daniel du Jardin Saheb Bahadur and Purcerrel Saheb Bahadur, to the effect that the amount for *fasli kharif* 1192 F (1784–5) in regard to the ta'alluqa of the villages of Pilwa, etc. has been deposited through the aforesaid person with the sarkar and no amount has remained unpaid. Consequently, these few lines have been

written by way of complete discharge so that it may remain as proof for future use.
Dated: 24 *Jamada* II, 1199 *Hijri* (3 May 1785).

## *Taqavi* documents

One of the most important functions of an *ijaradar*, it seems, was to make agricultural credit (*taqavi*) available to the villages. Forty actual documents are available from ta'alluqa Jarara in tappa Khair of sarkar Kol, of which twenty-eight are for the kharif harvest of 1189 F and twelve for the rabi harvest of the same fasli year. Most of the amount for kharif 1189 F was disbursed in July 1781, while that for rabi in November 1781. There is almost incomprehensible variation in the amount given per village—from Rs 4 to Rs 137–14–2. Taqavi was generally given for seeds or for cultivation or without stating any purpose; it was also rarely given just as loan or to pay cesses.[18]

## The Document

I am, Sanwant and Girdhari and Malu, etc., *muqaddams* of Jarara, *tappa* Khair. A sum of rupees one hundred and thirty-seven, fourteen and half annas (Rs 137–14–2) has been taken in *taqavi* for the harvest of *rabi* 1189 *fasli* from the *sarkar* of du Jardin Saheb, by way of loan. (This amount) is being brought under my control and used by me. It is promised that the above-mentioned sum, along with a quarter as interest (*sud sawa'i*), shall be deposited in the treasury of the *sarkar* at harvest time, and no excuses will be put forward. Consequently, these words have been written so that they may serve as proof. Written on 2 *Zilhijja* equivalent to 18 November of the (regnal) year 23 (18 November 1781).

The document has been witnessed by Raja Ram, the *qanungo*. In the right hand margin, in Modi script, the names of the recipients, the amount, the rate of interest, and the year (*Vikram Samvat* 1838) are given.[19]

It would be seen from the document mentioned above that taqavi was given to the muqaddams of the village by the ijaradar (working on behalf of the zamindar). There are some documents in which taqavi was given to actual tenants or peasants (*asamiyan*), but their number is small (six out of forty). Of these three are referred to as *asami*, two as simply residents (*sakin*) and in one case they are referred to as grocers (*baqqalan*), and so is the amount given to them (*asamis* receive Rs 5, 2, and 4; *sakins* receive Rs 5 each; while the *baqqalan* receive Rs 15).[20]

A closer examination of the Account Books reveals the fact that the amounts given in taqavi were not as small as would appear from the actual documents available, and therefore it would not be possible to assert with much confidence that the amount given to the *muqaddams* (who presumably distributed it to the cultivators) was small. For example, during the kharif season of 1779, the amount given in taqavi was Rs 6295–10–0 for different villages. For the ta'alluqa of Jarara, it amounted to Rs 1839–14–2 (June—Rs 1191–3–2; July—Rs 648–11–0), while for du Jardin Nagar, etc., it was Rs 1666–3–3 (June—Rs 95–14–3; July—Rs 1570–5–0). Taqavi for June-July 1780 for *ta'alluqa* Jarara amounted to Rs 2210–14–0.[21]

Contrary to the usual practice of the taqavi forming the first charge at any harvest, we actually have evidence of considerable arrears accumulating on this account.[22] For example, in the eleven villages of ta'alluqa Jarara, the total amount of taqavi during kharif 1188 fasli amounted to Rs 3227–6–3, out of which only Rs 541 was realized while Rs 2686–6–3 remained in arrears. One, however, need not labour the point that part of the taqavi was realized in kind, which was not always advantageous to the peasant or the muqaddam, because at the time of harvest prices usually fell.[23]

In spite of the very important role that taqavi played in the process of agricultural production, it brought sizeable profits to the zamindar because *sud sawa'i* amounted to about 50 per cent per annum. However, if the amount taken at the time of the kharif harvest was paid along with the revenues of rabi, the rate of interest was charged in the case of late payment. Even then, profits from taqavi were considerable (the total from ta'alluqa Jarara during 1187 fasli was Rs 861–4–1).[24]

In whatever manner one may explain away the important part played by the zamindar (or the ijaradar as his representative), one cannot ignore the fact of the utter poverty of the villagers who were forced to take only small amounts as agricultural loans, and were not always in a position to pay it back in time.

It may nevertheless be recorded that the zamindar (or his agent, or the zamindar as the agent of the state) had definite responsibilities in encouraging and extending cultivation, which included the expenditure of considerable sums on irrigation. For example, in December 1784, in Pilwa, a sum of Rs 1225–5–2 was spent as *khareh bar kulab*.[25] In March 1787, a sum of Rs 1836–13–1 was spent on the same item, presumably in *ta'alluqa* Marehra.[26]

## Indigo Cultivation

A reference has been made above to the enormous increase in the sum of ijara per year and it has been suggested that part of it may be explained in terms of indigo cultivation. Let us examine the income of the ijaradar from the ta'alluqa of Pilwa in 1193 fasli. After deducting minor expenses amounting to Rs 7–13–3, the total income amounted to Rs 5290–13–2. This comprised the following:

| | |
|---|---|
| For the cultivation of indigo (by the *ijaradar*) | Rs 4659–12–2 |
| *Zabti* | Rs 345–6–1 |
| *Kankuti* | Rs 250–7–1 |
| *Siwai* (extra) | Rs 35–3–2 |
| | Rs 5290–13–2[27] |

Thus, from the revenue of Rs 5290–13–2, the *ijaradar* paid to the zamindar Rs 5225, and was left with a net profit of Rs 65–13–2 on account of *mal* alone. The main reason for taking *ijara* was presumably the cultivation of indigo and the profit that it brought. Except for the year 1195 *fasli* (1787–8), the cost of cultivation of indigo is also available to us although it is from different though neighbouring villages.

| | |
|---|---|
| Ploughing: 570 bighas 18 days @ per 100 bighas Rs 4 | Rs 22–13–1 |
| Seeds: 1 *maund* 1 1/4 *seers* @ Rs 5–8–0 per *maund* | Rs 5–10–3 |
| 2 *maunds* 7 1/2 *seers* @ Rs 5–8–0 per *maund* | Rs 12–0–2 |
| Ploughing, levelling, and weeding: | |
| 30 bighas 11 *biswas* @ Rs 1–8–0 per bigha | Rs 45–13–1 |
| Levelling, and weeding: | |
| 33 bighas 5 *biswas* @ Re 0–13–3 per bigha | Rs 28–11–1 |
| Irrigation: | |
| 258 bighas 6 bighas per rupee | Rs 41–15–2 |

Harvesting:
Plouging *khatauni* (not clear):
 678 bighas 7 *biswas*             Rs 25–7–0
Payment to landowners (*mahsul arazi*):
 To Miyan Ihsanullah for *imlak*
  of 22 bighas 3 *biswas*      Rs 11–1–2
  Tawfiq of Shah Darwesh     Re 0–8–0
  To Raunaq Ali         Rs 6–0–0
                Rs 17–9–2[28]

## Prices of Principal Food Grains

Since du Jardin was deeply involved in food grains trade, his
Account Books contain details of food grains bought and sold,
at each of his major depots (*kothars*) month by month for almost
the entire period of about eleven years, and the amount spent
on purchase or realized from the sale of each of the grains. We
can thus reconstruct a complete picture of food grains market
conditions.

Only a few points are being made in this paper to illustrate
the nature of information available. The volume of profit earned
from this trade compared favourably with the revenues available from land. For example, profit from the purchase and
sale of grain between August 1779 and March 1780 amounted
to Rs 2,899–14–1, presumably from ta'alluqa Jarara alone.[29]

Table I
Average Price of Principal Food Grains in the area
1778–87[30]
(after each harvest was in)

|  | Bajra | Jowar | Wheat | Gram |
|---|---|---|---|---|
|  | (In maunds and seers per rupee) | | | |
| 1779–80 | 1.15 | 1.70 | 1.00 | 1.03 |
| 1780–1 | 1.10 | 1.80 | 1.00 | 0.36 |
| 1781–2 | 1.20 | 1.13 | 0.32 | 1.00 |
| 1782–3 | – | 0.14 | 0.27 | 0.35 |
| 1783–4 | – | 0.14 | 0.13 | 0.15 |
| 1784–5 | 2.00 | 2.10 | 0.13 | 0.10 |
| 1785–6 | 2.00 | 2.00 | 1.22 | 1.10 |
| 1786–7 | 2.05 | 2.30 | 1.25 | 1.20 |

Table II
Monthly Fluctuation in the Price of Food Grains, 1782–3[31]
(Wholesale Purchase Price of Gram at Farrukhabad)

| Month | Price (in *maunds* and *seers* per rupee) | Month | Price |
|---|---|---|---|
| July 1782 | 1.00 *maund* | January 1783 | 0.38 *maund* |
| August 1782 | 0.35 *maund* | February 1783 | 0.35 *maund* |
| September 1782 | 0.35 *maund* | March 1783 | 1.00 *maund* |
| October 1782 | 0.35 *maund* | April 1783 | 1 *maund* 5 seers |
| November 1782 | 0.38 *maund* | May 1783 | 1 *maund* 16 seers |
| December 1782 | 0.39 *maund* | June 1783 | 1 *maund* |

Table III
Wholesale Sale Price of Wheat at Different Depots[32]
September 1786

| | |
|---|---|
| *Kothar* Marehra | 1 maund 22 1/2 seers |
| *Kothar* Pora | 1 maund 10 seers |
| *Kothar* Kusganj | 1 maund 20 seers |
| *Kothar* Pilwa | 1 maund 35 seers |

In examining the average level of prices between 1777 and 1787, one has to take into account the severe famine of 1782–3, which was long remembered by the local people and the economic effects of which continued to be felt for another two years. However, it is significant that on an average, prices of the principal food grains were appreciably lower in 1787 than in 1777 (Table I). The average monthly fluctuation as revealed in Table II, shows the normal seasonal variation. The variation in wholesale prices in neighbouring markets (Table III) could perhaps be explained by difference in quality.

## Wages

These documents contain interesting data on wages of different classes.
*Kahars* (carrying a box of papers from Kanpur to Pora in 11 days)
      -per head Re 0–4–0 per day[33]

Masonry workers (11 persons @ Rs 1–5–0 per day)
-average per head Re 0–1–3 1/2 per day[34]
Workers of indigo factory (presumably supervisors)
-average per head Re 2–4–0 to Rs 2–8–0 per month[35]
Workers of indigo factory (43 ordinary persons, 1 July–8 October 1787)
-per head Re 0–12–1 per month[36]
Boatmen who came from Calcutta to Kanpur for September 1787:
Hazari Manjhi (cash Rs 6–0–0; expenses Re 1–0–0) Rs 7–0–0
Lausa Manjhi (cash Rs 5–0–0; expenses Re 0–13–0) Rs 5–13–0[37]
Badloo Oarsman Rs 3–0–0 per month
Troopers ranging from Rs 2–8–0 to Rs 5–0–0 per head per month[38]

## Salaries

Some figures of salaries of managers and minor officials may be compared with the wages mentioned above.

| | |
|---|---|
| Ratan Lal | Rs 10–0–0 per month |
| Jawahar Mal | Rs 7–8–0 per month |
| Manga Ram, *mutsaddi* | Rs 5–8–0 per month |
| Mir Abul Hasan, | |
| *kotwal sair*, Marehra | Rs 6–0–0 per month |
| Roop Chand, *kotwal* | Rs 4–0–0 per month[39] |
| Gulab Rai, *patwari* | Rs 2–8–0 per month[40] |

## Crafts

These documents contain interesting information about various crafts. For example, the cost of a gold ring made at Lucknow in March 1787 was as follows:

| | |
|---|---|
| Gold 9 *masha* and 1 *surkh* | —Rs 12–6–0 |
| Labour | —Rs 1–4–0 |
| Total | —Rs 13–10–0[41] |

Preparation of a piece of *than atlas* (brocade) *kalabattum tilai* (gold thread):

| | |
|---|---|
| 45 *tola* 1 *masha* @ Rs 1–3–0 per *tola* | —Rs 80–7–3 |

Silk                              —Rs 5-0-0

Wages of 420 persons @ Re 0-5-2 per head

                                  —Rs 134-8-2
Mahsul Arhat                      —Rs 5-0-0
Salahband                         —Re 1-0-0
Total                             —Rs 226-0-1[42]

## Personal Staff

We have an interesting list of the personal staff of Mr Perry during the years 1786-7. Since the salaries were not paid every month, it has not been possible to ascertain their monthly salaries but the number and designation of the staff are interesting.

Kundan, *baverchi* (cook)
Daulat, *khansama* (butler)
Ramzani, *nanpaz* (baker)
Jani (washerman)
Kallu (water carrier)
Jan Muhammad (tailor)
Jafar Khan, *khidmatgar* (valet)
Khuda Bakhsh, *palangbaz* (bedmaker)
Mohammad Azam, *huqqabardar* (hookah tender)
Lashkari, *mashalchi* (torch lighter)
Fath Muhammad, *farrash* (floor cleaner)
Bulaqi, *khakral* (sweeper)
Pir Muhammad, *sais* (syce)
16 *kahars* of *palki* (palanquin bearers)

The total amount paid in salaries varied because there was no regular monthly payment, as already stated. However, the total payments were as follows:

July 1786                         —Rs 132-15-0
December 1786                     —Rs 81-7-2
May 1787                          —Rs 71-14-0
July 1787                         —Rs 131-0-0

It appears that the highest paid of these servants was the cook whose salary was Rs 8–0–0 per mensem.[43]

This paper is being presented in the hope that this extremely valuable collection will be utilized by scholars of medieval Indian history to study economic trends, economic organization, production, exchange, handicrafts, wages, and prices.

## Notes and References

1. For details of the attempts of John Willes to pressurize du Jardin, see MSS SP no. 1582, documents nos 17, 28, 34, 35, 39 and no. 1581, ff. 35b and 48.

2. A certain Mr Grant was a well-established English merchant who had advanced money of the ships brought to Bengal by a certain Mr Bolts and the East India Company was interested in its cargo (25 August 1779, *Calendar of Persian Correspondence*, hereinafter *CPC*, v. no. 1570). Presumably, the same Grant was recommended by the Governor General to the Nawab of Farrukhabad, on 15 February 1782, to settle down in Farrukhabad for the sole purpose of trade, promising that he would have nothing to do with matters relating to revenue or administration (*CPC*, vi, no. 380). In case he was the same as Robert Grant, he had received the title of Sarfraz-ud-Daula, Mustaqim Jung, 'Servant' of Shah Alam Bahadur. An authorization written by him on 8 May 1782 directed the authorities concerned not to interfere with the passage of two Turki horses and two camels (MS. SP no. 1581, document no. 37).

3. Cf. MS. SP no. 1582, document no. 3.

4. Cf. a *parwana* of Muzaffar Jung issued to du Jardin in December 1786, and of Asaf-ud-Daula, at about the same time, MS. SP no. 1581, document no. 46 for the former and document no. 2 for the latter.

5. I am grateful to Dr S. P. Gupta. Reader in History, Aligarh Muslim University, for having shown the *arhsattas* of pargana Chatsu (eastern Rajasthan) of the seventeenth century, which contain this information.

6. MS. SP no. 1581, document no. 40. At this time, du Jardin held *ijaras* in Etah district not only from Raja Himmat Singh, but also from Miyan Almas Ali Khan, Ghulam Husain, and Shaikh Dayanat-ullah in pargana Marehra (SP no. 1597, f. 354b).

7. The Raja of Etah was of Chauhan descent. He succeeded to the *gaddi* shortly after Sabir Khan had overthrown his grandfather, Prithviraj Singh, in 1780. The *ijara* was terminated one year before the stipulated period, as a result of pressure exerted by the British agent, John Willes (MS. SP. no. 1582, document no. 7). Shaikh Dayanat-ullah, who had given himself a *ta'alluqa* in *ijara* to du Jardin, joined the British in pressurizing the French

traders (cf. Letter of Daud Beg to du Jardin dated 3 June 1786, MS. SP no. 1581, documents nos 31 and 33).

8. From the title *do nafar* (two persons) and even otherwise it seems clear that the *ijara* was given to Daniel du Jardin and Louis Purcerrel (cf. the next document which is quoted).

9. 1192 *fasli* was 1784–5, 1193 *fasli* was 1785–6, and 1194 *fasli* was 1786–7. Actually some villages in the neighbourhood belonging to Raja Himmat Singh, such as Nidhauli, had been taken in *ijara* for three years with effect from 1783–4 (MS. SP no. 1581, document no. 38). There is a discharge given by Raja Himmat Singh for the *ijara* of the same villages (of Pilwa, etc.) for 1191 *fasli* (1783–4) quoted below. Du Jardin therefore claimed that his *ijara* for four years was curtailed to three years (MS. SP no. 1582, document no. 7).

10. Literally 'earthly and heavenly calamities'. 'Earthly calamities' were defined as loss of crops due to ravages of war, or when destroyed by rodents or pests. 'Heavenly calamities' included hail storm, excessive rain, floods, drought, etc.

11. For the emphasis on the cultivation of indigo, cf. MS. SP no. 1581, document no. 34. See also *infra*.

12. Cf. *Siyaq Nama* of Munshi Nand Ram (Lucknow, 1879). In the document of 1104F (1696–7) quoted on page 37, while the *asl* of *tumar jama* is Rs 1,896–9–0, the *izafa* (increase) is Rs 450, i.e. 24.9 per cent. However, in another document of the same year quoted in the same work, the increase is 50 per cent (p. 50).

13. MS. SP no. 1596, ff. 318 *et seq.*

14. MS. SP no. 1597, ff. 354b–357a; cf. the figures in *Ain-i-Akbari* for c. 1595 in *dastur* Marehra, etc. (Tr. II/108) cotton: 93 dams 23 *jitals* (Rs 2–6–0 approximately): sugarcane (in the adjoining *dastur* of Akrabad): 223 dams 15 *jitals* (Rs 5–10–0 approximately). The increase in the rate of taxation over two centuries in the case of sugar cane is only marginal, while the increase in the case of cotton can be explained largely in terms of higher prices due to vastly increased demand of textile goods.

15. Cf. MS. SP no. 1581, documents nos 18, 19, 20, 21, 22, 30, 31, 32, etc.

16. Ibid., document no. 26.

17. Cf. MS. SP no. 1581, document no. 25.

18. These documents are given in MS. Indian 813 (no. 175 in the Catalogue of Indian MSS).

19. Ibid., document no. 3. The singular form (*manki*), even when used for more than one person, seems to be traditional. Cf. *Siyaq Nama*, p. 29.

20. Ibid., document nos 8, 17, 18, 29, 31 and 39.

21. MS. SP no. 1596, ff. 377b and 379b; no. 1601, f. 35. The total among distributed in *taqavi* in a single village generally did not exceed Rs 489.

22. For example, MS. SP no. 1598, f. 250.

23. MS. SP no. 1601, ff. 34 and 35. The eleven villages of *ta'alluqa* Jarara referred to here are: Jarara, Nigola, Bajhera, Naila, Andla, Kakola, Bhanera, Bamni, Kunwarpur, Bhogpur and Uswara. All these villages are still extant, but one village of the *ta'alluqa*, which was named after du Jardin and was called du Jardin Nagar, is no longer traceable. Maybe, its name has been changed. There is also a reference to village Jahangarh. Possibly, it is a misreading of Hasângarh, which may earlier have been pronounced as Hasangarh.

24. Ibid., f. 34.

25. MS. SP no. 1598, f. 225.

26. Ibid., f. 228.

27. Ibid. no. 1596, f. 355. The percentage of income from indigo plantation as a percentage of the total revenue may be seen from the following figures for 1193 *fasil*:

| Villages | Indigo plantation as percentage of total revenue |
|----------|--------------------------------------------------|
| Pilwa | 88 |
| Baragaon | 85 |
| Tatarpur | 87 |
| Jaisinghpur | 79 |

28. Ibid. The above figures may be seen on ff. 276b, 277a, 282b and 284a.

29. Ibid. no. 1601, f. 28.

30. Figures compiled from:
   SP no. 1597, ff. 356a, 362.
   SP no. 1599, ff. 190–2, 200, 211, 212, 214, 296.
   SP no. 1600, ff. 91, 94, 180.
   SP no. 1601, ff. 28.

31. MS. SP no. 1599, f. 200.

32. MS. SP no. 1600, ff. 91, 92, 93, 94.

33. MS. SP no. 1596, f. 36a, March 1787.

34. Ibid., October 1787.

35. Ibid., f. 285b, September 1787.

36. Ibid., f. 284b.

37. MS. SP no. 1597, f. 217a.

38. Ibid., ff. 274a, 300a, 301b, 326b.

39. Ibid., f. 327a.

40. This amount of the salary of a *patwari* does not of course represent his total income.

41. SP no. 1596, f. 24a.

42. SP no. 1597, f. 229b, December 1796.

43. SP no. 1577, 23a, 233a, 258, 296, 304a, 304b and 402a.

# Index

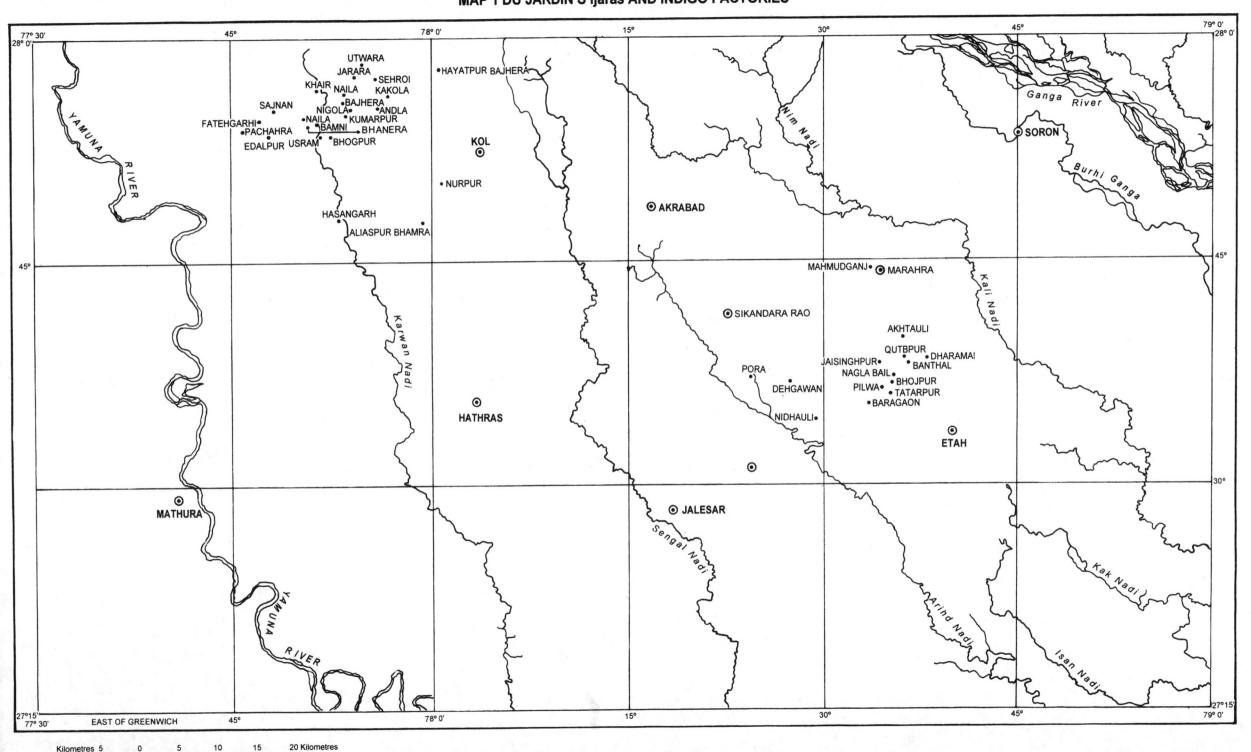

**MAP 1 DU JARDIN'S Ijaras AND INDIGO FACTORIES**

UTWARA
JARARA
SEHROI
•HAYATPUR BAJHERA
KHAIR NAILA KAKOLA
SAJNAN BAJHERA
NIGOLA ANDLA
FATEHGARHI NAILA KUMARPUR
PACHAHRA BAMNI BHANERA
EDALPUR USRAM BHOGPUR

KOL
⊙

•NURPUR

⊙ AKRABAD

HASANGARH
•ALIASPUR BHAMRA

Ganga River

⊙ SORON

Burhi Ganga

MAHMUDGANJ • ⊙ MARAHRA

⊙ SIKANDARA RAO

AKHTAULI
QUTBPUR
DHARAMAI
JAISINGHPUR BANTHAL
PORA NAGLA BAIL
DEHGAWAN PILWA BHOJPUR
TATARPUR
NIDHAULI• •BARAGAON

⊙
HATHRAS

⊙
ETAH

⊙

⊙
MATHURA

⊙ JALESAR

YAMUNA RIVER

Karwan Nadi

Nim Nadi

Kali Nadi

Sengal Nadi

Arind Nadi

Kak Nadi

Isan Nadi

YAMUNA RIVER

77° 30'   45'   78° 0'   15°   30°   45'   79° 0'
28° 0'                                    28° 0'

45°                                        45°

30°                                        30°

27°15'                                    27°15'
77° 30'  EAST OF GREENWICH  45'  78° 0'  15°  30°  45'  79° 0'

Kilometres 5    0    5    10    15    20 Kilometres

MAP 4 DU JARDIN'S *indigo* AND INDIGO FACTORIES